PRAISE FOR HOWARD GARDNER'S
Leading Minds

"[Gardner's] books are lucid, cross-disciplinary examinations of heady topics: *Creating Minds* . . . and *Leading Minds* . . . are rarities, being academic studies that are as readable as they are compelling. (Indeed, *Leading Minds* was the No. 1 seller on the Globe's local best-seller list last week.)"

—*The Boston Globe*

"At the heart of Gardner's thesis is a simple but unfamiliar idea, which forms the epigraph to one of the chapters: 'All leadership takes place through the communication of ideas to the minds of others.' . . . Armed with this idea of leadership Gardner is able to bring together leaders from very different fields, such disparate figures as Churchill, Einstein, the anthropologist Margaret Mead and Pope John XXIII. When viewed through the lens of the cognitive psychologist, they are all doing the same thing: all are telling, and embodying, stories."

—*The Independent* (London)

"In general, business people should read a lot more. I find it dangerous that many CEOs have no idea of the historical context of what they do. One book I recommend is . . . *Leading Minds* by Howard Gardner, a psychologist who teaches at the Harvard School of Education. He looks at 11 great leaders throughout history, people like Martin Luther King Jr., Maggie Thatcher, Eleanor Roosevelt, Harriet Tubman and Gandhi."

—Warren Bennis, interviewed in the *Los Angeles Times*

"Well and clearly argued."

—*The Irish Times* (Dublin)

"Fascinating. . . . Gardner analyzes the life and times of 11 modern leaders in search of how they managed to change our world."

—*The Gazette* (Montreal)

"A novel analysis of leadership. . . . The authors differentiate visionaries—leaders who create new stories, such as Gandhi and Jean Monnet, architect of a unified Europe—from such innovative leaders as Margaret Thatcher, who identify a theme latent in the population but neglected over the years and give it a new twist. Other leaders on whom they focus are George Marshall, Margaret Mead, J. Robert Oppenheimer, Pope John XXIII, former General Motors president Alfred P. Sloan Jr. and educator Robert Hutchins. This study will repay the close attention of aspiring leaders in many fields."

—*Publishers Weekly*

"A good test for me of a business book is whether I can remember anything important about it a couple of years after first reading it. . . . *Leading Minds* passes this test with flying colors. . . . Howard Gardner's striking insight, supported by his copious research, fed straight into my own thinking about brands."

—Hamish Pringle, *Marketing*

"[A] fascinating exploration . . . [*Leading Minds*] establishes a convincing middle ground between numbingly quantified studies and the unbounded impressionistic interview. . . . [It] illuminates the need for leaders to understand that part of the human psyche that holds on to the childish view of the world that yearns for certainty, and not to pander to it."

—*The Australian* (Sydney)

"The gamut of psycho-socio-scientific analysis applied to [leadership] routinely obscures its underlying diverse human dynamic. Making strides to reverse this state of affairs, Howard Gardner constructs a richly textured guide to the realm in which that dynamic plays out—within and between the minds of leaders and followers. . . . Supplemented with a treasure trove of appendices, Gardner's compelling portraits of leaders' minds offer an original framework for the understanding of the leadership process."

—*Industry Week*

"An imaginative book, filled with uncommon ideas."

—*Booklist*

"Howard Gardner has written another enthralling book. The eleven men and women he has chosen as his examples could hardly differ more widely, but Gardner has managed to define the common factors that made them all effective leaders."

—Anthony Storr, author of *Solitude*

"Immensely interesting, thought-provoking, and decidedly original. No one else could have written it."

—John Gardner, Stanford University

"Once again, Howard Gardner illuminates for us a crucial aspect of human behavior. If, as he claims, great leaders achieve power through the stories they tell, Gardner's own fascinating narratives of leadership show why he is one of the intellectual leaders of our times."

—Mihaly Csikszentmihalyi, author of *Creativity*

"Once again, Gardner brings his brilliant intuition and analytic skills to the study of human excellence. His diagnoses are of particular value today, when great leaders are both badly needed and unaccountably scarce."

—Edward O. Wilson, Harvard University

Leading Minds

OTHER BOOKS BY HOWARD GARDNER

The Quest for Mind (1973)

The Arts and Human Development (1973)

The Shattered Mind (1975)

Developmental Psychology (1978)

Artful Scribbles (1980)

Art, Mind, and Brain (1982)

Frames of Mind (1983)

The Mind's New Science (1985)

To Open Minds (1989)

The Unschooled Mind (1991)

Multiple Intelligences: Theory in Practice (1993)

Creating Minds (1993)

Extraordinary Minds (1997)

The Disciplined Mind (1999)

Intelligence Reframed (1999)

Good Work (with Mihaly Csikszentmihalyi and William Damon) (2001)

Changing Minds (2004)

Multiple Intelligences: New Horizons (2006)

The Development and Education of the Mind (2006)

Five Minds for the Future (2007)

Truth, Beauty, and Goodness Reframed (2011)

Leading
Minds

An ANATOMY *of* LEADERSHIP

HOWARD GARDNER

in collaboration with EMMA LASKIN

BASIC BOOKS
A Member of the Perseus Books Group
New York

Copyright © 1995, 2011 by Howard Gardner.

Published by Basic Books, A Member of the Perseus Books Group

The Library of Congress has cataloged the hardcover as follows:
  Leading minds : an anatomy of leadership / Howard Gardner in collaboration with Emma Laskin.
      p.   cm.
  Includes bibliographical references and index.
  ISBN 0-465-08279-3 (cloth)
  ISBN 0-465-08280-7 (paper)
  ISBN-13: 978-0-465-08280-3
  1. Leadership.   2. Leadership—Case studies.   I. Laskin, Emma.
II. Title.
HM141.G35 1995
303.3'4—dc20
95–12088
CIP

2011 paperback edition ISBN: 978-0-465-02773-6
E-book ISBN: 978-0-465-02777-4

10 9 8 7 6 5 4 3 2

In memory of Judith Krieger Gardner (1943–1994)
Who affected the thoughts, feelings,
and actions of everyone who knew her
and
Erik Homburger Erikson (1902–1994)
Teacher and friend
Who affected the thoughts, feelings,
and actions of a generation

CONTENTS

PART III
CONCLUSION: LEADERSHIP THAT LOOKS FORWARD

PREFACE TO THE
2011 EDITION

BACKGROUND OF THIS BOOK

Of the many books that I've written during the past forty years, *Leading Minds* may seem to have involved the biggest leap. Before its publication, I saw myself, and was seen by others, as a psychologist studying human development, particularly in the cognitive sphere. I had written a dozen books about the human mind, more than half of them featuring the word "mind" in the title. Until the early 1980s, I was primarily a research psychologist, writing for other psychologists. But after the publication in 1983 of my book *Frames of Mind: The Theory of Multiple Intelligences*, I became more focused on issues of education; indeed, the topics I wrote about, and the audience I was addressing, were drawn from the education sector.

But then, seemingly suddenly, in 1995, with the able assistance of Emma Laskin, I published a book about leadership. In that book, whose preface you are now reading, I focused on an issue traditionally regarded as within the purview of political science or history. Not only was I writing about a topic that seems remote from cognitive development in the individual, I also was writing about leadership in a way that addressed the general reader rather than the specialist. To top it off, my conception of leadership appeared idiosyncratic: What were people such as the anthropologist Margaret Mead, the physicist J. Robert Oppenheimer, or the intellectual Robert Maynard Hutchins doing in the company of a pope, a prime minister, and an army general?

Indeed, *Leading Minds* did constitute a turning point for me, an opportunity to address new audiences in policy and in business, and to "sound off" on topics in current events. Yet with the benefit of hindsight it is easy—at least for me—to see why, very much at midlife, I chose to write and publish a book about leadership.

Ever since childhood, I have been fascinated with politics and history; I have devoured newspapers and news magazines and compulsively tuned into broadcast news. The decision to write about leadership enabled me to exploit my passions as a history and news junkie. In that subterranean sense, I had already been working on this book for several decades.

The book also can be readily seen as growing organically out of my concerns in the immediately preceding years. Once I had published my book on different intelligences, I was frequently asked about whether there were different forms of creativity. I decided to focus on this issue in two ways: (1) formulating, with the help of colleagues Mihaly Csikszentmihalyi and David Henry Feldman, a general framework for understanding the emergence of new ideas and practices; (2) carrying out intensive case studies of individuals who, I hypothesized, stood out in terms of their creativity in several intellectual realms. Just two years before the publication of *Leading Minds*, I issued a book about my conclusions.

In *Creating Minds: An Anatomy of Creativity Seen through the Lives of Freud, Einstein, Picasso, Stravinsky, Eliot, Graham, and Gandhi* (1993; new edition 2011), I studied seven exemplary creative individuals, each of whom achieved his or her most stunning breakthrough in the shadow of 1900. Among these creators, many striking similarities existed, as well as some startling differences. But it became apparent to me early on that Mahatma Gandhi diverged in essential ways from the other six individuals, who were leaders *within* established domains of accomplishment, such as physics or painting or poetry. In contrast, Gandhi was trying to inspire and change an entire nation—indeed, as it eventually turned out, all human beings. *Leading Minds* represents an effort to go beyond the first six creators just listed and to understand what is distinctive about those who presume to provide leadership across domains and interest groups.

While thinking about individuals who stood out in terms of their creative or their leadership capacities, I was continuing my investigations of how best to educate young people.

In *The Unschooled Mind: How Children Think, and How Schools Should Teach* (1991; new edition 2011), I sought to understand why children absorb experiences and acquire diverse facilities so readily in the earliest years of life, and yet have such difficulty mastering the disciplines that form the core of common schooling. My research convinced me that, by the age of five or so, human beings already have a well-formed "unschooled mind" that consists of simple theories about mind and matter. The theories may be charming, but they are all too often misguided or plainly false. Although formal education strives mightily to refashion the mind of the five-year-old into the mind of a more sophisticated conceptualizer, most schools in most locales fail in this mission. Indeed, except for individuals who become expert in specific domains and actually come to think in a fundamentally different way about the world, most adults continue to theorize much as they did when they were young children.

The implications of this conclusion are startling from a scientific point of view and troubling from a societal perspective. If a leader presumes to speak to the masses of a nation or across the dialects of different domains, then, in effect, he or she must begin by addressing what I call "the five-year-old mind." The leader must either accept the mind of the child as given or, in the manner of a determined educator, try to remold that mind. As detailed in *The Unschooled Mind,* the task of guiding individuals beyond the purview of a preschool child's mind proves formidable.

THE ARGUMENT OF THE BOOK

Although I was initially unaware of it, the distinct lines of study I was pursuing almost simultaneously in *Creating Minds* and in *The Unschooled Mind* were destined to come together in *Leading Minds.* In this book I study a range of leaders from the last century in order to explicate what I see as the major facets of leadership, from the perspective of psychology. To summarize my formulation succinctly, a leader is an individual (or, rarely, a set of individuals) who significantly affects the thoughts, feelings, or behaviors of a significant number of individuals. Most acknowledged leaders—consider, for example, Franklin Roosevelt or Winston Churchill—are "direct"; they address their public face-to-face. But I have called attention to a hitherto unrecognized phenomenon—indirect leadership: In this variety of leading, individuals exert impact through the works they create.

Whether direct or indirect, leaders fashion stories—principally stories of identity. It is important that a leader be a good storyteller but equally crucial that the leader embody that story in his or her life. When a leader tells stories to experts, the stories can be quite sophisticated, but when the leader is addressing a diverse, heterogeneous group, the story must be sufficiently elementary to be understood by the untutored, or "unschooled," mind.

Far from being a motley crew, the leaders were carefully and strategically chosen in order to reinforce the argument of the book. I wanted to indicate through such examples that the gap between a prototypical indirect leader and a prototypical direct leader is not absolute; one can proceed in small steps from an Einstein or a Virginia Woolf all the way to a Margaret Thatcher or a Gandhi. What allows an Einstein or Picasso to affect others is less the words that they utter in the presence of others, and more the ideas and works that they, often working alone, create and make public. Cases such as Margaret Mead, J. Robert Oppenheimer, and Robert Maynard Hutchins represent intriguing intermediate cases: They begin by creating works that influence their colleagues in their respective chosen fields of anthropology, physics, and law. But eventually, owing to the power of their ideas and their decision to enter the public arena, they come to take on at least some of the traits of direct leaders.

Through this gamut of illustrations, I wanted to show the ways in which stories must be altered, as one moves from addressing a small and relatively homogeneous group (such as a set of scholars in a discipline or at a university) to a large and quite heterogeneous population (such as a multitude of dispossessed individuals or the citizens of a nation). Though I could have chosen different instances of a category (Henry Ford instead of Alfred Sloan as the head of a corporation, Ronald Reagan instead of Margaret Thatcher as the leader of a nation), the categories, and the order in which they are presented, are integral to the points of the book.

Along with detailed portraits of eleven leaders, I also include a survey of ten important political and military leaders of the twentieth century. Moreover, the detailed information in the Appendixes allows comparisons between my eleven leaders and a relevant "control group."

QUESTIONS RAISED

Upon publication of the book, a number of questions arose that I did not treat, or did not treat adequately, in the first edition. To begin with, I was asked about whether the choice of leaders did not reflect, chiefly, individuals whom I liked or admired. Certainly I prefer certain leaders to others, and my sample may be slanted to some extent in favor of individuals whom I admire. It is crucial, however, not to confuse the descriptive and the normative. My goal in *Leading Minds* is to describe features of effective leadership, irrespective of whether I happen to admire the individuals in question or the policies they promoted. Indeed, the analysis would be unacceptable as scholarship if it applies only to individuals for whom I have positive feelings. One purpose of the survey in the Appendix is to extend the framework to individuals, many of whom I, along with the rest of the world, consider loathsome.

Another issue that arose was whether, in my studies of leadership (and in my studies of creativity), I was simply being elitist. Without question, I am writing about individuals who are extraordinary. I do this in part to repair an imbalance in the behavioral science literature. The assumption has reigned that, if we understand ordinary forms of creativity or leadership, we will better understand the heights of achievement. I believe that this argument needs to be inverted. It is far more likely that we will better understand garden-variety forms of leadership if we have a deeper understanding of unambiguous examples of powerful leadership.

But I want to make an additional point. Extraordinary individuals may be the product of accident, but their accomplishments—positive as well as negative—constitute an important part of human history. Think of the nineteenth century without Napoleon or Lincoln, the twentieth century without Stalin, Hitler, or the Roosevelt family. Indeed, to be a tad provocative, think of the first decade of the twenty-first century without considering Osama bin Laden. In the grip of an ideology, postmodern critiques of leadership—critiques that question the role of the leader or any claims of extraordinariness—risk obscuring a vital enduring fact of life.

What of my focus, both in education and in the study of leadership, on the power of the unschooled mind? My treatment raises the question of whether one can *ever* persuade the general public to adopt a more sophisticated position on any issue. Indeed, all of my studies reinforce the power of the initial theories formed by young children as well as the difficulty of introducing a more complex and differentiated way of thinking. I would be untrue to my own findings if I were to intimate that greater sophistication can be easily attained.

Nonetheless, despite the horrors of human history and the swings of the pendulum, one can point to the gradual emergence of more sophisticated ways of thinking in the areas of morality and civility. My personal heroes are such individuals as Mahatma Gandhi and Jean Monnet and Nelson Mandela, who worked for decades to develop in their constituencies a more complex way of thinking about human relations. I find myself in agreement with Freud, who once wrote: "The voice of the intellect is a soft one, but it does not rest until it has gained a hearing. Ultimately, after endless repeated rebuffs, it succeeds." This is one of a few points in which one may be optimistic about the future of humankind.

REFLECTIONS ON THE PAST FIFTEEN YEARS

Though the topic of leadership and the field of "leadership studies" certainly existed in earlier times, few could have been prepared for the explosion of interest in the topic of leadership in recent years. In all probability, my book was a symptom of this new interest, rather than a prod to it. The contributions of certain key scholars—Warren Bennis, James McGregor Burns, John Gardner, and Barbara Kellerman—were one ingredient. The increasing dominance of the business sector in America and other developed countries, and the crucial role of the CEO and other members of the leadership team, doubtless contributed as well. Greater awareness of global problems—for example, poverty, climate change, the treatment of disease, and corruption—and the difficulties involved in tackling them also brought to the fore the need for skilled, informed, and fair-minded leaders. The various traumas of the period—the terrorist attacks of 9/11, the financial meltdowns of 2000 and 2008, the instability of large portions of Africa and the Middle East—all called attention to the costs of poor or ineffective leaders.

I am less certain about why, in the brochures and webpages of educational institutions, the training of leaders is so often featured. It is not clear to me to what extent the public is expecting our institutions to train leaders, as opposed to the institutions seeking to distinguish themselves by promising to cultivate an abundant supply, for which there may not be correlative demand. That said, it is difficult not to be struck by the near-universal claim, made by institutions from middle schools to graduate schools and across the globe, that they—and perhaps even they *alone*—have hit upon the magic formula for forging leadership.

The field—the collection of social institutions and gatekeepers concerned with the topic of leadership—has exploded. No one keeps up with the publications, journals, websites, institutions, organizations, and training programs that tackle leadership. The increase in knowledge—and in wisdom—about leadership is not nearly so striking, but I'd like to think that the avalanche of writings, including this book, may at least have sharpened and deepened our understanding of the nature of leadership, how best to cultivate it, and whether it is possible to prod leadership toward positive ends.

Having selected almost two decades ago eleven leaders on whom to focus, I think about whether I would today choose a somewhat different list. At least as examples of sectors, such as the military or the clergy, I think that I made reasonable decisions. Some names, such as Martin Luther King, Jr., are as eminent as ever. Others, such as J. Robert Oppenheimer or Robert Maynard Hutchins or Alfred Sloan, are far less known—and could easily be replaced by more contemporary figures, such as scholar Noam Chomsky, or university president Derek Bok, or business leader Bill Gates. Very different from Pope John XXIII, Pope John Paul II is equally worthy of study.

The one person who surely should be added is Nelson Mandela, justifiably the most admired person of our time. And the enduring legacies of Martin Luther King, Jr., and Nelson Mandela—and, less prominently, of Chinese dissident Liu Xiaboa and of Burmese dissident Aung San Suu Kyi—testify to the incomparable significance of Mahatma Gandhi, who in my view is the most important human being of the past millennium.

There has been considerable scholarship about the leaders portrayed here. At the conclusion of this preface, I list some of the writings that have advanced our understanding of these individuals and their capacity for leadership.

LEADERSHIP IN THE ERA OF TRUTHINESS, TWADDLE, AND TWITTER

Just as the political and economic spheres have been convulsed in recent decades, so, too, our world has been altered by technological, cultural, and even epistemological changes. I capture these changes by the trio of concepts of "truthiness," twaddle, and Twitter.

The term "truthiness" was popularized by the American television wit Stephen Colbert. Traditionally, we apply the predicate "true" to statements for which reliable evidence can be accrued. (Conversely, if it is impossible to imagine a situation where the statement could be disproved, we consider the statement to be an item of faith, rather than of reason.) People have always lied, and leaders have scarcely been immune from that sin—indeed, Nazi propagandist Josef Goebbels famously and cynically declared, "The bigger the lie, the more people believe it."

What Colbert has added is that, nowadays, the simple declaration of a state of affair by a person who is known suffices to confer upon it *truth value*. So whether a Republican leader is called a "war criminal" by a member of the Democratic Party, or a discussion of "end of life" procedures is called a "death panel" by a Republican spokesperson, these statements are deemed true simply because they have been repeatedly uttered in the public arena.

The cause of this state of affair is undoubtedly complex. In my *Truth, Beauty, and Goodness Reframed* (2011), I argue that the challenge to truth comes from three complementary sources: (1) increased knowledge about the wide range of cultures around the globe, many of which hold apparently incompatible views about the world; (2) the postmodern critique of such traditional notions as truth, according to which claims to truth are seen as simple assertions of power; and (3) the human tendency, particularly during adolescence and early adulthood, to adopt relativistic stances ("you've got the right to your opinion, just like I have the right to my opinion"). Whatever the relative contributions of these and other factors, it seems clear that leadership becomes more difficult when everyone's story is considered equally valid, independent of corroborating evidence.

Every observer of the contemporary scene notes the explosion of information, claims, and counterclaims in the air, or in its contemporary manifestation, cyberspace. No doubt at least some of that information is valuable, even invaluable. But much of what is available in the digital world is idle chatter, spreading of rumor, confusion of opinion with reason or evidence, and the like. I label this state of affair "twaddle." Ultimately, given enough time and investing enough due diligence, it is possible to arrive more reliably than before at the actual state of affairs. But for most of us, most of the time, we are drowning in twaddle.

Finally, as epitomized by the website Twitter, there is now a premium on messages that are brief, vivid, and memorable. Perhaps they need not be as brief as the 140 characters permitted in a tweet. But by virtue of the forces of advertising and entertainment on the one hand, and the unrelenting demands on time on the other, there is an enormous premium on getting to the point and avoiding complexity. Einstein famously quipped, "Everything should be as simple as possible but not simpler." Alas, the priority given to conceptualization of Twitter length makes the articulation of more complex stories, as well as less familiar stories, far more difficult.

No leader today can afford to ignore this powerful trio: the ease of pro-mulgating false statements, the detritus that permeates the blogosphere, and the prominence of the ad line and the gag line. Indeed, the challenge to the leader is to counter these forces when they are inimical to his or her goals and to put forth a powerful counter-story that highlights truth against truthiness, clarity against twaddle, and a developed and substantiated story as opposed to a Twitter-length teaser. As I write these words, U.S. president Barack Obama clearly understands these challenges, but it is uncertain whether he—or indeed any thoughtful leader capable of complex thought—can be heard and under-stood above the din.

At the very time that I was completing *Leading Minds*, I began to explore a set of issues that have occupied my thoughts and writing until today—a decade and a half later. In 1995, my colleagues Mihaly Csikszentmihalyi, William Damon, and I launched the GoodWork Project (see goodworkproject.org, goodworktoolkit .org)—a study of professions in our time. We asked whether, and if so how, pro-fessions may endure at a time when markets are very powerful, our conceptions of time and space are changing at warp speed, and there are few forces in developed countries to temper the market forces, let alone to channel them in socially re-sponsible ways, (Gardner, Csikszentmihalyi, and Damon, 2001).

Unless you believe in the innate goodness of human beings, the power of di-vine intervention, or the inherent wisdom of the market, there is no guarantee that human beings will use their skills and powers in positive ways. An emerging goal of the GoodWork Project is to familiarize individuals with what it means to use your capacities for goals that are larger than your own self-aggrandizement and that contribute to the broader welfare—and then to help these individuals move in that direction.

Some leaders seek power for its own sake; some leaders seek power in order to increase their own resources or those of family, friends, and close associates. Those are not the leaders whom I admire, nor are they the leaders that young people should emulate. As I make clear in the pages that follow, the key to effective leader-ship is amoral: The skills that I describe can be used for the ends of a Nelson Man-dela, or for the ends of Osama bin Laden. But once we turn from description to prescription, it is clear that, as individuals and as members of broader communi-ties, we should do all that we can to increase the incidence of good leaders—indi-viduals who are engaged, excellent, and dedicated to the pursuit of ethical ends.

CONCLUSION

In writing *Leading Minds*, my primary aim was to obtain a better understanding of the features of effective leadership. I certainly do not see the work as a guide-book that, once assimilated, will turn an ordinary citizen into a leader or an ordi-nary leader into an exceptional one.

That said, I believe that the cognitive view introduced here provides a fresh perspective on the nature of leadership. When one thinks of the leader as a storyteller whose newly fashioned stories must wrestle with those that are already operative in the minds of an audience, one obtains a powerful way of conceptualizing the work of leading. It is important for leaders to know their stories; to get them straight; to communicate them effectively, particularly to those who are in the thrall of rival stories; and, above all, to embody in their lives the stories that they tell.

At the conclusion of the book, I outline six constant features of leaders, as well as six features that have come to characterize leadership in our time. My hope is that the analysis will prove helpful to those who find themselves thrust into positions of leadership, and that it might also help those already in leadership positions obtain a better understanding of their task and, perhaps, suggest to them new ways in which to achieve success.

It is perhaps not surprising that we live in a time of disillusionment with our leaders. We are all too familiar with the evil that malevolent leaders can bring about, even as we are frustrated that individuals in whom we have placed hope so often disappoint. Many well-meaning individuals—both lay and scholarly—say that we have outlived the notion of leadership from the top and that we should embrace flattened or even leaderless institutions.

At such times, it is particularly important to return to fundamentals. Many assumptions about leadership in the political realm are superficial and unsubstantiated; there is no need to guide one's policies by the results of the latest poll or to force every complex idea into a sound bite. Here one can take inspiration from those individuals who have not accepted the conventional wisdom, who have risked defeat, rejection, obscurity, even their lives, in order to pursue ideas in which they (and perhaps a few followers) believe. To put it simply: Leaders can actually lead. One of the important roles that elders can provide in a society is to call attention to those figures from whom one may learn, and by whose lives one may be guided. Individuals the world over can be enriched by the words of Europeanist Jean Monnet, who declared, "I regard every defeat as an opportunity." The individuals portrayed in *Leading Minds* certainly have their flaws, but I believe that both ordinary citizens and aspiring leaders can also draw inspiration from their lives and from their stories.

REFERENCES

Cited in the Preface

Gardner, H. 1983/2011. *Frames of Mind: The Theory of Multiple Intelligences.* New York: Basic Books.

Gardner, H. 1991/2011. *The Unschooled Mind: How Children Think and How Schools Should Teach.* New York: Basic Books.

Gardner, H. 1993/2011. *Creating Minds: An Anatomy of Creativity Seen through the Lives of Freud, Einstein, Picasso, Stravinsky, Eliot, Graham, and Gandhi*. New York: Basic Books.

Gardner, H., M. Csikszentmihalyi, and W. Damon. 2001. *Good Work: When Excellence and Ethics Meet*. New York Basic Books.

Gardner, H. 2011. *Truth, Beauty, and Goodness Reframed: Educating for the Virtues in the Twenty-First Century*. New York: Basic Books.

Further Reading

Note: This is by no means an exhaustive list of works about particular leaders or about leadership in general. Rather, it features works that I have found helpful in thinking about the persons and issues treated in this book. I have avoided literature reviews, encyclopedic works, edited papers and letters, potted biographies, and hagiographies.

Leadership

Bennis, W. 2009. *On Becoming a Leader*. 4th ed. New York: Basic Books.

Bennis, W., and P. Biederman. 2009. *The Essential Bennis*. San Francisco: Jossey Bass.

Couto, R. 2010. *Political and Social Leadership: A Reference Handbook*. Thousand Oaks, CA: Sage Publications.

George, Bill, with Peter Sims. 2007. *True North*. San Francisco: Jossey Bass.

Gergen, David. 2000. *Eyewitness to Power: The Essence of Leadership*. New York: Simon & Schuster.

Goleman, D., R. Boyatsis, and A. McKee. 2004. *Primal Leadership*. Boston: Harvard Business School Press.

Kellerman, B. 2008. *Followership*. Boston: Harvard Business School Press.

———. 2004. *Bad Leadership*. Boston: Harvard Business School Press.

Keohane, N. 2010. *Thinking about Leadership*. Princeton: Princeton University Press.

Wills, G. 1995. *Certain Trumpets: The Nature of Leadership*. New York: Simon & Schuster.

Mahatma Gandhi

Andrews, C. F., and Arun Gandhi. 2003. *Mahatma Gandhi: His Life and Ideas*. Woodstock, VT: Skylight Paths. (In this book Gandhi's grandson updates a book by an associate of Gandhi's, looking at his ideas and their impact today.)

Lelyveld, J. 2011. *Great Soul: Mahatma Gandhi and His Struggle with India*. New York: Knopf.

von Tunzelmann, A. 2008. *Indian Summer: The Secret History of the End of an Empire*. New York: Picador.

Robert Maynard Hutchins

Hutchins, R. Maynard. 2007. *No Friendly Voice*. Hadamard Press. (This work is a collection of his talks.)

Pope John XXIII

Cahill, Thomas. 2001. *Pope John XXIII: A Penguin Life*. New York: Penguin.
Pope John XXIII. 2008. *Essential Writings*. Maryknoll, NY: Orbis Books.

Martin Luther King, Jr.

Frady, M. 2005 *Martin Luther King, Jr.: A Life*. New York: Penguin.
King, Martin Luther, Jr., and Clayborne Carson. 2001. *The Autobiography of Martin Luther King, Jr.* New York: Grand Central Publishers.

George C Marshall

Husted, Stewart. 2007. *George C. Marshall: The Rubrics of Leadership*. Carlisle, PA: Strategic Studies Institute.

Margaret Mead

Banner, Lois. 2004. *Intertwined Lives: Margaret Mead, Ruth Benedict, and Their Circle*. New York: Vintage.
Bowman-Kruhm, M. 2002. *Margaret Mead: A Biography*. Santa Barbara, CA: Greenwood Press.
Lutkehaus, N. 2001. *Margaret Mead: The Making of an American Icon*. Princeton: Princeton Univ. Press.

Jean Monnet

Fransen, Frederick. 2001. *The Supranational Politics of Jean Monnet: Ideas and Origins of the European Community*. Santa Barbara, CA: Greenwood Press.
Rousell, Eric. 1996. *Jean Monnet*. Paris: Fayard.

J. Robert Oppenheimer

Bird, Kai, and M. Sherwin. 2005. *American Prometheus: The Triumph and Tragedy of J. Robert Oppenheimer*. New York: Knopf.
Cassidy, David. 2009. *J. Robert Oppenheimer and the American Century*. Baltimore: Johns Hopkins Univ. Press.

Eleanor Roosevelt

Cook, Blanche Wiesen. 2000. *Eleanor Roosevelt: Volume 2, The Defining Years 1933–1938*. New York: Penguin.
Roosevelt, Eleanor. 2000. *Empty without You: The Intimate Letters of Eleanor Roosevelt and Lorena Hickock*. New York: Da Capo Press.
———. 2001. *My Day: The Best of Eleanor Roosevelt's Acclaimed Newspaper Columns, 1936–1962*. New York: Da Capo Press.

Alfred P. Sloan/General Motors

Farber, David. 2005. *Sloan Rules: Alfred Sloan and Triumph of General Motors*. Chicago: Univ. of Chicago Press.

Freeman, Allyn. 2005. *The Leadership Genius of Alfred P. Sloan*. New York: McGraw-Hill.

Margaret Thatcher
Berlinsky, Claire. 2010. *There Is No Alternative: Why Margaret Thatcher Matters*. New York: Basic Books.
Campbell, John. 2004. *Margaret Thatcher: The Iron Lady*. New York: Vintage.
———. 2008. *Margaret Thatcher: The Grocer's Daughter*. New York: Vintage.
Wapshott, N. 2008. *Ronald Reagan and Margaret Thatcher: A Political Marriage*. New York: Sentinel Trade Books.

PART I

A FRAMEWORK
FOR LEADERSHIP

1

INTRODUCTION

A Cognitive Approach to Leadership

With words we govern men.

—Benjamin Disraeli

Practical men, who believe themselves to be quite exempt from any intellectual influences, are usually the slaves of some defunct economist.

—John Maynard Keynes

EUREKA AND EINSTEIN

At the end of November 1943, three men, already figures of historical significance, met in Tehran, the capital of Iran. Now that the tide of the Second World War had finally turned in favor of the Allies, Prime Minister Winston Churchill of Great Britain, President Franklin D. Roosevelt of the United States, and Premier Josef Stalin of the Union of Soviet Socialist Republics sat down together for the first time to address a number of crucial issues. During the four-day meeting that came to be called the Eureka Summit, they and their representatives tackled such topics as the opening of a second Western front against the Germans; the policies to be pursued with respect to Poland, France, Turkey, and China; the treatment of Germany's leaders after the conclusion of the war; and the prosecution of the war against Japan, the other major Axis enemy. In addition to reaching various military and diplomatic decisions, the trio of leaders became better acquainted and placed the Alliance on a firmer footing.

At the time of the Eureka Summit, Albert Einstein was living quietly in Princeton, New Jersey, continuing to work, as he had been for over four decades, on fundamental questions about the nature of physical reality. In the early years of the century, Einstein had almost single-handedly brought about a revolution in physics, first with his special theory of relativity in 1905, and

3

The leaders of the Allies at Tehran, 1943: (seated left to right) Stalin, Roosevelt, Churchill

then with his general theory of relativity a decade later. When initially propounded, these theories had seemed primarily of scholarly interest, as Einstein was rethinking the nature of space, time, gravity, and other fundamental forces of the universe. But various implications of his work proved to be of the utmost practical consequence, as Einstein himself came to realize. In a 1939 letter to President Roosevelt, he called attention to the possibility that extremely powerful bombs might be constructed if one could set off nuclear chain reactions in a mass of uranium: Einstein's message proved a crucial factor in the authorization of work on nuclear weapons. By the end of 1943, work in Los Alamos, New Mexico, on the development of an atomic bomb had advanced to a crucial point; this work would have been inconceivable in the absence of Einstein's revolutionary insights about the relationship between matter and energy.

When we think of leaders, we usually envision the political or military giants of an era—Alexander the Great, Napoléon Bonaparte, Abraham Lincoln, or the generals of the Civil War. The familiar photograph of Stalin, Roosevelt, and Churchill seated alongside one another on a veranda in Tehran epitomizes this common conception of what leaders look like, even as the agenda at the Eureka

Albert Einstein/The Bettmann Archive

Summit reflected the kinds of strategic preoccupations that we attribute to those in leadership positions.

At first blush, few individuals could seem more remote from this conception than Einstein, who worked on issues so abstruse that, even today, few individuals understand them completely. In addition, he preferred to ponder issues in the laboratory of his own imagination, and then perhaps discuss them with one or two close associates. During the First World War, Einstein had been a pacifist; only because of Hitler's rise, and against his strong personal inclinations, had Einstein become drawn into political issues on the eve of the Second World War. When he was approached about becoming the first president of Israel, the armchair thinker was both amused and alarmed by the idea, and immediately declined—to the relief, it is said, of both parties.

In light of the deep differences among the Eureka Summit leaders, on the one hand, and Einstein, on the other, one may well ask whether it makes sense to contemplate these individuals in the same breath (or in the same prose passage). After all, one readily applies the name *leader* to Roosevelt or Churchill; to call Einstein a leader seems a stretch, unless one adds a descriptor such as a "leading physicist."

In this book, I argue that we can understand the achievements of such figures as Churchill and Einstein better if, first, we recognize the ways in which they were similar and, second and more importantly, we survey strategic intermediate points between these such prototypical figures. To anticipate my argument very briefly, I see both Churchill and Einstein as leaders—as individuals who significantly influence the thoughts, behaviors, and/or feelings of others. Churchill exerted his influence in a direct way, through the stories he communicated to various audiences; hence, I term him a *direct* leader. Einstein exerted his influence in an *indirect* way, through the ideas he developed and the ways that those ideas were captured in some kind of a theory or treatise; hence, he qualifies as an *indirect* leader.

Einstein and Churchill mark two ends of a continuum that denotes the capacity of a person (or a group of persons) to *influence* other people. (Indeed, I could have termed this study "An Examination of Influence," but that lexical move would have undermined the reorientation in thinking about both creativity and leadership that is my goal.) One way to understand a continuum is by examining its poles; and, indeed, I return to Churchill and kindred leaders in chapter 13. However, we can gain a better understanding of the crucial phenomena of leadership if we instead scan a range of cases—a set of twentieth-century individuals who span the continuum from individuals whose leadership is primarily indirect (like Einstein or Virginia Woolf or Charles Darwin) to individuals whose leadership is unambiguously direct (like Josef Stalin or Margaret Thatcher or Erwin Rommel).

The individuals I have chosen are not all household names, but they effectively represent the central question that arises when one contrasts Einstein and the Eureka Summit leaders: Who ultimately had the greater influence—the three most powerful men of their time or a solitary thinker armed with only a succinct physics equation? This tantalizing question, reframed to encompass various leaders, is one I revisit throughout the book.

ELEVEN CHARACTERS IN SEARCH OF A LINK

In all likelihood, the eleven individuals whose leadership I probe have never before been linked. One might well ask a set of enthusiastic parlor-game players (who had not read the opening pages of this book) to identify the features the following individuals have in common:

> Margaret Mead (1901–1978), who was trained as a cultural anthropologist, became famous for both her pioneering studies of adolescence among islanders in the South Seas and her wide knowledge about changing mores in the twentieth century. Through tireless speech making and writing over a fifty-year period, she influenced views about childhood, family life, and society all over the world.

J. Robert Oppenheimer (1904–1967), the theoretical physicist, is best known for his scientific directorship of the Manhattan Project. From 1943 to 1945 he led an unprecedentedly large and diverse team of scientists involved with this project as they succeeded in constructing the first nuclear weapons. Entering after the war into the highly charged world of scientific politics, he was eventually judged a national security risk. Oppenheimer spent the last years of his life out of the public eye, as the esteemed director of the Institute for Advanced Study in Princeton.

Robert Maynard Hutchins (1899–1977) became the University of Chicago's president when he was thirty. He propounded an influential, tradition-based view of higher education rooted in the study of classical texts and the discussion of philosophical issues. Always a controversial figure, he became in his later years a foundation executive and the founding director of the Center for the Study of Democratic Institutions.

Alfred P. Sloan, Jr. (1875–1966) was one of the founders of the modern corporation. As the head of General Motors, he set up an organizational structure that exploited the strengths of both centralized and decentralized institutional arrangements. As a principal spokesman for American business, he encouraged the belief that America's strength emanated from its capitalistic system. In the latter years of his life, he became a major philanthropist.

George C. Marshall (1880–1959) was a highly effective chief of staff of the U.S. Army during the Second World War. After the war, as the secretary of state, he first called for and then helped to direct the recovery program in Western Europe. For many around the world, Marshall embodied the disinterested public servant. Nonetheless, he became, in the early 1950s, the subject of attack by Joseph McCarthy, the red-baiting senator.

Pope John XXIII (1881–1963), born Angelo Giuseppe Roncalli, was one of the most important, and certainly one of the most popular, popes of modern times. Appointed at age seventy-seven as an interim pontiff, he surprised his colleagues by immediately announcing plans for a Vatican Council that would examine the Catholic Church's role in the modern world. He called for a return to the simple messages of early Christianity, instigated efforts to reduce tensions between the political superpowers, and built bridges that spanned many faiths, nations, and ideologies.

Eleanor Roosevelt (1884–1962), the niece of one U.S. president and the wife of another, was a leading advocate of liberal and humanitarian causes both in the United States and abroad. Often positioned politically to the left of her husband, Franklin D. Roosevelt, she became a lightning rod for criticism. A role model for many individuals, and particularly for American women, she was long touted as the "most admired woman in the world."

Martin Luther King, Jr. (1929–1968), who was trained as a minister, became the most articulate and successful advocate of the cause of African Americans in the middle years of the twentieth century. His massive 1963 March on Washington constituted a milestone in the history of the civil rights movement. In light of his decision to focus on broader domestic and international issues, his position as a black leader became more tenuous. His assassination by a rabid segregationist left a void in leadership that has yet to be filled.

Margaret Thatcher (1925–) rose from modest origins to become the Conservative prime minister of Great Britain from 1979 to 1990. As prime minister, she inspired a fundamental reconfiguration of social, economic, and political forces in her country. The defining moment of her tenure was her decisive leadership during the 1982 Falklands War. While resisting closer ties with Western Europe, she helped forge new relations with the Eastern bloc of nations.

Jean Monnet (1888–1979), a French economist and diplomat, played a crucial but largely behind-the-scenes role in the reconstruction of his country following both world wars. Well connected to business and political figures on both sides of the Atlantic, he was often cast in an oppositional "internationalist" role to the more nationalistically oriented Charles de Gaulle. Because of his efforts over half a century to bring people and nations together, Monnet is generally credited with being the chief architect of a united Europe.

Mahatma Gandhi (1869–1948) was the political and religious leader who guided his native India to independence in the first half of the twentieth century. He developed and practiced an ascetic philosophy of living, which many of his close associates also followed. His innovative approach to the resolution of conflict—*satyagraha,* or nonviolent resistance—rarely prevailed in India after his assassination, yet it has inspired political activists and dissidents throughout the world.

Coming from different countries and social backgrounds, and trained in a range of vocations, these eleven individuals all became leaders in the sense that I am using the term: *persons who, by word and/or personal example, markedly influence the behaviors, thoughts, and/or feelings of a significant number of their fellow human beings* (here termed *followers* or *audience members).* The leaders' voices affected their worlds, and, ultimately, our world.

The tension aroused in linking these individuals reflects the varying topographies of their major enterprises. Especially at the beginning of their careers, Mead and Oppenheimer worked chiefly within scholarly domains: they exerted influence largely by virtue of the quality of their research within those domains. They qualified, in the early years of their careers, as *indirect* leaders. Hutchins,

Sloan, Marshall, and Pope John operated in increasingly comprehensive institutions, where they had to communicate with individuals of different backgrounds and perspectives. Yet, within a university, a business corporation, the military, or the church these leaders still could assume a certain commonality of interest among their respective constituents.

The remaining leaders addressed much wider constituencies. Roosevelt played a special role in the lives of women, a population that had been largely disenfranchised in the United States and throughout the rest of the world. King assumed a leadership role among African Americans, who had been subjected to unprecedented mistreatment over several centuries. Most ambitiously, leaders like Thatcher seek to provide direction for a whole nation, while visionaries like Gandhi and Monnet deliberately seek to encompass collections of nations, if not the whole world.

A word on exposition. Reflecting the movement from domain to nation, I devote separate chapters (4–12) to Mead, Oppenheimer, Hutchins, Sloan, Marshall, Pope John XXIII, Roosevelt, King, and Thatcher, respectively. A brief reprise after chapter 11 allows me to review the argument. In chapter 13 I survey the activities of ten national leaders, each of whom played a decisive role on the world scene during the first half of the twentieth century. In chapter 14, moving beyond the nation-state as usually defined, I review the achievements of Jean Monnet and Mahatma Gandhi. Each of these men sought to provide leadership that spoke to the wider world.

RELATING AND EMBODYING STORIES

Leaders achieve their effectiveness chiefly through the stories they relate. Here, I use the term *relate* rather than *tell* because presenting a story in words is but one way to communicate. Leaders in the arts characteristically inspire others by the ways they use their chosen media of artistic expression, be they the phrases of a sonata or the gestures of a dance; scientists lead through the manipulation of the symbol systems favored in their domains, be they the mathematical equations of theoretical physicists or the anatomical models of neurophysiologists. In addition to communicating stories, leaders *embody* those stories. That is, without necessarily relating their stories in so many words or in a string of selected symbols, leaders such as Marshall convey their stories by the kinds of lives they themselves lead and, through example, seek to inspire in their followers.

The ways in which direct leaders conduct their lives—their embodiments—must be clearly perceptible by those whom they hope to influence. If a military leader like Stalin calls on his troops to be courageous, it matters whether he comports himself bravely. Similarly, if a religious leader like Pope John calls on Catholics to act generously toward those of other religious and ideological persuasions, his actual behavior toward Protestant pastors or Communist workers becomes significant. People who do not practice what they preach are hypocrites, and hypocrisy mutes the effectiveness of their stories.

In contrast, the personal lives of indirect leaders are not germane to their influence; strictly speaking, it did not matter to fellow scientists whether Einstein loved his wives, tormented his children, or never spoke to others. Nonetheless, the embodiments of an indirect leader are important. What matters to fellow physicists are the particular *approaches* to science embodied in Einstein's work. Just as his successors have been influenced by the conclusions that he drew, they have also been affected by the ways that he posed questions and the ways that he formulated, approached, and solved problems. By the same token, the conceptions and methods created by Igor Stravinsky and Martha Graham have affected succeeding generations of creative composers and dancers, respectively. If such creators had achieved their products through illegitimate means—for example, through fudging of data or through plagiarism—their leadership status would have been challenged.

It proves useful to align leaders in terms of the innovativeness of their stories. The *ordinary* leader, by definition the most common one, simply relates the traditional story of his or her group as effectively as possible. An ordinary political leader like Gerald Ford or the French president Georges Pompidou or an ordinary business leader like Roger Smith of General Motors does not seek to stretch the consciousness of his contemporary audience. We can learn about the commonplace stories of a group by examining the words and the lives of ordinary leaders; we are unlikely to be able to anticipate the ways in which that group will evolve in the future. In this book I have not focused on ordinary leaders.

The *innovative* leader takes a story that has been latent in the population, or among the members of his or her chosen domain, and brings new attention or a fresh twist to that story. In recent world history, neither Thatcher nor de Gaulle nor Ronald Reagan created wholly novel stories. Rather, it was their particular genius to have identified stories or themes that already existed in the culture but had become muted or neglected over the years. In the arts, individuals who style themselves as neoclassicists, neoromantics, or even neomodernists are also attempting to revive themes and forms that have fallen into disuse. In trying to capture the glory or the innocence of an earlier era, in the face of rival contemporary currents and counterstories, these innovative leaders may succeed in reorienting their times.

By far the rarest individual is the *visionary* leader. Not content to relate a current story or to reactivate a story drawn from a remote or recent past, this individual actually creates a new story, one not known to most individuals before, and achieves at least a measure of success in conveying this story effectively to others. The great religious leaders of the past—Moses, Confucius, Jesus, Buddha, Mohammed—certainly qualify as visionary; on a more modest scale, I view individuals like Gandhi and Monnet as visionary leaders for our time.

The question of just where to draw the line between innovative and visionary is not easy to determine and is not, in any case, crucial for this study. Readers may well quarrel with my suggestion that Thatcher is *innovative,* while Gandhi and Monnet earn the appellation *visionary.* Also, a story that appears visionary to most followers may strike the knowledgeable few as "merely innovative." What does emerge from this study is that visionary leadership is far more readily achieved in specific domains (like particular arts or sciences) or in specific institutions (like a university or a corporation) than in the guidance of an entire society. Indeed, in any century there may be only one or two effective political or religious leaders who are genuine visionaries.

LEADING A DOMAIN, LEADING A SOCIETY

The specter of the visionary leader touches on a fundamental distinction between leadership of a domain and leadership of a wider society, a distinction that I explore throughout this book. When it comes to providing leadership *within a traditional domain or discipline,* one can assume that one's audience is already sophisticated in the stories, the images, and the other embodiments of that domain. To put it simply, one is communicating with experts. Especially in the contemporary, "hungry" era, vision is at a premium within most domains. And so, while it is hardly an easy matter to become a visionary, such an individual stands at least a reasonable chance of successfully reorienting a domain.

Six of the individuals I studied in my 1993 book *Creating Minds* did in fact create a new story—one that eventually refashioned the domains in which they worked. Sigmund Freud showed his colleagues (and, ultimately, the world) a new way to understand normal and neurotic individuals; Einstein conceived of time and space in a way that was radically unfamiliar but scientifically productive; Stravinsky, Graham, Pablo Picasso, and T. S. Eliot reoriented their chosen art forms in ways that were initially startling but that ultimately affected numerous successors' practices. Both their actual works and their processes of creating proved influential. Quite possibly, their respective audiences were "primed" for their appearance; their revolutionary accomplishments in turn "primed" their audiences for yet further breakthroughs at their hands, or at the hands of those visionary creators who came after them.

These leaders of recognized domains need to be distinguished sharply from individuals who would presume to *reorient* a political entity, like a nation, or a broadly based institution, like the church or the military. In the latter cases, the aspiring leader is dealing not with experts but with individuals who bring an ordinary, relatively undisciplined frame of mind to their audience membership. (Indeed, even if the audience member happens to be an expert in some domain, such incidental expertise does not ordinarily color his or her perceptions as a member of the nation or institution.) The voter Janet Q. Public is unlikely to be an expert in the domain of politics; neither were Freud, Picasso, or Graham when each was acting merely as a voting citizen. Accordingly, at least to begin with, the leader who would reorient an institution must be able to address a public in terms of the commonsense and commonplace notions that an ordinary inhabitant absorbs simply by virtue of living for some years within a society.

By and large, members of a society are not—except in times of crisis—searching for an unfamiliar story or a new form of understanding. Indeed, the situation is almost the opposite. As Richard Nixon once expressed it: "About the time you are writing a line you have written so often that you want to throw up, that is the time the American people will hear it." In this way, ordinary citizens differ markedly from experts in the arts and the sciences, who, at least in modern times, are ever on the lookout for new answers and, equally, for novel questions. And even at a time of crisis, a visionary leader rarely achieves his or her desired effect. Thus, while visionaries like Gandhi or Buddha or Christ prove fascinating to study, they are also extreme rarities—mutant leaders, one might say.

In *Creating Minds* I focused on those individuals who ushered in the major artistic and scientific breakthroughs of the twentieth century, rather than on their contemporaries who represented the status quo or whose reaches toward breakthroughs were not successful. In this book, as I have noted, I focus on leaders who may be termed innovative or visionary—leaders who profoundly affect other people. I strive to understand Hutchins instead of his Harvard counterpart Nathan Marsh Pusey; Sloan rather than his General Motors' successor Harlow Curtice; Thatcher in lieu of her fellow prime ministers Neville Chamberlain, James Callaghan, or John Major. Part of the difference clearly lies in the minds, personalities, and ambitions of the more successful leaders, whether they operated in traditional domains or sought to address diverse publics. However, the needs and demands of the audiences, and the nature of the times in which leaders and audience members live, prove at least as important a factor in determining leaders' ultimate effectiveness.

As a rule of thumb, creative artists, scientists, and experts in various disciplines lead indirectly, through their work; effective leaders of institutions and nations lead directly, through the stories and acts they address to an audience. This distinction is not, however, rigid. A leader of a nation may lead indirectly; for example, de Gaulle's writings represented an important contribution to the French people. By the same token, a leader within a domain may lead his audience members directly—for example, by assuming the presidency of a professional organization. Note, however, that the leader within a domain is unlikely to be taken seriously by her colleagues unless she herself has created within that domain—and, preferably, has done so innovatively. Mead, for instance, could become an effective president of the American Anthropological Association because she was a widely esteemed practitioner of that discipline.

In addition to its focus on leaders with innovative messages, my sample is also distinctive in certain other ways. The leaders whom I study achieved their positions within democratic societies, largely because of their persuasive powers. I term them *leaders by choice*. Moreover, with certain noted exceptions, their view of their constituencies was typically *inclusive*—they sought to draw more people into their circle, rather than to denounce or to exclude others. By the same token, while they may have sought and enjoyed power, they were motivated in large measure by the desire to effect changes, rather than simply by a lust for more power. It is possible that the conclusions I draw about leadership might not apply in equal measure to individuals who, for example, achieved their positions by force or who were sustained chiefly by a hatred of others or by the thirst for absolute power. My review of the leaders of the Second World War helps to place in perspective the in-depth portraits of the eleven leaders I have selected; the survey in chapter 13 brings to the fore some characteristics of leaders who are obsessed with power or who gain advantage by setting groups against one another.

As with *Creating Minds,* I deliberately focus on individuals who have lived in the twentieth century. I sought individuals about whom biographical materials were readily available, whose claims to be influential were not controversial, and whose achievements and failures lay sufficiently in the past that historians have already attained distance from them. Because these individuals have lived roughly during the same epoch, I could be confident that differences among them did not reflect their having been subjected to contrasting historical conditions. It remains to be seen whether the generalizations that emerge also apply to earlier direct leaders like Oliver Cromwell or Napoléon Bonaparte, or to earlier indirect leaders (or creators) like Albrecht Dürer or Jane Austen.

THE STORY AS CENTRAL

The ultimate impact of the leader depends most significantly on the particular story that he or she relates or embodies, and the receptions to that story on the part of audiences (or collaborators or followers). What links the eleven individuals with whom I lead off, and the score of others from this century whose names could readily have been substituted for them, is the fact that they arrived at a story that worked for them and, ultimately, for others as well. They told stories—in so many words—about themselves and their groups, about where they were coming from and where they were headed, about what was to be feared, struggled against, and dreamed about. My analysis of leadership comes to focus, therefore, on the stories conveyed by representative leaders.

The audience is not simply a blank slate, however, waiting for the first, or for the best, story to be etched on its virginal tablet. Rather, audience members come equipped with many stories that have already been told and retold in their homes, their societies, and their domains. The stories of the leader—be they traditional or novel—must compete with many other extant stories; and if the new stories are to succeed, they must transplant, suppress, complement, or in some measure outweigh the earlier stories, as well as contemporary oppositional "counterstories." In a Darwinian sense, the "memes"—a culture's versions of genes—called stories compete with one another for favor, and only the most robust stand a chance of gaining ascendancy. I focus here on stories that worked, but I do not neglect those narratives that proved less compelling.

I deliberately use the terms *story* and *narrative* rather than *message* or *theme.* In speaking of stories, I want to call attention to the fact that leaders present a *dynamic* perspective to their followers: not just a headline or snapshot, but a drama that unfolds over time, in which they—leader and followers—are the principal characters or heroes. Together, they have embarked on a journey in pursuit of certain goals, and along the way and into the future, they can expect to encounter certain obstacles or resistances that must be overcome. Leaders and audiences traffic in many stories, but the most basic story has to do with issues of *identity.* And so it is the leader who succeeds in conveying a new version of a given group's story who is likely to be effective. Effectiveness here involves fit— the story needs to make sense to audience members at this particular historical moment, in terms of where they have been and where they would like to go. Consider the capsule version of Eleanor Roosevelt's story—that a woman who was at once ordinary in appearance and extraordinary in background and re- sources could improve the lot of disadvantaged people. Such a story was appro- priate at mid-century; the same story might have seemed unrealistic fifty years earlier and patronizing a half-century later.

As one comes to focus more closely on individual examples of leadership—tra- ditional or visionary, direct or indirect, inclusionary or exclusionary, successful or ineffectual—one must consider not only the particular stories that are already "in the air" but also the niche that the leader's set of stories ultimately occupies. By the same token, the particular embodiment in the life of the leader stands in competi- tion with a myriad of earlier images and stereotypes that already stock the con- sciousness of audience members. Through her daily mode of existence, Roosevelt had to refute the notions that only men can lead, that persons of privilege are sus- pect, and that only persons of extraordinary appearance and talents can inspire a revolution. To prevail, stories need enough background, detail, and texture so that an audience member can travel comfortably within their contours; only when these accompanying features are already well known can the leader count on an au- dience to "fill in the text." In chapter 3, I more closely examine the nature of sto- ries related by leaders and their various realizations and embodiments.

A COGNITIVE APPROACH TO LEADERSHIP

To summarize thus far: Our understanding of the nature and processes of leader- ship is most likely to be enhanced as we come to understand better the arena in which leadership necessarily occurs—namely, the *human mind.* Perhaps this characterization should be pluralized as *human minds,* since I am concerned equally with the mind of the leader and the minds of the followers (whom I sometimes refer to as *audience members* or *collaborators*). Accordingly, this book is a sustained examination, first, of the ways in which leaders of different types achieve varying degrees of success in characterizing and resolving important life issues in their own minds and, second, of how, in parallel or in turn, they attempt to alter the minds of their various audiences to effect desired changes.

By focusing on the mind and invoking the word *cognitive,* I make deliberate contact with an approach to the study of mind that has developed rapidly in the last few decades. In contrast to the behaviorists, who have focused only on overt actions, and the psychoanalysts, whose interest has been directed chiefly at personality and motivation, cognitive psychologists examine how ideas (or thoughts or images or mental representations)* develop and how they are stored, accessed, combined, remembered, and (all too often) rearranged or distorted by the operations of the human mental apparatus. Many researchers in the cognitive tradition have studied relatively simple stimuli such as single words or simple geometric forms; yet the compleat cognitivist aspires as well to explain more complex and more highly meaningful forms of information, such as stories, scenarios, dreams, and visions.

Confronted with the phenomenon of leadership, a cognitively oriented scientist is likely to ask such questions as, What are the ideas (or stories) of the leader? How have they developed? How are they communicated, understood, and misunderstood? How do they interact with other stories, especially competing counterstories, that have already drenched the consciousness of audience members? How do key ideas (or stories) affect the thoughts, feelings, and behaviors of other individuals? Precisely such questions concern us in the pages that follow.

While I am comfortable in describing the approach as *cognitive,* I do not wish to raise certain expectations. My model is not the familiar information-processing approach in which the generation or comprehension of a story is traced on a step-by-step basis (input to output). Rather, the approach is cognitive in a generic sense: an active mind is comparing stories with one another and highlighting some features, while downplaying others. My cognitive approach to leadership emphasizes a set of considerations that has received short shrift in the otherwise-ample social-scientific literature on leadership. The bulk of this literature falls into four categories, each of which is worthy of consideration, but each of which can be enriched by a consideration of cognitive dimensions.

Some authorities approach leadership primarily in terms of the acquisition and utility of *power.* Every society requires a political apparatus, and certain individuals either choose or are selected to direct the social and political structures. I do not for a moment underestimate the importance of power as a motivation or a force in its own right, but I insist that, of itself, power—as opposed to terror—

---

*All these words are used routinely by cognitivists and are often employed interchangeably as well.

cannot bring about significant changes. The vantage point of power, however achieved, needs to be yoked to specific messages—to stories—that can direct and guide an inner circle and a wider polity. This principle holds even with respect to individuals who gained enormous power in the twentieth century such as Stalin, Hitler, and Mao Zedong.

From a related perspective, others emphasize the role of specific *policies.* Recognizing that power must be used, proponents of this perspective focus on the decisions to be made about policy and the processes whereby the designated policies are more or less successfully implemented. At an extreme, such a policy orientation minimizes the role of a specific political leader; interest groups have their favored policies, and these groups will find instruments or vehicles to help institute those policies; decisions are made according to some kind of rational calculus.

While acknowledging the role of policies, I stress that the pursuit of certain practices or initiatives (promoted by certain societal events or certain interest groups), as opposed to others, is not a matter of chance; the articulation of policy alternatives by leaders proves a crucial element in determining the course of affairs that is ultimately pursued. Thus, Reagan may well have voiced the views of wealthy southern Californians who encouraged him to enter politics; but his own idiosyncratic skills, priorities, and persuasive powers left their marks on late-twentieth-century America. Reagan was not indistinguishable from the entrepreneur-politician Barry Goldwater or the actor-politician George Murphy.

Another perspective that calls into question the importance of the specific leader is one grounded in an examination of the *public,* or *audience.* Complementing those who see policies as having a life of their own, other authorities focus on the needs and fears of the general population, or of specific groups within the population. In this analysis, the mass of citizens senses, with some degree of precision, its most important goals, which could relate to policies or to grievances, goals, or anxieties. While the public may need ultimately to rally around some kind of a central figure, the choice of a specific leader is largely accidental. The leader who would succeed, then, is the one who best senses and delivers what an audience already desires.

I agree that at times the successful leader is the one who most keenly senses the wishes of a potential audience. But this act of intuition does not relieve the leader of the need to articulate a message clearly and convincingly, and to combat other contrary themes reverberating in the culture. In the 1920s and early 1930s, Germany may have been searching desperately for a new order (and a newly ordered society), but the emergence of leaders other than Hitler most assuredly would have changed the course of world history.

A final viewpoint is distinctly psychological. Unlike the other perspectives, and closer to my own set forth here, this one acknowledges the central role played by leaders. In most psychological studies of leadership, however, researchers have focused on the *personality* of the leader: his or her personal needs, principal psychodynamic traits, early life experiences, and relationship to other individuals. In what follows I often use insights drawn from this complementary approach. Yet, as with the other approaches, the personality emphasis cannot explain the particular course called for by a leader and the degree of success achieved with various audiences. Here, again, a concern with cognition—with the mental structures activated in leaders and followers—constitutes the missing piece of the puzzle.

In this book I say relatively little about how other authorities have approached the issue of leadership. In no way is this limited discussion meant to question the importance of earlier contributions to this much-studied topic. Indeed, as made clear in the reference notes to this and many other passages, I have learned a great deal from those authorities who have probed the personal traits and personal histories of leaders, different forms of leadership, and the crucial roles of the audience. I owe a special debt to my own mentor, the late psychoanalyst Erik Erikson, who in many ways inspired this study. But the existence of many excellent compendia on leadership, and my own focus on the cognitive dimensions of leadership, relieves me of the need to review critically other scholarly traditions in this field.

One more word on the study of leadership. In one sense, my study is conservative; it builds on the assumptions that there are individuals called leaders, who have stories and goals, who strive to achieve them, and who are sometimes successful in this pursuit. This stance will perturb those of a more radical stripe, who question whether leaders actually influence events, whether leaders *should* actually be allowed to influence events, or whether the conception of leadership itself deserves to survive. While acknowledging the rhetorical appeal of such accounts, I find them unconvincing in the light of human biology and human history. I invite those who question this enterprise to offer their own "leaderless" accounts of the success of the Manhattan Project, the early course of the civil rights movement, or the securing of independence for India.

THE PLAN OF THIS BOOK

In the concluding chapters of part I, I consider those components that make leadership possible. My analysis proceeds in two initially separate streams. In chapter 2, I review the features of human development that make possible the phenomena of leadership. In chapter 3, I consider the nature of the story making that leaders are engaged in and delineate the major kinds of stories that leaders have worked with over the centuries. A merging of these developmental and narrative streams facilitates an investigation of leadership as embodied in the lives of several influential twentieth-century leaders.

In the second and most extensive part of this book, I apply my framework by delineating the nature of leadership in varying domains. Proceeding from the most sharply delineated to the most expansive domains, I present a set of case studies, as well as some more general considerations of leadership processes associated with each kind of domain. First, I examine leadership within classic domains of scholarship, as represented by Mead's anthropology (chapter 4) and Oppenheimer's physics (chapter 5). At the start of their careers, these individuals exerted the kind of leadership that has traditionally been exercised by great artists like Picasso, Stravinsky, and Graham, or by exceptional scientists like Einstein or Darwin. Unlike these prototypical indirect leaders, however, Oppenheimer and Mead sought eventually to extend their influence, first by assuming direct leadership roles within their scholarly domains, and then by expanding beyond their scholarly domains, in the manner of a broad-gauged direct leader. They serve, accordingly, as exemplars of the central "Einstein-Eureka" tension being explored in this book.

In chapter 6, I begin my examination of leadership within institutions that pursue specific missions and that involve a set of interlocking constituencies. Institutions of this sort include schools, universities, and foundations. My chosen vehicle is Hutchins, who harbored awesome ambitions for the several institutions that he led but who ran into revealing difficulties as he attempted to implement his central ideas.

In chapters 7 through 9, still focusing on relatively circumscribed domains, I turn my attention to three classic institutions or "estates": the business corporation, the military, and the church. For many commentators, these organizations are synonymous with leadership; but as I try to show, the three estates exhibit interesting similarities with and differences from more narrowly, as well as more broadly, conceived institutions. My examples are Sloan (chapter 7), Marshall (chapter 8), and Pope John XXIII (chapter 9).

In chapters 10 and 11, I consider leadership for groups that have until now been considered nondominant, marginal, or "dissenting," to borrow the term created by the historian Bruce Miroff. In my study the two selected groups are women and African Americans. Both groups have spawned gifted leaders for at least a century, but no individual leader has successfully captured and held the national consciousness until the last half century. While the women's movement has lacked a single central figure, Roosevelt in many ways played a crucial role in the formation of feminine consciousness both in this country and abroad (see chapter 10). By nearly all accounts King has been the most important leader of the African American community (see chapter 11).

In chapter 12, following a brief reprise, I turn to what is generally considered the prototypical instance of leadership: the direction of a nation. This arena of leadership foregrounds the challenge a political leader faces in addressing a number of distinct constituencies while at the same time giving voice and direction to a recognized political entity. Epitomizing my argument that certain leaders must create and convey an innovative story to their constituencies is Thatcher.

Even more emblematic of political leadership are those individuals who preside over great nations during periods of crisis. A consideration of the individuals who led their respective nations during the Second World War provides an opportunity to comment on leadership at a time of "high stakes" and to consider the most malevolent, as well as the most heroic, forms of leadership. In chapter 13, I consider briefly not only the three Allied leaders at the Eureka Summit but also Chiang Kai-shek, de Gaulle, Hitler, Vladimir Lenin, Mao Zedong, Benito Mussolini, and Hideki Tojo. This survey gives me an opportunity to supplement knowledge of prototypical indirect leaders gained from the studies in *Creating Minds* with knowledge of prototypical direct leaders, who are drawn from the opposite end of the continuum. The review also provides a chance to revisit some of the hypotheses about leadership that have emerged from the earlier, more intensive case studies.

Part III extends the study in two ways. In chapter 14, I examine what may be the most important, but rarest and most elusive, variety of leadership: the form that goes beyond the nation-state and seeks to address all human beings. In recorded history, the chief epoch for such leadership occurred roughly two millennia ago, when a number of the major world religions were launched. Scattered attempts in more recent centuries have had relatively little long-term impact. For this reason, the case of Gandhi proves particularly telling—less, perhaps, because of its immediate success than because of the promise it may harbor for the coming centuries. On a somewhat more modest scale, the efforts of Monnet point to the kinds of leadership that may transcend national boundaries and rivalries.

In the concluding chapter 15, I take stock of the major findings that have resulted from the study. Included are a portrait of an exemplary leader, a survey of generalizations about leadership that have emerged, and a consideration of constants and new trends in the domain of leadership. In conclusion, I make some suggestions about how effective leadership might be facilitated.

A FEW WORDS ON METHOD

Let me comment on the methods I used in studying the individuals highlighted in this book and the kinds of conclusions that may accordingly be drawn. In general, I relied heavily on the published biographies of these individuals, as well as general histories of the period. Especially valuable were autobiographical accounts, which were available in nearly all cases. I also consulted, as needed, original documents—particularly speeches, popular writings, audiotapes, and videotapes—in which the protagonists have told their own stories in their own words. For better or for worse, Hitler's *Mein Kampf* and Gandhi's *Autobiography: The Story of My Experiments with Truth* are worth many secondary sources.

In much scholarly work, reports are written as if a study were primarily inductive (one reads many biographies of leaders and waits—with an innocent eye—for the proper generalizations to emerge) or as if it were an exercise in hypothesis testing (one proposes a model of a leader and then tests it systematically by examining "the data"). It would be misleading to absorb the present study into either camp. I began with some general ideas about leadership—in particular, with the notion that stories were important for all leaders and that leaders who wanted to influence wide audiences would find themselves drawn to the enunciation of simple stories. Based on my earlier study of creative individuals, I also had in mind some factors to monitor: for example, the kinds of families from which the leaders came, the cognitive strengths or "intelligences" exhibited by leaders, the crucial role played by other supportive individuals, and the length of time that it takes to develop and disseminate novel ideas.

In the course of the study, however, some of these themes receded in importance, while others emerged as worthy of more extended consideration. For instance, before beginning the case studies, I had not thought much about the contribution to effective leadership of travel in one's youth, the capacity to challenge figures in authority, a focus in early life on moral and spiritual issues, or the ways in which public figures apportion their time.

While it is not easy (and perhaps not even wise) to attempt to capture this oscillation between expectations and surprises, I believe that some of my own process of discovery does come through in this book. In this chapter and in the remaining chapters of part I, I lay out enough of my general background thinking so that readers can approach the case studies with the same "frame of mind" that I brought to them. Then, in the concluding part of the book, I turn more explicitly to the patterns and generalizations that have emerged from the study.

In this and the next two chapters, I introduce a set of distinctions that figures in a cognitive approach to leadership: such factors as direct/indirect forms of leadership, leadership within and across domains, inclusionary/exclusionary kinds of stories, identity stories, the embodiment of stories, and resistances and counterstories. Some readers will ponder these categories critically, while others may become somewhat impatient with what may seem like nitpicking or the proliferation of social-scientific jargon. I sympathize with both kinds of readers, for I harbor each of them within my own mind. Sometimes, I like to read as an accountant would, keeping careful track of every entry in some kind of ledger. At other times, I prefer to take in information as an audience member at a concert would, allowing the analytic themes to operate as they play freely within my imagination.

I have sought to accommodate both perspectives. In part I, I describe my conceptual categories as clearly as possible. From then on, however, I focus on the creation of effective music, with only the occasional introduction of program notes. In order to satisfy my own accountant tendencies, and those among the readership who share this actuarial proclivity, my collaborator and I have prepared appendices that delineate the key distinctions for each of the figures portrayed in this volume.

The world may continue to change rapidly, but we can expect to participate in that world as the same kinds of beings. Any psychologically informed discussion of human leadership should begin with a consideration of the nature and limitations of the species that encompasses leaders and followers.

2

HUMAN DEVELOPMENT
AND LEADERSHIP

*A leader is a man who has the ability to get other people to
do what they don't want to do and like it.*

—Harry Truman

Human beings are cultural creatures, growing up in societies formed over the centuries by other human beings, and participating more or less energetically in institutions that have evolved over equally long periods. For most of this book, I write within the cultural perspective, simply assuming that humans have been adequately socialized so that they can join these institutions, typically as followers but occasionally as leaders.

As noted in chapter 1, I apply a perspective that is cognitive as well as cultural. I view leadership as a process that occurs within the minds of individuals who live in a culture—a process that entails the capacities to create stories, to understand and evaluate these stories, and to appreciate the struggle among stories. Ultimately, certain kinds of stories will typically become predominant—in particular, stories that provide an adequate and timely sense of identity for individuals who live within a community or institution. This focus on stories presupposes that some individuals are in a position to convey these stories to others, that other individuals can identify with these stories, and that various individuals feel included or excluded once these stories have spread.

Just what kind of a creature can participate in such a community, enter into a world of narrative, and ultimately assume a position as follower, leader, or perhaps both? What sort of mind is needed to gain nurturance from at least certain kinds of stories told by certain kinds of people? I see at work four principal factors, outlined respectively in the next four sections. Two can be summarized briefly; two call for more extended discussion.

21

HUMANS' PRIMATE STATUS

The first factor is our *primate heritage.* In contrast with most other species, the order of primates is organized into hierarchies with *clear dominance relationships among its members.* Primates recognize individual members of their species from an early age, compete with one another for positions within the hierarchy, and ultimately assume specific relationships of dominance or submission to conspecifics.

These processes are most pronounced among males who live on savannah—at first during the rough play of childhood and later, during the serious competition for control of the colony, protection of offspring, and possession of the most desirable females. But dominance hierarchies are also found among female members of various primate species. In comparison with nondominant males, dominant males exhibit characteristic patterns of neurotransmitters (substances that transmit nerve impulses across synapses), such as a greater production of serotonin, and lower overall levels of stress. Intriguingly, when a male's position shifts in the hierarchy, so do these physiological markers. Primates often organize themselves into in-groups and out-groups; there may be an evolutionary advantage in remaining near those to whom one bears the greatest genetic similarity.

The second important component of our primate heritage is the *proclivity to imitate.* The decision about which model to imitate and when to imitate becomes crucial. Imitation is almost always unidirectional: that is, lower-status primates imitate the actions of higher-status conspecifics. However, the choices of behaviors to be imitated are made from a relatively narrow set of options; it would make little sense, for example, to speak of nonhuman primates as putting forth "stories" about their group that can lead other members of their species to develop a new sense of identity or a reconceptualization of the purpose of life.

While seemingly remote from the central topic of this book, our primate heritage is actually fundamental to an appreciation of leadership. For instance, the "dominance processes" observable in nonhuman primates are evident even among preschoolers. Dominant youngsters control toys, initiate and organize games, and help to keep the group together; less-dominant children orient themselves with reference to the more dominant ones and spend much of their time imitating and attempting to curry favor with the more dominant ones. Size, strength, skill, intelligence, attractiveness, and gender all contribute to the determination of which organisms will occupy superior positions in the emerging social hierarchy.

More generally, as primates, we expect a leadership/followership social structure. We also expect struggles for positions of dominance, and we frequently compute our positions within various hierarchies. This is *not* to say that we are slaves of our species membership. Nondominant cooperative groupings are possible. But those who expect such uncontoured structures to arise easily or to remain unchallenged are innocent of human history as well as human biology.

EARLY SOCIALIZATION:
SELF-DEFINITION AND GROUP IDENTIFICATION

The second of the four factors provides further clues about the origins of a sense of group identity. Researchers studying *early socialization of human children* have documented the importance of the establishment in early life of a strong and secure bond of attachment between infant and caretaker. Such an incipient sense of trust—or (less happily) of mistrust—colors the way that individuals react to authority. One's feeling of comfort in the presence of others or, correlatively, one's estrangement from others contributes powerfully to how one aligns oneself in later life with members of one's own group or with more remote groups.

Two other facets of early socialization are also crucial for understanding the processes and phenomena of leadership. One feature is the gradual emergence in the young child of a *sense of self.* As early as the age of eighteen months, young children have already become aware that they exist as separate entities. This awareness is revealed not only in a youngster's accurate use of names and other labels that refer to individuals, including herself, but also in her marvelous sense of affirmation when she peers into a mirror and notices that a mark placed surreptitiously on her face has marred her own appearance.

The other feature of critical importance in early socialization is the *appreciation of how one is similar to certain other individuals.* While youngsters naturally imitate a great deal of what they observe in the behavior of conspecifics who happen to be in their vicinity, this apprehension of similarity soon transcends sheer imitation. Indeed, since Sigmund Freud's time, researchers have spoken about a more complex process called *identification:* a youngster goes well beyond merely recognizing certain properties in common with another and comes to feel akin *in general* to an older model or set of role models. The young child may well *imitate* a person on the street or a puppet on television; but the child *identifies* with an older sibling or with the parent of the same sex, to the extent that he or she internalizes crucial features of that "role model." (Less frequently, youngsters come to identify strongly with age-mates.)

Once such identification begins to consolidate, the child need not directly monitor every action of the model. Instead, he or she can begin to imagine what the model *would do* in a given situation; the identifier can gain pleasure, or suffer shame or guilt, to the extent that he or she succeeds in living up to the expectations—the ideals—of the role model. Ultimately, effective followers no longer require the regular presence of the leader; they can anticipate his or her stories and themselves inspire other potential audience members.

In general, youngsters identify with those in their immediate circle. It is therefore of great interest when a child comes to identify with someone more remote—for example, the leader of a political or religious group. A fascinating "marker" of many future leaders is their capacity to identify with a more distant authority figure. This identification manifests itself both in efforts to emulate the leader and in a willingness to challenge that leader under certain circumstances.

Two parallel social processes are at work during the early years. The child develops an increasingly complex and differentiated sense of self as an individual; and the child comes to feel an affinity to older individuals in particular, and to one or more social groups in general. These processes continue to unfold throughout childhood and, indeed, for much of the rest of life. In youth, they are often referred to as the formation of identity; in middle age, as components of citizenship; in old age, as a sense of responsibility to succeeding generations.

The end product of these processes of self-definition and identification is an individual as part of a group; as a holder of certain beliefs, attitudes, and values; and as a practitioner of certain behaviors. It is the particular burden of the leader to help other individuals determine their personal, social, and moral identities; more often than not, leaders inspire in part because of how they have resolved their own identity issues.

But role models obviously can exert a range of influences. The growing child may evolve thoughts and actions that are either praiseworthy or undesirable or, as so often happens, simultaneously admirable and loathsome. Moreover, consequences ensue if role models worthy of emulation are not present, or if role models themselves exhibit inconstant or destructive behaviors. In these latter cases, the growing child will probably lack a coherent or integrated sense of self or a developed sense of group membership, and amoral or antisocial actions are likely to emerge. All too often, such an individual is likely to be attracted by demagogues rather than by saints.

THE MIND OF THE FIVE-YEAR-OLD

Courtesy of our primate heritage and the relatively predictable events of the first few years of life, one can anticipate the formation of the prototypical five-year-old child—someone who, amazingly enough, already possesses the basic ingredients necessary for entering into a leader-follower (or a peer-peer) relationship. That is to say, the five-year-old child already has a sense of himself and of other individuals, as persons and as members of the group. Children of this age can appreciate simple stories and, indeed, even create simple patterned narratives of their own. In addition, they already have assumed positions (still relatively flexible ones) within various dominance hierarchies and are becoming proficient at recognizing signals of leading, following, and relating as equals in peer-peer interactions.

Thanks to Sigmund Freud and his followers in the psychoanalytic movement, many observers have at least one relatively articulated view of the personality of the young child: an individual who is driven by strong urges, knows what she wants and will strive to get it, has a limited capacity to empathize with others, and exhibits rivalry with siblings as well as strong and often-contradictory "Oedipal" feelings toward her mother and her father. Thanks to the Swiss psychologist Jean Piaget and his fellow cognitive researchers, many observers also have a sense of the thought of the young child as an individual who sees the world largely from her own perspective and who knows the world chiefly through the operation of her sense organs and her motor systems.

Freud and Piaget introduced us to the third of the crucial basic ingredients of leadership—*the mind of the five-year-old child.* But these renowned authorities disagreed on a central point. While both theorists believed that children pass through "stages" in early childhood, they viewed the nature of those stages differently. Freud's affective, or emotional, stages are cumulative. That is, even when a growing individual apparently advances beyond his Oedipal strivings, he continues to experience a similar ensemble of feelings in analogous situations. For example, as an adult, he may well relive his affects of early years when he encounters a demanding boss or a sympathetic therapist.

In contrast, Piaget held that once a child achieves a more advanced cognitive stage, she no longer retains access to the cognitions of an earlier stage. As an example, consider what happens once a child is able to achieve conservation—that state of mind where she appreciates that liquid does not change in amount just because it happens to be poured into a new and differently shaped vessel. According to Piaget, the "more-developed" child no longer retains access to the prior mental state wherein the amount of liquid was judged by its apparent height or width inside a clear container ("it's more because it looks taller"). In fact, the child becomes incredulous when confronted with evidence that she at one time denied the principle of conservation.

As it turns out, neither Freud nor Piaget, the two greatest scholars of human development of our century, had it completely right—or, to phrase it more generously, each was right about his principal concerns. As Freud thought, individuals never lose access to the emotional states and strivings of their childhood. Thus, even renowned and powerful world leaders can reactivate their own feelings of infantile omnipotence (or helplessness), even as they can play on or rekindle the euphoria or rage their followers experienced in early childhood.

By the same token, Piaget correctly described stage transformations in certain "universal" cognitive spheres. Achievements such as gaining an appreciation of the conservation of liquid are essentially permanent; barring dysfunction of the nervous system, individuals retain these more sophisticated belief structures indefinitely. Older persons experience great difficulty in acknowledging that they ever entertained different views about the objects or states of the world—and they cannot, as a rule, think of the world as a young child does.

But these two explorers of the child's mind failed to account adequately for another crucial set of phenomena. From early childhood, children exhibit a keen interest in understanding the world about them—the physical objects (entities ranging from atoms to cars to suns); the biological objects (entities that are alive and entities that move on the basis of their own metabolic energy); and the mind (the existence of mental objects, like thoughts and dreams, as well as the mental receptacles that are metaphorically assumed to house them, like one's memory or one's imagination).

Even without formal instruction, youngsters develop quite powerful notions—often termed "theories"—about these several realms of existence. So, for example, children come to think that heavier objects fall more rapidly than lighter objects; that entities that move are alive, while those that do not, or cannot, move are dead; and that all individuals have minds, but that individuals share similar minds to the extent that they look alike, have the same name, or come from the same neighborhood.

It was to Piaget's great credit that he sensitized child-watchers to these incipient theories held by untutored children. Where Piaget fell short was in his assumption that such misconceptions would necessarily dissolve. By and large, it has now been established that youngsters' initial notions about the physical, biological, and psychological worlds are remarkably robust. Indeed, even students who have taken courses in the formal disciplines typically continue to believe—contrary to fact and contrary to teaching—that an object's mass determines its acceleration; that evolution leads to an optimal species; and that certain valued beliefs are a necessary correlate of membership in a particular family or community group. In fact, the only individuals who seem genuinely and comprehensively to change their views on such topics are the persons that we label as "experts." Only the physicists, biologists, and social analysts in our midst are apparently able to relinquish completely the astonishingly strong and enduring theories of early childhood.

Just as they develop "theories of the world," children also develop coherent notions about everyday activities. Children as young as two or three already have keen and reliable memories of series of events. By the age of four or five, most children have constructed a large number of "scripts" or "stereotypes" or "scenarios." These cognitive frames capture the regular features, as well as the optional ones, that come to mark such recurrences as birthday parties, trips to the supermarket, or dinner at a fast-food restaurant. In the face of much contradictory evidence, the "facts" of such scripts do change. One can come to accept—and even to expect—birthday parties that feature a dessert of fruit rather than cake or ice cream, or restaurant sequences where one pays upon ordering rather than after eating the meal. But by and large, early scripts, stereotypes, and scenarios prove surprisingly impervious to change.

In many ways, the mind of the five-year-old is wondrous, and it can be strikingly imaginative. It exhibits an adventurousness, a willingness to entertain new possibilities, and an openness to unfamiliar practices that is most attractive and that older individuals are well advised to try to maintain—in the way that the Picassos and Einsteins among us seem able to do. At least at times, the young child probes to the essence of the matter in a way that eludes more jaundiced adults (in the phrase of an old radio program, "Kids say the darndest things"). Yet, in an uncomfortably large number of cases, one may say that the five-year-old has already made up his or her mind. The theories and scripts of the young child are already consolidated and, in the absence of compelling circumstances that are repeated frequently, the growing individual shows little inclination to change.

This state of affairs proves crucial for an investigation of leadership. When an individual provides leadership for a group of experts in his chosen domain, he typically does so by virtue of the work that he executes—thereby exemplifying *indirect* leadership. But even when the leadership takes place through the *direct* and explicit communication of a message, it is possible for that leader to address fellow members of the domain in a sophisticated way. A physicist talking to physicists can assume that his audience members understand the principles of gravity, acceleration, and relativity; a diplomat or a social analyst speaking to peers in her craft can assume that her audience members can transcend stereotypes associated with different national or cultural groups.

The case is completely different, however, for individuals who presume to provide leadership across domains. Those who address a more broad-based institution like the church or a large and heterogeneous group like the inhabitants of a nation must at least begin by assuming that most of their audience members have a well-stocked five-year-old mind. So long as one traffics chiefly with theories and views already possessed by the five-year-old, one should be able to bring about modest change. Thus, when a political leader stresses the importance of supporting one's own group, while another leader emphasizes the importance of helping others, both can expect to engage the five-year-old mind. But when a leader seeks to promulgate a story that is more sophisticated—that calls, for example, for a broader definition of one's social group—she can succeed only if she educates the unschooled minds of the audience. In what follows, my frequent references to the "unschooled mind" serve as an encapsulation of ideas that children develop in the opening years of life.

THE ATTAINMENT OF EXPERTISE IN DOMAINS

The five-year-old has advanced as far as she can on the basis of information that is readily accessible to her senses and her motor systems, as well as the set of concepts and theories that are most readily (and un-self-consciously) acquired by members of our symbol-using species. However, self-education can go only so far. It is not surprising that most societies initiate some kind of formal education in the years following the first half-decade of life. The results of this process of education—*the attainment of expertise in various domains*—constitutes the fourth ingredient crucial to the explication of leadership.

In preliterate or traditional societies, an apprenticeship is the preferred method of education. Youngsters are placed near "masters"; and through example, practice, and occasional explicit testing, they eventually attain the traits and practices associated with one or more varieties of expertise. In literate societies, those who are expected ultimately to attain influential positions almost invariably attend school. There they acquire the basic literacies, a certain mode of comportment, and, insofar as possible, the skills that allow them to pursue a vocation valued in the broader society. When youngsters work comfortably and productively with masters and teachers, they are likely to identify with them, to feel akin to them, and to anticipate that they may one day be able to fill their shoes.

Domains vary widely. Piaget specialized in the study of domains that are considered to be within the purview of every ordinary human being—such as an appreciation of how to classify objects or how to make inferences from a scene or story. Accomplishment in certain domains is considered virtually mandatory within a culture—for example, in a modern industrial society, it is expected that everyone will attend school and at least master the basic literacies.

But most cultures also feature a host of domains that are neither universally nor culturally mandated. Modern industrial cultures, for example, offer people the option of mastering domains that will lead to articulated career paths, such as those of a biologist, a lawyer, or an educator; and they also feature domains that call on idiosyncratic skills, such as chess or the cultivation of roses.

Just which domains or disciplines ought to be mastered by a particular individual turns out to be a complex issue. Some domains are mandated by an individual's culture or subculture. For example, most youngsters schooled in China are able to make ink-and-brush paintings of flora and fauna, and most Russian Jewish boys were traditionally expected to play the violin and to be at least passable chess players. However, other domains are distinctly optional, depending on the given interests and tempos of the family, the moment at which one happens to be born, or the particular aptitudes, interests, and skills displayed by an individual.

Becoming a viable member of the adult culture involves the identification of domains in which one will achieve expertise. In most cultures throughout history, the decision has been made as a matter of course, either by the accident of birth or on the basis of a mandate issued by a parent or a chief. In modern circumstances, the selection of domains is more likely to be made by the individuals themselves, though often in consultation with (and perhaps in identification with) knowledgeable adults. As an individual becomes an expert, he becomes able to appreciate the accomplishments of the masters of his chosen domain, including feats sufficiently novel to change the topography of that domain. He has truly transcended the limits of the five-year-old mind.

However, in areas where he is not expert, or in areas where he is considered as part of a heterogeneous and largely unschooled group (and may be content to be so considered), he is likely to encounter (and to apprehend) messages that are much simpler. Most individuals today deal daily with two contrasting presentations: sophisticated indirect leadership in their domains of accomplishment; and relatively "unschooled" messages from direct leaders of large-scale institutions.

EXPERTISE IN THE REALM OF PERSONS

Until recently, observers have searched for early signs of gifts primarily in two sorts of domains. One group of youngsters is singled out as potentially accomplished in school activities; these are the culturally gifted children who are picked out by the schoolteacher or, more recently, identified by use of an intelligence test or some cognate measure of scholastic aptitude. Another group of youngsters comes to be identified because of a burgeoning talent in a specific domain, such as music, chess, sports, or mathematics. Because of acute pattern-detection capacities or mnemonic skills or physical dexterity in these domains, and often aided by parents or masters who are skilled in instruction and ambitious for their charges, these youngsters are deemed "at promise" for outstanding achievement in these domains.

Certain societies may display comparable concern with individuals who have special gifts in the personal realm (which I have elsewhere termed the "personal intelligences"). I have in mind here individuals who are exquisitely sensitive to the needs and interests of others, and/or individuals who are correlatively sensitive to their own personal configuration of talents, needs, aspirations, and fears. One might assume, for example, that those societies which search among scores of youngsters for future religious or military or political leaders (a pertinent case being the selection in early childhood of the future Dalai Lama, the spiritual leader of Tibet) have become superbly attentive to telltale "markers" for these talents.

Many organizations in our contemporary society have the potential to pick out individuals who may ultimately provide leadership, either the indirect variety that operates chiefly within a domain (like a particular science, art, or craft) or the direct form that has the potential to cut across different skill and knowledge bases (such as leadership of a political entity). Athletic teams, scouting troops, religious groups, various kinds of extracurricular clubs, and even the regular classroom are breeding grounds for future leaders. Sometimes the search for future leaders is explicit; more frequently, leaders are allowed to emerge and are informally identified as such. And certainly, specific institutions—such as the elite independent schools in Great Britain—have long thought of themselves as trainers of future leaders: legend has it that the epochal Battle of Waterloo was won on the playing fields of Eton.

While most individuals clearly do not attain expertise across diverse disciplines and domains, perhaps they do become expert in the ability to understand other persons. After all, we all interact with others from an early age, and perhaps we all gain significant skills in the human realm. I think it is reasonable to conclude that, as we mature, nearly all of us become familiar with certain more complex scripts (such as those involving ambivalence or jealousy or altruism), and nearly all of us develop some capability in appreciating the minds and motivations of other people. Yet, a myriad of social-psychological studies have revealed that most of us are not very skilled at detecting deception or the underlying motivations for actions; perhaps even more troublingly, most of us are not nearly as good at such detection as we *think* we are. Apparently, not even social expertise can be attained in the absence of dedicated study.

But social expertise does appear to be achieved by certain individuals. During the Florentine Renaissance, Lorenzo de Medici carried out a complex diplomatic negotiation at the age of fourteen. A readily recognizable example from recent American history is President Lyndon Johnson. Often called a legislative genius, he had an uncanny ability to put together unlikely coalitions that would support controversial bills. He once explained how he succeeded in securing passage of the 1964 Civil Rights Act: "The challenge was to learn what it was that mattered to each of these men, understand which issues were critical to whom and why. Without that understanding nothing is possible. Knowing the leaders and understanding their organizational need let me shape my legislative program to fit both their needs and mine." Unfortunately, this skill did not help him in the prosecution of foreign policy.

THE ANTECEDENTS OF LEADING

Earlier in this chapter I reviewed four factors that make possible the phenomena of leading and following in our species. To my knowledge, however, few systematic efforts have been undertaken to pinpoint the early markers of leadership. Some of the leaders-to-be I studied were clearly popular among, and sought after by, their peers from an early age; but many others had childhoods that were marked by loneliness, isolation, or frankly antisocial (if not criminal) behavior. Churchill spent much of his time alone, and Mussolini was twice expelled from school for stabbing fellow students. Some future leaders within domains, like Freud, reported an early fascination with issues of power and strategy, while others, like Einstein, were essentially uninterested in the world of other human beings.

Still, a few promising generalizations have been proposed. Future leaders have often lost fathers at an early age. According to one study, over 60 percent of major British political leaders lost a parent in childhood, more often the father. It may be that children with surviving parents take their social cues from the behaviors and attitudes of their mothers and fathers, while those who have early been deprived of a parent are stimulated (or feel pressured) to formulate their own precepts and practices in the social and moral domains. Their precocious dependence on themselves may place them in a favorable position for directing the behaviors of others. The French philosopher and writer Jean-Paul Sartre claimed that in the absence of a father, an individual is forced to make his own choices. However, the pain associated with the early loss seems to endure, and many of the once-bereaved leaders have reported never having lost a pervasive feeling of loneliness.

Another recurrent pattern among future leaders is a contrasting set of relations with their parents. According to the historian James McGregor Burns, Gandhi, Lenin, and Hitler each enjoyed a positive relationship with one parent and a negative relationship with the other. Stalin's mother doted on him, while his drunken father beat him savagely. Feelings of ambivalence accordingly predominate, and, it is conjectured, the impulse to wield power represents an attempt to resolve this anxiety-producing conflict. From all indications, President Bill Clinton's childhood was rife with parental tensions: he never knew his biological father, he did not get along at all with his violent stepfather, and he was called on increasingly to mediate among the adults in his household. He reportedly first began to consider a career in politics when he discovered, as a schoolchild, that he was able to resolve conflicts among his peers.

Some individuals have traits that make them stand out even at an early age. At least some charismatic leaders, such as Charles de Gaulle and John F. Kennedy, are blessed with a striking appearance that draws others to them. Others, like Gandhi or Hitler, are ordinary or even peculiar in appearance. Their charisma may stem from their unusual personalities or mien or from a remarkable life course. The psychologist Mihaly Csikszentmihalyi has pointed out that some leaders have distinguished themselves precisely because they have long spurned the socially accepted manner of achieving one's goals and yet—despite such defiance—have achieved success. These iconoclasts therefore strike observers as having privileged knowledge about the future, even though their stories may ultimately lead audience members down destructive pathways.

Scholars have discerned among leaders an inclination from early childhood for risk taking and a willingness to go to great lengths—often in defiance of others, including those in positions of authority—in order to achieve their ends. A motive to gain power—either for its own sake or in pursuit of a specific aim—is invariably present. The capacity to take risks speaks to a confidence that one will at least sometimes attain success; implacability in the face of opposition likewise reflects a willingness to rely on oneself and not to succumb to others' strictures and reservations.

Such toughness may be achieved by leaders at some considerable cost to themselves. Leaders often exhibit the wounds from their early losses and have a tenacity, even a ruthlessness, that may prove difficult for others to comprehend. In his biography of John Churchill, Winston Churchill commented:

Famous men are usually the product of an unhappy childhood. The stern compression of circumstances, the twinge of adversity, the spur of slights and taunts in early years are needed to evoke that ruthless fixity of purpose and tenacious mother-wit without which great actions are seldom accomplished.

Both the indirect and the direct leaders I studied seem from an early age to have stood apart from their contemporaries. They have felt that they were special and, at least in some cases, capable of feats beyond those achieved by normal individuals. In cases where this sense of specialness was not an early attribute, one can identify moments when the perception of being "chosen" was confirmed. For Martin Luther, it occurred when he became overwhelmed by especially flagrant abuses of the church; for Martin Luther King, Jr., it occurred when he discovered that he was capable of leading the Montgomery, Alabama, bus boycott. For creative individuals—indirect leaders who work in circumscribed domains of expertise—this feeling of "difference" need not pose any particular problem. Direct leaders, however, must feel simultaneously apart from yet constantly in touch with their contemporaries.

My theory of multiple intelligences points to a hitherto missing and possibly important piece of the puzzle. Most leaders obviously have gifts in the realm of personal intelligence—they know a lot about how to reach and affect other human beings. Such knowledge, however, stands in danger of being locked inside, in the absence of a way of expressing it. As I illustrate in subsequent chapters, nearly all leaders are eloquent in voice, and many are eloquent in writing as well. They do not merely have a promising story; they can tell it persuasively. A mark of the future leader is a generous degree of linguistic intelligence—the capacity and the inclination to use words well. When such linguistic intelligence is yoked to considerable personal intelligence, one has the makings of an effective communicator and, perhaps, a promising leader.

THE ANTECEDENTS OF FOLLOWING

Just as the origins of outstanding leadership have been little studied, the features of those who become followers remain shrouded in mystery. One might, of course, extend the term *follower* to all individuals who are not formally designated as leaders, in which case the "problem" of followership per se evaporates. Accordingly, it is useful to distinguish between two groups: those who are especially prone to enlist as followers in a cause, and those who exhibit the proclivity to follow that exists, at least latently, in every human being.

All notable leaders have had their followers, of course; and in some cases, one can identify individuals who have devoted their lives—who have even given their lives—in support of the story propounded by "their" leaders. Napoléon attributed half of his genius as a general to the fact that he could inspire individuals to give up their lives to aid his cause; the other half, he is reputed to have said, lay in his ability to figure out with great accuracy just how long it would take to transport a herd of elephants from Paris to Cairo.

Two possibilities about the "gift" of followership merit consideration. On the one hand, it seems likely that followers are cut from a different cloth than leaders—that, for example, they are perennially searching for the very authority figure that the leader has spurned. Many "believers" migrate from one group to another, always in search of the perfect community, perhaps ever destined to be disappointed. However, chronic followers may share some important properties with leaders. Napoléon quipped that he had become a great leader because he had been an outstanding follower. A leader of the French Revolution echoed: "You know, I must follow the people; am I not their leader?" And many future leaders, like the young George Marshall and Angelo Roncalli (when he was a fledgling priest, long before his selection as the pope), gained inspiration from the model leaders whom they themselves "followed" or identified with during their formative years. What may bind "born" leaders and "born" followers together is their common need for a structure, a hierarchy, and a mission—needs stemming from a primate heritage that may be less binding in those who can "take or leave" membership in a group.

Followers may differ from one another in their attitudes toward power. Some, like the youthful Stalin or Mao Zedong, are attracted to movements that feature strong leaders because they themselves are ultimately (if still unconsciously) interested in achieving and deploying power. Others may prefer the role of a follower precisely because they wish to see (and to feel) the reins of power being held by someone else. The physicist-turned-anthropologist Richard Morris has indicated that most people do not attempt to attain leadership of a social group: "most individuals will placidly accept whatever status they have attained . . . after they reach a certain age, most of them lose their drive to struggle upward." Both groups of followers probably differ from those who turn out to be "rescuers," such as the otherwise-unexceptional individuals who, during the Nazi era, risked severe penalties as they helped those whom they considered to be unfairly singled out for persecution.

While chronic followers may find themselves attracted to a parade of disparate leaders, most potential followers prove more discriminating. As for features that make certain leaders appealing, young children are attracted to the overt features of individuals: size, strength, physical attractiveness, and control of desired resources. By adolescence, additional features become important: the power of the individual's ideas (or stories), their coherence, and their appropriateness to a particular historical moment. And, equally, an ensemble of personal characteristics may enhance the leader's status: those leaders who exhibit charisma, spirituality, and an enigmatic blend of ordinariness and extraordinariness often appeal to others.

Two final points about followership: First, some followers are attracted to certain features (for example, perceived strength or power), while others are attracted to quite different features (for example, originality of ideas or spiritual luminosity).

Physical charisma differs from intellectual or spiritual charisma. Second, effective leaders are often distinguished by the fact that they exhibit an ensemble of these traits (Robert Maynard Hutchins was both physically attractive and intellectually scintillating) or that they can appeal simultaneously to different kinds of people (Margaret Mead's lifestyle magnetized certain followers, while her ideas about cross-cultural investigations impressed others).

THE DEVELOPED LEADER

In considering the features that attract followers to leaders, I have touched on the "end state" of development—the question of what it means to be a full-blown leader. In one sense, this question may seem premature; after all, I am examining a range of leaders precisely so that I can extract the most important features. Also, no leader is ever fully realized; at most, one can observe individuals who are in the course of attaining greater skills and heightened effectiveness. Still, if one keeps in mind these reservations, one can identify four factors that appear crucial to the practice of effective leadership.

1. *A Tie to the Community (or Audience).* It is a truism that a leader cannot exist without followers. What needs emphasis is that the relationship between the leader and the followers is typically ongoing, active, and dynamic. Each takes cues from the other; each is affected by the other. In the various case studies, we can observe the kinds of concerns, needs, and stories that animate members of the community; and we can note the way in which the leader may alter his stories to take these changing features into account. Such ongoing intercourse with members of one or more groups characterizes leaders as diverse as Robert Hutchins and Jean Monnet from an early age. Ultimately, if the tie is to endure, leaders and followers must work together to construct some kind of an institution or organization that embodies their common values.

2. *A Certain Rhythm of Life.* A leader must be in regular and constant contact with her community. At the same time, however, the leader must know her own mind, including her own changing thoughts, values, and strategies. For that reason, it is important that the leader find the time and the means for reflecting, for assuming distance from the battle or the mission. I term this tendency "going to the mountaintop," with the understanding that such a retreat (or advance) can occur literally—as in the case of Moses—or metaphorically, as in the case of de Gaulle and his daily walks. Periods of isolation—some daily, some extending for months or even years—are as crucial in the lives of leaders as are immersions in a crowd.

The relationship between isolation and immersion differs appreciably between two kinds of leaders. For the individual who leads indirectly through his work in a domain, most time is spent working alone or in small groups; only occasionally is it necessary, or advisable, for the individual to expose himself directly to the reactions of a larger and more diverse audience. In contrast, the individual who would directly lead a diverse and changing ensemble needs to spend considerable time in the company of her followers; but this individual requires time and space in which to reflect as well. When an individual like Clinton seemingly avoids opportunities for solitary reflection, there arises the possibility that he may not wish to know his own mind.

3. *An Evident Relation between Stories and Embodiments.* Throughout this book, I argue that leaders exercise their influence in two principal, though contrasting, ways: through the stories or messages that they communicate, and through the traits that they embody. Sometimes, the single leader alternates in emphases. For example, as prime minister, Churchill first developed a story about the need to maintain the glory of Great Britain, and he then embodied a courageous stand through his activities during the Battle of Britain. Some leaders, like J. Robert Oppenheimer or Ronald Reagan, place a greater emphasis on the stories that they tell; others, like George C. Marshall or Pope John XXIII, are valued more for the traits that they embody than for the already established, though recently neglected, stories that they relate. Some features, such as an explanation of the factors leading to a current imbroglio or window of opportunity, lend themselves to the relating of stories, while others, such as the importance of courage or of innovation, are better conveyed through embodiment.

A tension may develop between stories and embodiments. Indeed, many political leaders have gotten into trouble when the facts of their own lives seemed to contradict the stories that they were conveying. For example, it became difficult for Richard Nixon to champion the theme of "law and order" when his own administration was under attack for lawless acts. But in the happier event, stories and embodiments reinforce one another. For example, Martin Luther King, Jr.'s story about the willingness to withstand pain and criticism was exemplified in his actions. Moreover, it is a stroke of leadership genius when stories and embodiments appear to fuse, or to coalesce, as in a dream—when, as the poet William Butler Yeats would have it, one cannot tell the dancer from the dance.

As for the possible interactions of stories and embodiments in the earlier lives of leaders, I must again speculate. Alas, this kind of information has not been highlighted in most biographical accounts. My expectation is that individuals' stories often grow out of life experiences and therefore come to be naturally embodied in the presentation of self. Moreover, at times when an individual's stories clearly clash with his or her embodied behaviors, a hostile response on the part of audience members is likely to discourage such blatant disjunctions.

4. *The Centrality of Choice.* Within a primate horde, an individual organism may prevail through brute force. An analogous instance exists among human beings

when an individual finds himself in a leadership position because he has complete control over the instruments of power and/or maintains his position through violence, terror, and total ruthlessness.

In this study my focus falls on those individuals who have attained positions of leadership in a situation where they and their followers exerted some kind of choice, and where a measure of stability exists, without the temptation or need to invoke instruments of terror. Only in such instances of "leadership-through-choice" does it make sense to think of stories being told, virtues being embodied, or opinions being changed through example and persuasion. Nonetheless, it is worth keeping in mind the Stalins and Saddams of the world, for they did pursue paths to their positions of authority that in some respects resembled those taken by less brutal leaders. They, too, had to persuade, to adjust, and to highlight or mute nuances, depending on the predilections and anxieties of those whom they aspired to lead. In their cases, however, attainment of absolute power ultimately corrupted them absolutely. And it is also worth noting that some individuals who remain in temporary or elective offices may come to think of themselves as omnipotent and then act accordingly. President Franklin D. Roosevelt pulled back (as in the case of the scheme to pack the Supreme Court) when he had gone too far; Margaret Thatcher (as in the case of an unpopular, regressive tax) did not.

SYMBOLS AND COMMUNICATION

During the first few years of life, an individual's knowledge is secured primarily through the operation of sensory and motor capacities—the only cognizing capacities available to other organisms, including nonhuman primates. What distinguishes us from all other creatures, of course, is our ability to deploy, understand, and even create whole ensembles of symbols and symbol systems.

By the age of five or so, most normal children have already become experts in "symbolizing." They have attained a distinct grasp of a whole gamut of symbol systems, including natural language; gestural language; and the symbolic systems involved in picturing, numeracy, music, and other means of communication favored in their society. Equally remarkably, they attain this "first-order" symbolic mastery with almost no formal tutelage. Indeed, as has often been pointed out, if we had to understand the nature and operation of natural language in order to teach youngsters to speak, the species would long since have become extinct or at least mute.

It is scarcely an exaggeration to say that, after the first few years of life, cognitive development becomes equivalent to symbolic development. Moreover, this process of ever-heightened symbol use continues unabated when the child enters school or other educational milieus. In any modern society, a primary burden of schools is to teach second-order symbol systems—those written notations that themselves refer to the first-order symbol systems like spoken language and number systems. More esoteric symbol systems, ranging from those employed in the physical sciences to those used in music or dance or football notations, may also be acquired. And whether she is enrolled in formal schooling or in some kind of apprenticeship, the student comes to learn the various moves entailed in the symbolic systems that she must master.

Symbol systems are means of thinking and categorizing; equally, they are means of communicating. Nonhuman primates lack these means and thus must achieve their influence largely through the exercise of brute power. Human beings, in contrast, have options for asserting leadership. As discussed later, the mastery of the linguistic symbol system is crucial for most direct leaders, since leadership is maintained largely through the creative use of stories. Many leaders—ones I term "linguistically intelligent"—are distinguished early on by the mastery of storytelling; and many others make the mastery of storytelling—whether through persuasive oratory or through well-crafted written documents—a primary goal. It was said of de Gaulle that his political destiny

> depended most constantly on words. The soldier—brought out of obscurity by writing a book; the rebel—made into the leader of a nation by a speech; the man in opposition—who survives politically because of a few interviews with the press; the President, ruling by radio and television; and finally, the lone wolf—in touch by words alone with the fickle mob.

In contrast, individuals working in traditional domains and disciplines need not be masters of natural language or prodigies of storytelling. It did not matter how well Einstein spoke German or English or how well Picasso wrote French or Spanish. What mattered for these indirect leaders was their mastery of the symbol systems of twentieth-century physics and painting, respectively. Such individuals might have eventually become known through their person; but they were already known, by proxy, because their thought processes and experiences were conveyed in the strings of symbols—more informally, the works—that they produced. They were fortunate to live in cultures that have evolved several powerful modes of communication.

Leaders traffic as well in another kind of communication—communication through embodiment. Sometimes leaders communicate by the most elegant and simple of symbols—Gandhi nakedly facing his enemies, Churchill issuing a defiant sign for victory, Martin Luther King, Jr., standing resolutely behind bars. One may ask whether such symbolic communication, such embodiment of virtues, qualifies as a story. While the answer to this question is to a certain extent a semantic one, I suggest that these visual presentations, in and of themselves, cannot send an unambiguous message. It is only because these individuals are already recognized, and their causes already understood, that these images of embattlement can function in powerful ways. We might say that since the story has already been assimilated, an illustration of it suffices.

Any scholar who produces a work for publication is, however modestly, making a bid for indirect leadership. I would not have written this book if I did not want my words to affect the way that my colleagues—and the general public—think about phenomena of leadership. In particular, my decision to survey the continuum from indirect to direct leadership represents an effort to change conceptions of leadership, to bring out, through an ordered set of case studies, the array of stories and embodiments that link the accomplishments of an Einstein or a Picasso with the feats of a Thatcher or a Monnet, that give flesh to the words of Keynes at the head of chapter 1.

While I have resisted the temptation to propose a "model" of leadership, I have introduced a number of themes that have guided my thinking. In this chapter, I have reviewed those facets of human development that seem most germane to an understanding of leadership: humans' primate heritage; the early emergence of a sense of the self and of others; the development in early childhood of powerful theories or "scripts" about the world; the marks of emerging expertise in the domains valued in one's society; and the specific ensemble of traits that may mark the emerging leader and the emerging follower. We may think of these elements as basic ingredients out of which a comprehensive model of leadership can be constructed.

Whatever facets of leadership may be shared by humans and other primates, the importance of symbolic communication is essentially restricted to our own species. Only we humans spend the bulk of our time trafficking in symbols. While human cultures host a variety of symbolic systems and messages, all place a special premium on those strings of words that we call stories. It is appropriate to turn at this point in "my story" to the compelling stories that lie at the heart of leadership.

3

THE LEADERS' STORIES

All leadership takes place through the communication of ideas to the minds of others.

—Charles Cooley

In a wonderfully evocative short story, the Chilean writer Isabel Allende relates the tale of Belisa Crepusculario, a beautiful young woman from a desperately poor background who makes a living by selling words. She sells memorized verses for five centavos, improves the quality of dreams for seven centavos, writes love letters for nine centavos, and, for twelve centavos, invents insults that can be directed toward mortal enemies.

Belisa's life changes dramatically when she is seized by a ferocious warrior known simply as "the Colonel." After his men rough her up and almost kill her, the Colonel explains the reason for this unwarranted and wanton treatment. "I want to be President," he declares. Moreover, he explains, he wants to become president not by seizing power but by gaining the majority of the popular vote—in my terms, he wants to become a leader, to gain authority by choice. "To do that I have to talk like a candidate. Can you sell me the words for a speech?" he implores.

Belisa creates a tapestry of words that promise to touch the minds of men and the intuitions of women. She then reads the speech aloud three times to the illiterate Colonel so he can memorize and deliver it. And deliver it he does, countless times during the election season, in an effort to convince citizens to vote for him. As Allende's narrator indicates: "They were dazzled by the clarity of the Colonel's proposals and the poetic lucidity of his arguments, infected by his powerful wish to right the wrongs of history, happy for the first time in their lives." In the canonically happy ending to this fable, the candidate wins the voters' support, and Belisa gains the Colonel's love.

Epitomizing this chapter's epigraph, from the American sociologist Charles Cooley, this brief story captures important truths about language and leadership. Through sheer physical power, one can gain—and maintain—a position of authority over other people. This is how the Colonel had proceeded in the past. If one wishes to persuade others, however, it is necessary to convince them of one's point of view. Illiterate and inarticulate ("War's what I know," he admits to Belisa), the Colonel finds himself at the mercy of a woman who knows how to string words together compellingly. By using her words, he gains legitimacy. Homer underscored these complementary strands when he said of the heroic warrior Achilles that he was trained as a doer of deeds and a maker of speeches.

In recent years, social scientists have come to appreciate what political, religious, and military figures have long known: that stories (narratives, myths, or fables) constitute a uniquely powerful currency in human relationships. Many scholars have pondered whether the essence of the story is the existence of a sympathetic protagonist, the positing of plans and goals, the onset of a crisis that must be resolved, the initial buildup and subsequent release of a feeling of tension in an audience member, or the creation of a distinctive narrational voice. Many have sought to identify the prototypical narrative—the hero's quest, the journey away from home followed by the ultimate return there, or the clash between good and evil. Some have looked at the means available to the storyteller: logic, rhetoric, characterization, humor, and manipulation of the audience's mood and expectations. And still others have investigated the primary purposes of stories—the binding together of a community, the tackling of basic philosophical or spiritual questions, the conferral of meaning on an otherwise chaotic existence.

A definitive account of the nature and purpose of stories, scripts, and/or narratives may prove elusive. As the British philosopher Ludwig Wittgenstein showed in his analysis of the concept of "games," kinds of stories may bear at most a "family resemblance" to one another. For my purposes, this state of affairs is perfectly acceptable. In this study, I use the term *story* in a broad sense. While I focus on *narratives* in the linguistic sphere, I include *invented accounts* in any symbol system, ranging from a new form of explanation in the physical sciences to a novel mode of expression in dance or poetry. In addition, I span the poles introduced in chapter 2: the *overt* or *propositional account* communicated directly by the leader and the *vision of life that is embodied* in the actions and the life of the leader. True, I could create a separate term for each of these variants of the story. However, this tack would not only complicate the account but also suggest, misleadingly, that it is readily possible to distinguish a story from a fable or a structured dance sequence, or a message from an embodiment, a vision, or a dream.

I wish to underscore a contrasting claim. Using the linguistic as well as the nonlinguistic resources at their disposal, leaders attempt to communicate, and to convince others, of a particular view, a clear vision of life. The term *story* is the best way to convey this point. I argue that the story is a basic human cognitive form; the artful creation and articulation of stories constitutes a fundamental part of the leader's vocation. Stories speak to both parts of the human mind—its reason and emotion. And I suggest, further, that it is *stories of identity*—narratives that help individuals think about and feel who they are, where they come from, and where they are headed—that constitute the single most powerful weapon in the leader's literary arsenal.

STORIES THROUGH THE LIFE CYCLE

Infants and toddlers communicate with their caretakers, often in surprisingly sophisticated ways. They can indicate want, fear, surprise, regret, and emotional well-being. By the age of five or so, the young child has already become a creator and a consumer of stories. These stories may be punctate, consisting of a single happening; or they may be picaresque, containing a large sequence of loosely coupled vignettes. For all their variety, stories at this time of life share a basic simplicity. In one especially common story, which I have termed the "Star Wars" plot, two forces or individuals (A and B) are opposed to each other (as in the series of *Star Wars* movies). There may well be a protracted struggle between A and B. In the end, A—generally identified with the good—is likely to prevail, though there are instances where B triumphs, most often temporarily. In nearly all cases, the child identifies strongly with the individual(s) and the cause(s) of Force A.

So powerful a place does this Star Wars scenario occupy in the mind of the child that it tends to impose itself on other narratives that enter the child's consciousness. In its initial form, a story may actually feature three or more protagonists, and the struggle among forces may be multifaceted, protracted, and indecisive. When it comes to the re-creation or retelling of this story, however, the revised version tends to coalesce around a simpler form: multiple participants are reduced to two (or to two "teams" or "forces"), and a subtle and ambiguous conflict reverts to a Manichaean struggle between good and evil.

One can behold this simple form at work both in the realm of imaginative play and in the child's reasoning about everyday events. Five-year-olds, with their *rigid dualities,* cherish fairy tales and other magical adventures where the forces of light and darkness clash. They can identify with the light, while both learning about and being attracted to the dark. By the same token, when asked about situations that arise in their own lives, youngsters also bring to bear this dualistic form of thinking, this construction of the world in terms of binary conflicts. And so, queried about friendship, they are prone to consider peers as all benevolent or, more rarely, as totally malevolent. By the same token, when pondering a moral dilemma, they are likely to see an issue in stark terms. For example, the decision to steal a drug in order to save someone's life is seen, alternatively, as a heroic act or a dastardly one that merits Draconian punishment.

Why zoom in on the narrational proclivities of young children, when I am concerned here with the stories told by disciplinary or national leaders? The answer is central to my purpose: Adults never lose their sensitivity to these basic narratives. And it is often the leader who can draw on or exploit the universal sensitivity to a Star Wars plot or a Grimm's fairy tale—the leader who can speak directly to the "unschooled mind"—that succeeds in convincing an audience of the merits of his or her program, policy, or plan. It is surely no accident that President Ronald Reagan's Strategic Defense Initiative—an effort in the mid-1980s to build a shield that would protect the United States from a nuclear attack by the Soviet Union—quickly came to be known as the "Star Wars program." Reagan's so-called Star Wars initiative, often derided as simplistic by his political opponents, was considered by Margaret Thatcher to be the most important decision of Reagan's entire eight-year presidency.

But while they often remain "unschooled" in various domains, individuals can go beyond the five-year-old mind, and, indeed, many do so in the realm of narrative. If the five-year-old sees matters in terms of black and white, the ten-year-old is likely to exhibit a much more measured and evenhanded view of events. Indeed, the ten-year-old is *fair to a fault*. In considering two characters, she embraces the possibility that each harbors facets of both goodness and evil. The ten-year-old takes into account the intention underlying an action, as well as the consequences thereof.

If the five-year-old tends to be ruthlessly rigid, and the ten-year-old to be excessively fair, the adolescent—to be dubbed here as a fifteen-year-old—is superbly appreciative of a multiplicity of interests and perspectives. In formulaic terms, we can say that the fifteen-year-old *revels in relativism*. No matter how strongly a certain personality or position might be promoted, the fifteen-year-old remains a tad skeptical of that perspective. Gods have flaws, devils harbor virtues, and the grass is always greener on the other side. If an entity appears in one way, it can also be conceptualized in a very different manner. Friends are seen as capable of many kinds of acts, and a friendship is conceived of as a dynamic and changing relationship. Any seemingly moral act may harbor in it the seeds of iniquity, just as the apparently amoral act may be justified in the light of some hitherto-unrecognized principle.

Not every adolescent achieves the stance of the relativist. Some individuals remain as egocentric as the five-year-old; quite a few more never transcend the conventional morality of the ten-year-old. In our contemporary society, many fifteen-year-olds flirt with relativism, but they often revert within a few years to an earlier, less fluid form of understanding and reasoning. Nascent tendencies toward relativism are slapped down quite decisively in traditional or in totalitarian societies. The unschooled or the less schooled mind beckons seductively and persistently.

Still, it is worth mentioning a more sophisticated stance toward the world, one that we might associate with the discerning twenty-five-year-old or the mature fifty-year-old. Such an individual can be said to synthesize two apparently warring sentiments: on the one hand, an awareness of the relativity of values and, on the other hand, the need to take a stance and to declare a specific position as more appropriate, at least in a given context. In his most eloquent speeches, the Roman master rhetorician and advocate Cicero sought to present the rounded view of each of the warring positions, but in the end he always came down squarely on one side of the dispute. I term this perspective a *personal integration.*

Let me put these four perspectives to work on a single example, Isabel Allende's Colonel on the campaign stump. Suppose that he is representing the interests of the peasants in a Latin American society that has hitherto been dominated by the proverbial twenty wealthy families. He directs Belisa Crepusculario to create speeches for four different audiences.

Appealing to the five-year-old Star Wars mind, the Colonel paints the peasants as towers of virtue, while tarring the wealthy families as the root of all the country's problems. In this stark and simplistic rendition, the only solution is for the peasants to overthrow the plutocrats, replacing the Awful Oligarchy with Delicious Democracy or with a Dictatorship of the Peasantry. Observers of twentieth-century history recognize this story as one told by totalitarian leaders on the left and on the right, by Mao no less than by Hitler.

Addressing the ten-year-old mind, which is "fair to a fault," the Colonel proposes that the wealth of the nation be divided equitably. The estates of the wealthy should be broken apart and divided equally among all the peasants. At the same time, he emphasizes, it is important to take into account the prior rights and obligations of the wealthy families. And so, for the next ten years, each wealthy person is allowed to keep twice as much land and twice as much money as his impoverished neighbor (shades of liberal democracy in a reformist mode—the kind of political compromise favored by a Franklin Roosevelt or Lyndon Johnson).

Now invited to convince the adolescent minds of the republic, the Colonel adopts a relativistic ploy. To begin with, he concedes that there are more than two interest groups in the country and that each of them has something to be said in its favor. To be sure, the peasants have been deprived of their fair share, but many have not taken their duties of citizenship seriously and have even failed to vote. For their part, many wealthy families have been selfish and exploitative, but some of them have been charitable as well, and others have represented their nation effectively at international gatherings. Moreover, other stakeholders, such as the church, the educational system, and the communications media, need to be taken into account in any redistribution of resources.

Trying to mediate among these forces turns out to be a complex undertaking—one that taxes the problem-solving abilities of most of the audience. And so, after broadly describing the parameters, the Colonel proposes a sensible, relativistic solution: in an effort to honor the special perspectives of the various interest groups, each party will be given the power to veto measures affecting those issues that it especially cherishes. In reviewing sex and temperament in different societies, Margaret Mead sought to introduce her audiences to such a relativistic stance, in which multiple perspectives were jointly honored and no group was assumed to have a monopoly on the proper way to live.

Finally, the Colonel has the opportunity to address the wise elders of the land, women and men ranging in age from twenty-seven to seventy-two. In a polyphonic presentation, he touches upon the grave injustices that are manifest to the Star Wars mind, the need for fairness that animates the ten-year-old mind, and the recognition of relativistic claims that dominates the thinking of the adolescent. While acknowledging merit in each of these perspectives, he rises to the challenge of presenting a personal integration, which he hopes will appeal to the most mature minds in his land.

In this particular instance, he calls for a form of representative government, in which the claims of each of the constituencies are recognized as legitimate. At the same time, however, he espouses a radical transformation in the governmental processes. From now on, the claims of the peasants will receive first consideration, for they represent not only the numerical majority but also the group that has been discriminated against most consistently over the centuries. The status of every other party is determined by an analogous calculation. In making such a complex statement, the Colonel has in effect left the land of electoral politics altogether; he (or, most likely, a ghost writer) is ready to author a document like a federal constitution or a philosophical tract or equity, and thereby become the indirect leader of a domain.

STORIES STRUGGLING WITH ONE ANOTHER

This study—and for that matter, life in general—would be simpler if one could hear and evaluate one story at a time. Such a scenario would be possible if the mind were a blank slate, if the mind could focus on one story alone, or if each new story were to topple or erase all of its predecessors or competitors. But none of those conditions holds.

By the age of four or five, most youngsters have constructed dozens of scripts based on daily experience; moreover, they have heard dozens of stories from their elders and perhaps scores from the communications media that happen to be prevalent in their societies. No doubt, the number of scripts and stories continues to mount in the years thereafter; and, as already suggested, these narratives become more complex, subtle, and ambiguous. I would not be surprised if most adults in Western society possess a hundred or more regular scripts and have internalized several hundred stories. And in the fabled country inhabited by Belisa

Crepusculario and the Colonel—one still rich in the oral tradition—inhabitants no doubt carry within their heads an even larger ensemble of stories.

The challenge confronting the storyteller becomes clear. To the extent that she creates a familiar or formulaic story, it will be readily assimilated. No one will object to it, but its distinctiveness and power may prove minimal. To the extent that an innovative story is created, it may well attract initial attention; after all, the new creation differs from earlier stories, so it cannot simply "pass" for one of its predecessors.

However, decided risks attend the creation of a new story, which might well be misinterpreted; erroneously assimilated into an old story, one with which it was meant to be contrasted; or seen as irreverent or even blasphemous. To be concrete: If the Colonel is the first person to suggest that members of the twenty most powerful families should be required to carry out community service, his proposal is likely to attract the interest of journalists and of peasants who have felt disenfranchised. But he runs the risk either of being misinterpreted as saying that the twenty families should simply continue their earlier noblesse oblige or of being attacked verbally or physically by members of the leading families, who do not appreciate being told what to do, particularly by an upstart, hitherto-illiterate colonel in *their* army.

What happens when a number of different—and often frankly contradictory—stories are competing for attention, acceptance, and ascendancy among the various members of an audience? This situation resembles the usual state of affairs in most contemporary societies, including the ones encompassed in this study; every story encounters *counterstories,* and every new story engenders resistances. Authorities differ dramatically in their views, depending on whether they adopt a cognitive or an affective perspective on the issue. In short, what happens in a struggle between the schooled and the unschooled mind?

As espousers of the rational tradition, cognitivists are inclined to believe that the more sophisticated story will prevail. That is, because the mind prefers to function in its most developed form, more primitive expectations and explanations tend to be overridden by more complex and subtler ones. According to this argument, youths who have held the Star Wars position will tend to be convinced when they hear a spokesperson embrace "fairness to a fault," but few believers in fairness will be persuaded by a more primitive appeal to good/bad dualism.

The strongest evidence in favor of the cognitivist position comes from experimental studies. As children get older, they tend to espouse more sophisticated accounts and to spurn especially simplistic ones. More dramatically, when youngsters of different degrees of sophistication debate some point, it is more probable that the less sophisticated youngsters will come to adopt the more sophisticated argument than that the more sophisticated youngsters will be "dragged down" by the reasoning customarily invoked by their less sophisticated contemporaries.

Rationalistic considerations, however, do not always carry the day. Individuals argue positions for a variety of reasons, and their stances are prompted by a plethora of goals. Cases are made by implicit as well as explicit arguments, and unconscious as well as conscious factors drive conclusions. Stories appeal at least as strongly to listeners' emotions as to their calculation. Social psychologists have shown repeatedly that the prestige of a spokesperson, the identities of a speaker's friends and enemies, and the exploitation of nostalgia or grievances more strongly shape attitudinal change than the sheer merits of a rational argument do.

When it comes down to it, the argument that carries the day may well be the one that exerts the strongest affective appeal, rather than the one that triumphs on debating points. For every Abraham Lincoln, whose speeches were more tightly reasoned than those of rival Stephen Douglas, we must countenance the possibility of an Adolf Hitler, who baldly appealed to the lowest common denominator of the German citizenry and found that he could dissolve reason by arousing passions.

The limitation of a purely rational analysis of argument was brought home dramatically in the presidential debates of 1960 between John F. Kennedy, the Democratic candidate, and Richard M. Nixon, the Republican candidate. Nixon was the more experienced politician and, as a trained debater, took pains to answer, point-by-point, the various arguments Kennedy put forth. Those who heard the debate on the radio generally believed that Nixon had won. A quite different result occurred among television viewers, who had been positively affected by Kennedy's appealing appearance and manner, his capacity to speak directly to an audience, and his ability to convey—indeed, to embody—the points that were central to his vision of a new frontier. In contrast, viewers were put off by Nixon's haggard "five o'clock shadow" appearance and antagonized by the harshly pedantic style in which he sought to refute Kennedy's points: consequently they did not focus on Nixon's positive program. Far more people watched the debates on television; they considered Kennedy to be the winner and, by a narrow margin, awarded him the presidency.

I have delineated contrasting outcomes of what might happen when stories compete. On the one hand, considerable developmental evidence indicates that older individuals are capable of apprehending and creating more complex and multiperspectival stories than are their younger counterparts. Under certain idealized conditions, the more developed stories and the schooled mind carry the day. And so, for example, in debates within Margaret Mead's anthropological community, relativistic interpretations and personal integrations may well prevail over power- or fairness-based perspectives.

However, rational considerations do not stand alone. Stories can appeal for a variety of reasons, and listeners harbor a multitude of motives for attending, apprehending, and acting. Particularly once one ventures beyond a domain or discipline, particularly when one is confronting the diverse population within an institution or a nation, developmental dimensions become attenuated. The leaders of Weimar Germany may have offered a more sophisticated vision of a functioning society, but to many citizens it was not as persuasive as the simple picture of Aryan superiority and German retribution communicated by Hitler and his Nazi supporters.

A final point: In the cases reviewed so far, stories are seen as struggling against one another, with one or the other ultimately prevailing. Some storytellers are so skilled, however, that they are able to create narratives that appear to satisfy both parties in a controversy or to operate effectively at more than one developmental level. Through choice of words, through selection of examples, and through the use of nonlinguistic cues, a leader may be able to convince adherents of each perspective that he or she is on *their* side. The delivery of stories—for example, biblical parables—can be sufficiently polyphonic so as to please individuals of different ages, persuasions, and sophistication. Indeed, precisely this feat has been achieved by such superlative speakers as Franklin Roosevelt and Ronald Reagan, and by such skilled negotiators as Jean Monnet and Mahatma Gandhi.

To summarize the discussion to this point: Throughout life, individuals hear stories and have to evaluate their merits consciously and unconsciously. There is always the chance that a more sophisticated story will prevail, particularly when the teller is skilled and the audience is sophisticated. However, my study provides abundant evidence that, more often than not, the less sophisticated story remains entrenched—the unschooled mind triumphs.

THE SUBJECT AND THE CONTENT OF STORIES

Individuals create stories on every conceivable topic—and indeed on some topics that are barely conceivable! The very absence of a story on a topic provides a tempting stimulus for a born (or made) storyteller to concoct a new one on the spot. Belisa prided herself on giving every person his or her own special word, his or her own unique story, for "it was not her intention to defraud her customers with packaged words." Whether the Colonel would find a new story appealing is another matter; as a leader, he sought not to be original but to be convincing. Piggybacking on entrenched stories has often proved an effective route to a presidency or a prime ministership; this tack permits ordinary (as compared with innovative) leaders to achieve their ends.

While it would be futile to attempt to delineate all possible stories, it is important to chronicle the major topics and kinds of stories that leaders have related. In my analysis, these stories address the most essential questions raised by human beings and seek to provide comprehensive and satisfying answers to those questions. By and large, the origins of stories go back to the concerns of early childhood, and they focus on the issues that themselves arose at that time and continue to endure throughout one's conscious existence—issues of self, identity, group membership, past and future, good and evil. In the mid-1960s, the African American leader Malcolm X summarized well the mission of the story-teller when he asked his followers: "We want to know what are we? How did we get to be what we are? Where did we come from? How did we come from there? Who did we leave behind? Where was it that we left them behind and what are they doing over there where we used to be?"

In 1992, the presidential candidate Ross Perot described in equally vivid terms the answers that are sought by such audiences: "We owe it to the American people to explain to them in plain language, where we are, where we are going, and what we have to do. Then we need to build a consensus to do it." And from her different vantage point, the literary critic Diana Trilling has put it this way: "This is the unresolved question that imaginative people will always have in every time of life, in every part of the world: Where do I belong? And what price do I pay for where I choose to stand?"

In what follows, I delineate stories in three broad categories: stories about the self, stories about the group, and stories about values and meaning. I intend no suggestion that a story can fit in only one category, nor, indeed, that all stories told by leaders necessarily fall neatly under this taxonomy. But I believe that most of the stories that leaders tell are created in response to the pervasive human need to understand better oneself, the groups that exist in and beyond one's culture, and issues of value and meaning. Indeed, stories in the broadest sense—narratives, visions, dreams, embodiments—are most effective when they provide at the same time nourishment for the mind (or the understanding), on the one hand, and a feeling of belonging and security, on the other. In that sense, irre-spective of purpose and complexity, the stories of the leader revisit the basic agenda confronting each young child as he takes his first steps into the larger community. For each topic that I survey, audience members encounter stories at many levels of sophistication. These stories struggle with one another, with the presumption being that the less schooled versions (those that address the five- or ten-year-old mind) will not readily be replaced by the more schooled versions.

THE SELF

Initially, one establishes clues about one's identity on the basis of information given by those closest to oneself—parents, other relatives, or distinctively clad representatives of the religious and social communities within which one lives. But particularly as they venture forth from home, individuals also look to the leaders of the wider social and political entities (the head of the church, the leader of the country, and so on), and to others with whom they identify (often including individuals from sports or the media), for clues to the perennial question "Who am I?"

A concern with the delineation of one's identity is scarcely a new phenomenon. The Athenians took an oath that stated: "I inherit from the past of my family, my city, my tribe, my nation, a variety of debts, inheritance, rightful expectations, and obligations. These constitute the given of my life, my moral starting point." I am reminded as well of Diogenes' more visionary challenge to his countrymen: "I am not an Athenian or a Greek but a citizen of the world."

When confronted by stories of apparently greater cogency and sophistication, many individuals find it comforting to adhere to simple, black-and-white stories. Still, as a means of conveying the kinds of answers that have been given to the question of personal identity, we can consider different levels of developmental sophistication with respect to a sense of self:

- With young children, answers in terms of physical attributes and simple psychological traits constitute the point of departure. A five-year-old sees herself as a short (or tall) individual, a white-skinned (or black-skinned) person, and an individual who resembles (or does not resemble) others in her family and her community. Racial or ethnic stereotypes are readily grasped. Perhaps compensating for their still-diminutive stature, such youngsters (or older individuals who favor the five-year-old story) often see themselves as heroes who are strong and for whom right derives from might.

- Going beyond manifest physical attributes, the identity of ten-year-olds encompasses psychological traits such as honesty, dutifulness, and fairness. The schoolchild considers it important that one be seen as a person who behaves properly and helps others. By the same token, the growing child spurns individuals, including aspiring leaders, who defy these attributes of the "good boy" or the "good girl." It is disconcerting to think of oneself as a bad person, though some individuals, including future leaders of a destructive turn (like young Benito Mussolini, who stabbed fellow students), may gain a perverse pleasure in a label of this sort.

- By adolescence, the individual becomes capable of a far more differentiated view of self. A person can exhibit a variety of traits, including ones that may be in conflict with one another—such as generosity in certain circumstances and stinginess in others. One can have certain surface traits (being tall) that are either reinforced or undermined by underlying psychological traits (being timid or being tough). And one may oscillate between competing identities, one of which is regarded positively by the rest of the society, another of which is considered antisocial or eccentric. The adolescent is struck by the realization that a person who has been portrayed in one way (say, the U.S. president or the queen of England) actually exhibits many contradictory features, and the same ambiguity can characterize the adolescent herself. Monnet faced the challenge of convincing citizens of

49

once-warring European nations that they could also think of themselves as part of a larger unified entity called Europe.

- Finally, in one's adult years, the range of traits can be seen as summing up to reflect a certain kind of person. In the happier case, a person feels integrated, at peace with what he has accomplished and how he is regarded in the community. In the less happy event, a person feels frustrated or desperate, either because the traits do not sum up at all or because they yield a kind of individual with whom the individual feels little sympathy. In either case, however, there is at least an effort to form a composite identity; aspiring leaders must convey this coherent sense to a wider public and must help members of their audience achieve a comparable sense of integration. As Stephen Skowronek says in his study of the American presidency, every successful president must present "a coherent and compelling narrative about his place in history."

It should be evident that much of the task of creating a sense of self belongs to the individual himself. And especially in societies that are skewed toward the recognition of individual rights and obligations, the task of creating an identity proves to be a major and consuming one for most people. Nonetheless, there is no need for the individual citizen to engage in a solipsistic endeavor. Leaders who help individuals conceptualize a personal identity perform a crucial function. Thus, when Lenin saw himself not as an ivory-tower theorist, but rather as a student of history, an extrapolator from events, and a man of action, he conveyed a potent and enabling sense of self to his followers. Similarly, when in 1992 Bill Clinton presented himself to the electorate as a "new Democrat" who would not repeat the mistakes of previous unsuccessful Democratic presidential candidates, he induced many voters to think of themselves in new and more positive ways, not just as persons with views more liberal than those of the rival Republicans. Most memorably, when Franklin D. Roosevelt declared in his first inaugural address that "the only thing we have to fear is fear itself," he gave new hope to millions of citizens who had been mired in an economic and psychological depression.

THE GROUP

Every individual's sense of identity is rooted largely in his or her place within various groups. Nearly every individual belongs to several groups, whose missions and memberships may or may not overlap. A significant portion of early socialization consists in the discovery of the groups to which one belongs, a determination of one's feelings toward the various groups, and, ultimately (if ideally), the melding of one's several group memberships into a coherent whole.

Bearing in mind that views considered more developed will not necessarily triumph in a "Darwinian competition" among stories, one may consider a variety of perspectives on membership in groups:

- The five-year-old, while dimly aware of membership in multiple groups, has difficulty in comprehending the implications of such multiple identities. It is easiest for that child to see herself as a girl or a member of the Greenspoon family or a resident of Georgia than as someone who belongs to a number of separate but partially overlapping collectivities. By the same token, the child of this age is prone to deal with group membership (and group leaders) in stereotypical terms: girls are all good or all bad; Daddy Greenspoon can do no wrong (or, less frequently, nothing right); individuals from Georgia will either inherit the world or go to the devil. The eighteenth-century pamphleteer Tom Paine evoked this sentiment in the minds of his American compatriots when, in the influential essay "Common Sense," he portrayed the British as a group of tyrants and argued self-servingly that "the cause of America is in great measure the cause of all mankind." Paine was certainly not the last political figure to press this "unschooled" case.

- By the age of ten, the youngster can easily appreciate the existence of different groups and the possibility of overlapping memberships and conflicting loyalties. The individual wishes to believe that the groups he is affiliated with are positive ones, while hoping to have a minimal connection with groups that are alien or antagonistic. At the start of the American Civil War, southerners felt pulled in two directions: as American patriots and as loyal children of the South. Many southern patriots struggled to reconcile the rival accounts set forth by Abraham Lincoln and Jefferson Davis. To maintain a sense of security and intellectual coherence, many sought to resolve their conflicting loyalties expeditiously by abrogating one set of ties.

- The adolescent is aware that groups have long and complex histories and that no group has a monopoly on either virtue or vice. This individual also accepts the fact of membership in multiple groups and may even gain a measure of stimulation from their apparent inconsistencies, and, indeed, from contradictions in general. (J. Robert Oppenheimer and Robert Maynard Hutchins often reveled in such contradictions.) The adolescent is also capable of thinking of groups as deviating from their current status or practices. However, this gift of hypothetical or visionary thinking is sometimes purchased at the cost of unwarranted idealization of certain practices or philosophies. The adolescent will instantly give her life for a cause, in the way that neither a child nor a middle-aged person is likely to comprehend. The same adolescent who can appreciate, intellectually, the merits of the claims of the several parties involved in the French Revolution or the Iranian Revolution may end up embracing an absolutist position. Relativism and absolutism are not always mutually exclusive; the skilled leader of a terrorist group can exploit the adolescent's blend of idealism and cynicism.

- Finally, the seasoned adult can assume a distance from his group memberships and appreciate that he might well have belonged to a different set of groups, and thence have entertained a quite different philosophy of life. But rather than defending each set of groups as equally viable (as the relativistically oriented counterpart is wont to do), such an adult at least attempts to justify the particular ensemble of group memberships to which he is fated to belong.

And what of those cases where the ensemble of group memberships does not add up to an acceptable package? The reflective individual will clearly be on the lookout for the leader who offers a different set of options with respect to group memberships, including the possibility of creating new groups. No doubt the unhappy experience of being a German citizen in punitive post–First World War Europe engendered many political options, ranging from a liberal Weimar Republic to a Soviet-style Communist regime to the molding by Hitler of a new National Socialist Party. The choice made by an individual reflected his or her willingness to be inclusionary—to tolerate a range of viewpoints.

While it is tempting to highlight the positive facets of group membership, one must keep in mind as well the malevolent uses to which collective identities can be put. Reflecting on the post–cold war era, when nationalism and tribalism have reemerged as potent political forces, one sees all too clearly how group identity can be exploited in an exclusionary fashion. Because of the propagation of myths on the state-owned and -operated television system in the former Yugoslavia, for example, the Serbs have come to believe that they have been systematically targeted for extinction, so they have retaliated by attempting to eradicate the rival Muslim group. The novelist Kurt Vonnegut has written of "Granfalloon"—the deliberate invention of alien and unsympathetic groups, such as "those liberals" or "those Washington insiders." And the influential Russian poet Yevgeny Yevtushenko captures well the ambiguity of group membership during the Soviet era. He salutes the country's symbol:

> *Goodbye our Red Flag.*
> *You were our brother*

But then he voices the crushing disappointment of the Soviet people:

But like a Red curtain you concealed behind you
the Gulag
Why did you do it, our Red Flag?

It is one of the ironies of the age that the end of the struggle between the two superpowers should give rise to heightened group tensions rather than to the forging of broader identities.

VALUES AND MEANING

Most individuals attach meaning and value to the ideas that they develop, with or without formal tuition, about themselves and their group. Indeed, it is more difficult—if not unnatural—to think about these realms in a value-free way than it is to attach some kind of a weighted significance to thoughts about oneself, one's group, and the world of other individuals.

But most human beings also crave an explicit statement of value—a perspective on what counts as being true, beautiful, and good. Traditionally these views have come from art or religion; more recently, they have come as well from philosophy, science, and newly constituted secular groups. Personal introspection and discussion are additional sources of value systems. At times of stability, the accepted norms may be adhered to without discussion. But particularly in times of crisis or cataclysmic change, individuals crave a larger explanatory framework. They pay special—and perhaps undue—heed to those who can provide some kind of broad orientation, if not definitive answers, to essential questions: the purpose of work, the value of prayer, the just distribution of rewards and punishment, and the stance to assume in the face of death and other ultimate human concerns.

Again, one can discern developmental trends that occur with respect to values. The young individual expects an unambiguous panorama of the good and the bad; he or she attributes all values and judgment to some kind of overarching and unquestioned world intelligence. Somewhat older children become aware of competing value systems; they hope that reconciliation among them may prove possible. By adolescence, the plethora of meaning systems has become all too evident, and most youngsters despair at any kind of a synthesis: they are likely either to abandon any pretext of a coherent philosophy or, as a reaction, to embrace a momentarily appealing one uncritically.

A genuine synthesis—in part personal, in part extending beyond the person—becomes a more plausible goal in later life and, especially, as the end of life draws near. Most individuals ultimately embrace some kind of organized religious or philosophical system even as they retain the option of conferring a personal touch on this already available synthesis. The formidable challenge confronting the visionary leader is to offer a story, and an embodiment, that builds on the most credible of past syntheses, revisits them in the light of present concerns, leaves open a place for future events, and allows individual contributions by the persons in the group. Martin Luther's ideas, for example, spread with such amazing rapidity partly because he built on the strengths of Catholicism, addressed the legitimate concerns about inequity on the part of a pious community, and invited personal thoughts and personal callings. Contemporary leaders as diverse as J. Robert Oppenheimer, Pope John XXIII, and Martin Luther King, Jr., all sought to create a worldview that was adequate to their tumultuous times and meaningful to their troubled constituencies.

OTHER TOPICS, OTHER STORIES

While the realm of personal relations has always held special appeal, human beings have also been enormously curious about the other realms around them: the world of naturally occurring physical objects, the world of manufactured objects, the world of living nonhuman entities, and the worlds of time, space, and the various enigmatic forms of internal reality (such as dreams, fears, and memories). Toddlers play, often tirelessly, with instances of these various worlds. Young schoolchildren pose dozens of questions about these entities and ponder the often unsatisfactory and sometimes contradictory responses that they receive. Older schoolchildren try to master the explanatory systems that have been created within their culture. And adults hope that they will eventually synthesize the explanations offered by their culture with more personal answers that they have evolved on the basis of their own experiences and reflections.

Through prehistory and much of recorded history, the pictures of the world put forth by individuals have come from two primary sources: their own imaginative constructions, and the images given in the art and mythology of their society. While not necessarily at odds with one another, these lines of explanation can be thought of independently. Imaginative constructions emerge from commonsense observations: the world looks flat; entities that move on their own seem different from entities that do not; one cannot proceed backward in time in mundane reality, though one can do so in dreams or films. While Piaget thought that such ideas tended to disappear with age, they have proved to be enduring even among citizens of a complex, contemporary society.

Artistic and mythological explanations constitute distillations of the thoughts and experiences of individuals who lived in earlier eras. Thus, those living in ancient Egypt believed in an afterlife buried underground, while those living in a Christian society locate an afterlife in a blissful heaven or a punitive hell. The ancient Greeks saw human beings as unique creatures, while those who lived in the surrounding pagan societies discerned more of a continuity between humans and nature.

The various academic disciplines and specialties that evolved in the last two millennia have led to a conception of knowledge as constructed by communities of experts and as subject to continuing change and expectable (if often surprising) modifications in the light of new data and new theories. Within the disciplines, individuals look to the leading practitioners for a "readout" on the current state of knowledge about the various worlds (and microworlds) in which we live.

Most individuals harbor deep questions about the nature and future course of the world. But there is a gap, ever widening, between the disciplined perspectives embraced by experts and the unschooled opinions held by the rest of us. Given this state of affairs, direct leaders must select from among options. They must master the insights of the disciplines, in the process becoming experts themselves; cede this territory to the expert, parroting her findings and offering no personal view; or, spurning the apparent progress of understanding within the disciplines, embrace a more traditional or more personal philosophy.

This last option is often followed by those of a fundamentalist persuasion. Ignoring the overwhelming scientific evidence for the existence of processes of evolution over the millennia, for example, these individuals cling to the notion of a Creator who caused the world to come into being at one moment a few thousand—or perhaps a few million—years ago. Those who do not wish to offend fundamentalists hold their tongue whenever they encounter a tension between scientific and religious beliefs.

More generally, leaders face a set of choices when they enter realms in which disciplinary expertise has developed. Stories about identity—individual and group—are essentially personal ones, to which disciplinary experts have no unique contributions to offer. But traditional stories about the objects and the course of the universe have been radically altered by the work of scholars over the centuries. Domain experts like Oppenheimer or Mead must decide how much of this discipline-based story to promulgate when they address broader audiences. And leaders who presume to lead across domains must situate themselves with reference to domain expertise, on the one hand, and the overwhelmingly unschooled perspective of their audience, on the other.

CULTURAL STORIES

Whether living in bucolic Samoa, peasant China, tribally constituted Africa, or a modern Western industrialized city, an individual will in some way confront the ensemble of issues that I have just reviewed. However, these themes are unlikely to be encountered in explicit form—in a naked discussion of issues like identity, group membership, the spectrum of values, or the ontology of the world. Most people avert abstract theories, and most storytellers revel in the concrete—be it the colorful details of specific narratives or the vivid virtues embodied in a dramatic life. We encounter the themes of life and death on television, in the movies, and on the pages of the daily newspapers—and not, primarily, in lectures by learned philosophers or theologians.

Over the millennia, leaders and storytellers have created characters, settings, and events to crystallize these issues and convey a perspective on them through a kind of shorthand that works well for members steeped in a specific culture. Like other founding civilizations, the Greeks and the Romans constructed extensive mythologies, within which issues of life and death, the physical and the spiritual world, individual and group identity were vividly explored. The formal Christian religion performed much the same function for nearly two thousand years in the Occident, just as Buddhism, Islam, and Confucianism accomplished similar missions in the great Oriental civilizations of the last two millennia. Pope John XXIII built upon the Christian heritage, while Mahatma Gandhi fused several spiritual traditions.

Each nation has its own set of cultural heroes and villains. In the United States much of political experience is interpreted in the light of George Washington, Benedict Arnold, or Robert E. Lee; Otto Bismarck, Adolf Hitler, or Konrad Adenauer assumes a symbolic role in Germany; Joan of Arc, Napoléon, or Charles de Gaulle constitutes a point of reference in France. Within intellectual circles, specific artists, writers, and thinkers (William Shakespeare, Isaac Newton, Virginia Woolf, Martha Graham) serve as comparable overarching figures. Mere allusions to these figures may suffice to elicit a rich narrative fabric. A century ago in the United States, one could expect even a moderately educated person to be able to quote at length from the Bible and the plays of Shakespeare; in his speeches and writings, Martin Luther King, Jr., presupposed his audiences' familiarity with biblical stories and foundational American documents.

In more recent times, a different set of cultural stories has increasingly taken over. The creations of the media (such as the personae conveyed by the movie stars Clint Eastwood and Marilyn Monroe) and the successful products of the consumer society (like Coca-Cola or Nike sneakers) have come for many to crystallize notions of heroism, beauty, and the good life. In fact, youngsters today, in many countries, move more comfortably through the worlds contrived by Walt Disney, George Lucas, or Jim Henson than through the realms of classical mythology, religion, or literature.

For the most part, the messages concerning values that are embodied in daily interactions the world over have stressed the virtues of one's own group and the vices of others' groups. In this sense, the messages blend all too easily with the prejudices of the unschooled mind. Of special interest, accordingly, are those worldviews that are more moderate—those that discern strength in the golden mean; that recognize a value in grayness, as well as in black or white; that speak to interpretation, reflectiveness, and self-consciousness, rather than to absolute truth and unremitting falsity. Those who promote a more inclusionary sense of identity are always clashing with those who foreground older, deeply entrenched senses of exclusivity. Nuanced, pluralistic, and "open" perspectives become especially important when, in chapter 14, we turn our attention to those leaders who aspire to address the concerns of the planet.

MEDIA: THE VEHICLES OF STORIES

Traditionally, a story is told by a parent to a child as they sit near a fire or, perhaps, by a political or religious leader to his or her flock. Contemporary political leaders seek to recapture this atmosphere when they speak informally to their constituencies, through devices such as a "fireside chat," an "open town meeting," or an apparently spontaneous conversation with a reporter that just happens to be broadcast nationally.

In recent times two factors have combined to complexify, in fascinating ways, the communication of stories from leaders to their groups. The first has been the proliferation of technological media. The first megaphones and microphones seem but the most primitive modes of communication when contrasted with radio, network television, cable television, electronic mail, and other recent points of access on the global information highway. Gandhi may have despised the accoutrements of Western civilization, but his protests would have failed utterly had they not been communicated instantly by telegraph all over the world. King assumed that his confrontations with racist officials would be widely viewed. Through her exquisitely staged documentaries, the German filmmaker Leni Riefenstahl contributed materially to the myth surrounding Hitler and the Nazis. And the careers of contemporary martyrs—as well as current terrorists (who may see themselves as martyrs)—would be unthinkable without their ready access to media that broadcast their inspiring or nefarious messages around the world. Visual media obviously have a tendency—perhaps approaching compulsion—to reduce information to the sharpest and most pithy sound bite. This proclivity makes it difficult to deal, except in a ridiculing way, with issues of any complexity. And for better or worse, most mass print media have begun to follow the examples of the visual broadcast media.

The second factor has to do with the construction and manipulation of the image of the leader. Leaders have always had advisers, and occasional leaders like the biblical Moses are said to have had spokesmen (in his case, his more loquacious brother Aaron). Today, however, it has become the job of dozens of "handlers" to compose every word and to script every nuance in the public appearance of a national leader in accord with what the public is supposed to crave. The role of the citizens who constitute "focus groups" has become so important that the influential Republican media adviser Roger Ailes was moved to quip: "When I die, I want to come back with real power. I want to come back as a member of a focus group."

Accordingly, it is no longer clear to audience members whether they are being exposed to an authentic individual, speaking her actual words, or to a personage created by media advisers. More than one leader has *become* the persona that was initially invented by those expert in the creation and transformation of images. The desire for authentic experience—for direct contact with the genuine, unadorned leader—remains a positive motive. Politicians like Perot gain points when they can claim that they are *not* the creation of the media or its myriad of advisers. Yet even the claim for authenticity can be manufactured (good actors know how to feign sincerity), while many "authentic" individuals simply look awkward or amateurish when sitting under klieg lights.

KINDS OF SYNTHESES

As individual members of an audience confront various stories and storytellers, and the ensemble of messages and embodiments that populate their society, they are inevitably called on to make some kind of judgment, to reach some kind of synthesis. Early in life, people can easily live with contradictions, because they do not sense the tension between a belief in "A" and a belief in "Not A," or they sense it slightly and fleetingly. However, with the advent of greater cognitive sophistication, most individuals experience at least some tension between apparently contradictory propositions or schemes and some impulse to reconcile these perspectives.

Individuals differ enormously from one another in the extent to which they take up the challenge of synthesis. For one thing, cultures and subcultures do not necessarily draw explicit attention to consistencies and/or contradictions, nor do they necessarily place a premium on efforts to reconcile these tensions. Just compare for a moment a Cartesian society, which prides itself on regulation by logical consistency, and a Hindu society, where different beliefs are allowed to accumulate haphazardly, or even productively, alongside one another. Or consider the difference between a society that berates individuals for expressing contradictory beliefs and one that, with Ralph Waldo Emerson, dismisses consistency as the "hobgoblin of little minds."

But apart from different cultural norms, individuals within a society also differ in the extent to which they search for synthesis and the extent to which they can live with contradiction. In the psychological parlance, these variations in threshold constitute "individual differences." Some individuals, of the sort that the Greek poet Archilochus called foxes, like to immerse themselves in the details of many competing systems; others, whom he dubbed hedgehogs, prefer to believe in "one big thing." Individuals also differ in the extent to which they can tolerate ambiguities. Again, borrowing from the archives of psychological analysis, we can contrast two groups. Those who score high on the psychological scale that measures fascistic tendencies crave order and organization above all; those with modest scores on this scale are comfortable with, or even look out for, a degree of chaos, inconsistency, and contradictory minutiae.

Leaders both exemplify and play into these individual differences. Even as they themselves differ in the personal drive for synthesis, they will differ in the extent to which they attempt to provide a well-organized and internally consistent narrative for their followers. Some American presidents, such as Reagan, were not bothered in the slightest by apparent contradictions: Reagan could swear his undying allegiance to a balanced budget at the same time that he smilingly signed in a bill that in effect increased the deficit. Other presidents, such as former engineers Herbert Hoover and Jimmy Carter, were conscious of apparent inconsistencies and sought whenever possible to be consistent, even at the cost of awkward moments and ultimately unsuccessful bids for reelection.

Earlier, I pointed to the appeal of those individuals whose stories and embodiments are consistent with one another; such a synthesis satisfies the aesthetic sense of many leaders and many followers. Here I must acknowledge that such coherence is not a necessary mark of success. Many, if not most, auditors would prefer to hear a number of individual stories that are singly appealing than to obsess about a possible inconsistency between story A and story F. And many auditors are happy to ignore inconsistent embodiments so long as they find each story appealing enough in itself.

ISSUES ABOUT STORIES

Time for a brief summary: I have argued that a key—perhaps *the* key—to leadership, as well as to the garnering of a following, is the effective communication of a story. While my definition of a story is broad, it calls attention to a common core. I maintain that the most fundamental stories fashioned by leaders concern issues of personal and group identity; those leaders who presume to bring about major alterations across a significant population must in some way help their audience members think through who they are. Given this analysis, the prominent featuring of stories raises a number of searching issues.

To begin with, determining the stories of the leaders is not necessarily a straightforward task. Leaders say many things, at many times; not everything said is a story, nor is every story in the repertoire coherent or consistent with others. In this study, with rare exceptions, I do not consider statements or stories that have been mentioned only once; instead, I look for those stories and those embodiments that occur frequently, those that can be said to define the individual, at least during a particular historical epoch. Understandably, I am also concerned chiefly (though not exclusively) with those stories that seem to be effective in their context. It is my contention that any set of judges who examined the historical and biographical record would arrive at a similar set of stories; moreover, if one were to interview associates of the leader, they too would mention the stories and embodiments that I have singled out.

A second point has to do with the way in which stories are characterized. Here I take the liberty of expressing stories in as elemental a way as possible, often using words and images that are even more basic than those offered by the leaders themselves, and typically not spelling out the moves of particular versions. While each story could be drawn out in length, number of characters, episodes, and crises, I count on readers to fill in the background texture. I do this so that I can discuss the stories in terms of the framework introduced in this chapter: the particular content (for instance, about identity or group membership), the level of sophistication (for example, the struggle between good and evil, the relativistic perspective), and the kind of value system that is embodied.

My approach exposes me to two probing lines of criticism. First, it can be argued that the meaning and use of stories are chiefly in the ear of the beholder. A story that is about identity for one person touches on issues of value or group membership for another; what is simple for one person is complex for another. The occasion on which a story is used, the identity of the person who is telling the story, and the status of the audience hearing the story prove at least as important as the manifest (literal) content of the story.

Rather than rejecting this contextualist position, I wish to embrace it—though with reservations. Not only do stories always represent an interaction between the words of the teller and the ears of the audience, but many of the most skilled leaders play on this ambiguity, hoping that an apparently singular message will exert desired but different effects on diverse audiences. Certainly, when Martin Luther King, Jr., gave a major speech, it was crafted for the ears of numerous audiences, ranging from those sympathetic to segregation, to committed civil rights workers, to funders and politicians drawn from the middle of the ideological spectrum. Far from ignoring this multiplicity of goals and meanings, we, as analysts, must try to understand it. At the same time, I must assert my own, decidedly non-postmodern conclusion: Humanistically oriented scholarship would grind to a halt if we could not determine some meanings that transcend the specific contexts in which words are uttered or messages are conveyed.

The second vexed issue about stories concerns my adoption of a developmental stance. It is developmental both in the sense that I am studying the development of leaders (and their followers) and in the sense that I have characterized particular stories in terms of their supposed developmental sophistication.

To my mind, many advances in the social sciences have come about because of scholars' willingness to look at organisms and institutions in their initial form and to trace the continuities and discontinuities in the course of their evolution to some version of maturity or disintegration. The potential for leadership (and followership) exists early in most of us; but full leadership is never achieved—it always remains "in formation." By the same token, it is only through the vigilant maintenance of a developmental perspective that we can appreciate the constant dynamic that unfolds between leaders and their followers over significant stretches of time.

More controversial is the decision to characterize stories as reflecting different levels of sophistication. I could justifiably point out that this claim is an empirical one that has already been borne out. In dozens of studies, researchers have spelled out the ordinary differences among the schemes and the worldviews of the five-, ten-, and fifteen-year-old. Yet, in fairness, I should point out as well that most of these studies have been carried out in modern Western societies and that they have tended to be based on dilemmas posed in laboratory settings rather than on ethnographic work in natural settings.

However, my use of a developmental descriptive scheme has other rationales. At the least, it provides a convenient way of analyzing stories that can be employed whether or not one believes that the scheme exhibits universality. (Thus, for example, the scheme could be used even if, in some newly discovered society, young children were found to be relativists and senior citizens emerged as absolutists.) Relatedly, the scheme provides a way of comparing the stories that often compete and clash with one another, for those stories may differ not only in purpose or content but also in the cognitive mechanisms entailed in their comprehension and transmission.

My primary purpose for using the scheme, however, is to challenge conventional theorizing. Among developmentalists, it is generally assumed without argument that individuals pass through stages; that the later stages subsume the earlier ones; and that, in any competition, more developed forms are likely to triumph. My iconoclastic conclusion, mentioned earlier, is quite different.

As I see it, stories operate in many ways and compete with one another at many levels, unconsciously as well as consciously. Developmental sophistication along some metric is one factor, but it is not the only one. And in many, if not most, instances it is not the determining one. Among experts, to be sure, there is a reasonable chance that the more sophisticated version will prevail. But once one moves beyond the realm of expertise, and, indeed, once the expert herself is addressed as a member of a heterogeneous community, then "all bets are off." In addition to the diverse motives that may induce individuals to be attracted to one story or embodiment rather than another, every leader must somehow deal with a potent fact: the enduring strength of the unschooled mind. Because of this fact, those who fashion a more sophisticated account of identity are often bested by those whose identity stories are simpler, if not simplistic.

In what follows, I make no effort to categorize each story and counterstory in terms of its specific developmental level—that is both unwarranted and unnecessary. Instead, I speak in terms of the relative sophistication of stories that are enunciated by leaders; and I record their fate as they compete with other stories in the culture and other stories that are put forth by rivals. As shown repeatedly, a more sophisticated account of identity (or values or meaning) is often bested by an account that is simpler and has a broader appeal. A convenient summary of major stories and counterstories is provided in appendix I.

Enough for preliminaries. It is time to turn to the issue at hand—the study of different kinds of leaders. As we turn our attention, in part II, to particular leaders in particular situations, we see at work the various kinds of stories that have, in bare-bones form, been outlined here. We witness the ways in which these stories struggle with other ones, in the minds of aspiring leaders no less than in the minds of potential followers. And we have a chance to consider the scope of the stories created by leaders and the extent to which leaders and their followers feel the impulse to integrate the individual stories into some kind of overall coherent framework.

As I have noted, this particular study grew out of an earlier study of creative individuals, ones who were instrumental in transforming the domains in which they worked. Appropriately, then, the current survey begins with two leaders who, in early life, were considered among the most creative workers in their respective domains. If Margaret Mead was not quite the equal of Sigmund Freud, she changed conceptions of human nature; if J. Robert Oppenheimer was not quite the peer of Albert Einstein, he added to our understanding of the physical world.

But neither Mead nor Oppenheimer was content to remain as a disciplinary expert, addressing those trained in one domain. By paths that I trace, both found themselves addressing increasingly wide audiences, on increasingly broad topics. Indeed, by the end of their careers, they had made the transition from indirect leadership to direct leadership. At the heights of their public careers, they were speaking directly to audiences about those fundamental questions of identity and value that most deeply affect the human condition. Thus, while representing one end of the continuum of leadership, they also embodied over the course of their lives the full sweep of that continuum.

PART II

CASE STUDIES: FROM DOMAINS TO NATIONS

4

MARGARET MEAD

An Observer of Diverse Cultures Educates Her Own

I have spent most of my life studying the lives of other peoples, faraway peoples, so that Americans might better understand themselves.

—Margaret Mead

In September 1929, one month before the crash of the New York Stock Exchange, Margaret Mead, an anthropologist in her late twenties, returned to America from her second trip to the field. She was surprised to learn that, thanks to the enormous success of her first book, *Coming of Age in Samoa,* she was becoming well known. The book was considered at once of scientific importance and of unprecedented interest to the general public. Mead was able to save her earnings from the book and thus gain a freedom that was unusual for a young scholar, particularly during the Great Depression. She also faced a fateful choice: Did she want to devote her life to "pure" scholarship, speaking primarily to other experts in the domain of anthropology, or did she want to address the broad American public?

There are always many more young individuals of promise than there are ones who taste success, particularly at so young an age. Still, Mead seems to have been especially marked for achievement. By all accounts, including her own, Mead had a privileged childhood. Her parents, both trained as social scientists, focused considerable attention on her, their firstborn. They documented the details of her childhood in thirteen notebooks, treated her from an early age as if she were an adult, and transmitted their expectation that she would accomplish something of significance in life. Her paternal grandmother, a teacher, provided support as well as a powerful model of thoughtfulness, integrity, and a balanced life. In fact, much of Mead's schooling occurred at the feet of her beloved

Margaret Mead. UPI/Bettmann Newsphotos

"Grandma." Energetic, bright, curious, and active, Mead was blessed with many opportunities, as well as an abundance of social and artistic talents. A friend compared her to a brilliant but initially undirected missile, waiting to be launched: "She was going to be something; it didn't so much matter what."

One of the few times in her life when Mead was a genuine misfit occurred during her freshman year at DePauw University in Indiana. This precocious and intellectually oriented young woman found herself totally at odds with the partying-and-sorority life there and proved unable to cope with the scene. While, much later, she came to feel that she had benefited from the one-time experience of being a pariah, young Mead was delighted by the chance to transfer to Barnard College in New York City. In that metropolitan milieu, she, like so many other talented youths, found a set of like-minded and like-spirited intellectual young women—nicknamed the Ash Can Cats—and fell in love with intellectual and artistic life as it was realized in Morningside Heights and in the already fabled Greenwich Village. Although she traveled all over the world for the rest of her days, she always returned to New York City.

Upon graduation Mead also entered into the first of three marriages—to a childhood sweetheart named Luther Cressman—but gave little indication that marriage would ever occupy center stage in her life. Rather, in reviewing Mead's life, one gets the impression that marriage was something that one did at a certain point in one's life before moving on to other things and, perhaps, to other spouses.

Of epochal importance for young Mead were her initial contacts with the renowned German American anthropologist Franz Boas, then at the height of his career as the chairman of the anthropology department at Barnard's affiliate, Columbia University. Boas was widely admired for his mastery of the entire field of anthropology and his scientific contributions in the subspecialties of linguistics, archaeology, and physical anthropology.

Over the years Boas had developed increasingly strong views about the controversial issues of race and culture. He became an outspoken critic of the claim that human nature was determined by genetic factors, as well as an implacable opponent of all attempts to interfere with evolution through the controversial policy of eugenic breeding. He saw human beings as formed largely by particular historical, social, experiential, and cultural factors, and he was determined to garner further evidence in support of this perspective through comparative studies of indigenous societies around the globe.

Mead dropped her initial flirtations with the field of psychology and proudly elected to become an anthropologist. In her early twenties, now a graduate student at Columbia, she began to work directly with Boas; she also joined the circle of his talented associates, the linguist Edward Sapir and the cultural anthropologist Ruth Benedict. Mead admired the achievements of these three scholars, and they in turn were charmed by her enthusiasm, energy, and brilliance.

It became clear to Mead that one could not hope to be a significant anthropologist unless one undertook fieldwork and acquired one's own "people." Himself an Americanist, Boas preferred that Mead study an American Indian tribe, but the determined student had her heart set on work in the South Seas. Promoting her own desires strongly, as she invariably did, Mead prevailed in the choice of a site. At the surprisingly young age of twenty-three, she set sail for Samoa.

Mead's topic was child rearing in Samoa, with a particular focus on adolescence among Samoan girls. She spent a year conducting her fieldwork, interviewing many informants, and undertaking a number of case studies of particular Samoans. As proved true throughout her life, Mead worked tirelessly, filling many notebooks and making careful observations of everything that caught her ever-alert eyes and touched her commodious sensibility.

But Mead had another, equally important mission, which emanated from her association with Boas: to undermine the claims of biological determinism. Earlier writers in the century, particularly the American psychologist G. Stanley Hall, had posited that adolescence was a biologically programmed period of life, with "storm and stress" as inevitable handmaidens of puberty. Boas had planted in Mead's mind the idea that perhaps the rebelliousness and romanticism found so widely among Western adolescents might be absent in a "primitive" society. He directed Mead to examine critically the life experiences of the young women in Samoa.

On the basis of her fieldwork, Mead concluded that childhood and adolescence spent in Pacific Samoa were entirely different from youth lived in a modern and complex Western society. Rather than growing up in a nuclear family, the Samoan child was reared by an extended family of perhaps fifteen or twenty individuals. Relations between children and adults were informal, multiple, and diffused, rather than focused on one or two nuclear bonds and charged with strong passions; by and large, the Samoans' relations were free of the guilt that plagues Westerners. Of special interest, the teenage years in Samoa emerged as a time of relaxation, playful sexuality, and absence of vexing issues or lasting trauma. Neither pressures for celibacy nor visions of romantic love nor the burdens of lingering Oedipal complexes were readily discerned. Mead glorified the casual attitude among Samoans toward sexual relations and compared it favorably to the tension and remorse that had wracked the lives of so many young people reared in a Puritanical tradition. In the end, Mead rejected the idea, put forth by Hall and others, that adolescence had to be a turbulent period, and she characterized the Samoan experience as "freer and easier and less complicated" than in the West.

Upon her return to America, Mead instituted a practice that she was to sustain throughout her life: she wrote up her field notes in monograph form before undertaking a new expedition. In this case, she penned *Coming of Age in Samoa,* a highly evocative book addressed as much to the general public as to her anthropological colleagues. The manuscript, initially rejected by Harper's, was accepted by the publisher William Morrow. Her editor, Thayer Hobson, made the fateful suggestion that Mead add two concluding chapters, in which she would consider the implications of her anthropological findings for child rearing in contemporary America.

These chapters gave the book its special flavor and force, making Margaret Mead virtually a household name in literate America by the time that she was thirty. In the closing pages Mead compares the life in the South Seas favorably to an existence in twentieth-century America. She contends that Americans, in their heterogeneous, choice-filled, and rapidly changing society, pay a high price in terms of crime and delinquency, interpersonal conflicts, neuroses, and the collapse of a coherent tradition that fosters artistic expression. She gazes nostalgically at the South Sea paradise, where life is informal, there is little hurry and scant psychological maladjustment, and "the greatest cause for tears, short of death itself, is a journey of a relative to another island." Mead does not urge the adoption of a Samoan way of life—ever practical, she knew this was not an option for her fellow citizens, let alone for her high-strung and protean self—but she strongly urges her compatriots to draw lessons about alternative ways in which they might better rear their children and lead their own lives.

Looking back at *Coming of Age in Samoa* thirty-five years later, Mead wrote: "This was the first piece of work by a serious professional anthropologist written for the educated layman in which all the paraphernalia of scholarship designed to convince one's professional colleagues and confuse the laity was deliberately laid aside." Advertently or not, Mead had written a book directed at two separate audiences that brought to their reading diverse expectations and that may have drawn different conclusions from that reading. As we probe the contrast between leadership in an established domain or discipline and leadership of a wider, more diffuse public, it is important to acknowledge these two separate avenues of communication.

Let me begin by sketching the expectations of Mead's scholarly colleagues. Aware that Mead was a student of Boas, her colleagues had every reason to anticipate that she would execute a careful ethnographic study, in which she would chronicle her observations of a society that was comparatively unstudied. Aware as well of Boas's strong theoretical inclinations, they could expect that her conclusions would give little comfort to those bent on an explanation of Samoan behavior in terms of genetic-hereditary, evolutionary, racial, or other biologically tinged factors.

But Mead also surprised her colleagues. Such sharp and decisive conclusions were not to be anticipated in the writings of a new and still-inexperienced anthropologist, one younger than almost all of her collegial readers, and one who was a member of that still very small group—female scholars. After all, scholarship was (and remains) generally conservative, hedged in qualification, and deferential to precedent. Spurning these cautious traditions, Mead treated her single case study of Samoa as disproof of the biological conception of adolescence. As she was to recall many years later: "In anthropology you only have to show once that it is possible for a culture to make, say, a period of life easy, where it is hard everywhere else, to have made your point."

Mead's manner of presentation also embodied a message for her colleagues. It was not necessary, the Mead example showed, to present one's findings in the usual technical language of scholarship, with jargon, footnotes, and an overt theoretical framework. Rather, one could express "data" and conclusions in plain English—indeed, in graceful tones. Mead's first substantive chapter was called "A Day in Samoa" and began with an elegiac passage:

> The life of the day begins at dawn, or if the moon has shown until daylight, the shouts of the young men may be heard before dawn from the hillside. Uneasy in the night, populous with ghosts, they shout lustily to one another as they hasten with their work.

Yet Mead's work could not be dismissed as a potboiler. She was a keen observer of daily life, and she was at home with conceptual issues in anthropology. In one section she describes a native dance in exquisite detail; she then moves on with seeming effortlessness to an analysis of the dance's significance in the education and socialization of young Samoan children. A description of the ways in which older Samoan girls rear their siblings stimulates more general reflections on responsibility and authority. As if to anticipate possible scholarly criticisms, Mead featured no less than five appendices, which included a description of her methodology, maps of the housing arrangements in the villages, kinship structures, and even a discussion of "mentally defective" people in the population.

In writing her book as she did, Mead exhibited a behavior that characterizes major creators and leaders: a willingness to take risks and to challenge authority. Mead showed little hesitation in attacking the prevailing anthropological accounts that attributed culture differences to racial factors or that posited powerful biological constraints on adolescence. Only someone with self-confidence, only someone with a feeling that she just might "pull it off," would be willing to take on both the anthropological establishment *and* the general public. In the manner of an indirect leader, the young Mead challenged others through her writings, rather than through more direct conversations with an audience. Had Mead failed miserably, we can only speculate about whether she would have withdrawn to the world of the guarded, dusty monograph or bounced back with even greater panache. But given the striking success of this volume, Mead's evolutionary path toward more public forums seems to have been set.

In subsequent years, some of Mead's anthropological colleagues became critical of her popularization in general, and of her particular methods and conclusions in *Coming of Age in Samoa*. It is important to underscore, then, that the collegial response to this first book was actually quite favorable: the slim volume was recognized immediately as an important work, casting new light on an intriguing society and also addressing controversial scientific issues in a relevant and constructive manner. Such formidable scholars as the American anthropologist Alfred Kroeber, the British anthropologist Bronislaw Malinowski, and the British physician and scientist Havelock Ellis all praised the book. At the time of publication, *Coming of Age in Samoa*'s popular appeal was considered a bonus, rather than a source of irritation, within the anthropological profession.

While presumably aware that Mead's book was a contribution to her chosen discipline, members of the general public were drawn in by other factors. Mead's graceful writing style brought home, in a manner more typically associated with a work of fiction, the rhythms of life in a part of the world that had hitherto been known chiefly through the paintings of Paul Gauguin and the stories of Somerset Maugham. The exotic picture of youths gamboling in a tropical clime, eating yams and taro and bananas, fishing and weaving as they achieved a relaxed and comfortable livelihood formed an alluring contrast to America's pervasive industrialization, commercialization, and rapidly paced daily life. The apparently less regulated lives of Samoan youths seemed compatible with ideas of progressive education that were popular at the time. (Had television miniseries existed then, one can readily imagine a lurid adaptation of Mead's chronicles.)

The image of Mead also clashed with the stereotypes of the academic scholar. Neither a stuffy Germanic professor nor a shy spinster, Mead was a vigorous, attractive, adventurous, and courageous young woman. The "girl in the neighborhood" whom most might have expected to work at the corner store, become a teacher, or perhaps attempt to break into the movies had dared to travel alone to a far corner of the world, live among "savages" (cannibals as well as noble ones), learn an arcane language, and write up her impressions in vivid, easy-to-digest prose. Not least, Mead's provocative writings held promise that one could achieve a better vantage point on one's own society, thanks to the comparative edge provided by a study of a contemporary but decidedly different culture.

Over the next decade, Mead continued to follow the trajectory that had been launched with her study of Samoa. She made a series of trips to the South Pacific, where she conducted fieldwork among the Manus, the Arapesh, the Mundugumor, and the Balinese. While continuing to examine child development and family life, she now concentrated her attention on the behavior of males and females in different cultures. No longer traveling alone, she was accompanied in turn by two other anthropologists—Reo Fortune, her second husband, and Gregory Bateson, her third husband. With Bateson in particular, she pioneered in new methods of ethnography, photographing and filming for posterity the play and artwork of the Balinese.

The opportunity to visit a number of different cultures, some quite close geographically and yet distinctively different in their practices, positioned Mead well to analyze the "patterns of culture." While her genius lay in exquisitely careful observation and in lively and allusive writing, rather than in theoretically sophisticated disquisitions, she worked with Bateson (and also Fortune) to create a schematic analysis of the similarities and contrasts among the cultures that she had studied. This analysis took into account the interplay between two dimensions that existed all over the world: one's sex and one's basic temperament type. Each culture had to work with these dimensions, of course, but the ways that they were patterned or configured differed across cultures.

Surveying the cultures that they had studied, Mead and Bateson were able to delineate how each one fit along these key dimensions. They encountered every pattern conceivable within their scheme. As Mead described them, the Mundugumor valued fierce and possessive men and women, whereas Arapesh men and women were gentle and caring. Despite these differences, each of these cultures expected similar behaviors on the part of its men and women. Other cultures, however, mandated a contrast between male and female behaviors. Among the Tchambuli, the expected relations between men and women reversed those found in many contemporary cultures: Tchambuli women, brisk and hearty, managed business affairs; the men, caught up in cattiness and in petty rivalries, exercised only nominal powers. Reflecting on the New Guinea tribes that she and Bateson had studied, and challenging the widely held notion of fixed sex roles, Mead issued one of her strongest and most-quoted statements: "We are forced to conclude that human nature is almost unbelievably malleable, responding accurately and contrastingly to contrasting cultural traditions. . . . Cultures are manmade, they are built of human materials."

The typology harbored implications for adjustment or conflict within a society. When the sexual and temperament profiles of an individual were consistent with the expectations within a society, rearing would proceed far more smoothly than on those occasions when the profiles clashed with the expectations of a society. Both Mead and Bateson felt that they themselves were to some extent deviants from the norms of their own culture, and they now understood the ways in which they failed to conform. Having arrayed the tribes that they had studied along a fourfold scheme, they remapped this scheme so that it also pertained to Western society and, indeed, to their own particular sex-and-temperament combinations. The potential of the scheme to apply to their own complex world as well as to primitive societies may be one of the reasons why they felt—and cabled home to Boas—that they had made an epochal discovery. Here was a story that they not only believed in but also embodied in their own beings. What better proof of the validity of the theory than that it helped to account for the unusual lives of its cocreators?

The particular scheme that Mead and Bateson developed did not strongly influence the field of anthropology. Indeed, even their own daughter, Mary Catherine Bateson, herself an anthropologist, suggests that it was not entirely coherent. However, thanks to the series of comparative studies that she had executed, Mead had accomplished a feat of great importance for her future enterprises. Based on seven societies with which she was becoming intimate, she assembled what one might term a mental file cabinet of different patterns of rearing and living. For the remainder of her life, Mead would be able to draw appositely on these patterns, making instructive comparisons and contrasts among various nonindustrialized cultures and at the same time casting unanticipated light on those Western cultures familiar to her readers.

To cite an example, Mead studied one Balinese trance state and showed how it grew out of a particular kind of taunting relationship between the mother and her growing toddler. Initially this teasing situation prompts hysterical delight or violent weeping on the part of the child, but the child gradually learns not to respond to the teasing. Ultimately, the Balinese youth withdraws more and more into himself or herself and becomes an insulated type of personality. As adults, Balinese are loathe to enter into close relationships with other individuals, preferring to employ ritual and art as vehicles for more distanced, more readily controllable emotional expression. In the trance state, however, the childhood experience is re-created and the once-sought-after emotional release is again achieved. Mead went on to discuss in more general terms the relationship between mother-child interactions in early life and the forms of sexual and ritualistic patterns that emerge in later life. Such speculative analyses at once stimulated her colleagues to undertake new observations and fascinated a lay audience that remained hungry for information about life in exotic societies and for insights they could apply to their own milieu.

During the 1930s, Mead accomplished a formidable achievement: she continued to carry out pioneering fieldwork, write lively ethnographies that could be appreciated by curious lay readers as well as crusty specialists, and contribute ideas of theoretical and methodological consequence to the field of anthropology. No doubt she was aided considerably by her two anthropologist-husbands, and particularly by her synergistic relationship with Bateson. But just as surely, by her energetic example and her insistent prodding, she also contributed to the intellectual and professional growth of the two men. As she once stated: "Reo had a better ear than I have and Gregory had a much better ear, but neither of them ever knew whose pig was dead. I always knew whose pig was dead."

Had events continued in this same pattern, Mead might have been able "to have it both ways"—to remain in the top ranks of her chosen academic discipline and to communicate with an appreciative and ever-growing general public. She could have been an indirect leader within and across domains. Indeed, far more than most other scholars who make the popular turn, Mead managed throughout her life to retain a position of power and influence within her discipline.

Yet, a number of events at the end of the 1930s effectively brought Mead's active days of anthropological fieldwork to a close. After having been told by medical authorities that she would not be able to bear children, she gave birth in 1939 to a daughter, Mary Catherine Bateson. In the same year, the Second World War broke out in Europe, and two years later, in the United States as well. Along with other colleagues, Mead joined the war effort, directing her own attention to issues of meal planning and nutrition. And, like other figures profiled in this book, she became a regular commuter to Washington and a member of many influential policy circles. Despite her critique of American society (as seen through a South Seas' lens), she remained a genuine, enthusiastic patriot throughout her life.

By the end of the war, her third and final marriage had broken up; Mead was in her midforties; and, perhaps in part because of the precocious start of her career, she was already considered an elder figure in the scholarly domain of anthropology. She continued to participate actively in the intellectual life of her discipline, but it was primarily as a valued participant in scholarly conferences and as a returning celebrity-visitor to "her" cultures. Mead was able to maintain this position both through indirect means—her provocative writings—and through an increasing willingness to assume direct public roles in professional meetings and organizations. Meanwhile, her status as a writer, commentator, and public spokesperson on issues facing American society continued to expand until her death. She was becoming a direct leader, without official portfolio, on the national scene.

In middle and later life, Mead's relationship to the discipline of anthropology was proceeding in directions rather different from her relationship to the broader public. Specialists in disciplines generally distinguish sharply between those who are active contributors to the field and those whose contributions either have ceased completely or have taken on a more derivative tone. Once her major monographs on the peoples of the South Pacific had been issued, Mead no longer was seen as a prototypical fieldworker, nor as a contributor to ground-breaking work in a library-based subdiscipline such as linguistics, kinship structure, or the analysis of myth. She did, however, occupy a number of roles that proved critical for the flourishing of the discipline.

First, Mead continued to argue strongly for, and to provide crucial guides to, studies that examined childhood, family life, sexuality, and other issues that had been virtually ignored in male-dominated anthropology. This line of work was stimulated by her monograph *Sex and Temperament in Three Primitive Societies* (1935) and by a more popular book, *Male and Female* (1950). Returning after the war to New Guinea, Samoa, and other societies that she had visited before, Mead called attention to the changes that were taking place in child rearing and other personal relationships. She also promoted the use of psychoanalytic concepts and methods of analysis, though she never subscribed uncritically to strong Freudian claims such as the universality of the Oedipal complex. She wanted to chart the range of human possibilities. She declared that "the biological bases of development set limitations which must be honestly reckoned with," though she added that these bases can also be seen as potentialities by no means fully tapped by our human imagination.

Second, Mead was an insistent and tireless worker for interdisciplinary studies and for the central role of anthropology within such studies. The period after the war was a time when scholars, many of whom had been working as members of interdisciplinary teams on applied problems during the war, acknowledged with new force the need to rub shoulders with other kinds of experts from other disciplinary areas. Mead loved to collaborate across disciplines; an observer of her at a conference compared her to a child at summer camp. She easily mastered new lingo and drew connections among concepts that promised to illuminate issues of broad interest. Also, she had a genius for starting conversations among disparate scholars and keeping them going in productive directions, even though she often dominated them. Mead pioneered in developing methods whereby groups could collaborate in the examination of contemporary cultures. By insisting that such groups span the range of individuals living in the culture, she transcended an "us/them" mentality, in the process broadening the scope and validity of scholarly inquiry. Especially in the field of human development, Mead inspired much high-quality collaboration. And she was even able to stretch to more remote disciplines, such as cybernetics and communications theory. In these respects Mead resembles other intellectual leaders whose interests naturally spill across an ensemble of disciplines.

Most important, Mead became the optimal ambassador for the discipline of anthropology—a powerful direct leader who promoted and embodied the identity of "anthropologist" within and beyond the domain. As she became a public figure, with ready access to print and broadcast media, she not only brought anthropology to the attention of the wider public but also impressed on that public the importance of studying remote, rapidly changing (and often rapidly disappearing) cultures. (Much the same kind of move has been initiated in recent years by scholars of biodiversity, who have striven to stem the imminent loss of unique flora and fauna.) Popularizing concepts that grew out of Boas's and Benedict's studies, Mead made the word *culture* and the concept "cultures" part of the American lexicon. Chiefly by implication, she suggested that anthropologists spoke about human affairs from a privileged position, because of their intimate knowledge of diverse cultures. And in a manner somewhat akin to the esteemed *National Geographic* magazine, Mead also helped to raise the American public's consciousness about the integrity and legitimacy of lifestyles very different from their own.

Thus, Mead began with one form of story line and stance within her discipline, and gradually effected a transition to a different perspective. Initially, Mead sought to convince other anthropologists that Boas's position on the determining role of culture was valid. With others of the "culture" school, she successfully combated the counterstory of a biologically based explanation and an implicit or explicit embracing of a single account of all human development and all human nature. Then, pursuing the Benedict tradition while working with Fortune and particularly with Bateson, Mead delineated a set of typologies that encompassed the gamut of sexual and temperamental factors. In this case, too, the counterstories either embraced a single view of development or questioned whether *any* kind of pattern could be discerned.

Both of these contributions were valued within the profession, though each eventually came under increasingly critical scrutiny (as do all influential positions). During this initial period, which ran roughly from the mid-1920s to the late 1930s, Mead was a proper (if more popularly oriented) member of her profession. And her relatively complex stories spoke to minds that were definitely schooled in the profession.

In the succeeding years, Mead moved away from the mainstream of practicing anthropologists. Whereas, before, her focus had fallen on South Sea cultures, with the United States introduced for comparative purposes, the accent in her writings came gradually to be reversed. Now, echoing the remark in this chapter's epigraph, Mead attempted to explain contemporary society to itself, using her experiences in the field as background and comparative material. She had always been a remarkably quick study when it came to the apprehension of patterns in exotic cultures; now, making shrewd use of her ever-expanding mental file cabinet, she turned this powerful intuition to her own society, in a way that many found effective.

Anthropologists continued to appreciate Mead, principally because of her uncanny sense of important problems and promising methods, and because of the public recognition that she brought to the discipline in which they were collectively involved. Mead provided two identity stories for her fellow anthropologists: first, in view of its unparalleled data sources, anthropology was a uniquely important discipline; and second, the anthropologist had a special vantage point with which to address issues in his or her own culture.

Fellow disciplinarians were less in sympathy with the simplifications necessary in addressing an unschooled audience and with Mead's willingness to address nearly every issue from a putatively scholarly vantage point. Many were also uncomfortable with the stress on interdisciplinary work; to them, such an inclusionary story threatened the purity and singularity of the field of anthropology. Having studied human development and sexuality in the South Pacific, Mead felt entitled to comment not only on human nature(s) but on nearly every other topic that impinged on world affairs. The cases reviewed in this book suggest that one can become a direct leader in one's own domain only if one has earned one's disciplinary stripes through indirect leadership; yet if one wanders too far from one's evidentiary base or threatens the core values of the discipline, one risks losing credibility within the domain.

Like many other specialists in disciplines who eventually become direct leaders of a wider group, Mead was a generalist before she became an anthropologist; and she returned comfortably—some would say, too comfortably—to the role of an overall sage. During the Second World War and thereafter, she issued a series of books that were increasingly accessible in message—closer to pop sociology than to professional anthropology.

For a country that was groping its way toward the proper role for a world power, one with active ties and commitments all over the globe, Mead performed a vital function. She skillfully challenged many unexamined "truths" and tried to impress on the public a more sophisticated point of view. As she put it:

> My experience as an anthropologist has led me to think that as we have
> come to understand more about the laws of the physical universe in which
> we live, we have also—significantly in the very recent past—acquired a kind

of knowledge that gives us choices human beings never before have had. This is our knowledge about our own humanity—our newly emerging understanding about the nature of human nature.

Beginning with the area of her special expertise, Mead demonstrated not only the many different kinds of roles that members of each sex could assume, ranging from female leaders to male caretakers, but also the acceptance in remote cultures of behaviors proscribed in our own, from youthful sexual exploration to institutionalized bisexuality. Challenging stereotypes about age, she indicated that young children could assume roles of responsibility, while older individuals remained capable of learning and of adapting to change. In educational matters, she underscored the great malleability of the young child and the virtues of a progressive education that built on this early flexibility. She showed that apparently ancient practices like witchcraft were still viable, even as she demonstrated that apparently simple cultures could feature social relationships and understandings as complex as those that are unraveled daily on the psychoanalytic couch.

Seeking to complexify the notions commonly held by laypersons, Mead warned against a "frightened retreat to some single standard which will waste nine-tenths of the potential of the human race." Addressing to her Western audience the universal identity question of "Who are we?" she combated the widespread belief that "we" are special and superior to other cultural groups. She did so both by indicating the ways in which other cultures had successfully coped with dilemmas that dog us in the West, and by stressing that all human beings belong to a single species. Her story about people was unambiguously inclusionary rather than exclusionary. "What distinguishes human groups one from another is not inborn; it is the way in which each has organized and perpetuated experience and the access each has had to other living traditions," she contended. Mead argued that human beings should not feel guilty about particular practices in which they engage—for instance, divorce or bisexuality—and that they should be willing to experiment with new family arrangements such as trial marriages or groups rearing children together. Just as many Americans were forming a new, ecumenical visual image of the human planet as a consequence of popular photographic collections like Edward Steichen's *The Family of Man* (1955), Mead was providing fresh texts about populations around the world, including her own.

The stories related by Mead clearly went well beyond the beliefs of the unschooled mind. She was presenting a distinctly relativistic viewpoint and, at times, a personal integration that went beyond the relativistic. To gain in credibility, this perspective had to overcome a simple counterstory, which held that there is a correct way in which to live, and that Americans (or some other group) have privileged insight into this recommended course. Mead was helped in this mission by the public revulsion toward the Nazi version of racial and cultural superiority, but, equally, by her own persuasive lines of evidence and her effective written and oral presentations.

Even as Mead conveyed certain narratives and images to the general public, she also came to embody certain messages in her person. This zestful, energetic, and (mostly) sensible American woman could journey around the globe, make keen observations, and share them directly and unsentimentally with other people. Her childhood, her fieldwork, her friends, her travels, her own child, and her own grandchild were all resources on which she could and did draw as she sought to communicate with the spectrum of human beings. Indeed, many of her recommendations emerged from her own life—how to raise children, how to deal with conflict, and so on. And because her life was in many respects representative of her times, such recommendations found responsive ears, particularly among middle-class readers and television viewers.

The need to communicate and to do so powerfully became Mead's watchword. She led indirectly through her writings and directly through her encounters with small and large groups. She gave hundreds of speeches and wrote hundreds of articles in which she preached her gospel of a varied but essentially unified human nature. She collected friends and acquaintances effortlessly and displayed a special sympathy for mavericks; unlike many creative individuals who shrug off once-useful associates, Mead tried to hold on to all of those persons. She once estimated that she made a new friend every few months and rarely lost track of any of them. She had the leader's gift for speaking to a collection of diverse persons, many of whom would have disagreed with one another on specific issues, and yet leaving almost every person with the feeling that she had honored his or her perspective. And she had a soothing way of expressing novel ideas that made them congenial, rather than alarming, to those who might be inclined to be hostile.

Nevertheless, Mead struck some as an overwhelming personality who had to dominate every exchange and put others in their place. She often resembled a director who found it necessary to call all the shots, rather than a nurturant leader who strengthened and empowered others. At the same time, she had a genuine sense of responsibility; in tense or difficult situations, she readily put herself forward as one who could be helpful. Taking charge came as second nature to her. Her close colleague Ted Schwartz called for a "Manhattan project to study the source of her energy, her creativity, and her appetite for and ability to encompass the complexity of very many lives within her own life and intellect." But because she apparently subordinated herself to the causes that she was embracing, and because, while not always kind, she did strive to be a caring person, most of her associates were willing to concede to Mead her place nearer to the sun.

While Mead struck others as a straightforward person, she actually harbored within her a number of tensions, which might indeed have crippled a weaker or less committed individual. J. Robert Oppenheimer, as I will point out, was less able to handle such tensions. Sensitive to the various pulls and pressures on her, she composed in her early fifties a letter to her loved ones, to be opened in case of her early death. In this testament, Mead confessed:

> I have become increasingly conscious of the extent to which my life is being segmented, each piece shared with a separate person, even where within the time and space of that segment, I feel that I am being myself and my whole self in that particular relationship. . . . Different parts of my work are shared with different people with special interest. . . . Since the breakup of my marriage, far less of my life has been shared with one person, and a multitude of special relationships, collaborations, slight gaieties, and partial intensities have taken the place of a marriage. . . . Distance now separates me from people who once were able to keep most of the threads in their hands.

Mead ended the letter with a curious acknowledgment: "It has not been my choice of concealment that anyone of you have been left in ignorance of some part of my life which would seem, I know, of great importance."

Freud warned us to beware of denials, and his warning is appropriate here. Mead did indeed harbor facets of her life that she felt compelled to conceal. Probably the most sensational was a love relationship with her mentor and friend Benedict, which had begun when Mead was young and had continued into the years of her marriage with Bateson. There were many other lovers of both sexes as well. Then there was the fact of her religious life. Mead rarely spoke or wrote about organized religion and her own religious beliefs; and yet, this maverick child of nonreligious parents was a practicing Episcopalian who attended services regularly and valued hieratic rituals. Furthermore, although most people knew Mead as a committed rational thinker, she denied her condition after having been diagnosed with cancer and went to see a traditional healer.

Had these situations become known, Mead's credibility as a public spokesperson could well have been undermined either among her secularly oriented colleagues or among judgmental segments of the American public. Bateson, her daughter, suggests:

> The letter she wrote in 1955 has seemed to me to be an expression of concern that, due to some accident, details of her life might be revealed under circumstances of scandal or notoriety, circumstances under which she was not there to provide explanations and reassurances to those she cared about.

Mead wrote about the great variety of humankind and ventured quite far toward embodying that variety in the chapters of her own life. One gains the impression that what began as spirited curiosity and experimentation ultimately acquired a more compulsive flavor, as Mead felt a need to challenge conventional wisdom in nearly every sphere of her own life. Mead's continuing adherence to certain traditional practices suggests that she may not always have reveled in a life of studied innovation. Ultimately, the embodiment that she felt duty bound to pursue took its toll.

Without question, Mead was a leader in the sense that I use that term in this book—a person who affects the thoughts, behaviors, and feelings of a significant number of individuals. Indeed, along with J. Robert Oppenheimer, she epitomizes the individual who begins by occupying a central role within her discipline but then moves on to leadership in wider communities. By dint of her pioneering fieldwork and her abundant and excellently written books, Mead had become a leading anthropologist by the age of thirty-five, a position that she retained until her death in 1978. Her leadership took both indirect and direct forms, and in her active and committed life, she embodied what she spoke and wrote about.

Mead's writings about the importance of culture in affecting the course of human development, the patterns imposed by culture on the givens of sex and temperament, and the need for interdisciplinary collaboration constituted the ways in which she affected the mainstream of her profession. Mead's recognized leadership, evidenced by her participation over the decades on countless panels and committees, culminated in her election during her sixtieth year to the most prestigious position in her discipline—the presidency of the American Anthropological Association. Topping this off, Mead's capacity to reach to other disciplines and audiences also impressed colleagues who did not measure worth solely in terms of the number of new articles published each year in peer-reviewed journals. Affected by Mead's identity story of the contemporary anthropologist, others followed her example of attempting to straddle the discipline and the wider community, though few approached her success in doing so.

Mead was also a prominent leader across the academy and in the broader society. When it comes to providing leadership in the social sciences, Mead emerges as one of a dozen or so figures after the Second World War who, with some success, sought to legitimate a comprehensive, determinedly interdisciplinary approach to the study of human nature. On the wider stage of affecting American public opinion about the options open to women, children, and families, Mead had few if any competitors. Her monthly column ran in *Redbook* from 1962 to 1979 and had millions of readers. Her books, from the earliest reports on life in the South Seas to her appealing autobiography, *Blackberry Winter: My Earlier Years* (1972), were widely read and discussed. She spoke to large and appreciative audiences around the country and around the world; and as television became the dominant mode of communication in America, Mead became a fixture on the heady—and some of the less heady—talk-and-opinion programs. No name from the academy was more likely to appear at the head of a phrase uttered at cocktail parties than "Margaret Mead said . . . " She was the "symbol of the woman thinker in America." Many of the positions in debates about sex and lifestyle that are now taken for granted were first brought to the attention of nonacademicians by Mead and are now defended—or attacked—by individuals who have never heard her name.

Just what was the fundamental story that Mead communicated to the broader public? I see Mead's message as growing initially out of her studies of other people, but as directed primarily to her own society. As she saw it, a single human nature, whatever its limits, could nonetheless spawn a large variety of cultures. None has a monopoly on wisdom; none is inherently superior on all dimensions to all others. We should learn from other societies, just as they can learn from us. The result, Mead asserted optimistically, will be a world in which mutual understanding may help to reduce conflict.

While seemingly innocuous and certainly inclusionary, this message was an innovative one for her time. It clashed, on the one hand, with the notion that there was a single best way to be and, on the other, with a kind of mindless relativism, where any behavior that existed was necessarily as good as any other. Virtually no one living in the shadow of the Nazi era wanted to endorse a totally culturally relative position. Mead also asked individuals to acknowledge certain constants and constraints in human nature—those of sex, those of temperament, those of kinship and rearing—that underlie the undeniable diversity. This embracing of constraints as well as varieties of culture was a complex idea, one requiring the synthesis of apparent antinomies. As noted, it could be interpreted at several levels, and it ventured well beyond the unschooled mind.

Of all the leaders considered in this book, Mead stands out particularly in one respect: she was able to provide indirect and direct forms of leadership both within and across domains. Certainly, Mead was helped by the fact that her messages about human nature and culture were consonant with broader trends in her culture. She also had the advantage that her within-domain identity stories could be apprehended by individuals beyond the domain of the anthropologist. This ready transfer would not be possible in a more arcane domain, such as quantum physics, within which Oppenheimer worked. But it would be unfair not to stress as well Mead's unusual giftedness with language, personal communication, and the recognition of cultural patterns.

Mead posited many ideas that influenced others. Yet part of leadership inheres in having a program and in setting up a structure or organization that helps to bring that program to fruition. This, Mead could not—or would not—do. Mead formed meaningful relationships with countless people, but they were not structured so that she would achieve effectiveness on a wider plane. Mead had a short attention span and flitted from one interest to another; she was impatient and far better on initial inspiration than on dogged follow-through. In her compulsive desire to make optimal use of every minute, she rarely gave others a chance to contribute, feel engaged, or become empowered. She distrusted long-term entanglements and, while skilled at kindling the original spark, rarely remained active in a group or organization over the long haul. (Her involvement with the American Anthropological Association was probably her major long-term organizational commitment.) Indeed, she once expressed relief that she was a woman and so was less likely to be called on to assume administrative posts. She preferred leadership that was informal and transitory to leadership that demanded long-term commitments within a prescribed structure. Indeed, in a deep sense, she felt that Americans did not crave leaders, and she would have been appalled by the notion that she had "followers."

Besides lacking an organizational disposition, Mead also lacked a program that could be effected. Except for very general (and laudable) messages of reason, cooperation, cultural relativism, and mutual respect for diversity, she was not calling on individuals to join a crusade. Where some of her colleagues dedicated their energies to a single cause such as health, the environment, civil rights, or nuclear disarmament, Mead would sample the issue for a month or a year and then move on to another, equally seductive one. Her messages amounted to those of a concerned and committed world traveler and world talker, rather than those of an issue-oriented specialist. As she grew older and, finally, became sick, she focused even less; on the contrary, her statements became briefer, her attention span yet more attenuated, her impatience to do all before it was too late more pronounced. It proves far easier to detect her general effectiveness in consciousness-raising than her impact on specific issues.

Surprising as it was to see Mead's name splashed across the front page of the *New York Times* on January 31, 1983, five years after she had died, it was even more surprising to discover the context of that news story. An Australian anthropologist named Derek Freeman, who had first visited Samoa in the early 1940s and had returned for an extended stay in the mid-1960s, had written the book *Margaret Mead and Samoa* (1983) as an attack on Mead's early fieldwork.

According to Freeman, Mead had gotten the story on Samoa entirely wrong. Far from being the tropical human paradise that she had portrayed, Samoa is described as a society wracked with conflict and anxiety. Systematically, Freeman takes on each of the claims put forth by Mead; and whether the issue concerns rank, cooperation, aggression, religion, child rearing, sexual mores, adolescence, or the Samoan ethos, the Australian anthropologist reaches conclusions that are the opposite of his predecessor's. Even worse than attacking her conclusions, Freeman questions Mead's methods (in his view, she did not know how to do fieldwork) and her motives. As Freeman portrays it, a relatively open-minded Boas had sent Mead to the field to challenge the claims of hereditarians. In a chapter dripping with sarcasm and innuendo, Freeman asserts: "Mead Presents Boas with an Absolute Answer." Thus are anthropological legends forged and shattered.

Freeman's attack evoked spirited defenses of Mead, with many knowledge-able scholars pointing out that Freeman's databases and sources were as skewed in one direction as Mead's earlier work may have been skewed in another direction. A formidable and prestigious male authority figure was as prone to be misled by informants as an entirely nonthreatening young woman; Freeman's doggedly pessimistic view of Samoan society was no less one-sided than Mead's unduly positive account. Still, her long-time authority was now attenuated in the eyes of the public. To complement this revisionism toward Mead's anthropological legend, probing studies in the early 1980s by Bateson and by biographer Jane Howard presented an individual far more complex and tormented than the globe-trotting, staff-grasping, "grandmother-of-us-all." Mead emerged as an individual who, while laudable in many respects, was demanding on others, not frank with intimates about the diverse facets of her life, and reluctant personally to confront truths about herself.

Even Mead's messages to the world fell on less sympathetic ears after her death. The continuing weakening of the nuclear family, the wretched performance of many American institutions, the rise of violence in the streets, and the resurgence of ugly nationalism around the globe—issues to which Mead had been attuned—nonetheless called into question the optimistic, activist, progressive, and "many peoples, one world" vision put forth by Mead. Not that the desirability of Mead's visions was necessarily questioned (though they often were challenged by conservative spokespersons); rather, they were seen as improbable at best, and virtually impossible to achieve and to sustain. And while Mead's personal example as a female scholar continued to be admired, her writings came to be seen as more individualistically oriented, more supportive of the "feminine mystique," and even more biologically oriented than many latter-day feminists desired.

We have come, then, in recent years to discern limits in Mead's messages and in her personal example. Yet, in my view, the impact of her leadership remains clear. More than any other person of her time, Mead called into question both for professionals and for laypersons the belief that there is only one way to pass through childhood and adolescence. While illustrating the varieties of human cultures, she insisted that no group has all the answers and that the varieties grow out of fundamental dimensions of human nature. And, more than any of her contemporaries, Mead demonstrated that a single behavioral scientist—indeed, a female behavioral scientist—could speak directly to a wide population, strike a responsive chord, and define issues—if not answers—in an enduring way. The fact that her scholarly and personal messages were seen as basically consonant is an enduring tribute to Mead's intellectual and communicative powers. As a consequence, both her ideas and her example have had a lasting impact.

5

J. ROBERT OPPENHEIMER
The Teaching of Physics, the Lessons of Politics

*Every poet is a bit of a Fuehrer himself; he wants to rule
minds for he is tempted to think that he knows better.*
—Joseph Brodsky

As its cover story of October 10, 1949, *Life* magazine featured a face that had recently come to be recognized by many Americans—that of the physicist J. Robert Oppenheimer, captured in a thoughtful pose, and surrounded by books and papers. Looking directly at the reader with a penetrating and yet strangely calming gaze, and gracefully holding a cigarette, "Oppie" or "Opje" (as he was widely nicknamed) had come to symbolize for the world a new phenomenon: the theoretical scientist immersed in public affairs.

Oppenheimer was the wizard who had masterminded the Manhattan Project—by far the most massive, coordinated scientific effort undertaken to that point in human history—wherein he and his colleagues had devised the atomic bomb. Now, along with other leading scientific and political figures who served on an interlocking directorate of commissions, he was pondering the implications of atomic energy for war and for peace. The handsome and still-youthful family man had recently taken the helm of the prestigious Institute for Advanced Study in Princeton, New Jersey. There, as the lead article phrased it, this man with a "Da Vincian" mind presided with intellectual power and personal charm over a collection of brilliant scholars, the most celebrated among them being his fellow physicist Albert Einstein.

Five years later, charges of disloyalty were leveled publicly against the man who had for nearly a decade been the most influential scientist in the world. The very man whose team had contributed so decisively to the Allies' victory stood accused of being a security risk, one who should no longer be trusted with the secrets of his country. And, indeed, after a strange semi-judicial proceeding, Oppenheimer's

J. Robert Oppenheimer. UPI/Bettmann Newsphotos

clearance was revoked. No longer would he be able to serve his nation in any sensitive position. Oppenheimer appeared again on the covers of the nation's leading news and opinion publications, but this time with a much less happy guise.

In the dozen years between his fall from power and his death from cancer, Oppenheimer remained the director of the Institute for Advanced Study. He continued to address various publics on the issues that concerned him, though never again with the same assurance or influence. In December 1963, shortly after the assassination of John F. Kennedy, Oppenheimer received a vindication of sorts when President Lyndon B. Johnson presented him with the prestigious Enrico Fermi Award, given annually by the Atomic Energy Commission. At his death in February 1967, Oppenheimer was seen by friends and admirers as a hero who had been cruelly scapegoated; by many observers and associates as an ambivalent and ambiguous figure who had contributed, if unwittingly, to his own downfall; and by inveterate anti-Communists as one of the villains in the cold war, his name to be uttered in the same breath as the convicted perjurer Alger Hiss, if not the executed spies Julius and Ethel Rosenberg.

Born in New York City in 1904 into a family of German Jewish extraction, Oppenheimer had an early life at least as propitious and privileged as that of Margaret Mead. His family was wealthy, cultivated, and civic-minded, and his parents doted on their firstborn son. Oppenheimer attended Fieldston, the charter school of the Ethical Culture Society. There, consistent with the precepts of the society and of his own family, he came to identify strongly with its non-sectarian, idealistic, and humanistic concerns.

Young Oppenheimer, singularly brilliant and precocious, always stood at the head of his class. He read voraciously and could recall virtually everything that he had read. When he entered Harvard College, he took twice as many courses as were required and excelled in nearly all of them. Mastering languages was child's play for him. He learned Sanskrit and enjoyed reading works in the original; when visiting Holland, he picked up enough Dutch in six weeks that he could lecture on physics. His major scholarly interests came to center on the sciences, first chemistry and then physics; but intoxicated by learning on a wide scale, he could not put aside other disciplines, and he cherished poetry with equal fervor.

It is not easy to get a feeling for the psyche of the young Oppenheimer, except to say that he was—and remained—a very complex personality. In this respect he was the child of his parents. Gracious on the surface, both parents seemed to be tense and troubled individuals; his father had to strain to be agreeable, while his mother's emotional intensity hid a mournful disposition. Oppenheimer remembered himself as an "unctuous, repulsively good little boy." Like many hypertalented youths, he seems to have been lonely and sickly, but he did have a few good friends and was close to his younger brother, Frank, who eventually became a physicist as well.

Oppenheimer's adolescence was troubled. Because of ill health and moodiness he had to spend a year at home and an additional summer away from home before he was thought fit to attend college. He was close to suicide on at least one occasion—he himself spoke of a "chronic" tendency toward suicide—and he tried to strangle his close friend Francis Fergusson on another. He engaged in bizarre and sometimes dangerous risk taking while driving and sailing, and he was prone to exaggerations that would sometimes get him in trouble. He had difficulty in sustaining relations with peers whom he often struck as impervious and arrogant. He confessed in later life:

> In the days of my almost infinitely prolonged adolescence, I hardly took an action, hardly did anything or failed to do anything, whether it was a paper in physics or a lecture, or how I read a book, how I talked to a friend, how I loved, that did not arouse in me a very great sense of revulsion and of wrong.

When his mother died in 1931, he wrote an older friend that he was the loneliest man in the world.

While conducting research at the Cavendish laboratory in Cambridge, England, after his graduation from Harvard, Oppenheimer saw a psychiatrist who concluded that the brilliant young American scientist was schizophrenic. Although the diagnosis seems to have been wrong, or at least unsubstantiated, one can see how Oppenheimer's tendency to live in an inner world, his inability to sustain ordinary social relations with others, his compulsion to control situations, and his almost superhuman discipline and powers of concentration might have led to that conclusion. More than once in later life, Oppenheimer tottered on the edge of breakdown; and there were signs of neurosis, bordering on psychosis, in other members of the family. In comparison to such relatively robust (if not untroubled) personalities as Margaret Mead and Robert Maynard Hutchins, Oppenheimer had to devote considerable energy throughout his life to warding off depression and preserving his psychological equilibrium.

Oppenheimer was rescued from uncertainty about his future career and from acute distress in his personal life by a growing fascination with physics. This field had been placed centrally on the scientific map by Einstein's work at the turn of the century. Now the even more recent discoveries of complementarity, indeterminacy, and other quantum mechanical phenomena attracted the best and the brightest of young scientific minds. Oppenheimer was clearly central in their ranks. His early career associations were prototypical for members of this talented circle: Percy Bridgman at Harvard; J. J. Thomson at Cavendish in Cambridge; and Max Born at Goettingen, in the company of such giants as Werner Heisenberg, Wolfgang Pauli, Eugene Wigner, Herman Weyl, and John von Neumann (several of whom later became colleagues at the Institute for Advanced Study).

As a young scholar, Oppenheimer wrote important papers on relativity and quantum mechanics, extending the quantum mechanical perspective to hitherto-unexplored realms. Returning home from Europe, he received job offers from Harvard, the California Institute of Technology, and the University of California at Berkeley. He eventually accepted the latter two appointments, dividing his time between the northern and southern California universities throughout the 1930s.

At Berkeley, Oppenheimer finally found an intellectual community and a home. He was widely respected as an important theoretical physicist, a broad-ranging scholar, an outstanding translator of the ideas of others, and, increasingly, a brilliant teacher. While somewhat impatient with lesser minds and not above arrogance and snobbishness, Oppenheimer developed superlative skills at introducing difficult physical concepts to promising students, exciting their interest, and inspiring them to execute superb work.

Oppenheimer was beginning to show that he could exert a powerful hold on other individuals, particularly younger students. His letters underscore a distinct improvement in his ability to handle social situations; in the letters, he demonstrates considerable empathy for other people, whether his superiors, friends, or students. In a manner reminiscent of other young creators, like Sigmund Freud and T. S. Eliot, Oppenheimer displayed a keen sense of how to maintain cordial relations with individuals representing different statuses and points of view. In person, he now seemed able to anticipate the needs and wishes of those around him. Perhaps Oppenheimer had always been attuned to the human realm, but this sensitivity may have been masked in his earlier years by his own shyness and severe personal pains; perhaps he was simply developing new skills that he needed.

For a person of Oppenheimer's accomplishment and ambition, however, some crucial element necessary for scientific greatness may have been missing. While unsurpassed by any of his peers in sheer brilliance and power of understanding, Oppenheimer was destined not to become one of the international stars of physics, and he was not Nobel Prize material. No one can pinpoint with certainty the reasons for this failing: perhaps banal factors of timing or luck; perhaps his relative weakness at experimentation and at laboratory work; perhaps his depressive strain or his skeptical temperament; perhaps his compulsive dilletantism, which stimulated him to reach more widely rather than to probe more deeply.

My own guess is that the single biggest obstacle to Oppenheimer's immortality as a pure scientist was his lack of scientific nerve—an ambivalence about taking risks or assuming controversial stances that eventually compromised his leadership capacity. He was simply more at home talking, translating, teaching, and understanding the ideas of others than he was at venturing further and further out on a theoretical limb of his own construction. This once-isolated person was becoming an increasingly social animal. He preferred to pose questions rather than devote his life—and risk his career—in an effort to solve just one of them. His colleague and friend I. I. Rabi, himself a Nobel Prize–winning physicist, maintained that, for all of his brilliance, Oppenheimer lacked the temperament for pursuing a scientific conundrum in whichever way the issues pointed, without regard for the consequences. Rabi once declared of Oppenheimer: "He was not an original. Most of the real ideas came from others, but he could open doors and present them." And Rabi felt that Oppenheimer had a tendency to romanticize mysteries, rather than a drive to dissolve them.

From the record it is not clear to what extent Oppenheimer was troubled by his inability to effect a major scientific breakthrough. It is evident, however, that, during the 1930s, while Mead was making her scientific mark, Oppenheimer was discovering worlds beyond pure science. This was a time when America was preoccupied with the damage wrought by the Great Depression and with the rise of fascism abroad. Oppenheimer's early girlfriend Jean Tatlock, his brother, Frank, and, later, his own wife, Kitty, were very much involved in the left-wing politics of the 1930s, and Oppenheimer came to share their interests and concerns. As he later recalled:

My friends, both in Pasadena and in Berkeley, were mostly faculty people, scientists, classicists, and artists. I studied and read Sanskrit with Arthur

Ryder. I read very widely, mostly classics, novels, plays, and poetry; and I read something of other parts of science. I was not interested in and did not read about economics or politics. I was almost wholly divorced from the contemporary scene in this country. I never read a newspaper or a current magazine like *Time* or *Harper's*. . . . I was interested in man and his experience but I had no understanding of the relations of man to his society.

Oppenheimer noted, however, that "in late 1936" his "interests began to change." By the end of the 1930s, Oppenheimer had become a different person. To his brilliance as a specialist in physics were added sensitivity to individuals who were less privileged and mastery of the current political scene in his country and abroad. His linguistic and logical prowess was leavened by increasing deployment of his personal intelligences. Wedding the Ethical Culture Society concerns of his youth with a growing anxiety about the ever more unsettled world conditions around him, Oppenheimer became unquestionably a man of the left. He devoured the principal Marxist texts, embraced socialist ideals, displayed a sensitivity to injustice, supported radical causes, and strove to build a better social order.

Oppenheimer had always struck those about him as special, and his reputation was now spreading beyond the sciences. Already a direct and an indirect leader within the domain of physics, he was beginning to influence the thoughts and beliefs of individuals who were concerned about the political situation at home and abroad.

Even before the Second World War had broken out, physicists had become aware of the potential for producing powerful weapons through the release of nuclear energy. In a now-famous letter of 1939, actually drafted by the physicist Leo Szilard, Einstein had alerted President Roosevelt to this possibility. Various efforts directed toward the creation of an atomic weapon were soon launched, and Oppenheimer was assigned a leading role in Berkeley-based research on the reactions of fast neutrons. One of his tasks was to coordinate theoretical calculations about basic nuclear reactions with experimental data; he was expected to estimate the critical mass of material needed for fission and to assess the efficiency of the proposed weapon. The national scientific leaders at this early stage of weapons research—Chicago's Arthur Compton, Harvard's James Conant, and Oppenheimer's close Berkeley colleague Ernest Lawrence—took note of Oppenheimer's scientific acumen and his capacity to accomplish challenging tasks quickly.

Still, considerable distance lay between Oppenheimer as a major academic researcher on the West Coast and Oppenheimer as a leader of arguably the most important scientific and military endeavor in human history. It was by no means a foregone conclusion that Oppenheimer would be asked to head the scientific mission of the Manhattan Project. To be sure, he was fully capable of understanding the technical issues involved in the building of an atomic weapon, he had the respect of his fellow scientists, and he was willing—indeed eager—to make a full-time commitment to the project. Yet, counting against him were his relative youth (he was not yet forty), his lack of experience in directing any kind of institution, his reputation as a theoretician rather than an experimentalist, and his stature as a scientist who ranked just slightly below the very best. Oppenheimer's well-known left-leaning sympathies certainly gave pause to the country's defense establishment. As General Leslie Groves, who was assigned to oversee the entire project, recalled two decades later: "No one with whom I talked showed any great enthusiasm about Oppenheimer as a possible director of the project." Moreover, reflecting on Oppenheimer's left-leaning political allegiances, Groves referred to "much that was not to our liking by any means."

Ultimately, early in 1943, Oppenheimer was named the scientific leader of the Manhattan Project. Despite his initial misgivings and a decided lack of enthusiasm on the part of several of his consultants, Groves became convinced that, among those who were available, Oppenheimer possessed the optimal combination of personal and intellectual gifts. Groves considered Oppenheimer to be a scientific genius—in a class by himself—and also took a personal liking to him. Considering the alternatives, it became clear to Groves that no one else was nearly as likely to be able to preside over a disparate collection of scientists and technicians and to get them to work together smoothly and effectively. And so, Oppenheimer, until then primarily an indirect leader in a traditional domain, instantly became a direct leader of a much broader endeavor.

By unanimous consent Oppenheimer proved a brilliant success as the scientific director of the Manhattan Project. He had all of the desired virtues. He understood the technical material perfectly, could assimilate new findings immediately, and could explain crucial issues to individuals from different fields and backgrounds, and worked tirelessly. Making it his business to worry about the living conditions in the isolated sites of Santa Fe and Los Alamos, Oppenheimer attended to everything from salaries to social activities to meals. He selected (often, it was more like a seduction of a reluctant party) the most talented upper-level personnel (average age twenty-five, highest age around forty) and maintained close personal contact with them and their uprooted families; and he was also impressively solicitous of the members of the support staff. The great physicist Hans Bethe reported:

> The success of Los Alamos rested largely on its teamwork and the leadership of its Director. It is not the primary function of the director of a laboratory to make technical contributions. What was called for from the director of Los Alamos at that time was to get a lot of prima donnas to work together,

to understand all the technical work that was going on, to make it fit together, and to make decisions between [*sic*] various possible lines of development. I have never seen anyone who performed these functions as brilliantly as Oppenheimer.

This positive characterization was echoed by nearly all observers. The physicist Victor Weisskopf alluded to Oppenheimer's "continuous and intense presence which produced a sense of direct participation in all" of the scientists. Oppenheimer's long-time friend Paul Horgan spoke of him as a "first class manipulator of the imagination and interpreter of it." Rabi called Oppenheimer a "born leader . . . [who, with the Manhattan Project] created an atmosphere of excitement, enthusiasm, and high intellectual and moral purpose that still remains with those who participated as one of the great experiences of their lives." And the physicist Edward Teller mused: "I don't know how Oppenheimer acquired this facility for handling people." The answer may have been given by another long-time friend, the writer Haakon Chevalier:

From the earliest age, I imagine, the need to be pre-eminent must have maintained itself. For a long time, probably, in school and college, the leading position came to him as a kind of natural due. He towered above his peers so unmistakably that no one challenged his leadership and he came to take this order of things as his due.

In Los Alamos, Oppenheimer faced an unprecedented challenge. In order to assemble a fission bomb as soon as the material became available, he had to construct a huge scientific and technical research apparatus in secret and maintain the interest, cooperation, and morale of forty-five hundred workers. He had to satisfy the demands of the military leadership for the most rapid possible construction of a weapon under conditions of utmost security. Yet, for most of the scientists, secret work on someone else's project represented a direct contradiction to the unfettered and frankly egotistical way in which they customarily worked.

Oppenheimer insisted on the greatest possible openness at Los Alamos, consistent with the understandable demands of security. He resisted the military's impulse to limit individuals' knowledge of the project. He maintained regular contact with scientists all over the country and, indeed, in parts of Europe as well. He planned gatherings where the scientists could relax and interact casually. He encouraged debate and participated catalytically, as well as substantively, in these discussions. When confronted with a difficult and competitive colleague such as Teller, Oppenheimer showed flexibility and imagination; he allowed Teller to act as a gadfly, to pursue some of his ideas about a "superbomb" (like the hydrogen bomb), and to grow intellectually; at the same time, Oppenheimer made certain that Teller did not interfere with other scientists and that the major missions of the laboratory continued to be pursued with single-minded intensity.

With unprecedented success, Oppenheimer controlled his own temper and hid his hitherto-undisguised tendencies toward arrogance and domination. Managing a neat and difficult trick, he succeeded in being both the unquestioned leader of the scientific effort and a colleague, ready to shoulder responsibilities and burdens along with everyone else, and reluctant to pull rank or express disdain.

In the terms of this study, Oppenheimer made an effective transition from being an indirect leader, working within a narrow (though pivotal) area of physics, to being a direct leader of a large and heterogeneous scientific establishment. In his scientific role, he was dealing with experts and could discuss scientific issues about nuclear physics in all their complexity. At the same time, however, as a direct leader of men and women, he also presented a far more elemental story of identity: We scientists and technicians are blessed with special knowledge and skills. As patriots, we must work together effectively, and as selflessly as possible, in order to produce a weapon that can help the Allies win the war. From all indications, Oppenheimer believed totally in this story, and his actions embodied his beliefs. It is difficult to imagine a more effective leader of a high-stake scientific mission.

Even a story of scientific cooperation during wartime will encounter pockets of resistance. Among the counterstories Oppenheimer encountered were narratives that stressed the division between "pure science" and practical applications, or between "pure science" and "science politicized." The need for secrecy also ran against the scientific credo that stressed the unrestricted sharing of all knowledge. As the successful construction of awe-inspiring weapons became more probable, scientists voiced increasing misgivings about the uses to which the weapons might be put. A leader less skilled than Oppenheimer might well have seen his own story overwhelmed by these competing agendas.

Leading Los Alamos was not without its costs. Oppenheimer drove himself to exhaustion and unstable health, became virtually emaciated, and chronically smoked and coughed. Because of some casual encounters at the time with old left-wing friends, suspicions about Oppenheimer's personal loyalty were rekindled among security forces; sometimes investigators would question him persistently after a grueling day at work. He confronted more than one personal crisis in terms of his ability to handle the work and provide the needed leadership. On several occasions in 1943 and 1944, he declared that he could no longer continue. Nonetheless, Oppenheimer remained at the helm and continued to grow steadily in skills and accomplishments until the climactic completion of his awesome task in the summer of 1945.

When the first atomic weapons were detonated, first as a trial run in the desert near Alamogordo, New Mexico, and then with fateful consequences on the Japanese cities of Hiroshima and Nagasaki, Oppenheimer stood at the height of his career. He had successfully led an enterprise of unequaled complexity and importance, and he had done so while maintaining the respect of his colleagues and subordinates. He had succeeded in bridging the enormous distance between scientific expertise and institutional leadership. Just as Mead had found herself faced with unexpected choices after returning from her second trip to the field, so Oppenheimer confronted a range of options, from returning to the world of academic physics to entering the political arena.

While the majority of his fellow scientists returned, often with undisguised relief, to their laboratories and universities, Oppenheimer elected to remain involved in the national policy arena. Because of his unchallenged expertise on atomic energy, his growing familiarity with the political scene, and his increasing intimacy with many leaders and policy makers, he found himself moving easily into positions of influence. In the years immediately after the war, he fulfilled a variety of such roles, ranging from membership on the United Nations Atomic Energy Commission's Scientific Committee, to chairmanship of the General Advisory Committee to the U.S. Atomic Energy Commission, to membership on the Scientific Advisory Committee of the Office of Defense Mobilization; in all cases he performed very ably. A colleague who served with him said: "He was so naturally a leader of our group that it was impossible to imagine that he would not be in the chair." Alice Kimball Smith and Charles Weiner noted:

> In fact, Oppenheimer became a kind of Grand Pooh-Bah of atomic energy: because he summarized discussions so succinctly and was often staying in Washington for another meeting the next day, fellow panel members gladly delegated report writing to him; sometimes this meant that Oppenheimer was reporting to Oppenheimer.

It was this Oppenheimer, a middle-aged man at the height of his powers and influence, who graced the cover of *Life* magazine in the fall of 1949.

Oppenheimer had a more troubled side, however. Even before the bombs had been assembled and detonated, Oppenheimer and the other scientists had been aware of the fearsome consequences of the bombs' use. Many in the scientific community had felt that the bombs should not be dropped at all—that a "demonstration weapon" should be detonated in front of the enemy, or that atomic weapons should be internationalized or banned. Oppenheimer himself appears to have had reservations about the decision to detonate the bombs over Japan, but he had not headed any kind of overt opposition, based on any moral qualms, as some of his scientific colleagues would have wished. Indeed, Oppenheimer had quashed a petition calling for a "trial demonstration" of the bomb. Instead, he had seemed struck—if not immobilized—by the tragedy of the situation and had cited, in a famous moment, a passage from the Bhagavad Gita: "If the radiance of a thousand suns were to be burst at once into the sky, that would be like the splendor of the Mighty One. . . . I am become death, the shatterer of worlds." And he had voiced his own view: "In some crude sense, which no vulgarity, no humor, no overstatement can quite extinguish, the physicists have known sin; and this is a knowledge which they cannot lose."

After the war, Oppenheimer wanted very much to represent the voice of rationality within circles of influence; he favored international control over atomic energy, peaceful use of nuclear energy, and the gradual processes of disarmament. In private, he counseled caution and expressed skepticism about the construction of more powerful weapons, such as the hydrogen (or "Super") bomb. But Oppenheimer often found himself in a minority when surrounded by individuals from the defense establishment, and he witnessed as well a steady, seemingly inexorable drift toward conservatism and jingoism on the American political scene.

Thus, Oppenheimer was placed in a quandary. To maintain his influence within the corridors of power, he often had to subjugate his private beliefs and align himself with a more militant majority. Propelled by guilt regarding his close association with the atomic bomb, uncertainty because of his compromised position on security matters, and an undeniable—if ambivalent—lust to remain near the centers of power, Oppenheimer was in many ways a tormented man, one more reminiscent of his youthful self than of the confident leader of the early 1940s.

Although his name was becoming a household word, Oppenheimer was never at ease speaking to the heterogeneous general public. Unlike Mead, who relished opportunities to appear on the mass media, Oppenheimer remained at his core an introverted scholar and intellectual leader, most comfortable in addressing those with whom he shared technical knowledge and cultural values. Nonetheless, because of his expanding niche in mid-century America, Oppenheimer had to be able to speak to, and provide some measure of leadership for, at least four different communities or audiences.

First, Oppenheimer continued to be an expert on the technical aspects of physics. Indeed, few of his generation rivaled him in his mastery of a range of fields, his ability to keep abreast of new findings, and his capacity to stimulate exciting new lines of work, as he was doing in his new position at the Institute for Advanced Study. His institute work was addressed to the most fundamental issues of existence: What is the universe made out of? How can we best think about matter and energy? How did the universe originate, and what will happen to it?

Oppenheimer remained an inspiration to members of his scientific peer group. On the final day of his Los Alamos service, he had given a presentation so brilliant that it remains stirring to read. Especially prized was his ability to help physicists see the "bigger picture"—how one physics problem or domain related to another, how physics connected to other sciences, to other areas of knowledge, and to the world of personal choices. He recognized the powerful bonds that existed among scientists, as scientists; he saw in this kinship the basis for a more rational world, in which knowledge could be pursued, shared, and harnessed for positive ends.

Oppenheimer added to this primary audience three other groups. He was comfortable in addressing the broader scholarly community—individuals representing other disciplines at the Institute for Advanced Study and scholars at other centers of learning. For them, he represented the literate, interdisciplinary individual, equally at home in the laboratories of the sciences, the ateliers of the arts, and the libraries of history and literature. Far more than Mead, Oppenheimer was an intellectual's intellectual. He was deeply interested in the nature of knowledge—and of ignorance—across scholarly fields. He liked to puzzle aloud about the mysteries of the mind and of the universe, and he gained as much pleasure from posing broad questions (such as "How can human morality be coded on a strand of DNA?") as from considering solutions that his scholarly colleagues put forth. With this schooled audience, as with his primary audience of physicists, Oppenheimer could anticipate a certain level of expertise and a fundamental allegiance to his cognitive enterprise.

Somewhat more challenging to work with were the policy makers who looked to Oppenheimer for explanations of the intricacies of atomic energy and for advice on what to do with instruments of mass destruction. These people wanted to know about the potentials, for good or evil, of the new weaponry that had been created; they searched at times for technical insight and, at other times, for moral leadership. While some admired the subtlety of Oppenheimer's mind, others grew impatient with his proclivity for raising questions rather than providing answers. Oppenheimer had an unfortunate clash with President Harry Truman, who became annoyed at Oppenheimer's chronic breast-beating. "Don't you bring that fellow around again," Truman muttered to his secretary of state, Dean Acheson. "After all, all he did was to make the bomb. I'm the guy who fired it off."

Finally, despite any personal misgivings, Oppenheimer did not shrink from addressing and attempting to educate the general public. Recognizing the gap that separated the professional scientist from the interested layperson, he energetically worked at explaining and justifying the world of science. In a way that seems difficult to re-create now (because those of us raised in an atomic age have come to take it for granted), Oppenheimer had to wrestle publicly with the issues posed by scientists' role as creators and bearers of power—as those who would be God.

With policy makers and the general public, Oppenheimer strove to simplify issues without distorting them. He was thus endlessly surrounded by paradoxes, which he patiently tried to unravel: How can a scientist relish open exchanges and yet engage in research that is top secret? How can scientists attempt to uncover the truth, and then confront the fact that they have stumbled on answers that could destroy the planet? What are the consequences of sharing technological know-how with one's enemies, and what are the consequences of an arm's race if we turn our back on such sharing? How can the terrible weapon of atomic energy also harbor within it formidable peacetime uses? One can see Oppenheimer struggling to make the shift from disciplinary questions about the nature of matter to the most fundamental universal questions about human nature and human identity. And one can see as well a shift from a simple, militarily grounded, exclusionary view of the political world (the Allies versus the Axis powers) to a more inclusionary view of all humankind.

Oppenheimer often turned to the fundamental insights of physics to explain his quandary—*our* quandary—to a wider world. Building on the Danish physicist Niels Bohr's epoch-opening discovery of complementarity, Oppenheimer commented:

> We are gradually coming to a critical awareness of the fact that it is much harder to tell the truth than we like to think. It is difficult even to be candid unless one has a vast community of experience and knowledge in terms of which to talk. In politics the great actions and the great men are those that reveal the relations and harmony between views, generalizations, and ideals which superficially appear neither compatible nor relevant. There is surely need for this today in coping with the question of the role of the individual in society—whether the individual is an instrument of society or an end of society. Neither the human soul as something to be saved nor man as a part of society can be ignored; it is not easy to consider these two concepts without some sense that each complements the other. We have been alerted to this kind of duality by our experience in science.

In his attempt to share with a wider audience the contradictions and paradoxes that he had encountered through his own life experience, Oppenheimer touched on some of the major themes that occupied many other twentieth-century leaders, and particularly those who aspired to leadership in the world of ideas. Oppenheimer was asking the inhabitants of the world to join him in grappling with the relationships among knowledge, power, and openness; the balance between purity and innocence, on the one hand, and pollution or skepticism, on the other; the proper ratio between secrecy and openness in a society, particularly one that is committed to freedom of expression; and the difficulties of making wise decisions about human life when so much of contemporary knowledge is so technical that only bona fide experts have the wherewithal to grapple with it.

As noted earlier, Oppenheimer was a complexifier, one attracted by riddles and even seduced by the mystical. The dominant story that he sought to convey represented a personal integration of elements of scientific knowledge, historical circumstances, and human frailty. Oppenheimer was true to his nature when he shared his intoxication with the enigmatic and the paradoxical:

- "A subject is much harder to understand when no one understands it."

- "The peoples of this world must either unite or they will perish. The war that has ravaged so much of the earth has written these words. The atomic bomb has spelled them out for all men to understand."

- "We have devoted effort, study, thought, and treasure to the quest for military security. . . . We have brought about the most fearful insecurity that has been known to man in what we know of his history."

- "No man should escape our universities without some sense of the fact that not through his fault, but in the nature of things, he is going to be an ignorant man and so is everyone else."

- "We have made a thing, a most terrible weapon . . . and by so doing . . . we have raised again the question of whether science is good for man, or whether it is good to try to learn about the world."

- "The atomic bomb . . . which owed its whole success and its very existence to the possibility of open discussion and free inquiry, appeared in a strange paradox, at once a secret and an unparalleled instrument of coercion."

In putting forth his deepest thoughts about the world, Oppenheimer was seeking to share his insights with a variety of audiences. One can see how physicists and other scholars would grasp, and perhaps sympathize with, Oppenheimer's attempts to extend the paradoxes of physics to the enigmas of contemporary life. Yet, these messages were not ones that could be readily apprehended by the unschooled mind: they far more closely resembled musings on relativity (physical or cultural), or attempts at a grand personal synthesis, than straightforward accounts of right and wrong. It is easy to see how Oppenheimer's nonexpert audiences—lay as well as political or military—would be confused, frustrated, or alienated by the complex issues that he sought to communicate.

In the late 1940s and early 1950s, the United States, incited by the demagogic senator from Wisconsin, Joseph McCarthy, underwent paroxysms of anti-Communist sentiment. Anyone with the slightest tinge of association with socialist or Communist causes became fair game for this latter-day witch-hunt. Oppenheimer had long been plagued by rumors and whisperings about his left-leaning tendencies and his sympathy for Communist ideas and institutions; as noted earlier, he had been under surveillance since the middle of the war. When it came time for Oppenheimer's security clearance to be renewed, his enemies decided to attack him—and the non-militant causes with which he was affiliated. In December 1953, associates on the Atomic Energy Commission notified Oppenheimer privately that his security clearance would not be renewed unless he was willing to undergo a hearing.

Eager to clear his name and to puncture any lingering suspicions of disloyalty to his country, Oppenheimer requested and was granted a hearing that took place in April and May of 1954. This hearing "In the Matter of J. Robert Oppenheimer" constituted the most stressful experience of his adult life. Oppenheimer was subjected to questioning that more closely resembled a criminal proceeding than an "inquiry," and yet he and his counsel were not permitted the rights and safeguards that are granted in formal judicial proceedings.

Oppenheimer was so shaken by this personal attack on his behaviors and motives that he did not perform well as a witness on his own behalf. He was evasive and occasionally contradicted himself. His lackluster performance fueled those critics who believed that he had been indiscrete—if not frankly disloyal—during the war, that he had ill-advisedly opposed the development of the hydrogen bomb after the war, and that he had failed to cooperate as a witness in earlier inquiries about his friends and family members. Those attuned to the troubled times and the inquisitorial tone of the hearing were not surprised when, on June 28, 1954, the Atomic Energy Commission formally withdrew his security clearance.

Few incidents in recent American political and intellectual history have been more scrutinized than the "Oppenheimer affair." Histories, novels, plays, and even a television movie have been produced, each reopening questions about Oppenheimer himself and about the broader issues of science, knowledge, and openness—themes that constitute leitmotifs of our times. Oppenheimer's fate in the matter might well have been sealed; perhaps neither he nor others could have said anything that would have prevented what he subsequently labeled "a farce."

My own conclusion, however, is that Oppenheimer was an agent, though clearly an unwitting one, in bringing about his own political downfall. A man of great subtlety and complexity, one who reveled in paradox and ambiguity, Oppenheimer was not able to step into another role—one necessary for a victory in this political inquiry. From a tactical point of view, Oppenheimer had two choices: He could ridicule the charges, and maintain so outraged a stance as to call into question the motives of those who would dog him. Or he could concede that, like any other human being, he had made certain mistaken judgments (as indeed he had), but that these were all well-motivated and harmless efforts to protect relatives and friends, that they were in any case decades old, and that his loyalty and patriotism had been established beyond question.

Neither of these stances was compatible with Oppenheimer's temperament. He was an extraordinary man who could deal with very difficult theoretical issues; moreover, he had shown that he could rise to the occasion in perilous times, particularly when he was convinced that the cause was just. He fell down in his ability to connect to the ordinary person, the person with a less subtle mind, the person who preferred to see events in black and white, rather than in exceedingly fine shades of gray. As the historian George Kennan, once a colleague of Oppenheimer's at the Institute for Advanced Study, remarked: "Curious mixture that [Oppenheimer] was of scientist, scholar, and aesthete, he was poorly armed for that sort of bureaucratic in-fighting."

Here the contrast between Oppenheimer and some of his colleagues becomes instructive. One of his staunchest defenders at the hearing was his old friend Rabi, who, as a street-smart New Yorker, was able to ridicule the accusers and keep them firmly on the defensive; he had the temperament to take risks to defend himself and his friends. Oppenheimer's most damaging critic at the hearing was his friend-turned-adversary Teller, the self-styled "father of the H-bomb," who had long doubted Oppenheimer's reliability. As he was to demonstrate time and again in forty years of influence over American defense policy, Teller had the ability to speak to politicians and generals in their language. Choosing his words carefully, Teller left little doubt that America's fate should not be allowed to remain within Oppenheimer's slippery and unreliable grasp. A Manichaean view, with the United States as good and the Soviet Communists as evil, proved to be an effective counterstory; it prevailed over a more nuanced point of view, which sought opportunities for dialogue and shunned jingoistic rhetoric and stereotypical thinking.

I do not believe that the charges against Oppenheimer were credible. But I am less certain that Oppenheimer thought of himself as completely innocent, and this ambivalence proved costly. I question the extent to which Oppenheimer was at peace with himself when not surrounded by scientists and intellectuals with whom he felt in deep sympathy. Except during the extraordinary two-year period of the Manhattan Project, Oppenheimer exhibited difficulty in relating to individuals as equals. Sometimes, especially in his youth, this took the form of arrogant put-downs, in which he made "giants feel like cockroaches." He once dismissed Philip Graham, the powerful publisher of the *Washington Post* and *Newsweek,* by noting that Graham must not have read something in the original Sanskrit. Sometimes, particularly in the presence of powerful political and military figures, Oppenheimer could be slavish and fawning as he sought to gain others' support. His personal family life was troubled: his wife was a heavy drinker, his daughter, Toni, committed suicide, and his son removed himself completely from the public eye. I believe that, despite his sensitivity to others in his circle, Oppenheimer was unable to place himself in the minds of his accusers (and of disinterested observers) and to appreciate what might make sense to them and what would drive them to distraction.

Oppenheimer was genuinely admired and respected by many academic colleagues. He was brilliant, versatile, a good conversationalist, a good listener, and a loyal defender of the fundamental principles of the scholarly academy. Yet, rather than striking his academic peers as serene, he emerges as more of a Svengali, a presence who mesmerized other scholars and intellectuals with his piercing eyes, incredibly broad and detailed knowledge, playful sense of paradox, and mastery of the issues and problems that occupied his audience members. Most scholars felt that they had never met anyone like Oppenheimer, and they were vaguely uncomfortable about the extent to which they fell under his spell. One of his Berkeley colleagues, Wendell Latimer, attributed the influence that Oppenheimer had over others to "elements of the mystic." Rabi spoke of a "spiritual quality" with "depths of sensibility and insight not yet revealed." John Mason Brown, the eminent literary critic, remarked: "The power of his personality is the strongest because of the fragility of his person. When he speaks he seems to grow, since the eagerness of his mind so affirms itself that the smallness of this body is forgotten." One can see how this type of appeal might be less potent among generals and politicians, where physical size and perceived power may be valued more than eagerness, subtlety, or mystery of mind.

I acknowledge a paradox here: Oppenheimer was not one of those persons incapable of adopting the perspective of others; indeed, in various circumstances, and especially during the Manhattan Project, he displayed an uncanny capacity to do so. Yet, this display of personal intelligence was perhaps an acquired skill, one that never became second nature to the man (as it did, say, to Franklin D. Roosevelt); or perhaps it was a cultivated politeness or kindness, rather than an instinctive sense of what would convince someone else. Something in Oppenheimer's personality warred against a natural sympathy with those beyond his narrow circle—possibly, a powerful motive to maintain control or an innate sense of difference, superiority, or even inadequacy. As with Hutchins (see chapter 6), this fundamental inability to align himself with certain of his audiences was to have fateful consequences.

Oppenheimer may have been partly a victim of timing. Immediately after the detonation of the bomb, there had been sympathy in America for a restrained use of power and perhaps even a system of international controls of nuclear weapons. Had Oppenheimer needed to defend himself at that time, he might have found a more sympathetic audience. But by the early 1950s, the Soviet Union had already exploded a hydrogen bomb, and most Americans believed that the struggle between the United States and the Soviet Union allowed for no middle ground: Oppenheimer's measured tones fell on increasingly deaf ears.

Severely shaken by the hearing and its ultimate damning judgment, Oppenheimer never again sought the public stage in America. He remained as the exemplary director of the Institute for Advanced Study, where he recruited superior thinkers as permanent members of the faculty, nurtured the young scholars who visited for brief periods, and encouraged a level of dialogue among staff and visitors that was equaled in few other locales around the world. He delivered many addresses in front of learned societies, where he reflected with insight, humility, and keen intelligence on the scientific and ethical issues of the time, the growth (and the dilemmas) of knowledge, and the many continuing puzzles of lives. There were few more eloquent speakers on these topics in the 1950s and 1960s.

Showing admirable restraint, Oppenheimer never commented publicly on the hearings. Those close to him said that in some ways the harrowing experience had actually strengthened him, permitting him to focus on areas where his powers were beyond doubt and sensitizing him to human frailties. Even when presented with the Enrico Fermi Award—certainly as much of a public vindication as anyone in his position might expect to receive—he contented himself with the brief and tasteful remark: "I think it is just possible, Mr. President, that it has taken some charity and some courage for you to make this award today. That would seem to me a good augury for all of our futures."

Strange bedfellows, Mead and Oppenheimer were similar in some ways, but strikingly different in others. On one side is a man, European in manner, a theoretical physicist, an introvert with a tendency toward brooding pessimism, a restrained commentator, and a pursuer of elite specializations. On the other side is a woman, patriotically American, a cultural anthropologist, an eager extrovert of optimistic tones, an instinctual activist, an inveterate publicist, and an expert on popular cultures. They probably would not have often sought the same experiences or genuinely enjoyed each other's company over the long haul.

With regard to leadership, however, Mead and Oppenheimer represent exemplary and parallel figures. As youths, both displayed formidable intellectual gifts, sensitivity, and curiosity, and they easily stood out among their peers. When they attended college, it was not clear which fields of study would attract their attention—they could each presumably have achieved success in a number of scholarly pursuits, and perhaps in a variety of other professions as well.

Having chosen their respective fields, they easily rose to the top of their professions. Few thirty-five-year-old physicists or anthropologists had greater prospects than Oppenheimer and Mead, respectively. Both had also established their capacity to lead—both indirectly and directly—within their own professions: Oppenheimer as a teacher and synthesizer; Mead as a fieldworker, writer, and organizer. But the events of the Second World War, in different ways, propelled them to a wider arena. Oppenheimer became the director of a project of incalculable importance, and Mead devoted her efforts to understanding the mores of her own society and communicating her insights to an increasingly attentive American public.

After the war, Oppenheimer and Mead each had to address and satisfy contrasting constituencies. These ranged from traditional academic domains, with their technical language, to constituents who harbored some scholarly pretense but lacked expertise, to the broader literate public. The two scholar-leaders dealt differently with this challenge. Mead moved away from the anthropological mainstream and eventually, after her death, was even challenged as a reliable authority on Samoa. She avoided formal institutional affiliations and founded no school. Her ultimate audience became American readers and viewers, who looked to her for exotic information and, perhaps even more, for guidance about their own daily lives. She became valued as a scholar-intellectual who could speak comfortably to the wider public; and if some of her solutions now seem dated, she helped to define cultural issues for decades.

Oppenheimer remained centrally involved in physics, though as a teacher and interpreter rather than as a benchtop or blackboard scientist. He was called on with increasing frequency to address a broader public. He did so with success when confronting serious scholars from the disciplines and laypersons with strong intellectual grounding and personal sympathies. But he was never able—and perhaps never truly wished—to communicate directly with the wider public; and because of his security problems and the increasingly polarized time in which he lived, he achieved far less success than Mead did in dealing with political leaders and their constituencies. He remained committed to dealing with questions in their complexity and subtlety, a highly schooled stance that proved attractive within the academy but not sustainable on the streets. His colleague and nemesis Teller achieved greater long-term success by working directly and indirectly with political and military leaders, creating stories that were simpler and less inclusive.

Mead and Oppenheimer came to embody different messages in their manner of presentation. Mead reached out to touch people, and they reached back. Communication was her central theme, and she was brilliant at it. Oppenheimer, reserved and contained, could not slap backs or wade into audiences or participate convincingly in what he called the "common discourse." He framed this problem himself in a 1960 address in Berlin:

> I have been much concerned that in this world we have so largely lost the ability to talk with one another. In the great succession of deep discoveries, we have become removed from one another in tradition, and in a certain measure even in language. We have had neither the time nor the skill nor the dedication to tell one another what we have learned, nor to listen nor to hear, nor to welcome its enrichment of the common culture and the common understanding. We hunger for nobility: the rare words and acts that harmonize simplicity and truth.

How to understand the world in its complexity and subtlety, and yet communicate directly to dispersed individuals with limited expertise, is perhaps the fundamental issue facing leaders today. In their respective ways, both Oppenheimer and Mead addressed this issue and set models—inspiring as well as troubling—for how specialists in disciplines might transcend their ranks. Mead extended common sense; perhaps characteristically, Oppenheimer called his collected papers *Uncommon Sense.* If Oppenheimer, a troubled and poetic spirit, more eloquently expressed the dilemma of communication in our time, Mead, essentially comfortable with herself, more adeptly showed how effective communication could actually occur.

In presenting the cases of Mead and Oppenheimer, I have begun my survey of the continuum of leadership. Both Mead and Oppenheimer were creative individuals whose influence initially came from their thinking and writing. Thus, they represent that pole of the leadership continuum epitomized by Albert Einstein—the solitary scholar (or artist) with little inclination toward direct leadership. As they moved to assume more overt leadership roles within their disciplines and then venture beyond disciplinary boundaries, Mead and Oppenheimer embodied two important shifts: from indirect to direct forms of leadership, and from leadership within a domain to leadership of a broader unschooled society. Yet, they remained a considerable distance from political leaders at the opposite end of the leadership continuum—those who would find themselves representing a nation at an international conference, such as the fabled Eureka Summit.

In the next four chapters, continuing this journey, I examine leaders who are placed explicitly at the head of circumscribed institutions—first, the small institution of an American university, then the larger and more complex global corporation, and finally the massive institutions of the United States Army and the Roman Catholic Church.

6

ROBERT MAYNARD HUTCHINS
Bringing "The Higher Learning" to America

Presidential power is the power to persuade.
—Richard Neustadt

Almost any educated person can deliver a lecture entitled "The Goals of the University." Almost no one will listen to the lecture voluntarily. For the most part, such lectures and their companion essays are well-intentioned exercises in social rhetoric, with little operational content. Efforts to generate normative statements of the goals of a university tend to produce goals that are either meaningless or dubious.
—Michael Cohen and James March

At the height of the Second World War, a less epochal battle was being waged—a battle for the soul of one institution of higher learning. Robert Maynard Hutchins, the long-time president of the University of Chicago, found himself in conflict with many of his faculty. Hutchins and his colleagues were trying to create the optimal education for undergraduates. The purist view, embraced by Hutchins, most of his hand-picked administrators, and a minority of the faculty, held that students should follow a prescribed course: they should study classical disciplines as conveyed in "great books" and receive a single bachelor of arts degree as soon as they had demonstrated intellectual readiness. Arrayed against this position was a more pluralistic—or at least more practical—view that embraced a number of viable curricula. Proponents of this view held that students should be permitted to follow various paths to their respective degrees and that it was perfectly acceptable for one student to specialize in science, another in the humanities, and a third in the social sciences or the arts.

In the early 1940s, Hutchins, who had been named president of the University of Chicago before he was thirty, was already a famous and much-honored

Robert Maynard Hutchins. UPI/Bettmann

figure in American public education. A veteran of many campus and national debates, he was widely esteemed as a proponent of high intellectual standards and a certain kind of philosophically grounded liberal education. And yet, Hutchins was to lose this battle with his faculty by striking an unsatisfying compromise—much as he was to fail in other reform attempts at the university and, later, at other institutions that he directed.

It may seem odd that a university president could not sell his ideas to his own faculty, particularly when these ideas had been widely and favorably commented on and even adopted on other campuses. Part of the problem lay in the specific circumstances at Chicago—notably, in Hutchins's high-handed governance style and his overpowering personality. But a more entrenched problem, in my view, emanated from the challenge of directing a circumscribed institution.

Those at a university are thought to be engaged in a single common pursuit—after all, they are broadly known as the professoriate. Yet, unlike the anthropologist who speaks to other anthropologists or the physicist who addresses his or her physics colleagues, the head of a university must be able to convince an often-unruly group of individuals who represent different disciplines, hold conflicting loyalties, aspire to diverse educational goals, and are often a rambunctious lot to boot. Schooled and expert they are, but each one only in her or his chosen academic subject. When it comes to more general issues of education, they may be no more knowledgeable or reliable than other individuals. Nor does it help, as a wiseacre once quipped, if each of the faculty members is convinced that he or she is the smartest person in the room.

Hutchins's intellectual skills and commanding presence earned him a university presidency at a young age and, eventually, the directorship of other institutions as well. Yet, he lost far more battles than he won and eventually was more sympathized with than emulated. In coming to understand better his unusual path and his ultimate plight, we can gain insights into the considerable challenges entailed in guiding even a relatively small and circumscribed institution—one seemingly less demanding than a corporation, a church, an army, or a nation.

If ever an American youth was targeted for future leadership, it was Hutchins. Born to an established New England family (Hutchins's father was a Presbyterian minister who himself would eventually preside over a college and head a foundation), Hutchins was a tall, handsome, ambitious, assertive, and decidedly brilliant boy. His family, at least as loving and supportive as the Mead and Oppenheimer families, was committed to hard work, high ethical standards, and relentless self-criticism. Although not personally committed to church activities, young Hutchins was much influenced by the religious rhetoric that he heard, and he even considered becoming a missionary.

Hutchins first attended Oberlin College, an evangelical Protestant institution, for two years. Oberlin stressed the link between the pursuit of knowledge and the use of that learning in public service, and Hutchins was deeply affected by this philosophy. Then, following a stint in the army, Hutchins completed his undergraduate education at Yale College, where he easily established himself as one of the most important figures on campus by excelling in nearly every pursuit except athletics. His college classmates included the future publishers Henry Luce and William Benton, as well as the playwright Thornton Wilder, who was to become one of Hutchins's lifelong friends.

During his collegiate days, Hutchins displayed notable skills as a public speaker and debater. Perhaps taking a leaf from his eloquent preacher-father, he spoke clearly, without undue emotion or histrionics, and marshaled from memory relevant facts and vivid examples. Aided by an admirable and quick wit, an ability to provoke without offending, and an enduring sense of irony, he readily maintained sympathetic contact with his audience.

After a brief and unpleasurable experience as a high school teacher, Hutchins received an invitation that changed his life. President James Angell of Yale University asked Hutchins to serve as the secretary for the Yale Corporation, the hallowed group of individuals responsible for operating the university. Hutchins's principal jobs were to raise funds and to handle publicity for Yale, and he became a skilled public advocate for the university. One of his biographers, Harry Ashmore, reports that "in these public utterances, Hutchins gave free rein to a restless and skeptical intelligence, yet his wit and charm were so disarming that his frequently caustic observations aroused no protest and he turned out to be an entirely successful public relations man."

While at Yale College, Hutchins had already begun to study the law. During his service for the Yale Corporation, Hutchins further pursued his studies at the Yale Law School, where he once again distinguished himself. He concluded that law school was the best place in an American university for one to achieve excellence in literary expression. Elected the most likely to succeed by his classmates, Hutchins, a *magna cum laude* graduate, was immediately offered a faculty position at the Yale Law School. There he taught courses in procedure and public service law and aided Dean Charles Clark in instituting some reforms in legal education.

Hutchins barely had time to settle down as a faculty member before yet another opportunity came his way: Clark resigned to serve on a court of appeals, and Hutchins was named as the acting dean. In this position he immediately engaged in a flurry of activity, churning out a set of position papers, making a number of appointments, and displaying a knack for handling the ordinary business of budgets, curricula, and faculty meetings. (No doubt he had been "primed" by his service with the Yale Corporation.) He also proceeded on two pet projects—encouraging psychological research that was relevant to the laws of evidence and seeking financial support for an Institute of Procedure. In December 1927, members of the Yale Corporation voted to install Hutchins as the permanent dean.

We generally think of individuals as becoming prodigies in certain domains—in music, chess, or mathematics, for example. Because all of these are computational or algorithmic, young people can progress rapidly if they can figure out the laws or patterns that are at work. Such prodigies do not need much experience in dealing with other people—at least, not until they aspire to operate at the highest levels of the domain.

It is exceedingly rare, even in a society that has been oriented toward youth, for an individual to emerge as a direct leader—indeed an institutional leader—at so early an age as did Hutchins. Even given Hutchins's models in his own family and his own singular abilities and traits, other people at Yale undoubtedly could have filled the exalted positions to which Hutchins was appointed. Part of Hutchins's success lay in the excellent chemistry between President Angell and himself; even today, a well-regarded university president has considerable latitude in making senior appointments. No doubt his unusually attractive looks and gracious, patrician manner were pluses. But the key to Hutchins's meteoric ascent seems to have derived from his amazingly rapid learning curve in an area where most take years to learn the ropes and many months to recover from their mistakes. In less than a decade Hutchins apparently achieved the administrative expertise that eluded so many other, more seasoned individuals.

Not only did Hutchins look the part from the very moment of his appointment as law dean, but he had the skills to size up the situation, to figure out what was wanted, and to pursue that goal in a convincing and often-effective way. Like other precocious "natural" leaders, including some examined in this book, he had a rare and useful combination of intelligences: the logical capacity to figure out options, the linguistic capacity to persuade others orally and in writing, and the interpersonal knowledge to appreciate what was likely to work with a certain cast of characters in a given situation.

This is not to suggest that Hutchins was a flawless corporation secretary, professor, or dean. On the contrary: He made mistakes, he was often stronger on promise than on delivery, he exhibited more enthusiasm than technical knowledge, and he often misjudged what it would take to implement a policy once it had been adopted. In addition, he displayed some of the naïveté and impetuousness of youth, and he lacked a coherent philosophy and a reliable set of methods for proceeding.

Yet at the Yale Law School under Hutchins's leadership there was a clear sense of excitement, a feeling that things were happening, a conviction that the school was *the* place to be. There was an honors program one day, a link to the medical school the next day, and a program in legal realism whose traces remain even today. "We do not care much whether all our experiments are successful," he characteristically declared. "We shall be satisfied if other law schools can profit by them if only to the extent of avoiding our mistakes. After all, the great thing about a university is that it can afford to experiment." Hutchins could challenge authority and dogma, but he knew when to be modest and humorous about himself. Regrettably, some of his appealing, self-deprecatory features became less manifest with the passage of time.

One feature of Hutchins's tenure at the Yale Law School is worthy of special note. Hutchins clearly aligned himself with the progressives on the faculty. He wanted students to have choices; he encouraged them to become involved in the wider community. He criticized the dryness and predictability of the case method, the nonintellectual "trade school" aspects of the law school, and its isolation from the rest of the university. And he forged a strong alliance with the newly developing behavioral and social sciences. Hutchins believed that the findings of social science should be relevant to legal decisions; methods of psychology should be used, for example, to assess the reliability of evidence, the effectiveness of rules, and the appropriateness of punishments. Accordingly, he encouraged—and sought to secure funding for—the establishment of institutions that would infuse the law with empirical data.

Thus, as Hutchins's reputation began to grow in legal and university circles, it was as a future-directed, practical, progressive innovator. In the Hutchins of the late 1920s I discern few if any harbingers of the decidedly conservative educational theorist who was soon to impress himself on the nation.

Once again, opportunity knocked for Hutchins. The University of Chicago, one of the most celebrated educational institutions in the country, was searching for a new president. Its turn-of-the-century founding president, William Rainer Harper, had been a young and innovative educational leader who had brought much prestige, support, and intellectual strength to the campus, and particularly to the graduate school; but his successors had been a disappointment. The university trustees were particularly keen on securing an individual who would rekindle the excitement of the Harper era and bring attention and resources to undergraduate education.

In April 1929, Hutchins appeared before the search committee. Although clearly young and short on years of administrative experience, he made a powerfully positive impression on the members, and especially on the most influential trustee, Harold Swift, the scion of the famed meatpacking company. After consultation with Yale colleagues yielded a positive, if somewhat guarded, evaluation, the youthful Hutchins was offered and accepted the presidency of one of the major institutions of higher learning in the land—a school of 14,000 students, 780 faculty, and a budget of $7.4 million a year.

Hutchins brought to Chicago the same excitement or turbulence—depending on one's tolerance for chaos—that had surrounded him at Yale. His early honeymoon years saw a flurry of innovations that caught the imagination of those (including funders) interested in higher education: faculty members appointed exclusively to the College, admission of high school juniors to the College, two-year as well as four-year college programs, the grouping of the departments into four overarching divisions, and a distinct tilting toward interdisciplinary (nonspecialist) courses. Hutchins believed in controversy, actively promoted debate, and displayed considerable skill in advancing the causes that he most favored. As one of his biographers, Mary Ann Dzuback, summarized it: "The undergraduate program moved from the fringes of the university to center stage, from a largely elective program offering three bachelor's degrees to a fully prescribed program offering one degree, and from ten-week discrete courses to year-long interdisciplinary courses coordinated across the curriculum."

But while the organizational changes were an important—though controversial—part of his program, Hutchins's emerging philosophy of education became his central contribution to the ongoing debate about the mission of the university. This part of his story cannot be told without introducing Mortimer Jerome Adler, a Jew from New York who had studied philosophy and psychology at Columbia University and also had participated in John Erskine's fabled Great

Books seminar. Adler was permanently influenced by the latter experience, where small groups of students carefully read and discussed major texts from Western thought and literature—works that would be today considered "the canon." An autodidact by inclination and a renegade by temperament, Adler was discomfited by many of the intellectual and cultural trends of his time. He looked back to the classical eras of Greece and Rome for the founding ideas of his civilization, and to the organization of knowledge and the relation among institutions of the Middle Ages for his vision of society.

Hutchins and Adler had first met in the late 1920s at Yale, where they had been drawn to each other because of their mutual interests in psychology and the law. Although virtual opposites in background and personality—Hutchins was gracious, reserved, and at least superficially accommodating, whereas Adler was abrupt, self-promoting, and cantankerous—Hutchins and Adler had hit it off immediately and remained close associates for the next half century. Indeed, at Chicago they cotaught a Great Books seminar for eighteen of those years. More than any other person, Adler shaped Hutchins's ideas about general education. And these ideas centered around the reading and dialogic discussion of classical texts and the attempt to embody in one's living the key ideas and processes exemplified in these books.

In 1936 Hutchins published *The Higher Learning in America,* a set of lectures in which he presented his newly congealed ideas about education to a wider public. These ideas were conservative in substance but radical in tone, because they called for a major reorientation of the institutions and values of American higher education.

Hutchins began his tract by vociferously attacking American colleges as vacuous sites that exhibited neither ideals nor coherence. "The most striking fact about the higher learning in America," he declared, "is the confusion that besets it." He criticized the emphasis on fun, vocationalism, misguided ideas of progress and utility, and clumsy attempts to mold "character" directly. Furthermore, he decried the lack of standards, the total dependence on money, the hegemony of sports, the rampant anti-intellectualism, and the unexamined assumption that all individuals deserve an education, whether or not they choose to apply themselves to the task.

In the place of these false gods, Hutchins, with Adler peering figuratively over his shoulders, called for an education that was centered on the nurturance of the mind. "An intellect properly disciplined, an intellect properly habituated, is an intellect able to operate well in all fields," he contended. Hutchins did not hedge. He asserted that "the unifying principle of a university is the pursuit of truth for its own sake." In confident, lapidary phrases he went on: "Education implies teaching. Teaching implies knowledge. Knowledge is truth. The truth is everywhere the same. Hence education should be everywhere the same. I do not overlook the possibilities of differences in organization, in administration, in local habits and customs. These are details."

Building on a curriculum of great books—works that had stood the test of time—Hutchins endorsed a course of study that featured the arts of reading, writing, thinking, speaking, and mathematics. Such a course of study would engender a common stock of ideas and common methods for dealing with them. The systematic thinkers of the past, most notably Aristotle and Aquinas, emerged as the guiding lights of this enterprise.

Most interestingly and most controversially, Hutchins argued that the curriculum had to be coherent and that the foundation of this coherence ought to be metaphysics. By metaphysics, Hutchins meant the area of knowledge that draws out the basic principles and causes underlying our world, our existence, and our individuality. Waxing grandly, Hutchins pointed out: "Metaphysics then, as the highest science, ordered the thought of the Greek world as theology ordered that of the Middle Ages. . . . Without theology or metaphysics a unified university cannot exist." More concretely, through immersion in metaphysics, students would come to understand the nature of the various disciplines and their relationships to one another.

And so, whether they were studying physics or politics or poetry, students would come to grips with the principles that undergird concepts and practices in those disciplines, and perhaps even discern the similarities and differences between a scientific and a humanistic view of the world. Similarly, in comparing natural sciences, social sciences, and metaphysics, the student would learn that these areas "deal with the same propositions and facts, but with different ultimate references." Hutchins concluded that "the fundamental problems of metaphysics, the social sciences, and the natural sciences are, then, the proper subject matter of the higher learning."

Far more than might have been anticipated in an America mired in the Great Depression, Hutchins's ideas captured the attention of the educated public. They were widely discussed and debated. Taking a deliberately provocative stand, this youngest of major university presidents had reopened the debate about the nature of the university. Those who admired such calls to arms, as well as those who hankered after the tidier cartography of knowledge associated with an earlier era, were especially enthusiastic. Echoes of this intellectual event were discernible fifty years later when Allan Bloom, a philosopher rooted in the classics and also ensconced at the University of Chicago, published *The Closing of the American Mind* (1987). While Bloom's diagnosis and cure were not identical to Hutchins's, they appealed to similar audiences and evoked analogous criticisms.

Hutchins's ideas certainly did not please everyone. Some were satisfied with the status quo or were reluctant to reorient the prevailing practices radically. Some admired the vision in the abstract but thought Hutchins's proposal impractical or financially untenable. But the grittiest critiques came from those who disagreed with the substance of Hutchins's ideas and put forth their own counterstory. Foremost among this group was one of Hutchins's own faculty members, the economist Harry D. Gideonse, who within a year published *The Higher Learning in a Democracy* (1937).

The tipoff to Gideonse's objections lay in his emphasis on the word *democracy*. After attacking Hutchins's presentation for being vague and underspecified— "What is metaphysics today, and how many different metaphysics can there be?" he pointedly asked—Gideonse attacked Hutchins's argument as being inherently elitist, reactionary, and antidemocratic. He contended that Americans were living in a time when science had undermined many established truths, much new knowledge had been proposed, and understandings in general were seen as tentative and changing. Many ways to study the world and many ways to organize knowledge had evolved. "Unity imposed by authority is only another term for uniformity," declared Gideonse. Also, he held that education has more than one purpose: introducing an individual to current thoughts, problems, and living conditions and educating the whole person are as important as cultivating the mind along certain preordained lines. Reformist Hutchins at Yale might have considered such sentiments; traditionalist Hutchins at Chicago found them anathema.

Against Hutchins's monism, Gideonse put forth the more dynamic and pragmatic views of the widely respected philosopher of education John Dewey. Already a legend in the 1930s, and one who had exerted a major impact on American precollegiate education through his progressive views, Dewey stood as a powerful and credible counterforce to the scholasticism embraced by Hutchins, Adler, and their compatriots. Gideonse quoted from Dewey's Gifford Lectures: "[Such a progressive view] . . . renounces the traditional notion that action is inherently inferior to knowledge and preference for the fixed over the changing; it involves the conviction that security attained by active control is to be more prized than certainty in theory." And ultimately Dewey himself entered the fray:

> I would not intimate that the author [Hutchins] has any sympathy with fascism. But basically his idea as to the proper course to be taken is akin to the distrust of freedom and the consequent appeal to *some* fixed authority that is now overrunning the world. . . . As far as I can see President Hutchins has completely evaded the problem of who is to determine the definite truths that constitute the hierarchy.

Thus was framed an educational debate whose reverberations have continued, almost without interruption, until this day.

What might have been a parochial debate among philosophically oriented educators actually addressed broader issues. Hutchins was critiquing the university system (a stance that garnered wide support) and defining what education ought to be like (a vision that elicited much scorn). Fully aware of the competition, he was making a play to become the leading voice in American higher education. We should try to discern the message, its audiences, and its fate.

In the innovative story that Hutchins told to his colleagues and the wider community, we in American higher education have lost our way. We have followed many false gods—sports, vocationalism, and cafeteria-style electives—that could lead to passing successes but that ultimately will yield a vacuous existence. What is needed is a serious new vision—or, perhaps, a return to a classical one—that is focused and coherent. Hutchins's recommended version was grounded in the conviction that education should focus sharply on the life of the mind; that the reading and discussion of great books is the preferred route; and that this purposefully general education would produce an educated citizenry that, Oberlin-style, could be entrusted with the public good.

As I have suggested, Hutchins's account had to contend with various counterstories. Some of these did not harbor any alternative positive vision: their adherents were mired in the status quo, either because they preferred that or because the status quo, flawed as it was, seemed too difficult to alter. But the counterstory associated with Dewey and other progressive educators embraced a distinctly different view. Knowledge was seen as tentative, pluralistic, dynamic, ever-changing; it was more likely to stem from observation of the natural and man-made worlds and from interaction with diverse individuals than from intense study of classics written hundreds or even thousands of years ago. Proponents of this view said that many worthy educational paths existed, not the single one prescribed by the Chicago philosophers. While neither of these visions completely carried the day, only a small minority of American educators aligned themselves explicitly with the position that Hutchins embraced, and that state of affairs remains until this day.

The question of which story was more sophisticated or more "schooled" remains vexing. At first thought, Hutchins's story appears more straightforward, with its clear idea of what is right, important, and worth pursuing. The progressive/ Dewey story calls for a more pluralistic and relativistic view of knowledge. Yet, in practice, implementation of Hutchins's program—with its highly intellectual content and its sophisticated lines of argument—would place great demands on both students and teachers. In contrast, the progressive/Dewey program could readily be used as a pretext for a permissive atmosphere, one devoid of standards, one all too easy to implement. Perhaps the fact that the two stories each feature aspects of complexity and aspects of simplicity helps explain why they have continued to struggle with each other over the decades, with neither ultimately triumphing.

If the position that Hutchins defended was clear enough, the role that he embodied proved less easy to characterize. Whereas Dewey (as the prototypical indirect leader) preferred to teach and write and, for the most part, avoided heated public debate, Hutchins was a natural and comfortable public figure. Attractive, gracious, eloquent, and persuasive, he often disarmed those who expected him to be a curmudgeon or a troglodyte. Like the Hutchins of the previous decade, he still valued experimentation and debate; in that sense, he remained an activist and won the admiration of those who were young in spirit. But now, he was defending a different faith, one at odds with the practical, social-scientific orientation he had championed at the Yale Law School. As his long-time associate and biographer Milton Mayer declared: "The ardent advocate of the scientific approach to the law was, almost overnight, to be seen as the implacable enemy of science."

Part of Hutchins's appeal lay in his clarion message, but part of it lay as well in his attractiveness and his gently aristocratic manner. He was the darling of individuals who were attracted to one or another of those features and the special favorite of those who, like later admirers of American conservative spokesmen William F. Buckley or George Will, were charmed by both—those who found comfort in The Tradition. As is often the case with such magnetic and mercurial figures, Hutchins was appreciated more by those who were at a distance from him than by those on his own university campus. However, his clashes with faculty involved more than issues of turf; many professors sincerely felt that Hutchins was guilty of vast oversimplification or even that his analysis was dead wrong. From their point of view, it was *his* position that was unschooled and devoid of nuance—and perhaps, indeed, that is why it appealed to individuals who were removed from the daily canons and practices of scholarship.

It is tempting to conclude that the once-liberal Hutchins was converted to a scholastic educational philosophy by the Mephistophelean Adler and his coterie, which included the literary critic Richard McKeon, the historian Stringfellow Barr, and the philosopher Scott Buchanan. But such a verdict would distort matters. For one thing, Hutchins had immediately taken to Adler and his iconoclastic ideas. For another, Hutchins's own family background and his early education had in some ways been conservative, and he was instinctively an institutional man rather than a countercultural rebel like Adler. Recognizing (and to some extent ruing) this paradoxical state of affairs, Hutchins once explained to Adler that it was not always possible to be both a university president and an educational philosopher.

Without wanting to accuse Hutchins of insincerity, I would say that he was susceptible to opportunism, lured by the search for the "effective story." I propose that Hutchins was perennially on the lookout for ways to define his institution, on the one hand, and to make a mark for himself in the public consciousness, on the other. At Yale, the move toward legal realism seemed to be indicated; at Chicago, a call for a sharply delineated general education was in order. I also feel that he was attracted to the certainty of Adler—the evangelist in Hutchins sought a strong platform on which to preach. At times, there appeared to be a disjunction between the positive, upbeat experimentalist of his Yale days and the conservative advocate that he became; Hutchins's manner did not always match his words. Still, I do not see Hutchins as a man so devoted to a certain educational philosophy that he would adhere to it no matter what messages resonated with his audiences. Rather, I see him as a pragmatically tinged idealist who enjoyed advancing a powerful position and running with it, and one who could probably have defended a number of possible story lines.

Known first to the country as a persuasive spokesman on educational matters, Hutchins soon—and perhaps gladly—assumed the role that is typically conferred on Americans who have achieved prominence: he addressed a wide range of matters of public concern. During much of his active professional life, he received over a thousand invitations to speak per year and accepted about one hundred, and he presided over a weekly radio program, *The Chicago Roundtable*. In a manner that we associate more with politicians than with university presidents, more with direct than with indirect leaders, Hutchins spoke out on the great topics of the day, ranging from civil liberties to the nature of democracy to issues of war and peace. Despite his conservative educational views, he was generally on the liberal-democratic side of public debate: he staunchly defended the First Amendment, freedom of the press, and civil rights for various minority groups. He was an articulate expositor and defender of the Constitution and a courageous foe of red-baiting.

In an extremely well-received 1932 speech, he inspired the Young Democrats, fueling rumors that he might be appointed to the Supreme Court or even run for vice president. Any prospect that he might aspire to elected or appointed office (and Hutchins did not try to quash such rumors) was probably ruled out, however, by Hutchins's strong isolationist views. In the years and even the months before the Second World War, Hutchins spoke out at length in public against any U.S. involvement in the European war.

Hutchins saw himself as defending long-term American interests against the transient appeal of jingoistic rhetoric. He said that Americans should achieve democracy at home before seeking to export it abroad; he set high standards for what he termed a "just war." Asserting that "the path to war is a false path to freedom," Hutchins called instead for the creation of a new order at home. He contemplated writing an article with the title "Where Hitler Is Right." And in a phrase that he was destined to regret, he characterized Hitler as "half right" for challenging his people to pursue an ideal higher than comfort.

Once Pearl Harbor had been attacked, Hutchins's antiwar campaign became moot. "Long run activities must be sacrificed to the short run activity of winning the war. . . . What the country must have we must supply," he said. As it happened, the University of Chicago's scientific laboratories were crucial for the war effort, and Hutchins saw to it that they were placed fully at the nation's disposal.

He took pride in the university scientists' creation of the first controlled atomic chain reaction on December 2, 1942; and he noted that the University of Chicago handled more military projects than any other single institution of education.

Even during the war, Hutchins continued his campaign for educational reform. In one controversial speech in January 1944, he stunned his own educational community by calling for the abolition of tenure and for the payment of faculty on the basis of need rather than seniority. Hutchins claimed to be shocked by the hostile reaction to this speech, but he was of course attacking the faculty in the most sensitive areas of job and financial security. It is not clear whether Hutchins's surprise reflected naïveté, disingenuousness, or a strange brew of both.

After the war, Hutchins once more turned his sights fully onto issues at the university, especially completion of a restructuring of the curriculum that he had launched in the 1930s. Yet the times were not with him. Members of the faculty were tired of having been treated so long in a manner that they regarded as high-handed, particularly regarding issues of appointments and curricula, which members felt lay within *their* expertise. Philosophers challenged his narrow Adlerian view of their field; social scientists resented his disdain for their empirical work; natural scientists rejected his absolutistic views of the nature of knowledge. And nearly all faculty members—no matter their disciplinary or ideological stripe—reacted against his occasional threats to change the ground rules of their employment. The youths returning from battle who were now entering college were older and more attuned to professional advancement and to getting on with their personal lives; a philosophically centered education in a self-styled ivory tower was not for them, and they flocked to institutions that could help them become reintegrated into the larger society. During this sensitive period Hutchins remained a civil presence and, for the most part, desisted from acrimonious confrontations. Yet, to avoid downright defeat, Hutchins had to give in on most of the issues that mattered most to him—and this Protestant evangelical personality was not gratified when he received half a loaf.

Hutchins was personally tired as well. He asked to be given the title of chancellor of the university so he would be freed of administrative responsibilities, took the 1946–47 academic year off to try (unsuccessfully) to repair a failing marriage, and offered his resignation in the mid-1940s (it was not accepted). He spent more of his time on outside activities, such as the directorship of the *Encyclopaedia Britannica* and various efforts to promote the cause of great books with the less well-educated "middle-brow" public. Indeed, for an increasing proportion of this public, he became associated more with Adler's educational causes beyond the university walls than with those of the University of Chicago. After the war, he confessed to a friend: "The vital juices are dried up. The spirits are low. I am inventing all kinds of excuses for myself." Finally, in 1951, after two decades at the helm, Hutchins resigned from the university.

Whether one judges Hutchins's tenure at Chicago to be a success or a failure depends on one's viewpoint. Some of the programs and policies Hutchins advocated were indeed adopted, and a few of them survived his departure from the university and continue to this day. His courage, especially in defending faculty members who were charged with being Communists, was widely admired. His ability to appoint people of quality, even when they did not endorse his positions, was also appreciated. And despite his own misgivings about the practice of science as a meritorious intellectual activity in and of itself, he made it possible during the 1940s for the university to become one of the leading centers of scientific research in the world.

Within the university he is seen as having made the University of Chicago into a place where debates about the purpose of education were central, where the task of educating youth was taken seriously, and where there was at least a place—if not as central a place as Hutchins and Adler might have wished—for great books, interdisciplinary courses, and metaphysical themes. During Hutchins's tenure, Chicago was considered a special kind of university, with appeal to a particular kind of faculty and student body—serious, committed, and interested in ideas. It was, in Hutchins's phrase, "a specialized institution for unspecialized men . . . citizens who would ideally be able to move from one specialty to another as their interests and the needs of the community might recommend." When in 1993 the university was voted last in a survey of the amount of fun available at each of three hundred American institutions of higher learning, the soul of Hutchins must have beamed down on Chicago's midway.

Assumption of a broader viewpoint confirms Hutchins's unique status. Among U.S. leaders of higher education in the first half of the twentieth century, Hutchins earned his title of "the last of the titans"—those leaders who presided over their own campuses with personal authority and personal vision, and who spoke as well to the nation. Hutchins was admired throughout the land as an articulate and convincing spokesman for higher education. Whatever the actual fate of specific Hutchins-endorsed programs, Chicago was widely seen as a university that was committed to educational excellence and opposed to intellectual faddism. The list of graduates from the Hutchins (and the immediate post-Hutchins) era is impressive. And for those who wanted a vintage Hutchins-Adler education, Hutchins lent his prestige to a number of undertakings. There were Great Books and Paideia programs in high schools and colleges throughout the land; and as an enduring monument, there was the campus of St. John's College in Annapolis, Maryland (and later, a sister institution in Santa Fe, New Mexico), which constructed its four-year curriculum around the reading and discussion of great books.

After leaving the university presidency in 1951, Hutchins assumed a string of influential positions. From 1951 to 1954 he served as an associate director of the newly affluent Ford Foundation, with special responsibility for projects in publication, education, and technology. From 1954 to 1977 he presided over the

Fund for the Republic, an institution created by the Ford Foundation that awarded grants in civil rights and civil liberties. He also served from 1959 to 1973 and again from 1975 to 1977 as the founding president of the Center for the Study of Democratic Institutions, a residential institution in Santa Barbara, California, where distinguished permanent faculty and visitors discussed and wrote about the major issues of the day. In his spare time, Hutchins also chaired the advisory board of the *Encyclopaedia Britannica* from 1947 to 1977 and continued his long stream of talks, publications, and seminars, including four ambitious Pacem in Terris conferences, inspired by the influential encyclical of Pope John XXIII.

One might have thought that, freed of the burdens of running a university, raising money, and dealing with an often-fractious faculty, Hutchins would have had a marvelous time. But, as the University of Chicago sociologist Edward Shils once quipped, Hutchins after 1951 was like a "prince in exile." Hutchins continued to be an exciting and charismatic individual who inspired loyalty, issued a fount of sparkling ideas, and spoke and wrote grandiloquently about world issues. In a manner more reminiscent of the adventurous law school dean than of the traditionalist university president, he supported a series of quintessentially liberal causes.

Hutchins's ideas in the post-Chicago period, which he articulated well and appropriately, appealed to those of a liberal persuasion. But except for his educational ideas, which were already well known, there was little that sharply distinguished Hutchins's issues and opinions from those of other intellectual and political leaders such as Adlai Stevenson, Father Theodore Hesburgh, Margaret Mead, or Eleanor Roosevelt. As a public figure, Hutchins was not particularly innovative; and since his ideas ran into increasingly stiff opposition as the 1960s gave way to the 1970s, he became anachronistic before his death in 1977.

As he grew older, Hutchins also provided additional evidence that he was more interested in contributing to public controversy than in laying out a consistent point of view. For example, in the aftermath of the detonation of the first atomic weapons, Hutchins warned about the possibility of world destruction and led calls for world government. Yet, at the same time, he spoke about the wonders of atomic energy (it "promises fertilizers and soil balancers more powerful than any known today") and said that nuclear energy "could usher in a new day of peace and plenty." But Hutchins also worried that this new wealth would bring about "boredom and suicidal tendencies." Not surprisingly, he invoked education as the solution to all of these problems.

There proved to be a surprisingly limited market in the world of ideas for an aging *enfant terrible* with a set of views that ranged from the highly predictable to the seemingly contradictory. Hutchins thought that the philanthropic institutions would allow him free rein, but he discovered that even the great foundations—and perhaps especially the Ford Foundation—had their own agendas, as well as a reflexive fear of nearly any controversy. He found himself constantly in turmoil with boards of directors and boards of trustees. Since launching new institutions was (and is) expensive, Hutchins, never as successful a fund-raiser as his reputation suggested, found himself constantly dunning the wealthy for money. Hutchins came to think of himself as a failure and was wont to quip, "Down the hill with Hutchins."

Perhaps most tragically, Hutchins never found (or founded) the educational environment that could work for him *and* for others. His center, secluded in the luxuriant hills of southern California, held tremendous promise: in a scheme worthy of the ancient Greeks, great minds were expected to aggregate; discuss important issues; and, inspired by the magnetic Hutchins, formulate decisive recommendations. But Hutchins could never attract a permanent faculty of quality, and the many distinguished visitors did not necessarily share his vision of conversation and action. Administrative debacle followed administrative debacle. Sadly, most of the center's publications were more reminiscent of foundation boilerplate than of important public documents crying out for national debate (redolent of the presidential addresses satirized by Michael Cohen and James March in this chapter's epigraph). Just as the post-Hutchins University of Chicago had lapsed in many ways, the center did not survive in any meaningful way after Hutchins's illness and death in the late 1970s. As biographer Mary Ann Dzuback declared: "In the end, by placing the Center so at odds with academic life and with the organization of modern higher educational institutions and the needs of their constituents, Hutchins unknowingly guaranteed its demise."

To his grave, Hutchins probably thought that the time or the circumstances were not right for his plans. But we must face the possibility that Hutchins himself was not right. Hutchins was an intelligent and inspiring person, but he was not an analyst or a scholar. He had difficulty entering deeply into topics, mastering them at expert level, and creating new and enduring intellectual frameworks. As he himself had intimated in *The Higher Learning in America,* he was a person for the general picture, and not for details. And, contrary to the popular view, Hutchins was not a man to build and cultivate institutions. He was gifted initially at generating excitement and getting people on board, but like Margaret Mead he was impatient and wanted soon to move on to new projects and fresh ideas. Perhaps his rise had been too meteoric; he had never quite mastered the many steps that can translate a vision into reality.

Most damagingly, Hutchins was too involved with Hutchins. As John Gardner, the acute observer of leaders and himself a distinguished public servant, has suggested, Hutchins was too brilliant and too arrogant. He liked others' ideas, but not as much as his own; he liked debate, but on his own terms; he could listen superficially—perhaps even charismatically—but he was more interested in being listened to. According to Shils, "He always argued like a man reasonably explaining obvious things to the wrong headed." Enamored of reason, he had little sensitivity to the irrational or spiritual dimensions of human relations. He gained pleasure out of going against the grain, even when that ploy ended up undermining his own goals. He spoke of dialogue, debate, controversy, and compromise, but these notions did not well describe his own mode of operation, which began as authoritative and became increasingly authoritarian over the years.

In the end, Hutchins deserves to be judged as a leader—a leader for twenty years of a major educational institution and a leader, for an even longer tenure, of enlightened American opinion in the areas of education and public policy. His leadership proved most effective under two conditions: first, when it was directed to an audience that was ready to appreciate it (which most often turned out to be a certain portion of enlightened middle-brow citizenry rather than his own, possibly overeducated and overcritical faculty); and second, when the messages that it conveyed were consistent with those embodied in his own traits and actions.

Hutchins as a student of great books or as a defender of civil rights was convincing because he sought to honor these causes in his own life. But Hutchins as a model of debate, consensus building, and democratic processes was less effective, because of his own decidedly ambivalent position on these issues. Underneath it all, he was one who stood apart—an elitist in democratic clothing.

Indeed, in reflecting on the three figures portrayed so far in this book, I discern three distinctive styles of relating to a wider audience. Mead was an accumulator, a simplifier, and a director—one who sought to bring people together under a single consensual theme. Oppenheimer was a complexifier—one who was more interested in articulating and enjoying puzzles than in solving them decisively. For all of his charm and leadership qualities, Hutchins was essentially a divider—one who liked to sharpen contrasts and, in exclusionary fashion, to align himself with the angels and his opponents with the devil. He once gave vent to his strong philosophy on this point:

> I have come to regard educators as a lost cause. I have felt that the only chance is to call the public of whom the educators live in deathly fear. When I am conciliatory, nobody pays any attention. . . . When I am vicious, the teachers at least have to answer the questions of their constituency.

Indeed, at times, as regarded the merits of science or the uses of atomic energy, he could not even resist arguing publicly with himself.

The task of building and leading an institution is complex and difficult, even for an institution as relatively small and circumscribed as a college or university. While the members of the community are all scholars, their scholarly predilections and views about education are not necessarily consonant with one another. The task becomes even more daunting when one acknowledges that institutions of higher learning in America have had to change constantly during this century.

Once they were bastions of privilege for scions of affluent families, comfortable settings for future professionals, and oases removed from urban problems. Now "multiversities" serve many national constituencies, redress wrongs among various populations, and provide universal postsecondary education.

In this historical welter, a few figures do stand out: the initial generation of giants, like Charles Eliot at Harvard, who introduced the elective system and eased the transition from College to University; the experimentalists such as Harold Taylor at Sarah Lawrence, who introduced artistic courses and practices into the liberal arts curriculum; the creators of small and clustered gems such as Frank Aydelotte at Swarthmore, who established a tutorial system for the student body; the builders of the large national universities and multiversities of today, such as Herman Wells at Indiana University, John Hannah at Michigan State University, and, above all, Clark Kerr at the University of California.

Nearly all of these individuals eventually ran into problems that they could not solve to their satisfaction—that is perhaps the fate of all innovative leaders. But during the time of their greatest effectiveness, they had to succeed in two important, but not necessarily confluent, assignments: first, creating a story that made sense to the variety of constituents, ranging from crusty trustees to impressionable prospective students; second, providing enough direction and support to those under their charge so that the institution could operate effectively on a daily and yearly basis. The first assignment called for a public presence with some articulateness; the second called for the ability to remain in the background, to provide rewards and sanctions when needed, and to create long-term loyalty to the institution, if not its leader.

For much of his life, Hutchins succeeded in creating an effective story for some individuals residing at his home institution and for many others in the nation. Over the long run, he proved less successful in creating the institutions that could carry on his mission and do so enthusiastically. (Eliot's Harvard and Aydelotte's Swarthmore may have survived with less alteration than Hutchins's Chicago). Yet Hutchins may have achieved something even more important: he propounded one powerful view of education—a broad general education of high standards for the serious citizen in a democracy—with enough flair and enough appeal so that it remains today as a contender, even if it is honored more in the breach than in the observance.

7

ALFRED P. SLOAN, JR.
The Business of America

*Today it is clear that every man, woman, and child, includ-
ing generations yet to be born, has a stake in the power of
General Motors.*

—Alfred P. Sloan, Jr.

In the thirteenth century, Europe's once tightly integrated feudal society began
to crumble, slowly giving way to a number of different sectors. Three sectors, often called "estates," came to the fore: the nobility, the clergy, and the commons—the latter consisting of merchants. While initially the estates only
provided advice to the sovereign, they steadily gained influence. And while
membership in a particular estate was hardly an option for every free individual,
let alone any serf, offspring eventually came to exercise some choice concerning
the estate to which they would belong. Thus, in a family having several sons, one
might end up in the clergy, while others would enter the merchant class.

Nowadays, we no longer invoke the language of estates, but instead recognize major clusters of professions. So far in this study, we have considered
three individuals who elected to join the ranks of scholars—either as a practitioner of a specific discipline, such as physics or anthropology, or as the president of a major institution of higher learning. Such individuals, as I have
noted, begin by providing indirect leadership within a specific discipline; they
gain effectiveness as direct leaders to the extent that they can speak with conviction to their scholarly colleagues; and their influence may spread beyond a
university setting if the stories that they have created "speak" to the wider educated public.

In this chapter, I focus on Alfred P. Sloan, Jr., a leader of the contemporary
"estate" of the corporation. In the next two chapters, I examine leaders of two
other estates of our era—George C. Marshall of the military and Pope John

Alfred P. Sloan, Jr. UPI/Bettmann

XXIII of the Catholic Church. There are intriguing similarities among the three leaders. Each was born of unremarkable origins in the closing decades of the nineteenth century. Each showed mettle at an early age and yet marked time until he assumed a series of positions of authority within established institutions. Each was somewhat restrained in temperament, yet willing to confront authorized leaders on important issues. Each contributed to the definition of his chosen institution for the modern era. And each helped followers understand the evolving nature of the institution to which he and they belonged. While all three institutions have been distinguished by their hierarchical nature, these leaders led primarily by persuasion rather than by the bald assertion of authority; they assumed an inclusionary stance toward others. Yet, none could escape entirely the aura of competition; after all, businesses, armies, and even churches vie with one another.

Finally, while each of the three contemporary estates governs only certain facets of a member's life, they all aspire to be more comprehensive than a scholarly domain. In contrast to domain leaders, the three individuals considered here had to address a wider and more differentiated audience and to craft messages that could be understood even by individuals who were not expert in a domain. The order of treatment here follows the increasingly expansive spheres of influence, with a corporation representing the most constrained domain, and a church touching (at least potentially) on the deepest and most pervasive spheres of a person's existence.

The early history of the automobile industry is dominated by the saga of Henry Ford. A brilliant inventor and an equally brilliant entrepreneur, Ford conceived of the Model T Ford, an inexpensive and functional automobile that far outsold competing vehicles in the early 1900s. Indeed, during the early 1920s, the Ford Motor Company produced 50 percent to 60 percent of all cars that were made in the United States.

Ford, who had little formal education, derived his views from personal experience. He came to formulate distinct and often idiosyncratic ideas on most topics, ranging from politics to design to corporate life. He strove to ensure that the average person could afford an automobile. Ford strongly opposed organized labor unions. Although he offered generous wages to his employees, he ran his company paternalistically; in the terms of this study, he embodied his views in the ways in which he dealt with others. And he looked with particular disdain at competitors who attempted to introduce organizational strategies into their companies, declaring at one point:

> To my mind there is no bent of mind more dangerous than that which sometimes is described as the "genius for organization." This usually results in the birth of a great big chart. . . . It takes about six weeks for a message from a man living in one berry at the lower left-hand corner of the chart to reach the president or the chairman of the board.

Despite his conviction and charisma, Ford had bet on the wrong model of the consumer and the wrong model of the corporation. By the late 1920s, the Ford Motor Company's hegemony was waning; by the Second World War, Ford's market share had been reduced from 60 percent to 20 percent, while rival General Motors' market share had jumped from 12 percent to 50 percent. By the 1950s, GM was the largest and richest corporation in the world. This radical change in fortune was the result of many factors and the efforts of many individuals, but the key person unquestionably was Alfred P. Sloan, Jr., who presided over GM from 1923 to 1946 and chaired the corporation's board until 1956.

Sloan was born in New Haven, Connecticut, in 1875. His forebears were ministers and schoolteachers, and his father was in the wholesale tea, coffee, and cigar business. In contrast to our three precocious scholars, Sloan's childhood and early adult years seem to have been unremarkable. Shortly after receiving a degree in electrical engineering from the Massachusetts Institute of Technology, he went to work for the Hyatt Roller Bearing Company of New Jersey. In the ensuing years an antifriction bearing produced by the Hyatt Company became an important component of the automobile.

When Sloan joined it, Hyatt was a small company that employed about twenty-five people. Sloan soon became the general manager of the company and rapidly learned about the world of business, and especially about the explosive growth of the automobile industry. Under Sloan's shrewd and demanding leadership, Hyatt grew rapidly and soon was supplying both products and consulting information to various car manufacturers. Indeed, at one point Hyatt was Ford's sole supplier of ball bearings.

In 1916, William C. Durant, who headed the General Motors Company, approached Sloan and asked whether the Hyatt Company was for sale. Sloan concluded that his business, while profitable, could not long retain its size and form; he also disliked the crisis atmosphere, where the demand for his product varied precipitously and unpredictably from one season to the next. After some hesitation and bargaining, Sloan sold Hyatt to GM for $13.5 million. Durant placed Sloan in charge of a conglomerate called United Motors, and within a few years Sloan had become part of the executive committee that ran GM.

Sloan's shift to GM occurred at a time of enormous change in the automobile industry and in American industrial life more generally. Until the late nineteenth century, most American businesses were owned and managed by the same individuals, often members of one family. Only a few businesses, such as mills and plantations, were subdivided into sections, and even those tended to be supervised by a single manager or foreman or, at most, a small group.

This manner of doing business changed dramatically because of the rise of the railroads; the growth of the urban industrial economy, with its unprecedented demand for goods; the shift to new sources of energy like coal and oil and to new products like synthetic dyes; and the replacement of individual craftsmen by machine tools. By the beginning of the twentieth century, the United States was already dominated by a relatively small number of major corporations that were often monopolistic, such as the Standard Oil Company, the United States Steel Corporation, and the American Tobacco Company. Rather than relying on free agents to carry out various ancillary functions, these companies attempted to control all facets of their industry, from the securing of raw materials to the marketing of consumer goods. They hired specialists to handle such functions as bookkeeping, sales, and production. And in the tradition of American tinkering, they experimented with various organizational charts—the creation of divisions, management by committee, forms of centralization and decentralization. The historian of American business Alfred Chandler has said that "the major innovation in the American economy between the 1880s and the turn of the century was the creation of the great corporation in American industry." And, indeed, by 1900 the corporation—with purchasing and production of materials and parts, plus financing and marketing, all within the same infrastructure—had become the basic industrial unit.

Compared to oil, steel, and tobacco, the fledgling automobile industry was still wide open. In 1900 a mere 500 automobiles had been sold; the number had risen to 65,000 by 1907; in 1915 nearly one million passenger vehicles were purchased. The market was divided among a large number of companies, some of whose names (Buick, Ford) have endured, while others (Maxwell, Oakland) have long since been consigned to the historical junk heap. The individuals associated with these companies were as likely to be amateurs, speculators, or crackpot inventors as titans of industry or business. Financing was often idiosyncratic or ragtag; Wall Street financiers had not yet taken over.

Durant was one of the most energetic and farsighted of the early automobile moguls. Starting with the successful Buick organization, he was able to create and combine companies with great flair, and he boldly took risks that more often than not paid off. His General Motors Company—soon to be renamed the General Motors Corporation—was formed out of a combination of several leading producers of the day, including Buick, Cadillac, Oldsmobile, and Oakland.

Unlike Ford, who favored extreme centralization, Durant was partial to decentralization: he left the various companies under GM's control largely to their own devices. Where Ford expanded internally, perfecting the assembly line and rationalizing all aspects of production, Durant relied on external purchases to fill the needs of automobile manufacture. Observing Durant, his new associate Sloan concluded:

> I was of two minds about Mr. Durant. I admired his automotive genius . . . [and] his loyalty to the enterprise was absolute. . . . But I thought he was too casual in his ways for an administrator and he overloaded himself. . . . I was particularly concerned that he had expanded GM between 1918 and 1920 without an explicit policy of management with which to control the various parts of the organization.

Sloan tried to influence Durant's mode of operation; though not a confrontational individual by nature, he was not afraid to criticize company policy and even Durant's actions. But while Durant was respectful of his capable younger associate, he tended to follow his own intuitions rather than the advice of others.

In the aftermath of the First World War, GM almost collapsed because Durant had overextended the company. GM had to write off $100 million in losses, and Durant was personally in debt to his brokers for nearly $40 million. Decisive action was needed. In the fall of 1920, following a few weeks of tense negotiation, Durant, who had lost a personal fortune of more than $100 million, was eased out of the company. A sharply new course was struck—one that would decisively reshape not only the company but also, ultimately, American corporate life.

In GM's early years, Durant had looked for support beyond the New York financial community and had turned to the du Ponts of Delaware. The du Pont family, owners of a highly successful chemical and explosives company, became major investors in GM, owning 29 percent of the company by 1919. And Pierre du Pont, the president of the Du Pont Company, had, by dint of this investment, become a significant figure on the GM board.

Du Pont had presided over the conversion of a family business into a conglomerate of the scale, though not in the style, of United Motors and GM. Like Sloan, du Pont had attended MIT and combined a knowledge of the scientific and engineering processes with an interest in organizational structure; both men were organization builders, not (in contrast with Ford and Durant) eccentric individual geniuses. Indeed, as Sloan was to put it, both men preferred "the slow process of getting all the available facts, analyzing them as completely as our experience and ability made possible, and deciding on our course." The question of the hour was, Whose style would prevail at GM and, more generally, in the automobile industry of the future?

At the time of the GM crisis—one brought on by both external economic collapse and internal mismanagement—it was essential that GM appear to be in capable hands. "Pierre du Pont was the one individual in GM who had the prestige and respect that could give confidence to the organization, to the public, and to the banks," recalled Sloan. Over the next three years, du Pont, Sloan, two other board members, and a small number of key advisers worked on an almost daily basis to place GM on an even keel; 101 separate meetings were held in 1921 alone. Du Pont and Sloan tended to agree with each other, but Sloan stood by his opinions and prevailed in disputes.

The key ideas for the reorganization of GM came from Sloan, who actually had circulated his proposals in a 1919 memo. Sloan had been so dismayed by the condition of GM at the time that he had seriously considered resigning to join the banking firm of Lee Higginson and Company. Virtually the first act of the newly constituted board was to adopt Sloan's drafted plan in its entirety: thus, in the board's words, it endorsed "an organization for the General Motors Corporation which will definitely place the line of authority throughout its extensive operations as well as to coordinate each branch of its service, at the same time destroying none of the effectiveness with which its work has heretofore been conducted."

As Sloan saw it, the group of companies and the set of capacities that GM comprised were faced with a major challenge: how best to combine optimally features of both decentralization and centralized power and control. In particular, Sloan felt the need for some form of control of the individual operating divisions, which included those that made brands of cars and those that created specific parts and accessories. His solution was to allow managers of the separate divisions to have considerable autonomy over their daily operations, but to create simultaneously a sizable general office consisting of executives (a president, operating and financial vice presidents, and group executives) and advisory staff officers, who functioned as in-house experts. Also, each division was placed on its own profit-making basis, so that its contribution to the welfare of the organization as a whole could be judged. Surprising as it may seem, this relatively straightforward cutting of the Gordian knot proved revolutionary in the corporate world; it endured at GM and was also copied by many other organizations, small and large. Sloan's master stroke of indirect leadership—the creation of a viable organizational chart—had national reverberations.

The 1920s brought rapid (actually, overly rapid) expansion of the American economy as a whole and further expansion of the automobile industry; GM played the central role in both trends. Having achieved his stated purpose of bringing stability to GM, du Pont resigned the presidency early in 1923 and turned the reins over to Sloan. At the height of his powers, Sloan created a new and effective form of organization at GM.

Most significantly, Sloan and his close associates fully realized that there was no "best car" to be made. Instead, they focused on studying the market and creating a range of products that, collectively, would address the needs and desires of the full range of consumers. "A car for every purse and purpose"—an appeal to both "mass" and "class"—became their watchwords. Moreover, they recognized the need for a range of products for each market segment, and they deemed the quality of the product more crucial than a few hundred extra dollars in cost—a tilting toward the "top of the market." Sloan described it as "a comprehensive plan whereby the organization would go into the market with a properly designed car in each price position, something like a commanding general would have to have an army in every point of the front line so that he could not be attacked."

Ford, in contrast, aimed for economy above all else and once famously quipped that his customers could have any color that they wanted, "so long as it [was] black." Ford followed his intuition, which he assumed would coincide with that of the average consumer; Sloan and his associates proceeded by carefully studying the market and the policy alternatives. In the words of the historian

Alfred Chandler, Ford's policy—his counterstory, if you will—"proved to be one of the most costly mistakes in American business history."

There were many other facets to Sloan's achievement at the helm of what was fast becoming America's flagship corporation. GM devoted much effort to launching advertising and sales approaches that could saturate a large but fickle market. The creation of a cadre of good and loyal dealers was crucial in this campaign. The role of used cars was recognized early, and attention to this dimension of the automotive industry proved to be another effective way of showering the market with alternatives. Since the number of purchasers could not increase indefinitely, growth had to occur principally through intra-industry competition. Accordingly, GM established the practice of creating a new and distinctive annual line, encouraged people to trade in their vehicles, and secured a reputation for excellent service on demand.

Corporative initiatives proliferated. Separate organizations were created to finance car purchases (with little or no money down), to promote the solidarity among executives, and to facilitate links among dealers. Annual forecasting was initiated so that rapid adjustments to changes in the market could be made. A strong and largely self-standing research division was created and supported—although, after a number of costly debacles, Sloan made certain that it was not allowed to dictate policy to the firm. And far earlier than Ford, GM made its peace with labor unions, chief among them the United Auto Workers. Within a few decades Sloan's revolutionary steps became fixtures of the automobile industry.

And here we come face-to-face with the issue of Sloan as a leader—an individual who affects the thoughts, behaviors, and feelings of other individuals. From one perspective—one might call it a Ford perspective—a man like Sloan has an easy job. He has authority. He presides over a board of directors—particularly its executive committee—and prevails in most instances. Under individuals like Durant, such a setup could easily become autocratic. And indeed, one of the first actions that Sloan took following his ascendancy to the presidency was to increase greatly the power of the chief operating officer of the corporation.

Yet Sloan conceived of his position in a very different—and, perhaps, more modern—way. In his view, browbeating was not a desirable mode of operation. As he later recalled: "I never minimized the administrative power of the chief executive officer in principle when I occupied that position. I simply exercised that power with discretion; I got better results by selling my ideas than by telling people what to do." Sloan hired the most competent senior group he could assemble, placed them in responsible positions, treated them fairly and paid them well, and organized them into committees where they discussed issues and options in depth and attempted to reach agreement. "Our management policy decisions are arrived at by discussion in the governing committees and policy groups," Sloan noted. Thus, GM operated largely through administration by committee and decision by consensus.

Of course, nothing can more readily cripple an organization than a reliance on countless desultory, nondecisive committees that meet endlessly. Indeed, in the early 1920s Henry Ford viciously ridiculed GM's mode of operation. "The Ford factories and enterprises have no organization, no specific duties attaching to any position, no line of succession or of authority, very few titles, and no conferences." (A committee-based mode has also been blamed for the weakening in the 1990s of certain major American corporations, among them IBM and GM itself.) Sloan avoided such paralysis, constituting the committees' goals and membership carefully, giving them specific assignments, monitoring their progress, and, at a certain moment, guiding them toward decisions. "Much of my life in GM," he noted, "was devoted to the development, organization, and periodic reorganization of these governing groups." In a manner reminiscent of Margaret Mead's approach to the study of contemporary cultures, committees at GM intentionally were staffed with individuals from different divisions and spheres—balancing the sales manager's enthusiasm with the statistician's objectivity—so that these colleagues could educate one another and come to understand their problems, perspectives, and individual and collective opportunities. Sloan monitored these procedures carefully, intervening when necessary. He spoke often of the central enigma: "How could we exercise permanent control over the whole corporation in a way consistent with the decentralized scheme of organization? We never ceased to attack this paradox."

Leadership has crucial and indispensable human dimensions. Sloan may have been a pioneer of—perhaps even a genius in—the creation of organizational charts, but that "domain expertise" was not the principal component in his success. Sloan embodied the virtues that he sought in his associates. A tireless worker, he was invariably on top of all of the available information. He called for studies of key issues, mastered their data and details, and used their conclusions explicitly in making decisions. His participation in groups modeled the kinds of considerations that he deemed important and the mode of converging on a decision that he favored. For years, he wrote GM's annual report himself.

He also devoted time to getting to know his associates—not only the chief executives but also less highly placed individuals from other spheres of the company. He invited them in to talk, he wrote and responded to countless memos, and he visited them at their work sites:

> I made it a practice throughout the 1920s and early thirties to make personal visits to dealers. I fitted up a private railroad car as an office and in the company of several associates went into almost every city in the United States, visiting from five to ten dealers a day. I would meet them in their own places of business and ask them for suggestions and criticisms concerning their relation with the corporation, the character of the product, the corporation's policies, the trend of consumer demand, their view of the future,

and many other things of interest in the business. I made careful notes of all the points that came up, and when I got back home I studied them.

This interest did not go unrequited. When Sloan retired, the dealers honored him by contributing over $1.5 million to cancer research.

As with the other leaders considered thus far, Sloan must be seen in two contexts. On the one hand, he was an expert in a domain—the domain of organizing and then directing a complex industrial organization, perhaps the most complex business the world had known to that time. His expertise here grew out of his formal university training, on the one hand, and his experiences at Hyatt, United Motors, and the GM Corporation, on the other. In carrying out this part of his work, Sloan was functioning as an expert: it was crucial only that other members of the domain could appreciate and apprehend his message—his "story." In this variety of indirect leadership, it did not matter what Sloan was like as an individual—he could have exercised his influence completely behind the scenes or, indeed, through writing books (in the manner, say, of the currently popular business consultant and author Peter Drucker).

As GM's head, Sloan was also a direct leader of his institution. From this platform, Sloan conveyed a definite identity story to the thousands of employees. Part of the story was a general one: Every GM employee is part of the most important and dynamic business in America, perhaps in the world. But part of the story was a specific one: GM is not just another company; workers and managers alike are members of the world's most progressive and most powerful organization. The company invited participation by all of its members, no matter how humble their position, so that they could ensure the continued unequaled quality of their product. GM was a family, with Sloan as the benign patriarch. He embodied its virtues in his unstinting work for the company, and he expected his corporate offspring to do the same.

Sloan was also a public figure, a direct leader for millions of Americans involved in the world of commerce. He was not only the visible executive of GM, a public corporation with hundreds of thousands of employees and over one million stockholders; he was also a paragon of American industry, looked to during critical times (such as the Second World War), applauded by many of his fellow industrialists, and subjected to strong criticism from other businesspeople, writers, political figures, and segments of the general public. His successor "Engine" Charlie Wilson is said to have declared revealingly: "What is good for GM is good for the country."* And while Sloan might have avoided such grandiloquent word-

*Wilson actually said, "We at General Motors have always felt that what was good for the country was good for General Motors as well." It is instructive that the misquotation, rather than the original remark, has become part of American folklore.

ing, he was aware (and proud) of the unique place that "his" corporation had come to assume in American life.

What, then, was the story that Alfred P. Sloan, Jr., conveyed to the rest of the country? First, it was that business was a power at least equal to the political estate, and perhaps the principal power among the contemporary estates. John D. Rockefeller and his fellow "robber barons" had shown the power of American business; Sloan and his corporate colleagues could show that business was well organized and responsibly run, aware of its public responsibilities, and willing to provide leadership during times of crisis and to facilitate prosperity for the nation's working people. Critics of capitalism were simply misinformed or malevolent. GM had weathered the depression and had become the nation's leading manufacturer of war materials during the Second World War. Its leaders were the beacons of their community and also personally charitable. Embodying this point, Sloan gave his own wealth back to the nation through major philanthropic gifts. "The financial story of General Motors is a story of growth," declared Sloan. And he added: "We have done a very creditable job for the shareholders, without neglecting our responsibilities to our employees, customers, dealers, suppliers, and the community."

And so, Sloan was helping to define a nation—perhaps for the first time in human history—in terms of business and, for that matter, in terms of the giant national and international corporations. As Americans, he was saying, we belong to a society that believes in and fosters business—business where size can be an advantage, rather than a liability, and where prosperity for the company can go hand-in-hand with prosperity for the nation as a whole. Just as individuals looked to their automobiles as unique providers of privacy and mobility, they could look to the industry that produced cars as a principal vehicle in their personal prosperity. No wonder the eyes of the whole country shifted to Detroit when the new models were unveiled each fall.

Sloan obviously struck an expansive note. His audience grew from one corporation to an entire industry to the country as a whole (witness the epigraph to this chapter). And his message enlarged as well. Beginning with the theme of what it meant to be a worker in a certain kind of company, he ended up by suggesting that American business provided the basis for a good life. While this message did not touch all facets of life—neither political nor religious dimensions were highlighted, for example—it did provide a vision of a modern-day identity. And while it was an innovative story, it was not a threatening one, because it suggested that everyone could benefit from the success of capitalism.

Indeed, the genius of capitalism was Sloan's most pervasive message. He spoke of the "development of an industry that was to advance the economic and social status of humanity more than any other." Of the automobile, he said: "Humanity had never wanted any machine as much as . . . this one." He praised the capitalistic way of life: "The ambition . . . to rank high in the world of material accomplishment is not only a highly worthy objective but the fact that it has until recently been so regarded undoubtedly has been an important contributing factor in the development of America and of the highest standard of living." And he asked (rhetorically): "Can anyone see anything undesirable or anything contrary to the public interest in a process that permits and encourages the capitalization of the natural ability and industry of the unusual individual?" Sloan combined his own story with that of his company's when he reflected:

> No greater opportunity for accomplishment ever was given to any individual in industry than was given to me when I became president of General Motors. . . . As President of General Motors, I realized that our thinking affected the lives of hundreds of thousands directly and influenced the economic welfare of many important communities.

In speaking of business and automobiles, Sloan (and his colleagues and successors at GM) could invoke an inclusive rhetoric. Both the automobile industry and the business community as a whole could continue to grow indefinitely. As a leader, Sloan had the advantage that the story told within his home institution could be transported readily to much wider audiences throughout the nation. Yet, there was obviously a competitive dimension to the industry as well. GM's success had to come at some cost to others. The first and least visible losers were the many smaller companies that GM either bought out or allowed to die—monopolistic capitalism in its unvarnished version was at work. The most visible victim was the Ford Motor Company, which, in a remarkably short time, lost both its top executives and the lion's share of the sales market to rival GM. Labor unions were periodically locked into disputes with the Sloan-led management team. And to the extent that the country came to think of itself as a collection of profitable (and not-so-profitable) businesses, there may have been subtler losses as well.

Just as there were casualties of GM's power, there were also alternative stories that suffered when the saga of business-as-big-and-beneficent prevailed. In earlier times, Americans had wanted to think of themselves as interested in matters other than money and material success—selflessness, concerns of the spirit, aid to others who were less fortunate, and a life of modest communal and personal pursuits. While not directly challenging these components of identity, Sloan was putting forth a vision that was anchored in size, power, and dominance. Sloan tried to address issues of charity and was personally philanthropic, but a viewpoint anchored in capitalistic competition tended toward self-aggrandizement. Perhaps because it was a simpler and more selfish story, the materialistic story largely prevailed for many years. At times of prosperity, all could seem to benefit from a rising tide; but at times of economic stress, one person's or one company's achievement was likely to be at the cost of another's.

Sloan retired from the board chairmanship of GM in 1956 and lived for another decade. One of his chief activities during this period was to compose an interesting and influential autobiography, *My Years with General Motors*, a major resource for subsequent writing about the corporation. Sloan's lengthy book is almost an unalloyed chronicle of success and a hymn of praise to the American enterprise system. (What is most fascinating to me is that its nineteen-page index does not include a single entry under the label "Japan.")

The national and international business scene has changed almost totally since Sloan's prime. In the United States railroads are thought of derisively; airplanes are increasingly the vehicles of choice for travel of any distance; service and information, rather than heavy industry and commercial products, are seen as the businesses of the future; and the automobile industry in the United States has gone through a series of declines, largely because of the superior competitiveness of vehicles made in Japan and other foreign countries. GM (like IBM and a few other companies) has come to play the role of the fallen giant, the corporation that failed to notice what was happening in the wider world. It is the wizards of the computer companies—Steven Jobs of Apple and NeXT, William Gates of Microsoft, and Mitch Kapor of Lotus—who are looked to as harbingers of a new and leaner American competitive stance. Whereas Sloan was spoken of during his lifetime in terms of respect bordering on awe, one of his successors, Roger B. Smith, became the target of the full-length movie lampoon *Roger and Me*.

Whether Sloan (or his contemporary clone) could have written a happier chapter for GM today is anyone's guess. From what we know of human cognitive development, it is unlikely that an elderly person who had come to believe totally in the GM of 1930 or 1950 could have discerned within it the seeds of its own destruction and planned accordingly. Proper planning in this instance would include the ability to think at a meta-strategic level about issues ranging from the short-term financial markets to the niche and operation of the organization a decade or two in the future. In Sloan's day, GM was run like the military or the government—a vast flow of information passing up and down the bureaucracy, with countless checks and balances; nothing could be more remote from the intuitive entrepreneurship of a Henry Ford or a Thomas Edison. The young Sloan did, of course, see the weaknesses in the business that had been cobbled together by Durant. But whether his training at MIT and his apprenticeship at Hyatt and United would have allowed him to fashion a corporation that could thrive at the end of the century is questionable. Toward the end of his active corporate life, Sloan was most concerned with the styles of next year's models. Perhaps experience in the Wall Street junk bond and merger frenzy of the 1980s or thousands of hours spent as a hacker during one's college years constitute better preparation for the CEO of today or tomorrow.

Indeed, the question has been raised explicitly of the utility of "stories" in the contemporary business world. When the corporate manager Louis Gerstner was recruited in the early 1990s to rescue IBM, he declared: "The last thing IBM needs now is a vision: it needs lower costs and better market focus in every division." And Microsoft's Gates echoed this sentiment: "Being a visionary is trivial. Being a CEO is hard." One could counter that Gerstner's denial of the importance of a vision is itself a story—perhaps a postmodern business story. But it is perhaps better to listen to Gerstner himself a year later: "[Changing a culture] is not something you do by writing memos. You've got to appeal to people's emotions. They've got to buy in with their hearts and their beliefs, not just the minds." And so, armed with a new story about "market, execution, and teamwork," he toured the country and told his employees a new identity story: "I'm one of us now."

Sloan's own history underscores once more the powerful effect of the right skills in the right circumstances. In 1920, GM desperately needed the mastery of organizational structure and the willingness to act that du Pont and Sloan were able to furnish. In the succeeding three decades, as agrarian life continued to decline, both the corporate world and the country as a whole hankered for a story that would explain the modern world to its inhabitants—the world of mass transportation and communication, of business booms and busts, of periods of war, depression, and prosperity. For at least this short period of American history, a story centered on business, on the automobile business, and on GM in particular was the story that the citizens of the nation wanted to hear. That story could have been told by others, and embodied by others—and, indeed, people like Ford, du Pont, and the Rockefeller family members carried the torch of business with their own brands of effectiveness.

But through the concatenation of circumstances chronicled here, Sloan and his corporation were at midcentury probably the most influential fashioners of the story. Only when forces arose beyond the corporation's control—the threats posed by fascism and communism, the rise of Asia and the so-called third world, and the recognition of searing problems within the American economy and the American psyche—did it become clear to many that the business of America could not be simply business.

8

GEORGE C. MARSHALL
The Embodiment of the Good Soldier

My own definition of leadership is this: The capacity and the will to rally men and women in a common purpose, and the character which inspires confidence.

—Field Marshall Bernard Montgomery

Lt. Colonel (temporary) George C. Marshall was known as a temperate and composed man. His hero was General John J. "Black Jack" Pershing, the commander in chief of the American Expeditionary Force in Europe during the First World War. Yet in October 1917, at his first meeting with the formidable general, Marshall confronted Pershing sharply. Pershing had come to observe a military exercise, and he did not like what he saw. He berated the commanding general and his chief of staff. In view of the actual conditions at the front, Marshall felt the remonstrance was unfair and told Pershing so publicly, in no uncertain terms. He poured out "a torrent of facts"; and then when Pershing, taken aback, referred to the troubles that he was having at headquarters, Marshall retorted, "Yes, General, but we have them every day, and they have to be solved before night."

Over twenty years later, in November 1938, Marshall found himself in the presence of an even higher commander in chief—President Franklin D. Roosevelt. Roosevelt laid forth an ambitious set of plans for building ten thousand war planes. Marshall was shocked that Roosevelt apparently had no program for recruiting personnel and for servicing the planes. After the presentation, Roosevelt circulated among the listeners and asked Marshall whether he had made a good case for his program. Marshall replied sharply, "I am sorry, Mr. President, but I don't agree with you at all." Everyone else in attendance was shocked by Marshall's behavior, since Marshall apparently had never before had a briefing with the president. Indeed, after the meeting, Secretary of the Treasury Henry Morgenthau approached Marshall and said, "Well, it's been nice knowing you."

George C. Marshall. UPI/Bettmann Newsphotos

On yet a third occasion, in May 1940, Marshall (now the army chief of staff) had a public confrontation with his superior. The topic of the conversation was the mobilization of men and planes in anticipation of possible U.S. participation in the European war. The meeting was proceeding inconclusively when Roosevelt displayed a lack of interest in what Marshall had to say on the topic. Something in the usually controlled Marshall snapped, and he asked for three minutes. As his biographer Ed Cray tells it:

> Two decades earlier he had confronted General Pershing in the muddy field of Gondrecourt; now he challenged the president of the United States. . . . The words spilled out, precisely at first, then in a rush of frustration. Barracks, rations, weapons, all in short supply. New artillery and antiaircraft guns designed but not in production. . . . The Germans had a million men in 140 divisions massed in the West. What were five against that horde? On and on, well past the three minutes he had asked for, the chief of staff ticked off his army's deficiencies.

This time, Morgenthau had a different reaction. He wrote in his diary: "He [Marshall] stood right up to the President."

What does it mean when a usually reticent person who carefully monitors his behavior throws caution to the wind and publicly confronts his superior? It is not likely that the confronter is deliberately sacrificing his career, although he is presumably aware of the risk of demotion or even dismissal. Nor is it likely that the confronter is simply misreading the situation and believes that those in attendance will deem it appropriate for him to speak up in this highly charged situation.

It seems to me that Marshall spoke up when he had command of the facts, when he sincerely believed that he was in the right, and, above all, when no one else had been able or willing to articulate the position that he was defending. In each of these situations, Marshall beheld an apparently knowledgeable executive, who should have been capable of arriving at the proper course, but instead was proceeding in a seemingly misguided way. Absent some kind of demurral, the commander was likely to continue down this erroneous path. Marshall gambled that a concise statement of his own convictions, backed up with facts and figures, might affect the decision or at least allow a judgment to be made in light of a fuller grasp of the situation. One could say that he was speaking out of personal interest, but also out of a certain *disinterest*—out of the conviction that a contrasting perspective on a situation needed to be aired by someone.

There is another consideration as well. By speaking up, Marshall was announcing, in effect, that he was an equal of the others in the meeting, including his nominal commander. He was declaring a new collectivity—a new "we"—composed of those who were knowledgeable and responsible. Put in a more self-serving way, he was indicating that he thought of himself as capable of occupying a leadership position—he was embodying leadership by his words and actions. And he was leaving open to his superior the option of enlarging the leadership circle to include the intruder himself. In the cases of both Pershing and Roosevelt, such a reaching out to Marshall is precisely what transpired.

One of the most intriguing features of individuals whom we come to consider outstanding is that they themselves often fail to appreciate just how unusual they are. In their 1992 study of individuals who exhibit unusual moral responsibility, developmental psychologists Anne Colby and William Damon reported that these individuals frequently do not see anything unusual in what they are doing; an indigent moral exemplar, for example, assumes that anyone else would adopt a dozen foster children, just as she has done. In my own study of creative giants, I found repeated evidence that these individuals expected that *every* person working in their domain would want to be original, to defy current practice, and to make a statement that would be remembered for years to come. And they assumed that most any person would be willing to organize his or her own life, as well as the lives of others around them, to help ensure immortality for a given line of work.

Now, in this study, I have been struck by the extent to which future leaders have from an early age seen themselves as members of an elite group; more often than not, they feel that they can readily engage in conversations with those at the top of the authority hierarchy. These confident individuals sense that they are articulate and persuasive. Margaret Mead and J. Robert Oppenheimer, for example, had no compunctions about entering into debate with, respectively, the leading anthropologists or physicists of their time. Even in his youth, Robert Maynard Hutchins interacted readily with university administrators. Alfred Sloan, Jr., did not hesitate to express his views to William Durant or Pierre du Pont, and, as we have now seen, Marshall felt entitled to convey his reservations to those above him in the military and political hierarchies. Angelo Roncalli, who would eventually become the pope, was circumspect in what he said and to whom he said it; and yet one finds throughout his career the capacity to think for himself and to indicate—if only to the pages of his personal journal—that he would not be cowed by persons and policies of which he did not approve (see chapter 9). Perhaps such future leaders see what they are doing as natural and fail to appreciate—or appreciate only later—how bold they have actually been.

Marshall had little in his background or his early life that would suggest a promising future as any sort of leader. Born on December 31, 1880, in Uniontown, Pennsylvania, Marshall was the third child of a relatively prosperous family. Unfortunately for the young Marshall, he seemed less able and more awkward than his older brother and sister, and he grew up feeling inadequate and somewhat of an underdog, particularly in academic matters. His father, who owned a coke and furnace company, definitely favored Marshall's older brother, Stuart, and Marshall had to depend on his doting mother to protect him from his father's anger and occasional beatings. Marshall wanted desperately to be close to his father, but his mother seems to have been more important in stimulating his ambition and his fierce sense of integrity. When Marshall was ten years old, his family suffered a severe financial setback; this unanticipated reversal of fortune helped make Marshall into an extremely careful and frugal young man.

Marshall was spurred on by his difficult childhood. He could not stand to lose or to see himself as a failure. When his siblings or the youngsters in the neighborhood attempted to take advantage of him, he thought strategically and fended for himself. Adults often think back to defining experiences from their early childhood. Marshall liked to retell the story of how a group of young girls had reneged on an agreement to pay for a raft ride and how he had abruptly retaliated and sunk the raft on which they were floating. "I never forget that because I had to do something and I had to think quickly, and what I did set me up again as the temporary master of the situation."

Marshall decided early on that he wanted to be a professional soldier. Having neither the scholastic gifts nor the connections to secure an appointment to West

Point, he did not even apply there and instead became a cadet at the Virginia Military Institute (VMI). He continued to be an indifferent academic student—excelling only in history—but soon distinguished himself in other military virtues. He was considered excellent in drill, discipline, decision making, and leadership; he was always the senior officer of his class. Marshall also earned respect from both students and teachers when, after a particularly harrowing and painful hazing, he refused to point any fingers at the perpetrators and instead maintained his composure.

Marshall was already beginning to display the signs that would mark him as a mature adult. He was certainly not a scholar or an intellectual, and he would not have been considered academically intelligent; his strengths lay more in the sphere of "personal intelligences," in well-considered judgments about people and events. An extremely hard worker, he was very disciplined and reflective, and he expected these features in others as well. He learned the art of command and came to appreciate that he could not allow himself to become too intimate with those who would have to obey his orders and who might have to be disciplined or dismissed.

Marshall did have a temper that could erupt violently, but he learned to control it; indeed, he struck others, and particularly women, as being charming, witty, and persuasive. He was modest, but not shy about pursuing his own interests. For example, in April 1901, just before his graduation from VMI, he barged into President William McKinley's office without an appointment with the request to be allowed to take a special examination in order to be commissioned as a second lieutenant. Marshall may have commanded respect when he spoke out *precisely* because individuals knew of, or could sense, his normal restraint. Since he was usually such a controlled person, one could infer that he felt deeply when he did express himself and that he would not do so if he had not mastered the facts of the situation and felt committed to the words that he was uttering.

Marshall graduated from VMI in June 1901 and married Elizabeth Carter Coles the following year. For the next thirty years he held a variety of postings in many parts of the world. (In this respect his career exhibits strong parallels with that of another institutional man—the future Pope John XXIII.) In 1902 he was a commissioned second lieutenant of the infantry in the Philippines. From 1906 to 1908 he attended the Cavalry School and Army Staff College in Fort Leavenworth, Kansas. There, he diligently studied military strategy, had opportunities to teach and to lead, and ended up at the top of his class. Between 1913 and 1916, after having a variety of instructor positions in the United States, he was back in the Philippines. He was then promoted to captain and assigned to duty with the Allied Expeditionary Force in France during the First World War.

Viewed from one perspective, Marshall was pursuing a successful military career. The young officer rose steadily in the ranks and was widely respected as an excellent teacher and an effective leader. He knew how to select individuals for positions, inspire others to work together, and delegate authority or, when necessary, assert it. He was becoming an excellent briefer. He could work well with civilians as well as military personnel. Yet perhaps because of the widespread appreciation of his talents, and his own dawning knowledge of his special skills and understandings, Marshall was frustrated by the shape and pace of his career. For instance, although Marshall was capable of planning large-scale maneuvers, he had found himself in the Philippines in charge of fewer than a hundred men. By 1916, he was expressing distress about his lack of sufficiently rapid advancement:

> The absolute stagnation in promotion in the infantry has caused me to make tentative plans for resigning as soon as business conditions improve. . . . The prospects of advancement in the Army are so restricted by law and by the accumulation of large numbers of men of nearly the same age all in a grade, that I do not feel it right to waste all my best years in the vain struggle against insurmountable difficulties.

For all of its perils, the outbreak of war presents the one opportunity that ambitious soldiers await. And, indeed, promotions came quickly to Marshall after the outbreak of the First World War: he became a major and then a lieutenant colonel. Yet because of a minor injury, and the fact that he was not yet in a position to command troops, Marshall watched others, such as Douglas MacArthur, surpass him in rank and responsibility. Marshall requested a transfer to the European front lines, but it was denied on the grounds that he was too valuable to spare. "Lt. Col. Marshall's special fitness is staff work," declared General Robert Lee Bullard, the division commander. "I doubt that in this, whether it be teaching or practice, he has an equal in the Army today."

In this staff position Marshall played a crucial role in planning the delicate and complex Meuse-Argonne offensive in the fall of 1918, in which 500,000 men and 2,700 guns were transported within less than two weeks. He won the epithet as "the wizard" of "the most magnificent staff operation of the war"— but he had still not seen the thick of battle. And so, despite service of undoubted quality, Marshall missed the opportunity, in the wake of the First World War, to become one of the U.S. military's stars.

Despite—or perhaps because of—his sharp encounter with General Pershing, Marshall was named as the principal aide to the general, after Pershing became the army chief of staff in Washington during the early 1920s. The two men—similar in background, temperament, strengths, and deficits—gained deep and lasting affection for one another; Pershing became the father figure that Marshall had lacked. Marshall learned much about effective leadership from a master:

> I have never seen a man who could listen to as much criticism. . . . You could say what you pleased as long as it was straight, constructive criti-

cism. . . . General Pershing as a leader always dominated any gathering where he was. He was a tremendous driver if necessary, a very kindly, likeable man on off-duty status, but very stern on a duty status.

After a five-year stint with Pershing, Marshall served with the Fifteenth Infantry Regiment in Tientsin, China, in the mid-1920s, and he then had a series of postings in the United States during the early years of the Great Depression. In the early 1930s he served brilliantly as the head of an academic department at an infantry school in Fort Benning, Georgia. He attained the rank of colonel in 1933. In the mid-1930s he was named the chief of staff of the Thirty-third Division, based in Chicago. His last pre-Washington posting was as the commanding general of the Fifth Brigade in Vancouver, from 1936 to 1938.

Still, Marshall waited for the recognition that he (and others) felt was due him. Meanwhile, he had been experiencing a number of painful losses, including the death in 1927 of his beloved wife. He continued his exemplary teaching—no one could better summarize a complex battle problem in a few pithy sentences. Also, he helped to modernize and simplify the methods by which recruits were instructed in military procedures, and he developed an impressive cohort of younger officers, whose career trajectories he monitored in his famous "Black Book." But during a time of unprecedented domestic preoccupation and scarcity of resources, there were simply no pressures to make promotions within the military.

Paradoxically, Marshall finally received the promotion for which he had aspired for the same reason that he had been so long denied it: politics. So long as decisions about appointments were made by those who were partial to MacArthur, Marshall was destined to remain in the second ranks; while neither man would have admitted it, there was a long-simmering rivalry between them. (When MacArthur was finally relieved of his command during the Korean War, he characteristically blamed Marshall, although the then secretary of defense had actually argued against MacArthur's removal.) But when, at the close of 1935, Malin Craig, a "Pershing man," succeeded MacArthur as the army chief of staff, one of his first actions was to appoint Marshall as a brigadier general, thus giving Marshall a coveted star for the first time.

The crucial shift in fortunes for which Marshall had been waiting, sometimes patiently, sometimes impatiently, had finally occurred. Now in his midfifties, less than a decade from retirement age, he found himself at last within the corridors of power. In July 1938 he was appointed the assistant chief of staff; in October 1938, the deputy chief of staff. And in April 1939, reaching deep into the ranks of senior generals, President Roosevelt selected Marshall as the next army chief of staff. It would fall on his shoulders to prepare the army for the largest military effort in human history and then to assume the major role in planning the campaigns to defeat the Axis enemies. Indeed, the army of 200,000 in 1939 (the seventeenth largest in the world) was to become an army of $8^{1}/_{3}$ million by

1945. By the time Marshall was appointed a five-star army general, in December 1944, the promotion surprised no one.

Despite the well-motivated efforts of modern (and postmodern) historians to enlarge the reaches and transcend the limitations of traditional accounts, history remains primarily a record of the victors. Along with the other Allied powers, the United States won the Second World War, and so the names of Americans Franklin Roosevelt, Harry Truman, Douglas MacArthur, Dwight Eisenhower, George Patton, and George Marshall carry a sheen that they might not otherwise have attained. Each of these individuals was clearly a leader, and each made his distinctive contribution in shaping the Allied victory. But except for the nominal command, which belonged to the president, and the exquisite triumphs of battle victory, which belonged to the generals in the field, Marshall was undeniably the key American contributor to the Allied victory—as Winston Churchill put it, "the true organizer of victory."

In the early phases of his tenure as the chief of staff, Marshall was primarily responsible for alerting the American people to the dangers of the Nazi threat and to the need for a rapid mobilization effort. This was the point in his life where the creation and promulgation of a "story" was most critical. Americans had never been particularly interested in conflicts that were raging abroad, and considerable isolationist sentiment reigned both in Congress and among the general public. Moreover, the United States was officially neutral in the conflict.

Marshall proved equal to this task of rallying. Working both behind the scenes and through public testimony to Congress, Marshall was able to impress upon the majority of his fellow citizens the need to build up the army in size, to secure proper training for the new personnel, to authorize ample supplies of planes and tanks, and to support those abroad who were opposed to the Nazis. At the same time, he discouraged ill-advised operations and explained his reasons for doing so. He once declared: "I have but one purpose, one mission, and that is to produce the most efficient Army in the world."

This story of the need for a strong defense force was not novel, but it was one that Americans of a new generation had to learn. Marshall's combination of mastery of the facts, articulate testimony, and deep belief in the necessity of mobilization proved unprecedentedly effective; Marshall, who was correctly seen as nonpartisan, was able to dramatize the lacks in the American arsenal and to articulate the steps needed to correct them. He was able to appeal to the idealism of the members of Congress, praising those who went beyond partisanship and gently chiding those who put their own or their constituents' pet causes ahead of the nation's. Indeed, Marshall soon became a more effective spokesman for mobilization than Roosevelt himself.

Once the so-called "phony" war had become a real one, as a consequence of Hitler's blitzkrieg in the spring of 1940, and once the Japanese attack on Pearl Harbor in December 1941 had drawn the United States into battle, Marshall was designated to preside over the prosecution of the war effort. He conceptualized the various fronts, computed the needs for personnel and materials and saw to it that they were procured as efficiently and judiciously as possible, participated actively in decisions about tactics and strategy, made sure that the inevitable disputes among American commanders were kept within manageable limits, and pushed hard for an American point of view in negotiations with the other Allied powers' leaders. And once victory seemed assured, by the later months of 1943, Marshall had to participate in the equally difficult task of planning the "end game" and preparing for what was destined to be a perilous peace.

In this effort, of course, Marshall was aided by dozens of close associates, thousands of staffers, and, ultimately, millions of men and women, including those who served in other armed services and fought for other nations. Many associates shared the job of coordinating information and developing complex plans. Putting together this team was a herculean task. Yet, as in the presidency, the "buck" had to stop somewhere; and in the case of America's involvement in the Second World War, that somewhere was Marshall's scrupulously ordered desk.

Leaders exert their influence through the stories they tell and the ways they embody those stories. In Marshall's case, the stories were familiar, or at least not strikingly original; he was explaining to the armed forces and to the nation why it was necessary to mobilize and to go to war. Within the army, Marshall told his personnel that they had to act as disinterested professionals, not politicians; they had to be ready for anything that might happen militarily. To other Americans, Marshall explained the role of the military in a twentieth-century democracy and emphasized that the military had to press toward victory in a way consistent with the nation's democratic values.

None of these stories was unfamiliar, but each had to compete with counterstories that were simple and proved appealing to various audiences. American isolationists depicted the battles of Europe as remote and unconnected to American interests; from their perspective, it made sense to let the European (and later the Asian) states battle one another. Many military personnel felt that if they were to risk their lives, they had the right to participate in the political process and to oppose those with whom they had ideological differences. And once war broke out, many citizens and politicians were inclined to pursue victory at all costs. Only because he told his stories with exquisite persuasiveness, and because he embodied these messages so transparently in his own life, did Marshall succeed so remarkably in influencing American public opinion.

Once Americans were convinced of the need for a strong military in the event of war, Marshall had to provide more finely nuanced stories. One theme concerned the nature of the army. The army, he asserted, could no longer be a motley assortment of enlisted personnel; it had to represent the broad swathe of American life. Achieving this would require essentially equitable conscriptive processes. Army officers had to be well educated, and they had to direct operations on the basis of the best military thinking. Technology had to be state-of-the-art, and research had to mobilize the best minds to lay out future courses of action. Officers who had outlived their time had to be quickly eased out of the ranks, to be replaced by younger and more current thinkers and doers. Marshall portrayed a new army that discarded obfuscatory regulations, outmoded bureaucratic attitudes, and the "monotonous drilling which, to be honest, achieved obedience at the expense of initiative. It excluded 'thought' of any kind."

Another story concerned the nature of military service. Soldiers, said Marshall, were to serve their country—leaders and ordinary citizens—in a disinterested way, apart from political infighting. And he, as the chief of staff, was to present facts impartially and make recommendations when so requested, but he was to steer clear of partisanship.

Marshall embodied these stories in the simplest and most effective way. He became the country's number-one soldier, the ideal military man. Superlatively well informed, he knew his officers, his personnel, and his military needs. Like Alfred Sloan, Jr., he could answer almost any question about his formidably complex organization; and if he could not answer the question immediately, he would forthwith commission a study that could provide an answer. He understood the global complexities of the war effort, even as he had mastered the finest details of assignments and personnel. His "black book" contained information on every promising officer that he met, and his incomparable networking knowledge proved indispensable for the mammoth operation that he had been entrusted to lead. Indeed, Marshall's choice of high-level officers, often based on firsthand knowledge gained at Fort Benning in the early 1930s, was essentially unerring; almost never did he have reason to regret an appointment. (The contrast could not be sharper with the rapid turnover associated with American political appointments of more recent years.)

Marshall served as the ultimate model of integrity. His personal honesty and sense of honor were beyond question. He was universally seen as selfless, without a hint of self-promotion or self-pity. He bent over backward to avoid any kind of special favors for himself or for those associated with him. Indeed, he spurned even the slightest hint of any special treatment for the offspring of his second wife, one of whom ultimately died in combat; and he was equally unrelenting when asked to extend privileges to Kay Summersby, the driver and presumed lover of General Dwight D. Eisenhower.

Honing his linguistic skills, Marshall had become a superb briefer. He could address any audience effectively, respond to their questions, anticipate their concerns, and direct their attention to the relevant issues. Rarely did he use notes, and, supported only by his steel-trap memory, he could continue speaking for hours. He became the most sought-after witness in Congress. His testimony became legendary as, time after time, he addressed a skeptical committee and won it over to his cause. Marshall knew how to address the proud Congressmen as equals, never condescending to them and always taking their concerns seriously, yet sticking to his guns as well. He looked and talked as Congressmen believed a genuine leader should. An observer who had heard many presidents address the Congress said, "Not one of them could hold a candle to General Marshall when he wanted to make people do things."

Marshall could not have been effective if he had been perceived as partisan. Setting the standard, he did not even vote, and he expressed his strong displeasure when military men toyed with running for office or otherwise intruded into the political process. He was able to indicate his disagreements with a current governmental policy, though never in a disrespectful way, even as he indicated sympathy with viewpoints that were not widely known or supported. As Speaker of the House Sam Rayburn once pointed out, Marshall told the truth even when it hurt his cause.

Marshall had to demonstrate that he could get along with his superior, President Roosevelt. Tensions had existed from the beginning, as borne out by their early confrontations and by Marshall's reminder, when Roosevelt offered him the chief-of-staff position: "I have the habit of saying exactly what I think, and that, as you know, can often be unpleasing." Indeed, Roosevelt's mercurial temperament, reliance on intuition, and improvisational style of government clashed with Marshall's allegiance to organizational charts, clear lines of authority, and fixed spheres of responsibility.

Yet the two men came to know each other well and to respect each other's expertise profoundly. There is evidence that Roosevelt was somewhat envious of Marshall's great sway over Congress and of his capacity to convince others that he was operating in a completely non-self-serving manner; of course, Roosevelt—the master politician of his era—took every advantage of Marshall's skill. For his part, Marshall came to marvel at Roosevelt's capacity to win political support for a program and his ability to make and adhere to difficult decisions. Yet, characteristically, Marshall kept his distance from the president so that he would feel no inhibitions in offering advice, especially advice that might rankle his superior.

Marshall showed that he cared about the human dimension of soldiering. No matter how busy he was—and his day was booked to the minute—he always found time to meet with subordinates, to send a present to a deserving associate, and to extend his sympathy at times of personal loss. Until it became impossible, Marshall personally answered all of the mail that he received. (Thereafter, he still sampled correspondence each day and assigned to others those letters that he could not answer himself.) Marshall traveled around the country and the world to see officers and front-line soldiers; remembering his own initial clash with the seemingly remote Pershing, he took careful note of their complaints. He believed that one should prevail by cultivating respect, not by engendering fear. And he placed value "on the effect of good example, given by officers; on the intelligent comprehension by all ranks of why an order has to be and why it must be carried out; on a sense of duty, on *esprit de corps.*" He once commented: "To issue an edict or regulation would probably do more harm than good. The job must be a personal one, to be effected slowly."

Yet, Marshall was famous—infamous—for being a taskmaster. He demanded a great deal of himself and was equally demanding on those around him. He did not suffer fools gladly. He once declared: "I cannot afford the luxury of senti-ment. . . . Mine must be cold logic." Like his mentor Pershing, he was curt with those who were ill prepared or self-serving, but he sought to learn from those who disagreed with him, if they were respectful and well prepared. After his first week as the army chief of staff, he bawled out his senior staff for failing to *dis-*agree with him. Indeed, he disliked officers who flattered him in order to gain promotion, and he liked men who spoke up on issues that mattered to them. "Whenever I find these fellows who seem to have ability and a certain amount of disagreement with what we are doing," he once said, "I am always interested in seeing them and getting firsthand impressions."

Still, Marshall understood well the chain of command and did not toy with it. He had risen in a hierarchical organization, and he believed in the necessity of such an organization. The good soldier needs to be able to balance the support-ive, human dimension with the imperative for discipline and authority; and as the best soldier, Marshall showed others how to achieve and sustain this equilib-rium. His capacity to honor authority, without being cowed or crippled by it, embodied an important message for his fellow soldiers, his commander in chief, and other citizens.

Perhaps it was Marshall's exemplary soldiering that cost him the dearest prize of the war. By the time of the Tehran conference (or Eureka Summit) in Novem-ber 1943, the Allies had agreed on Operation Overlord, the complex landing on the beaches of France that would allow the Allies to attack Germany's western flank. It remained to select the general who would command the Allied forces, and by agreement, that officer would be an American. There were only two viable choices—Marshall or Eisenhower—and the choice was Roosevelt's to make.

Roosevelt agonized over the choice. On the one hand, nearly everyone ex-pected him to choose Marshall, who was not only Eisenhower's superior but the man who had earned the right to command what was certain to be the most im-portant and most memorable battle of the war—if not of all recorded history. But Roosevelt felt the continuing need to have Marshall at hand as his principal military adviser, and he knew that Marshall was far more removed from the bat-tlefields than the younger Eisenhower, who had shown his mettle as a com-mander in North Africa and in the Mediterranean.

A complex sequence of events followed. Roosevelt gave Marshall the option to select the commander; Marshall said that he could not exercise that option—it was a decision that could be made only by the commander in chief. Most observers believe that Roosevelt wanted to keep Marshall at home and gambled that the always modest and soldierly Marshall would allow him that option. There is little question that Marshall was personally disappointed by the decision; indeed, he disappeared for several hours without explanation after the selection of Eisenhower and then decided to leave the presidential party in Cairo and travel around the world. But in the public's view, Roosevelt had made the tough but right choice. As he put it to Marshall: "I feel I could not sleep at night with you out of the country." Marshall never disputed Roosevelt's choice and supported Eisenhower completely during the months ahead.

Even without the command of Overlord, Marshall's burden was overwhelming. It fell on his shoulders to balance the different political and military interest groups in the United States; and he had to manage the overall war effort and negotiate diplomatically with officials from the several Allied parties, including Churchill, with whom he often clashed, and Stalin, who treated him avuncularly. While the British commanders Viscount Bernard Montgomery and General Alan Brooke and the American commanders Patton and MacArthur were planning battle tactics, Marshall was confronting the relationships among these armies and the proud men who led them. When President Roosevelt died of a cerebral hemorrhage one month before victory was achieved in Europe, Eleanor Roosevelt immediately turned to Marshall to handle the funeral arrangements. There was little surprise that, when Americans were polled about the individual most responsible for the successful prosecution of the war effort, they chose George C. Marshall over Franklin D. Roosevelt.

At age sixty-five Marshall was fully ready to retire as chief of staff and spend the remaining days of his life with his beloved second wife, gardening and relaxing at his white Federal-style home in Virginia. But a calm retirement was not to be. With scarcely a few hours of retirement under his belt, Marshall was asked by President Truman to undertake a special expedition to China. Marshall remained there for a year, only to be recalled to Washington to serve as the secretary of state. In the wake of major surgery, he resigned the secretaryship in 1949, but a year later, after the outbreak of the Korean War, he agreed once again to serve in the president's cabinet, this time as the secretary of defense. He was in this sensitive position during the Korean hostilities and at the tense time when MacArthur was relieved of his command on the grounds of insubordination and yet returned home to receive adulation from much of the American public.

Marshall's postwar diplomatic career was not crowned with the same string of successes as his military career. (Like Oppenheimer and others who led in a variety of circumstances, he was more likely to succeed when his role was unambiguous, when good and evil were clearly delineated, when he could commit himself fully to a clear story, and when partisan politics were muted.) His expedition to China accomplished little; the Communists continued their inexorable march to domination. The army that he had fought so hard to establish and strengthen was rapidly demobilized and demoralized. Marshall strongly opposed U.S. recognition of the State of Israel, but President Truman overruled him. The Korean War did not go well. MacArthur's insubordination caused Marshall great pain, and he was widely—though unfairly—blamed for the dismissal of the beloved general.

Most cruelly, Marshall was one of the public servants vilified by Joseph McCarthy, the ruthless junior senator from Wisconsin. McCarthy engaged in character assassination as he spoke of "America's retreat from victory: The story of George Catlett Marshall." Comparing Marshall to the blood-stained Macbeth, he accused the general of being part of "a conspiracy so immense and an infamy so black as to drown any previous such venture in the history of man." Marshall looked to General Eisenhower, soon to be President Eisenhower, for a defense, but "Ike," more intent on securing votes than on ensuring justice, did not rise to the occasion. Confronted with McCarthy's venomous words, Marshall could only respond, "If I have to explain at this point that I am not a traitor to the United States, I hardly think it's worth it."

Yet, for all the vicissitudes of the Truman presidency and of Marshall's roles within it, the postwar period was also the time of one accomplishment so enormous that it vied in significance with the Second World War victory: the reconstruction of Western Europe, including both the victorious and the defeated countries, so many of which had been devastated by the war. This reconstruction had to be masterminded and funded by the United States, the only remaining power with the will and the means to oversee the process.

In a commencement address of historic importance, delivered at Harvard University in June 1947, Marshall laid out the dimensions of such an effort. He declared:

> It is logical that the United States should do whatever it is able to do to assist in the return of normal economic health in the world, without which there can be no political stability and no assured peace. Our policy is directed not against any country or doctrine but against hunger, poverty, desperation, and chaos. Its purpose should be the revival of a working economy in the world so as to permit the emergence of political and social conditions in which free institutions can exist.

While Marshall had shared both the conceptualization of this plan and the writing of the speech with other individuals, among them foreign policy experts George Kennan and Dean Acheson, the effort soon became dubbed (with Truman's blessing) the Marshall Plan. This acknowledgment was appropriate. In part, the labeling was designed to gain bipartisan support for ideas associated with an individual who was, yet again, more popular than the U.S. president.

However, the effort at reconstruction was properly associated with Marshall's personal philosophy as well. A pragmatic idealist who believed in the institutions of a democratic society and in the capacity to mobilize people for constructive purposes, Marshall had proposed a plan for Europe that represented the best of American instincts. People were being asked, in the name of an exemplary public servant, to look beyond their immediate, narrow interests. Just as Marshall had helped Americans to answer the question of what they were like in a time of war, the plan that bore his name helped to answer the question of what Americans could be like in a time of peace.

In the story for which Marshall would be most widely honored in the postwar era, he declared that recovery had to follow war and that victors and vanquished had to work together cooperatively for that end. Marshall asked Americans to go beyond a military defense of their own borders and their own values and to devote energies and resources to the rehabilitation of the wider world. Because this story asked people to go beyond themselves, to suspend old rivalries, to see themselves as citizens of the world, it was a story that demanded sophistication—one that merits the epithet "visionary." For Marshall's program to prevail, it had to counteract more primitive stories, which sought to glorify American power and to punish those who had not, or did not, completely support American causes. It is a tribute to Marshall's power—to his name and to his example—that this selfless story endured for as long as it did.

Resigning from public service for good in 1951, Marshall survived the McCarthy debacle and continued to be much honored. In 1953 he received the Nobel Peace Prize, a singular experience for a person whose initial fame derived from his prosecution of the most destructive war in human history. The Nobel committee spoke of the "most constructive peaceful work . . . in this century." Thereafter, he declined in health and died in Walter Reed Hospital in October 1959.

Marshall stands out among the leaders in my study—and indeed, among the full ensemble of American leaders—in the excellence of his direct leadership of a military institution, the army, and of his direct leadership role in the larger society, as a cabinet member with two portfolios. He assumed power because of his position in an institution, but he helped redefine that institution because of the way in which he filled his role. His messages were differently nuanced for various populations, but his personal embodiment—as an individual of integrity and nonpartisanship—served him well with a range of audiences. Marshall had skills of indirect leadership as well; for example, his written summaries were much valued. But it was as an individual who could speak directly to others—usually in persuasion but sometimes in confrontation—that he made his distinctive mark.

Seldom, if ever, in American history was a man more celebrated by the vast majority of his compatriots and by citizens throughout other parts of the world.

Truman pronounced him "the greatest military man that this country ever produced—or any other country for that matter" and concluded, "The more I see and talk to him, the more certain I am he is the great one of the age." Secretary of War Henry Stimson declared, "I have seen a great many soldiers in my life, and you, sir, are the finest soldier I have ever known." *Time* magazine twice named him its "Man of the Year." And nearly all of the American military leaders and diplomats who wrote their autobiographies recalled the unique effect that Marshall's person and example had exerted on their lives.

In 1953, Marshall was asked by President Eisenhower to represent the United States at the coronation of Queen Elizabeth II, the new young sovereign of its wartime ally. As he walked into august Westminster Abbey, Marshall noted that all of the audience members, representing the entire British commonwealth, had risen to their feet. When he asked what was happening, his neighbor pointed out that the assemblage had stood to honor their distinguished guest from America. First Churchill, then Brooke, and then Montgomery, in their robes as Lords of the Realm, broke ranks with the procession to shake Marshall's hand.

Churchill, with whom Marshall had often struggled, readily praised Marshall, calling him the "noblest Roman of them all." At the end of the war he had sent Marshall a simple message: "Thank you very much." Writing at greater leisure at the end of the summer of 1945, Churchill had added: "It has not fallen to your lot to command the great armies. You have had to create them, organize them, and inspire them. . . . There has grown in my breast through all these years of mental exertion a respect and admiration for your courage and massive strength which has been a real comfort to your fellow toilers, of whom I hope it will always be recorded that I was one." Because Marshall, like Churchill, embodied so much that other human beings admired, he influenced his fellow citizens constructively, in peacetime as well as during war.

9

POPE JOHN XXIII

Rediscovering the Spirit of the Church

All human cultures have infinitely more in common . . .
hidden somewhere deep in their sources and foundations.
                                                    —Vaclav Havel

Elected only on the twelfth ballot, and already seventy-seven years of age, Angelo Giuseppi Roncalli was an improbable pope. After the lengthy reign of Pius XII, whose influence was expected to last for one hundred years, most observers anticipated a brief and uneventful interim term, bereft of an appreciable legacy. In his journal, the man who chose to call himself Pope John XXIII reflected on this paradoxical situation:

> When on 28 October 1958, the Cardinals of the Holy Roman Church chose me to assume the supreme responsibility of ruling the universal flock of Jesus Christ, at seventy-seven years of age, everyone was convinced that I would be a provisional and transitional Pope. Yet here I am already on the eve of the fourth year of my pontificate, with an immense program of work in front of me to be carried out before the eyes of the whole world, which is watching and waiting. As for myself, I feel like St. Martin, who "neither feared to die, nor refused to live."

Although John's papacy turned out to be less than five years long, it was anything but uneventful. By the time of his death on June 3, 1963, he had challenged many of the unquestioned assumptions of the church and had launched initiatives that promised to change the church's presence throughout the world. He had begun the first Vatican Council in over eighty years and had issued two momentous encyclicals. He had taken important steps to bring about rapprochement between the antagonistic superpowers. And perhaps most important, he

Pope John XXIII. UPI/Bettmann

had touched the lives and the spirits of millions of ordinary individuals, including many who had no formal connection with Roman Catholicism. Like a few other figures of our time—Mother Teresa and Nelson Mandela come to mind—Angelo Roncalli was truly beloved across national and religious boundaries.

Roncalli had no firmer claim on the papacy than any other Italian Roman Catholic who grew up in the late 1800s. Born in 1881 in Bergamo, he was the oldest son in a family of thirteen children. The family earned a living as sharecroppers, and they were very poor. Thirty relatives lived together in an extended-family arrangement. Roncalli remembered his childhood as a happy one and particularly recalled his parents' generosity:

> There was never any bread on our table, only *polenta;* yet when a beggar appeared at the door of our kitchen, when the children—twenty of them—were waiting impatiently for the bowl of *minestra,* there was always room for him, and my mother would hasten to seat this stranger alongside us.

The young Angelo was not particularly enamored of school. Strongly influenced by his uncle Zaverio and by the local parish priest Father Rebuzzini, he much preferred church. He participated in early morning mass each day and was confirmed in 1889. He later said that he could never remember a time when he did not want to be a priest. There was little surprise when, on the eve of his twelfth birthday, he entered the Bergamo seminary.

Angelo was now removed from the rest of the world. The seminary was conservative, traditional, and counter-reformational in tone. Its avowed goal was to transform young men into model members of the church and to protect them from each and every worldly temptation. When he was but fourteen, Roncalli began a lifelong journal, and we know from this record that he took the process of "spiritual formation" extremely seriously.

The first eighty pages of this journal are a record of Roncalli's thoughts and experiences during his years in the Bergamo seminary. In the journal he interweaves quotations of important passages from the Bible and other unimpeachable sources, lists of resolutions, moments of insight or grace, records of trivial faults or momentary backslidings, and direct expressions of love to Jesus and to the Immaculate Virgin Mary. Roncalli is at once chronicling what has entered his consciousness and attempting to develop a set of habits that could last a lifetime. The portrait that emerges is of a serious youth who wants desperately to think and to do the right thing.

To readers unaccustomed to someone fully fixed on his spiritual growth, the journal can appear a boring, even lifeless record. It is tedious to read lists of behaviors to be carried out every day ("Meditate for at least a quarter of an hour," "Read some passage from the devout Thomas a Kempis in Latin"), every week ("Be diligent in attending the meetings of the Sodality and the study circles," "Fast on Fridays and Saturdays in honor of the Passion of Jesus Christ and of our Lady"), every month ("Read these little Rules several times, and it will be well to do this in the company of others, so as to check your observance of them"), every year ("Before leaving the seminary for the holidays, confer with your spiritual director about how best to spend them well in the Lord"), and all the time ("Have a special love for your companions and this mutual love must come from God and tend to God," "No one shall lay his hands on another," "Do not use the intimate 'tu' when speaking with one another and do not use dialect words or, worse, immodest expressions; if you hear these used by others, go away, showing that you will not take part in such conversations," "Evil companions must be shunned like vipers," "No books must be read that have the slightest taint of immodesty," "Do not attend public spectacles").

What is one to make of this document? The philosopher Hannah Arendt, one of the most insightful commentators about Pope John XXIII, has little patience for it. She describes it as "a strangely disappointing and strangely fascinating book. . . . For pages and pages it reads like an elementary textbook on how to be good and avoid evil. . . . It consists of endlessly repetitive devout outpourings and self-exhortations . . . with only the rarest references to actual happenings." On the basis of such evidence Arendt concludes that "whatever or whoever Pope John XXIII was, he was neither interesting nor brilliant, and this quite apart from the fact that he had been a rather mediocre student and, in his later life, was without any marked intellectual or scholarly interest whatsoever."

While it is probably true that Roncalli could not discourse probingly on philosophical issues, it is misleading to consider him uninteresting or even, as Arendt suggests, "a bit stupid, not simple but simple-minded." There is considerable evidence that young Roncalli was curious about the world and, indeed, that he even got in trouble because of reading and thinking that was judged too adventurous by his superiors in the church.

In the journal we glimpse the determined efforts of a serious young adolescent to make himself—to construct himself—into an individual that he could himself respect, in the way that great religious leaders, saints, or devout ordinary individuals might command respect. Part of this trek was guided by the regimen through which all seminarians pass; but the larger part of this mission had to be assumed by Roncalli himself—he had to undertake an "apprenticeship in spirituality." As Roncalli wrote in 1922: "The life of the spirit . . . is the gradual formation of habits of thought and action, in the light of higher principles which are revealed to the soul gradually. It is a life that has to be studied and practiced like an exact science, the science of the saints."

There are probably thousands, if not millions, of young seminarians around the world—as well as many nonseminarians—who have undertaken such an effort at remaking themselves as individuals with a highly developed spiritual dimension. But most of these youths have met other fates. They have given up this effort as hopeless or as fundamentally misconceived, and have gone on to other, more secular pursuits; they have gone through the motions of piety while becoming cynical (though they may not have confronted the cynicism in themselves); or they have become insufferable prigs who have first made their own lives miserable and eventually have sullied the lives of others around them.

Roncalli stands out because he neither gave up nor became cynical nor became a narrow and doctrinaire person. As Arendt points out, he succeeded in becoming a spiritual person who was at peace with himself and who could therefore inspire others. He genuinely drew his inspiration from the life of Christ—from His simplicity and divine humanity. Roncalli sincerely came to believe that being unknown and little esteemed was most desirable. His training for a life of spirituality took the proverbial decade, and his choices were renewed daily over each subsequent decade. By evolving into the kind of person to whose ranks so many initially aspire but so few reach, he became one of a tiny circle of people who embody spirituality and thereby—in the manner of a leader—affect those with whom they interact.

For all his sanctity and devoutness, Roncalli did tire of Bergamo ("bored stiff with sermons and reading") and was happy to have the "stimulus" of Rome. He met Monsignor Giacomo Radini Tedeschi, a canon of Saint Peter's. Tedeschi, a dynamic church leader, stimulated social action in the church, such as founding and maintaining hostels and soup kitchens for the poor. Roncalli was swept up by the desire to play a more active role in the community. Liberated from Bergamo, he found his interest in learning rekindled. "I feel a need and a passionate desire to study . . . a restless longing to know everything, to study all the great authors, to familiarize myself with the scientific movement in all its manifestations," he wrote. And he spoke positively about "the forward, upward movement of Catholic culture."

Yet a strong tendency to moderate, to mediate, to avoid the embracing of a strong position was already manifest. In a journal entry of December 1903 Roncalli writes:

> I shall study new systems of thoughts. . . . Criticism for me is light. . . . But I shall always try to introduce into these discussions, in which too often ill-considered enthusiasms and deceptive appearances have a part to play, a great moderation, harmony, balance, and serenity of judgment. . . . On very doubtful points I shall prefer to keep silent, like one who does not know, rather than hazard propositions which might differ in the slightest degree from the Church's orthodoxy.

It was just as well that Roncalli was searching for an intermediate course and that he preferred moderation to modernism. As he put it as early as 1904: "In the day of judgment we shall not be asked what we have read but what we have done; not how well we have spoken but how virtuously we have lived." Just as well, because a new pope, Pius X, was on the scene, and as a committed anti-modernist, Pius had no patience for Catholic social activism. He dissolved the Catholic social action group, thus causing "the hardest moment in the life of its chaplain, Radini Tedeschi"—an action of which Roncalli was to say that "it came like a thunderbolt in a clear sky." In an ironical turn of events, Tedeschi was reassigned as a bishop in the provincial diocese of Bergamo, and Roncalli, now twenty-four, was appointed as his secretary.

Just as Alfred Sloan, Jr., had learned about corporate America in his stints at the Hyatt and General Motors companies, and George Marshall was immersed in military leadership in his position as senior aide to General Pershing, Angelo Roncalli learned about the inside of clerical leadership while serving as secretary to Tedeschi. His personal spiritual apprenticeship was complemented by a more public apprenticeship as a young bishop. Roncalli was very fond of Tedeschi, whom he always referred to as "My bishop." He observed with keen interest as Tedeschi took over the Bergamesque realm in an authoritative and authoritarian way. In his new position, Tedeschi determined to re-create the thrust for Catholic social action. He visited all of the churches in his district and defended the rights of workers. Yet, in Roncalli's carefully formulated view, "he did not concentrate on carrying out reforms so much as on maintaining the glorious traditions of his diocese and interpreting them in harmony with the new conditions and needs of the time."

This statement communicates an important insight for Roncalli, one that remained with him and, in fact, was to inspire his own papacy half a century later. He concluded that one should be able to remain a loyal Catholic and adhere to traditions, and yet at the same time take into account changing historical and contemporary situations. He saw no need to activate disturbing reformist rhetoric. In later years his touchstone *aggiornamento*—often translated as "renewal" or "updating"—represented an effort to capture this sensibility of continuity in change.

During this time of fierce debate within the church about the acceptability of new ideas, especially those of a more social activist or socialistic tenor, Roncalli experienced the most severe testing of his own position. Taking an intransigent stance toward the newer intellectual winds, Pius X had issued an encyclical called *Pascendi,* which promised instant excommunication for anyone tainted with modernism. Roncalli, well aware of this policy, retreated and took refuge in the study of history, where precedents for a reform effort might lie. And, as if to draw inspiration, he undertook a decades-long study of Saint Charles Borromeo, who had presided over a religious renewal in the wake of the sixteenth-century Council of Trent.

Nonetheless, Roncalli did not escape unscathed from the modernist/antimodernist contretemps. A brouhaha surrounded the writings of the French historian Louis Marie Olivier Duchesne, whose *History of the Early Church* had been viciously attacked by an associate of Pius X and then placed on the index of proscribed readings. Members of the diocese of Bergamo were thought to be sympathetic to Duchesne, and Pius himself declared: "In no other diocese has Duchesne's *History* been so widely diffused and praised." Roncalli was admonished by Cardinal Gaetano De Lai, a close associate of Pius, to be careful in the teaching of Scripture.

Roncalli had not taught Scripture and considered this to be a case of mistaken identity. But when he protested to De Lai, the latter revealed to the young Roncalli the real reason for his chastisement:

> According to information that has come my way, I knew that you had been a reader of Duchesne and other unbridled authors, and that on certain occasions you had shown yourself inclined to that school of thought which tends to empty out the value of tradition and the authority of the past.

Roncalli was extremely upset. He wrote out many drafts of a projected response to De Lai. Finally, he posted a letter in which he denied under oath all the charges against him:

> I have never read more than 15 to 20 pages—and even then just as a sampler. . . . I have therefore *not read a single line* of Duchesne's history trans-

lated by [Nicola] Turchi and never had them in my hands or among my books . . . never read a single modernist book, pamphlet, or review, except for Fogoazzoro's *Il Santo* that I flicked through before it was condemned.

Roncalli learned from this brush with punitive authority that he needed to be cautious and keep any strongly held opinions to himself. Direct confrontations à la Pershing-Marshall were simply inconceivable in the church of the day. As Roncalli confessed in his journal a few years later: "It is my nature to talk too much. . . . I will be more and more careful to rule my tongue. I must be more guarded in the expression of my opinions, even with persons of my own household." At the same time, he could not hide his disapproval of those who denounced others with un-mitigated and ill-considered ferocity. As he put it: "The truth and the whole truth had to be stated, [but] I could not understand why it had to be accompanied by thunderbolts and stormclaps from Mount Sinai rather than by the calm and seren-ity of Jesus on lakeside or mountain." He felt that one should find ways of marking errors without devastating those who committed errors.

Reflecting on this difficult encounter, Roncalli searched for a more harmo-nious middle way. He would not identify with the judgmental people such as De Lai, nor with iconoclasts such as Duchesne. Instead, he would maintain his tra-ditional values while showing tolerance for those who might choose a less con-ventional path. As he was to write in 1938: "I can work in my own style, that is in the style of a Church, that is both teacher of all and always modern according to the demands of the times and the places."

The years following his stint in Bergamo were momentous ones for the world, and, like most of his contemporaries, Roncalli was deeply affected by the First World War, the worldwide depression, the rise of fascism in Italy and Ger-many, and the Second World War. During the early decades of the century, Roncalli had a series of postings. In the First World War he was first a sergeant in the medical corps and then a chaplain. He remained in Rome in the early 1920s as a part-time historian and as the director of an organization for the sup-port of foreign missions. Drawing on talents that had been nurtured, he gained a reputation at the time as a forceful speaker and a potential leader. Roncalli was stationed as an archbishop in Bulgaria from 1925 to 1935, and he then was as-signed to Turkey and Greece during the Second World War. In 1944, he was given the delicate assignment of serving as the first postfascist Vatican ambassa-dor in France and dealing with bishops who had been Nazi collaborators. In 1952, he entered what was putatively to have been his last assignment, as the pa-triarch of Venice.

From the specifications of his various assignments, one can infer something of the way in which Roncalli was regarded within the Vatican hierarchy. Clearly, he was not seen as prodigious; his position in Bulgaria was a backwater assign-ment, and he remained there for a long period. Turkey and Greece called for considerable diplomacy, particularly during the war years when the Balkan and Mediterranean areas were fiercely contested. It was doubtless Roncalli's success with various factions—or, at any rate, his ability to avoid debacles—that dictated his assignment to the vital but fragile Parisian nunciate. And it was fitting that, as his career was drawing to a close, he was assigned the attractive seat of Venice, close to his birthplace.

Given the unimpressive, timid record of the Catholic Church during the period leading to and including the Second World War, the question arises about Roncalli's own stance and activities during this time. The record is not complete. I think it is fair to say that Roncalli had few, if any, misgivings about Mussolini and fascism, but that he was distraught about the rise of Hitler, the turn to total war, and the effort to exterminate the Jews.

So far as can be determined, Roncalli did not venture beyond the position of the church as a whole. Roncalli may have helped save the lives of a large number of Jews in Turkey—perhaps as many as twenty-four thousand—during the war. But it is also part of the record that Roncalli felt he could not go further than he did and that he was far too credulous of the line fed to him by the German diplomat Franz von Papen. At one later point he said somewhat forlornly:

> Could I not, should I not, have done more, have made more of a decided effort and gone against the inclinations of my nature? Did the search for calm and peace, which I considered to be more in harmony with the Lord's spirit, not perhaps mask a certain unwillingness to take up the sword?

In general, he seems to have been willing to find solace from, and to hide behind, his religious face: "How I dislike politics! And nationalism is a real curse for a nation, when religion serves as its tool! We Catholics are blessed in finding in our religion an incentive to patriotism but no pretext for dominating other people."

What of Roncalli more generally during this period? Most of the time he apparently was at peace with himself, and he noted: "My own happy nature, which is a great gift from God, has kept me immune from those afflictions which accompany daring and generous spirits who hurl themselves like living flames into their zealous labor for souls." He did not mind getting old and was gratified that he felt less prey to the temptations of the flesh as he aged. Yet an occasional word or phrase from his journal reveals that he was not altogether pleased with his own relation to the powers of the church. In Bulgaria he referred to "many trials . . . which are not caused by the Bulgarians . . . but by the central organs of ecclesiastical administration." And he noted: "This is a form of mortification and humiliation that I did not expect and which hurts me deeply." He wrote at another point: "I feel quite detached from everything, from all thought of advancement of anything else. I know I deserve nothing and I do not feel any impatience. It is true, however, that differences between my way of seeing situations on the spot and certain ways of judging the same things in Rome, hurt me considerably; it is my only real cross." And he confessed in a note: "My ministry in Greece is once more beset with difficulties. For this reason I must love it more."

And what of the years immediately preceding his papacy? In his first speech in Venice, Roncalli declared characteristically that he would "stress what unites rather than what divides." He traveled widely both inside and outside the diocese. He wrote lengthy pastorals that, in retrospect, can be seen as preparation for the encyclicals he would issue as pope. More generally, he showed—after thirty years abroad—that he could handle a complex Italian diocese with efficiency, diplomacy, and even a certain flair.

After Pope Pius XII died, nearly half of the cardinals who journeyed to Rome to select the pope were actually older than the seventy-seven-year-old Roncalli. Hardly looking for change, they expected a continuation of the restrained policies of the much-admired Pius XII. They had come to view Roncalli as an amiable person—a safe choice—who would be liked by lay Catholics and pose no threat to their main concerns: the power of the Vatican curia and the hegemony of the established church doctrines. Roncalli himself did not campaign for the position—one might speculate that he had not foreseen the papacy in his lifeline—and seemed genuinely surprised at his selection.

Roncalli's first act as pope—choosing his name—signaled that he was not as predictable or as pliable as traditionalists might have wished. Spurning the names chosen by his immediate predecessors, he instead went back to the name of John, which had not been used for six hundred years. In selecting the name, he referred to two saints—John the Baptist, who "prepared the way of the Lord," and John the evangelist of Christ. He also pointed out additional motivations: John was also the name of his father, the person to whom the church where he had been baptized had been dedicated, and the name of innumerable cathedrals in the world. And he invoked the words of the Apostle John: "My children, love one another." Then, as if to tease the men who had chosen him, he pointed out that John was the most frequently chosen name for popes, that there had been many Johns whose terms were mostly undistinguished and mostly brief, and that the most recent employer of the name had been the antipapal Pope John XXII of Avignon.

Despite his age, the new Pope John XXIII made it clear from the first that his would be an active papacy. Perhaps, indeed, he felt freer than a younger man to "be himself," to leave administration to others, and to focus on the big picture. It was as if he had paid his dues over the years and had now been unleashed to act as he desired and to express his long-held but seldom-expressed views. Unlike his immediate predecessor, he ventured outside the Vatican walls to visit many shrines, parishes, hospitals, prisons, and other community institutions. Continuing many recently instituted liturgical reforms, he appointed fifty-two cardinals (as many as had been enthroned at the time of his election), canonized ten saints, issued eight encyclicals, and participated actively in negotiations for the release of church fathers held under Communist rule. An austere and hieratic church father had been replaced by a fat and genial uncle. Pope John XXIII's warm, friendly, open manner was immediately apparent to the faithful around the world, and he indeed was seen—and wished to be seen—as the humble and responsive "universal shepherd" of a flock of nine hundred million Catholics.

But, shortly after the beginning of his reign, Pope John raised the most controversy and ultimately exerted his greatest influence by convening the Second Vatican Council—the first such council since 1869–1870 and only the twentieth in church history. In Pope John's own words, the council came as "an inspiration which struck us, in the humility of our heart, like an unexpected and irresistible command." Subsequent historical studies have revealed that the idea had a more gradual origin, dating back to Pope John's earlier studies and writings, as well as to an impulse of his predecessor's; but the decision to convert a possibility into actuality may well have felt as spontaneous as is suggested by Pope John's testimony. Moreover, an important story such as the saga of a Vatican Council benefits from a decisive beginning.

Everyone realized that a gathering of church leaders from all over the world, representing many colors and many shades of faith, could have multiple purposes and numerous possible outcomes. Indeed, the uncertainty surrounding the first such convening in almost a century was part of the reason that many church leaders were nervous about Pope John's plan. The pope believed that the council should be a time of reaffirmation and renewal, and he felt that church leaders should look back to the founding ideas of Christian life—the key beliefs, rituals, and practices. At the same time, they should strive to understand the times in which they lived, the new demands and forces, and the ways in which the church might best meet them, while remaining true to its core doctrines.

Pope John did not see the council as an occasion to discuss or reformulate Catholic doctrine or, less still, to issue new condemnations; rather, he wanted to join other Catholics in reformulating truths in contemporary terms and determining how to explain these ideas in pastoral terms. He and his closest associates prepared assiduously for the council, appointed many commissions and secretariats, and determined seventy issues or "schemata" for discussion. When told that it would not be possible to get a council of this magnitude ready by 1963, Pope John reportedly answered, "All right, we'll have it in 1962."

An especially important element of this renewal was ecumenism. Pope John felt that the Roman Catholic Church should work closely and synergistically not only with the other Catholic churches but also with the "separated brethren" of other Christian denominations. He established a Secretariat for Christian Unity, which he hoped would become a permanent part of the Holy See. When he met with Protestants, Pope John made it a point to seat himself on the same level as the other delegates, not on his customary throne. And he even stepped outside Christianity by meeting with the head of the Shinto faith and with groups of Jewish leaders.

Pope John anticipated that the church fathers would find themselves in disagreement on many issues. But this state of affairs did not in itself disturb him. Indeed, he welcomed open discussion and respectful debate—"holy liberty"—among all the bishops in attendance. Recapping the first session of the council, he said: "There existed a sharp divergence of views. Such difference of opinion can be disturbing at times but it is no cause for surprise. In fact it was providential, for it served to clarify issues, and to demonstrate . . . the freedom of the sons of God." When he found that divergent opinions could not readily be reconciled, he arrived at the shrewd move of constituting a special commission that would comprise equal numbers of members from the competing perspectives. A supercommission was "to coordinate the work of the various commissions and determine more clearly what direction their work [should] take, having regard to the general aims and intentions of the Council as a whole." The legitimation of such a process of debate and consultation, including representatives of rival points of view, proved to be as important as the actual conclusions that were eventually reached. (It is reminiscent of similar measures introduced by Margaret Mead with respect to cross-cultural study, by George Marshall with respect to new officers on his staff, and by Alfred Sloan, Jr., with respect to the different General Motors stakeholders.)

In only a few other individuals (Marshall comes to mind) were the means and the messages more closely and more convincingly intertwined than in the person of Pope John. To the members of his church, Pope John decried bureaucratic intrigue among those at the top of the authority structure and called for a return to the simple teachings of Christ. The church had to go back to its roots, which acknowledged the essential worth of all human beings. Within the church, there were not to be privileged groups or orders; as he put it, the pope's love was not to be any greater for Italy than for the Philippines.

Pope John emphasized the story that he had been creating over many decades. It was possible, the pope believed, to be both traditional and modern. The church's ideas and practices were exemplified in the lives of Christ and the saints. But the church could not endure and remain meaningful unless it came to grips with the facts and conditions of the modern age, whether they were nuclear weapons, the cold war, or poverty in the third world. From its position of moral authority, the church had a special role to play in addressing these conditions and, when possible, in attempting to ameliorate them.

Pope John spoke as well to a wider religious community that extended beyond the church. He believed that individuals had to be seen first as human beings and then as members of religious groups. There was a place in the world for individuals of all religions, creeds, and philosophies, and the pope felt kinship to them all. Pointedly, he addressed his encyclicals to "all men of good will." Pope John expressed these views in his statements to the council, in other speeches and writings, and above all in two important encyclicals. In *Mater et Magistra*, of

May 1961, he embraced many social reforms, including assistance to third world nations, living wages for all workers, more equitable economic policies, and other socialist measures that promised to help individuals. In *Pacem in Terris,* of March 1963, he called for an end to the nuclear arms race, regulation of national affairs in the interest of humankind, and reconciliation between East and West—between the capitalistic and the communistic systems.

The very articulation of these ideas represented a distinct departure for a papacy in the middle of the twentieth century. Pope John's startlingly direct stories were innovative in the precise sense in which I have been using the term. He took ideas and themes that had long existed within Christianity—indeed, since the time of Christ—and gave them fresh expression and new meaning. His calls for love, a respect for all individuals, aid to those who were less fortunate, and a diminution of political and religious tensions were all in the spirit of a broader, more inclusionary sense of human identity. Perhaps not surprisingly, many of these themes spoke more directly to common people—to the unschooled mind—than they did to individuals who were searching for more complex messages or who had a stake in maintaining the status quo. Yet, Pope John's stories were not restricted to the simple-minded; like the most effective themes and allegories of the great religions, they could speak to, and be meaningfully interpreted by, individuals of different levels of sophistication.

It was not easy for Pope John's opponents to articulate counterstories, because they did not wish to appear ungenerous and unloving. Yet, many conservatives at various places in the church hierarchy were threatened by what Pope John was saying. If one broadened the notion of what it meant to be a good Catholic, a good Christian, a good human being, then those who had been singled out for this fidelity to a particular religious creed or set of practices could no longer claim uniqueness. By being inclusionary, Pope John was excluding "core Catholics" from their special status. Moreover, as had happened in Pope John's own youth, moves toward social justice were widely interpreted as radicalizing attempts, which might cause instability and undermine church traditions. The counterstory asserted that it was better to keep things as they were, rather than risk introducing chaotic changes in practice or in the hierarchy.

Pope John's leadership capacities inhered at least as much in the way he led his life. Recalling the pope, Dominican Yves Congar declared: "The opening toward the world and toward 'the others' was shown more by concrete gestures and by the very dynamics of this style, which was altogether pastoral, human, and highly evangelical, than in John XXIII's speeches." His gentle boldness empowered others in the church. One bishop at the council commented, "We heard men dare to say things we'd privately been thinking for a long time."

Pope John felt himself to be just another human being, and not a special member of a privileged elite. He liked to speak directly to people, and his humanity shone through. He related as much to bishops and the laity as to cardinals, and he refused to lash out at individuals just because he believed them to be in error. A person's honesty and love were more important than his or her membership—or nonmembership—in any particular order. Pope John accumulated no earthly possessions—he gave away everything that he received and, indeed, possessed less than twenty dollars' worth of material goods when he died.

As happens with other saintly individuals, stories about Pope John abounded, both during his life and after his death. While it is not possible to verify them all, in the aggregate they certainly create the impression of a human being without a shred of pretense—one who felt completely at peace with others and with himself. They could not have been told of other twentieth-century popes. I content myself here with citing just a few illustrative remarks:

- "I always try to show people that I am a regular person. I have two eyes, a nose—a very big one—a mouth, two ears, and so on. And yet people still sometimes remain rigid and non-communicative."

- To a group of prisoners: "Since you could not come to me, I came to you."

- About an elderly peasant woman: "She should get as close [to me] as [did] the King of Jordan."

- To a diplomat: "I know you are an atheist, but won't you accept an old man's blessing?"

- To a workman who had sworn in his presence: "Must you do this? Can't you say 'merde' as we do too?"

- To those who did not want him to be seen during his daily walks around the papal gardens: "Why should people not see me? I don't misbehave, do I?"

- To a young visiting priest who was very nervous: "My dear son, stop worrying so much. You may rest assured that on the day of judgment Jesus is not going to ask you: And how did you get along with the Holy Office?"

- To himself, when he realized that he was feeling overburdened by the responsibilities of the papacy: "Giovanni, don't take yourself that seriously!"

Pope John was also prepared to play for high stakes. In the tense years of the construction of the Berlin Wall and the Cuban missile crisis, Pope John sensed that John Kennedy and Nikita Khrushchev, the leaders of the rival superpowers, could be reached as human beings. The church was one major power in the world that could possibly transcend distance and ideology. Responding to a feeler from Khrushchev, he said, "The Lord is making use of this humble instrument which is my person in order to move history." Drawing on an intermediary, the American journalist Norman Cousins, Pope John was able to establish a communication link between the leaders of the superpowers. Both Kennedy and Khrushchev respected and admired Pope John. This emerging bond of trust led to the release of a Ukrainian metropolitan, Jusyf Slipyi, who had long been held in Russia; it contributed as well to a general lessening of tensions and culminated in the signing, shortly after Pope John's death, of a nuclear nonproliferation treaty. Through these actions, the pope was impressing upon the world a story that it had not yet understood: Representatives of the world's major antagonistic governmental entities would have to find ways of working together if we are to avoid nuclear annihilation and build a lasting peace.

Pope John was often able to achieve his goals without the support of those holding the most power in the church. The ultraconservative Catholic press second-guessed much of what he said and what he did; he was called "irresponsible" and "politically unprepared." The curia of the Vatican was as conservative as any entrenched bureaucracy and had had many hundreds of years of practice in undermining popes who had attempted to thrust in untested directions. Pope John was well aware of this tendency and devoted much effort to placating the curia, when possible, and to overpowering it, when necessary. He deliberately couched his first speeches in very cautious terms, as if to reassure the curia; he drew his first appointments principally from the moderate and the conservative wings of the Vatican; and he took traditional positions on certain flashpoint issues, as in opposing contraception and the entry of women into the ministry.

But when it seemed that the curia might deter Pope John from his most important goals, he was ready to take them on. Attacking an uncooperative biblical commission, he wrote his secretary of state: "The time has come to put a stop to this nonsense. Either the Biblical Commission will bestir itself, do some proper work and by its suggestions to the Holy Father make a useful contribution to the needs of the present time, or it would be better to abolish it and let the Supreme Authority replace it in the Lord by something else." And when he found that he had been deliberately misquoted by conservative associates, he simply quoted himself directly from the unbowdlerized original text.

When Pope John learned in late 1962 that he had terminal cancer, he redoubled his efforts. He continued the work on the council, as well as his efforts at international mediation. He relied even more heavily on an informal network of religious and diplomatic associates. And he voiced concern that his own work within the church and on the international scene might be undone. Speaking to a visiting father, Roberto Tucci, on February 9, 1963, he said:

> You see, my dear Father, I know that I have a very short time to live. Therefore
> I must be more than ever careful to weigh all undertakings in order to avoid

that the conclave which meets after my death is "against me" and thereby makes a choice that might destroy what I have tried to begin building.

Pope John XXIII was right to be concerned about the immediate fate of his legacy. Indeed, shortly after his death, he was called by one cardinal "the greatest disaster in recent ecclesiastical history—the last five hundred years." He was followed in office by his chosen successor, Cardinal Giovanni Battista Montini—Pope Paul VI—who tried to carry on his work with respect to the internationalization of the church. Yet many of his more liberal tendencies in church practice and in interpretations of doctrine were allowed to become attenuated, both through the efforts of subsequent popes and through the naturally conservative instincts of church leaders throughout the world. Even the most inclusionary figures eventually generate opposition, usually from those who want to feel special; and not infrequently that opposition suffices to undo a progressive tendency.

The legacy of Pope John XXIII has proved most enduring through the messages embodied in his own person. Pope John showed the world that the leader of the church need not be austere, distant, and hieratic; he could feel genuine affinities to ordinary individuals, and this feeling could be reciprocated. He demonstrated that the leadership of the Catholic Church need not thwart affinity with other churches—nor even with atheistic communism. In so doing, he made a tangible contribution in forging closer ties among sects, peoples, and even warring superpowers.

Pope John's simplicity was complete, pure, and eloquent. Ernesto Balducci wrote in *The Utopia of Pope John XXIII* that "the essential modernity of Pope John, which the world has grasped with immediate intuition, lay in the total sincerity with which he was able to accept the triumph of life, that of the child as well as that of the astronaut." Just as first Angelo, and later John, attempted to revive the spirit of Christ, many of those inspired by him have sought to keep alive the spirit and the message of Pope John XXIII.

In this part of the book, I have examined prototypical leaders of three contemporary estates. I have surveyed a wide geographical area, from middle America to modern Rome to the global reaches of a world war—and a sizeable span of estates, from the American corporation, to the U.S. Army, to the largest religious establishment in the world. The three leaders all attained their positions gradually by dint of their achievements in a variety of "trial" postings and the increasing respect that their close colleagues held for them. As members of a hierarchical organization, they confronted authority figures when necessary, but not gratuitously. Once in high office, they had to determine and depict what it meant to lead their respective organizations at a rapidly changing moment in history. They each confirmed certain traditional norms and yet helped to redefine the nature of their institutions in their times. And while each was placed in a somewhat competitive state vis-à-vis others in their chosen estate, they strove for broader and more encompassing definitions of their particular realms.

Alfred Sloan, Jr., described what it meant to live in corporate America; George Marshall explained the importance of a trained and devoted armed service; and Pope John XXIII portrayed the place of the church in the world of developing countries and nuclear warfare. Even more than by the stories they told, however, these men exerted an impact because of how they embodied the stories. Sloan was effective because of his incomparable knowledge about his corporation and his abiding interest in its members; Marshall affected others because of his embodiment of the quintessential soldier, patriotic and yet nonpartisan; Pope John showed the modern world what it was like to live as a true Christian. In this way each man's identity virtually merged with the institution whose essence he was trying to convey to its members and to the wider community.

Sloan, Marshall, and Pope John are alike in one other way. Each was placed in charge of a large, well-established hierarchical organization. Because of their status, they had the legitimacy to direct their enterprises; and any ceding of authority, any decision to avoid browbeating, was voluntary. To some extent their stories came with their positions, and their embodiment assumed relatively greater import. The prior existence of an organization provided them with certain staff support and relieved them of the necessity of constructing an organization afresh and worrying about its existence from one moment to the next. Also, each of the institutions has certain privileging features: the corporation can raise new moneys from stockholders and has various protections under the law; the military has numerous privileges during time of war and rarely has its legitimacy questioned; the church has significant financial resources and considerable spiritual authority as well.

In these respects, the leaders of established institutions differ sharply from the individuals I describe in the next two chapters. Neither Eleanor Roosevelt nor Martin Luther King, Jr., held elective or appointed office; they evolved into leaders because of the explanations—the apologias and the visions—that they had arrived at for their own lives and times, and the ways in which they were able to communicate those evolving explanations to others. Roosevelt and King are, in my terms, self-anointed leaders of nondominant groups—and in this respect they form a striking contrast with other leaders in this book.

10

ELEANOR ROOSEVELT
Ordinariness and Extraordinariness

What are the defining characteristics of a leader? At the top of the list, in my view, is the ability to inspire his own generation and generations to come, with a zest for living and a sense of high possibilities for his country and mankind in the future.

—George W. Ball

Each of the leaders examined so far in this study chose a career in which it was possible to occupy a role of leadership. The scholars Margaret Mead and J. Robert Oppenheimer could expect to exert influence on others in their chosen disciplines: they were able to build upon their positions as a leading anthropologist and a leading physicist, respectively, to move on to grander stages of "direct leadership." From an early age, Robert Maynard Hutchins sought to be a leader in higher education and he never strayed far from this role. The trio of leaders examined in the previous chapters had each joined a "major estate" by their early twenties and had embarked on paths that ultimately propelled them to the top of their chosen profession.

In their own ways, Eleanor Roosevelt and Martin Luther King, Jr., were both ambitious individuals. But the particular paths that their ambitions would take could not have been assumed, for the niches that they ultimately came to occupy had not existed in the societies in which they had grown up. They had to create a role, a powerful story, and an audience that would be receptive. In the psychiatrist Ronald Heifetz's terms, they sought to attain leadership even though they lacked formal authority.

Neither Roosevelt nor King ever achieved their youthful aspirations. In her early twenties, Eleanor wanted only to be an ideal wife who was supporting her talented and ambitious husband, Franklin, and a superb mother who was raising

Eleanor Roosevelt. UPI/Bettmann

an exemplary brood of children. In his early twenties, King wished above all to preside over a successful ministry, as his father had, before moving on to a teaching position at a prestigious university.

From her vantage point as the wife of a governor, then as the wife of a president, and finally as a woman on her own, Eleanor Roosevelt promoted a range of issues in which she strongly believed. She also showed Americans— and particularly American women—that it was possible for a woman-without-portfolio to exert a significant influence in the national and international political realms.

From his vantage point as the most prominent African American of his time, Martin Luther King, Jr., brought attention, first, to the plight of black* Americans and, ultimately, to the situation of other dispossessed peoples in America and throughout the rest of the world. Like Roosevelt, he embodied the principal stories to which he brought attention; and like Roosevelt, he arrived at conclusions largely as a result of reflections on the events of his own life.

In reviewing the paths taken by Roosevelt and King, one encounters many familiar themes. But because these individuals ultimately provided leadership in roles that had not existed before, they also deviated in instructive ways from other leaders of their time. They could not simply embody stories that were already known. Rather, as they began to discover their audiences, and as their audiences began to discover them, a delicate and elaborate set of interactions commenced. More so than in the case of other leaders, Roosevelt and King found themselves reinventing themselves from time to time—partly in response to the stirring events of their own lives, partly in response to reactions from the most responsive members of their audiences.

In the end, both figures aroused strong reactions—negative as well as positive. Not only were they providing sharp and challenging visions of personal and group identity; more provocatively, they were suggesting that neglected groups actually *had* identities, ones that all citizens needed to respect. I consider Roosevelt and King to be "leaders of nondominant groups"—"leaders of the dispossessed"—advocates for populations of Americans who in a significant sense had remained invisible to the self-styled dominant population. Archie Bunker, the television character of the 1960s who was generally seen as a bigot with redeeming features, inadvertently provided a pithy summary of this point. During an episode of *All in the Family,* he once declared: "Until Eleanor Roosevelt discovered 'em, we didn't know the colored folks existed."

Eleanor Roosevelt had one of the most remarkable childhoods of her time. Born in 1884 into a New York family of great wealth and political and social standing, she had available more opportunities as a woman than virtually any other woman of her generation. Yet Eleanor** had a singularly unhappy childhood, one that would have left any child scarred, if not permanently disabled.

Her parents, Anna Hall Roosevelt and Elliott Roosevelt, looked like an ideal couple. Eleanor opens her autobiography with the sentence: "My mother was one of the most beautiful women I have ever seen." Two pages later she declares: "With my father I was perfectly happy. . . . [He] was the love of my life." Yet,

---

*In this and the following chapter, I generally use the word *black* because of its increasingly common use during King's lifetime.

**To avoid confusion about which of the many Roosevelts is under discussion, I often use first names in this chapter.

beneath the glittering surface of the extended Roosevelt clan lurked extensive pathology. In the hard phrase of the biographer Blanche Wiesen Cook, "The Victorian world of her father, and subsequently her young uncles and aunts, involved alcoholism, adultery, child molestation, rape, [and] abandonment." Eleanor's mother, a cold and severe woman, died of diphtheria when her daughter was eight. Her well-meaning but increasingly self-absorbed, disturbed, and dissipated father died when Eleanor was ten. Until her teenage years, the orphaned Eleanor was raised, along with her siblings, by her maternal grandmother.

Eleanor Roosevelt remembered herself as an unattractive, almost ugly duckling child who felt chronically inferior to other members of her family, was always fearful, and craved praise and security. She disparaged her own psychological state ("the ability to think for myself did not develop until I was well on in life"), as well as her academic skills. Others noted that Roosevelt's height and sobriety made her seem adultlike and that she was often treated as if she were no longer a child. (Her mother nicknamed her "Granny.") Nonetheless, by the end of her elementary schooling, she was already beginning to show a command of language, an interest in moral issues, and other signs of leadership that would mark her in later life.

The most important event for Roosevelt's future development was her attendance, from 1899 to 1902, at the Allenswood School in suburban London. The headmistress of the school, Mlle. Marie Souvreste, was a remarkable person who expressed strong views about issues of the day; struck by Roosevelt's honesty and straightforwardness, the seventy-year-old Souvreste almost immediately took the young Roosevelt under her wing. Clearly attracted to each other, the two women remained close friends until Souvreste's death on March 19, 1905. Roosevelt traveled through Europe with this maternal figure, learning both about the cultural life of the Continent and about how a strong and independent woman could handle herself in a male-dominated world. Roosevelt declared without exaggeration: "Whatever I have become since had its seed in those three years of contact with a liberal mind and strong personality."

Her years abroad under Souvreste's tutelage gave Roosevelt a worldliness and a liveliness of spirit that she might otherwise never have achieved. When she returned to the United States, she immediately became involved in social service. It was the Progressive Era in Washington, with her uncle Theodore Roosevelt as a dynamic president, and it was the era of social reform in New York City, where the Roosevelt clan lived. Joining organizations such as the National Consumers' League and the Junior League, Roosevelt worked for better conditions for city dwellers, particularly those in the slums. She taught immigrant children at a settlement house on Rivington Street. Looking back on those years, Roosevelt commented: "I had been a solemn girl. My years in England had given me my first taste of being carefree and irresponsible, but my return to the United States accentuated almost immediately the serious side of life."

But such efforts in the public sphere, however absorbing and meritorious, were not meant to be the principal preoccupation of a young New York debutante. It was expected—and Eleanor did not demur—that she would soon fall in love, get married, and raise a family. Following this script, Eleanor in fact became engaged to her distant cousin Franklin Delano Roosevelt, an impressive, if somewhat superficial, Harvard undergraduate. They married in 1905, as Franklin was beginning his studies at Columbia Law School.

At age twenty-one, Eleanor would scarcely have bothered to ponder the questions of who she was and which group she belonged to. Such questions tend to arise most insistently for individuals who feel themselves marginal, distinctly outside of the comfortable mainstream. But Eleanor, both as a single person and as the new wife of Franklin, was about as much a part of the Establishment as one could get. Any thoughts of launching or leading some kind of iconoclastic enterprise would have been bizarre. It was her job now to serve her husband: "I listened to all his plans with great interest. It never occurred to me that I had any part to play. . . . I want him to feel that he belongs to someone." The wounds of her early childhood and the adventurous fling with Souvreste felt equally remote; within the Roosevelt patrician ethos, it would have been entirely inappropriate for her to speak of them, let alone dwell on them.

Though not without their surprises, their delights, and their problems, the next fifteen years did not suggest that Eleanor's life would ultimately take unusual turns—ones that would thrust her into positions of worldwide attention, approbation, and controversy. Eleanor gave birth to five children who survived past infancy. She did not have much of a flair for mothering, due no doubt to her own troubled childhood and her overly sober disposition, but she tried to learn from her mistakes and to keep her children on course. As a daughter-in-law, she had to contend with Sara Delano Roosevelt, surely one of the most dominating members of a dominant breed. Sara possessed much money and issued many opinions; she did not give Eleanor much breathing room, but Eleanor did her best to maintain a peaceful household.

Eleanor focused her surplus energies on her husband, whose career was advancing rapidly. According to the biographer Joseph Lash, Franklin had outlined to his fellow law clerks a career like his uncle Theodore's—"the state legislature, assistant secretary of the Navy, the governorship, and then, with 'any luck,' the presidency." True to this vision (and reflecting the incredible self-confidence and sense of destiny observed in other future leaders), Franklin was elected in 1910 to the New York State Legislature, and the family moved to the capital city of Albany. After Woodrow Wilson was elected president of the United States in 1912, Franklin was appointed as the assistant secretary of the navy, and the family moved to Washington. Eleanor was a supportive political wife and a tireless manager of the increasingly large family. She learned to move the small troop of

Roosevelts among the family households, including the homestead at Hyde Park, New York, the summer camp at Campobello in Maine, and the temporary home in Washington.

Through necessity, if not choice, Eleanor had placed her incipient public service interests of premarital days on hold at least temporarily. America's 1917 entry into the First World War afforded Eleanor the opportunity to serve, and she eagerly seized it. She worked at the Red Cross canteen, organized the Navy Red Cross, and supervised knitting at the Navy Department work rooms. She introduced strict food-saving procedures at home and sought to publicize this model of restraint to others. Her opinions about political matters grew increasingly liberal, and she became a supporter of women's suffrage. For the first time, she found herself able to confront more conservative family members who complained about the inconveniences of war or who longed for the days when one could purchase a substitute for oneself to avoid military conscription. Perhaps this burgeoning self-confidence, while emerging a bit late, presaged the capacity to challenge that marks leaders.

The end of the war in November 1918 might have allowed—or spurred—Eleanor to return to her role as a supportive but essentially apolitical wife. Instead, however, two dramatic events completely altered the nature of her marriage and launched her on the increasingly independent course that she was to follow for the rest of her life.

First, Eleanor discovered a cache of letters that revealed a serious romance between Franklin and Lucy Mercer, an attractive young socialite who served as Eleanor's social secretary. Eleanor had been completely trusting of her handsome and flirtatious husband, who had in recent years come home very late on many occasions; but now she held incontrovertible evidence that confirmed her worst fears. She later confided: "The bottom dropped out of my own particular world. . . . I faced myself . . . honestly for the first time. I really grew up that year." After a painful confrontation, in which all options including divorce were considered, Franklin agreed to cut off his relationship with Mercer, and Eleanor agreed to remain in the marriage. From this time forth, however, the marriage was devoid of passion—indeed it could be well, if incompletely, characterized as a marriage of convenience. Eleanor determined that she would have to gain sustenance from other relationships and activities. Franklin continued to become involved with other women and actually died twenty-five years later in the company of Lucy (by then Lucy Rutherfurd). And while it is not possible to document any physical involvement, some scholars now believe that Eleanor became intimate with a number of lesbian women and at least one or two younger heterosexual men.

The second climactic event was as dramatically public as the first was painfully private. In the summer of 1921, Franklin contracted a very serious case of polio, and it appeared doubtful that he would ever walk again. Many individuals, and particularly his mother, expected that Franklin would retire and remain as the charming but paralyzed seigneur of Hyde Park.

Eleanor threw herself into Franklin's rehabilitation with enormous energy and dedication. With perhaps unintended irony, she declared: "[The illness] made me stand on my own two feet in regard to my husband's life, my own life, and my children's training." She was determined that he would not remain an invalid. And while she was at best ambivalent about public political life, she wanted to ensure that Franklin's accomplishments would be preserved and that he would have the opportunity to reenter politics if he so wished. Eleanor was aided in these rehabilitative efforts by the journalist Louis Howe, whom the Roosevelts had known for a decade. Howe saw political genius in Franklin and was devoted to the still-young Democrat's resumption of his tremendously promising career; Howe also looked to Eleanor as an apt pupil, friend, and sustainer of Franklin.

Before studying Eleanor Roosevelt's life, I had assumed that much of her splendid career as a public figure had originated as a dress rehearsal during Franklin's term as governor of New York State (1929–1933) and during the opening years of his presidency. Once one examines the record, however, it becomes clear that Eleanor as the public eventually knew her actually came to the fore during the early 1920s and, perhaps surprisingly, during the period when her husband was too preoccupied with illness and recovery to be immersed in political matters. It was in the 1920s that Eleanor mastered the "domain of public service."

Eleanor was no stranger to the political scene, of course. The Roosevelt family had long been involved both in New York (the Hyde Park and Oyster Bay contingents) and in Washington. Eleanor had been a political wife and an observer of the scene during her husband's membership in the state legislature, his assistant secretaryship in Washington, and an ill-fated (but ultimately not damaging) run for the vice presidency in 1920.

Now, however, having gradually broken free from the dominance of her mother-in-law, Roosevelt could throw herself totally into the political process. And that is precisely what she did. During the 1920s, working closely with an impressive group of women in New York, she took on many issues that spanned the legislative agenda from health to housing to the protection of women workers. Roosevelt and her associates not only made progress in conducting research, holding hearings, and drafting bills but also supported one another personally. "Simple networks of shared work and friendship sustained many political women who struggled for change and equality in a world they were not supposed to organize, a world that constantly erected barriers."

Roosevelt came to conclude, however, that important changes could be made only through the political process, from which women had been largely excluded. (Women's suffrage had become a reality in 1920, around the time of her two major life crises.) And so Roosevelt graduated from the nonpartisan Woman's

City Club to the charged circles of New York State Democratic politics. She had learned how to research issues during her early collaborative work; now, carefully tutored by her husband and Howe, she learned (as other leaders in a democracy must learn) how to give speeches, court delegates, and count votes. Reluctantly, she learned to become direct and even confrontational with individuals who held power: "To many women, and I am one of them, it is difficult to care enough [about an issue] to cause disagreement or unpleasant feelings, but I have come to the conclusion that it must be done for a time so we can prove our strength and demand respect for our wishes."

Interest and motivation were important, but so were skills. According to the biographer Doris Kearns Goodwin, Roosevelt discovered that she had "a range of abilities she never had any idea of—remarkable organizing skills, superb judgment, practical insight, and astonishing endurance." Roosevelt's talents were soon recognized by her contemporaries, and she held offices in a number of non-political and political groups. The historian Elizabeth Perry declares that "as a result of her experiences in the women's political networks of New York City, she had become an accomplished, widely known and admired public figure in her own right." It has even been suggested that during the 1920s Eleanor was better known in New York political circles than her formidable husband.

And so Roosevelt completed her apprenticeship in the political realm and became a significant political figure in her own right. Despite having been brought up to think of herself in auxiliary terms consistent with traditional views of women's roles, she was becoming a major actor on the political scene. The innovative story that she told her associates—as well as skeptical citizens—was that a woman could become a major participant in liberal democratic politics; and she more perfectly embodied this story with every passing year.

Paradoxically, just about the time that Eleanor had found her political voice and bearings, Franklin was ready to return to the political scene. It was a most impressive recovery. He was elected governor of New York State in 1928, was re-elected by an overwhelming margin in 1930, and was the victor, by a landslide, in the watershed presidential election of 1932.

Whether during a time of prosperity (1928), depression (1932), isolationism (1936), fears of war (1940), or all-out conflict (1944), Franklin showed himself to be a tremendously appealing—indeed, singularly charismatic—figure to American voters, and, increasingly, a hero to many overseas. Still paralyzed from the waist down, he had triumphed over his illness, and his confidence gave hope to millions of individuals. Not incidentally, he was also a powerful analyst of the political scene, a shrewd judge of people, a brilliant orator, and an intuitive, masterly balancer of political forces. His formidable native talents had been complemented by a decade of careful study of American political realities, and he was now the consummate political figure of his time.

While Eleanor clearly admired Franklin's skills and had learned from him how to observe and analyze human situations, she secured remarkably little pleasure from his political victories. It was as if they had happened to someone else, a casual acquaintance, rather than someone with whom she had chosen—and then chosen again, after two searing crises—to share her life. One factor in this lack of engagement is that Eleanor, despite her gifts, did not really enjoy the hurly-burly life of politics, the need for composure, or the inevitable maneuvering and secrecy; and she actively disliked the life of an American political spouse, who was (and is) denied privacy. After Franklin's successful bid for the presidency, she declared: "I never wanted to be a President's wife and I don't want it now." But another factor must have been at work as well. Quite possibly, Eleanor was so hurt by the waning of their marital passion that she could not gain any direct pleasure from Franklin's achievements. More than one observer has suggested that Eleanor Roosevelt invested the passion that she could no longer direct toward her husband personally to the mission to which he was dedicated and to the many causes that they both supported.

Indeed, once Franklin was ensconced in powerful executive positions, to which he dedicated himself totally, Eleanor strove valiantly to construct her own life. Most important to her during the late 1920s and early 1930s were the activities that she could call her own—her lecturing, writing, occasional radio programs, and espousal of causes to which she felt personally close. She began to lecture on literature, history, and current events at the Todhunter School in New York City. No doubt this stint gave her the chance to transmit to teenage girls some of the lessons that she had gained during her own adolescence at Allenswood. And with two close friends, Nancy Cook and Marion Dickerman, she built her own home and a small furniture factory at Val-Kill Creek, a few miles away from the mansion at Hyde Park. These geographical and spiritual retreats meant a great deal to Eleanor, particularly at times when she and her husband were constantly in the public eye.

By the time Franklin was elected president, Eleanor had become a person very different from the young mother and housewife of 1910. To those who knew her well, she was not only an accomplished politician but also an independent person who no longer took orders from her mother-in-law and did not kowtow to her husband. She was now able to confront others in her personal and her professional contacts. In many ways, she had become the spiritual offspring of Souvreste and Howe, rather than one of the many children of the Roosevelt clan. Now, in what was perhaps her greatest challenge, she sought to become a viable first lady, on the one hand, and a person who could be faithful to her own principles, on the other.

When Franklin took the oath of office on March 4, 1933, in the midst of the country's worst recession, Eleanor could not possibly have anticipated what the next four years would be like—let alone the next twelve. She knew that she wanted to maintain some independence, but she also understood that such autonomy would prove elusive. She knew that she would be expected to occupy symbolic roles—national hostess, national figurehead—and she dreaded that ritualistic part of her new assignment. She also worried that she would no longer be able to choose issues or put forth her own (as opposed to her husband's) position on important issues. At the same time, she may well have grasped that some power was inherent in her position and that she might be able to marshal the power in personally meaningful directions.

Eleanor groped at the beginning. She attempted some public writing and broadcast formats that she eventually abandoned. She offered to be her husband's secretary, a suggestion that he wisely rejected. She took the risk of holding the first press conference ever given by a first lady, with attendance restricted to a group of women reporters, and found that platform to be effective. She sought to avoid the secret service and even undertook risky travel routes in an effort to preserve a modicum of privacy and autonomy.

These efforts sent a powerful message to the public. Just as Franklin had shown that he was willing to implement virtually any experiment that might help the nation during this perilous time, Eleanor made it clear that she would not simply stand on ceremony. The best-prepared wife of a president since Abigail Adams (one might now add, the best prepared before Hillary Clinton), she was determined to be a positive force on the national horizon. As she sought to forge a role, she was not afraid to embarrass herself—although she was extremely careful not to embarrass her husband publicly.

The Eleanor Roosevelt who emerged during the 1930s played at least four distinct roles, each with its characteristic messages, and she accomplished each with considerable distinction. In my terms, Roosevelt led directly; and while her stories were not in themselves visionary, her identity and her means of transmitting those stories were certainly innovative.

To begin with, Roosevelt was a staunch supporter of women's participation in government. Both publicly and behind the scenes, she lobbied for the inclusion of women in key positions, and she worked equally hard to make sure that women's views would come to be known and, insofar as possible, implemented. While the rate of increase of women workers was slow, more of them were placed in government agencies, ranging from venerable ones like the post office to new ones like the Works Progress Administration. The placement of women on the Democratic platform committee in 1936 was called by the *New York Times* "the biggest coup for women in years." Roosevelt's first message was "Politics must include women in significant roles."

A second role was as a public voice on behalf of liberal issues. Roosevelt had unprecedented access to the media, and she used it to the hilt. In addition to holding periodic news conferences, she wrote articles, books, and for many years a daily newspaper column entitled "My Day," which appeared in 136 news-papers. America had never seen a political woman in so public a way, and Roosevelt almost singlehandedly changed the public notion of what political spouses could know and how effectively they could marshal and affect public opinion, particularly regarding the rights of less-privileged citizens. Her second message was "America must be a progressive nation."

Her third role was as an ombudswoman who lobbied different agencies and served as a liaison between the government and the general public. Even looking at a fraction of the mail that she received alerted Roosevelt to issues that mattered to the public, and she did not hesitate to support those causes in which she believed. When she heard about a dubious policy of the Agricultural Adjustment Agency, she called up the administrator and said: "Why dump all these pigs into the Mississippi [River] when there are thousands of people in the country who are starving? . . . Why not give the meat away to them?" She also threw her weight behind certain projects, ranging from the National Youth Agency to a model community called Arthursdale. As the reporter Mary Beard wrote: "To an amazing degree, the White House has become a popular tribunal. Behind its portico the First Lady of the Land hears indulgently every case that comes before her." Roosevelt's third message was "The first lady is looking out for the interests of the forgotten American."

Eleanor's fourth role—perhaps her most important and in all likelihood her most delicate—was as an informal adviser to her husband. Eleanor always down-played her importance as a member of her husband's kitchen cabinet, and Franklin unquestionably kept his own counsel on most issues. Moreover, just as Eleanor may have tried to pressure Franklin in favor of one or another pet cause, Franklin often obviously valued Eleanor's taking publicly a position on issues like greater civil rights for minorities that, for one or another reason, he could not afford to assume.

Nonetheless, particularly during the first years of Franklin's presidency—when experimentation was the rule and domestic policies were on the front burner—there is every reason to think that Eleanor was a powerful voice in the inner discussions at the White House. She pushed regularly and hard for what she believed in, using every public and private opportunity to persuade Franklin of the merit of her perspective. Rexford Tugwell, a member of the original kitchen cabinet, minced no words:

> No one who ever saw Eleanor Roosevelt sit down facing her husband and holding his eyes firmly [and saying] to him, "Franklin, I think that you should . . . " or "Franklin, surely you will note . . . " will ever forget the experience. . . . It would be impossible to say how often and to what extent American governmental processes have been turned in a new direction because of her determination.

She was a cabinet minister, without a specific portfolio but perhaps with the most important of all portfolios—a record of service in the public interest. Eleanor articulated her fourth message as follows:

> [Franklin] might have been happier with a wife who had been completely uncritical. That I was never able to be and he had to find it in some other people. Nevertheless I think that I sometimes acted as a spur, even though the spur was not always wanted or welcome. I was one of those who served his purposes.

It is worth underscoring, sixty years later, how esteemed Eleanor Roosevelt was in her time. In nearly every poll, she emerged as the most-admired American woman and as one of the most-admired Americans of either sex, and, more often than not, she was also chosen as the most-admired woman in the world. In 1939 two-thirds of the U.S. public approved of her performance as first lady, and she was regularly named as one of the most powerful individuals in Washington. These regular tallies, which continued until her death, did not merely reflect the fact that she was well known—so were Queen Elizabeth, Mme. Chiang Kai-shek, and other first ladies. Roosevelt had succeeded in amalgamating the role of a supportive presidential wife with the persona of an independent individual who thought for herself and acted on the basis of her beliefs. Even those who often disagreed with her often indicated their admiration for her achievements. She affected not only people's beliefs about certain groups and certain issues but also their thinking about the permissible roles for an unelected figure who also was a woman.

Of course, Roosevelt was also vilified—sometimes as a means of attacking her husband, but sometimes because her strongly expressed views or her mien antagonized conservative citizens. The stories of women's roles in progressive government flew directly in the face of widespread beliefs—counterstories—that women should stay out of politics or that they should uncritically support their husbands' beliefs and programs. With some individuals objecting to Roosevelt's views, others objecting to her apparent deviations from her husband's, and some antagonized by the combination of factors, she emerged as well as a much-criticized figure. Yet, because she stood her ground, she ended up enlarging the public's notions of what a woman could achieve on the American political scene.

The events taking place in Europe eventually came to overshadow the concerns of both Roosevelts. Economic recovery and social reconstruction at home were important, but preserving democracy in a world threatened by totalitarianism became the overriding concern. The growing world crisis led to third and fourth terms for Franklin and came to occupy nearly all of his attention. In one sense, the advent of the Second World War enabled Eleanor and Franklin to join efforts in a way that they had not publicly done previously. Despite early pacifist leanings, Eleanor backed the war effort and zealously supported her husband's policies. She also believed, despite her personal wishes to escape the limelight, that he was the only person who could lead the country during the wartime. She supported him in very important ways, by undertaking exhausting visits to the troops in Asia and in Europe and performing well in assignments that Franklin physically could not execute himself.

Yet, the personal relationship between Eleanor and Franklin seems to have become even more attenuated during the last few years of Franklin's life. Eleanor had always been concerned primarily with domestic issues; she feared that the radically altered national agenda would crowd out her pet issues and limit her access to the president. Indeed, Franklin had less time and less patience for Eleanor's social views, which continued to be far more liberal than his own. He was so busy with the war effort that he had little time for any family life—even his children had to make appointments if they wished to see him. And, as already suggested, he continued to enjoy the company of other women. Eleanor made the necessary adjustment in her own lobbying, downplaying domestic concerns and focusing on the war effort, but she continued to focus on the plight of the disadvantaged at home and abroad.

When one is leading an established institution, one can assume a certain constancy in agenda and in mode of operations. Individuals without such authority find themselves much less in control of events and must be prepared to shift course, more or less radically, if they wish to retain any kind of audience and exert any kind of effect on the public. With sound political instinct, Eleanor synthesized her enduring concerns with the newly emerging priorities of war. While working tirelessly in support of the war effort, she concentrated her energies on behalf of two primary groups. First, she fought to make sure that women were active participants in all facets of war production, that they were recognized and rewarded for their efforts, and that they had support in their additional demanding roles as mothers and homemakers. Second, she struggled with equal energy for the right of black Americans to serve in the armed forces and to be treated as full Americans in their homes, at the workplace, and in public spaces. There was strong resistance to both of these causes, particularly among those who embraced an exclusionary view of America. Paradoxically, the pressures of waging "total war" may have done more to advance the status of both groups than any other single factor. Eleanor deserves enormous credit for her perseverance in these two often unpopular causes.

When Franklin died in 1945, Eleanor grieved for the country, but she seemed remarkably untouched personally. She spoke of an almost "impersonal feeling" in learning about his death and referred instead to "the sorrow of all those to whom the man who now lay dead, and who happened to be my husband, had been a symbol of strength and fortitude." She went on to say, "I am more

sorry for the people of this country and of the world than I am for ourselves."
And when the newly sworn-in president asked what he could do for her, Eleanor
responded to Harry Truman: "Is there anything we can do for *you?* Because you
are the one in trouble now."

After Franklin's death, Eleanor fully expected—and perhaps wished—to return
to a more anonymous, private existence in beloved Dutchess County, adorned
with occasional travels abroad and regular holidays with her children and grand-
children. She told one reporter that "the story [was] over" and according to
Henry Morgenthau, Jr., she questioned whether "now that she was the widow of
the President, anybody would want to hear her." If Eleanor had failed to anticipate her exacting tenure as first lady, she was completely mistaken about her
probable role and influence during the last seventeen years of her life.

At about the time that George C. Marshall had been called from retirement
to serve in the Far East, Eleanor Roosevelt was asked by President Truman to
become a member of the first U.S. delegation to the United Nations. Inas-
much as she was to be the only female member, this selection was a singular
honor, as well as a challenge. She commented, "If I failed to be a useful member, it would not be considered merely that I as an individual had failed, but
that all women had failed, and there would be little chance for others to serve
in the near future." Roosevelt performed well in this capacity for many years,
during both the Truman and the Kennedy administrations and showed herself
capable of being a tough negotiator who locked horns on more than one occasion with the Soviet Union's fearsome delegate Andrei Vishinsky. She was particularly notable as a member of the Human Rights Commission, where she
fought tirelessly for a declaration of human rights. Her contributions were
noted when "delegates rose in a standing ovation to the woman who more
than anyone else had come to symbolize the cause of human rights throughout
the world."

Roosevelt embraced many other causes beyond this official position. A regular figure on the American media, she added television appearances to her long-
time involvement with radio and print. She did not avoid the controversies that
swirled around recognition of the State of Israel and the anti-Communist hyste-
ria of the late 1940s and early 1950s. She became involved in public confrontations on such hot-button issues with New York's conservative Cardinal Francis
Spellman and with the far-right newspaper columnist Westbrook Pegler. According to the historian William Chafe, "In long letters to President Truman,
she implored the administration to push forward with civil rights, maintain the
Fair Employment Practices Committee, develop a foreign policy able to cope
with the needs of other nations, and work toward a world system where atom
bombs would cease to be negotiating chips in international relations." While
these issues were not hers alone—indeed, they were ones that she shared with

other liberal thinkers such as Robert Maynard Hutchins and Margaret Mead—Roosevelt's combination of fame, evident conviction and tenacity, and political savvy made her an effective direct leader.

Indeed, harking back to the Eleanor of the 1920s, the former first lady became deeply involved in Democratic city, state, and national politics. She was informed and well-respected, and she cared deeply about who led the party and who led the nation. She had a hot-and-cold relationship with President Truman, engaged in repeated battles with the bosses of New York's Tammany Hall, slowly distanced herself from the one-time vice president Henry Wallace, evinced a dislike of Eisenhower and Nixon, and initially expressed skepticism about John Kennedy. She was a highly visible and influential member of the new reformist group of the era, the Americans for Democratic Action, to which she was the first financial contributor. Many political figures turned to her for guidance and for mediation; she was clearly the "elder stateswoman," if not the "soul" of the Democratic Party.

But the central figure in Roosevelt's post–Second World War political life was the Illinois governor Adlai Stevenson, whom she supported in his first try for the presidency in 1952, fought valiantly for in 1956, and attempted to draft as a third-time Democratic nominee in 1960. She cherished Stevenson's style, and she loved his globally oriented, New Deal messages. Indeed, the passion that Eleanor directed toward the Groton-Princeton patrician Stevenson stands in beguiling contrast to her distanced views toward the candidacy of the Groton-Harvard patrician Franklin Roosevelt.

In her public life after Franklin's death, Eleanor continued to voice and to embody the principal messages of her earlier years. There were two major differences: she could speak in her own voice, without having to worry about the impact of her words on her husband's career; and she focused her energies increasingly on the world scene. Indeed, one can speak of a major shift in the later years of Eleanor's career, as she came to address a far wider audience on issues of global as well as national interest. Eleanor continued to call attention to the role of women in politics, the need for progressive policies, and the obligation to help the disenfranchised; but she spoke as well about newly emerged issues of disarmament, poverty, and hunger throughout the world. Just as had occurred during the Franklin Roosevelt presidency, she continued to be a thorn in the sides of less adventurous political leaders and of people who preferred the status quo.

Roosevelt slowed down after her seventy-fifth birthday and died after a lingering illness in the fall of 1962. To the end, she remained the most visible symbol of the New Deal and in many ways the major embodiment of her husband's legacy. At a memorial service, her friend Stevenson asked a question that was probably on the minds of many Americans: "What other single human being has touched and transformed the existence of so many others? What better measure is there of the impact of anyone's life?" The columnist Raymond Clapper called her simply "the most influential woman of our times."

Leaders appear in varied guises and exert different kinds of influence. Although sometimes pressured to run for office, Eleanor Roosevelt avoided any kind of official elected position; she was therefore not in a position to issue orders or to exercise formal authority. Whatever effects she exerted in her time came from the persuasiveness of what she said and from the messages embodied in the way that she lived.

I find Roosevelt's enduring effectiveness as deriving from three messages, which she embodied as much as she articulated. Although blessed initially with privilege and wealth, she struck individuals as very ordinary—plain in physical appearance, plain in dress, plain (if oddly high-pitched) in speech. Playing against the notion that leaders must somehow look the part, she convinced individuals that any person could exert influence:

> About the only value the story of my life may have is to show that one can, even without any particular gifts, overcome obstacles that may seem insurmountable. . . . In spite of a lack of special talents, one can find a way to live widely and fully. . . . I have had only three assets: I was keenly interested, I accepted every challenge and every opportunity to learn more, and I had great energy and self-discipline.

And she once said, "I do believe that even a few people who want to understand, to help, and to do the right thing, for the great number of people instead of for the few, can help."

Nowhere was the juxtaposition of ordinary and extraordinary more manifest than in Roosevelt's daily news column, "My Day," which ran for twenty-six years. She prepared the column herself every day, taking off only four days in 1945 when her husband died. The column was often mundane, as she described her impressions of a new city, events at an unremarkable meeting, or her routine experiences with family and friends. Many of the ideas expressed were simple, familiar, and, with the passage of time, frankly banal. Mixed in, unpredictably, were fascinating encounters with the celebrated and the notorious, as well as poignant and memorable (and controversial) thoughts about momentous issues. Few individuals would have been able to write a column like this; and Roosevelt did it with evident sincerity and with a desire to enlighten her fellow citizens—including the president.

Roosevelt's column offered her a unique avenue for communication with the public. Many individuals wrote to her, and she often answered in person or through her column. While she was helping to call attention to issues, and thereby participating in the shaping of American public opinion, this unprecedented "public colloquy" just as surely brought new issues to Roosevelt's attention and thus shaped the messages that she transmitted to others. Throughout her life, Eleanor's ability to listen, observe, and learn from what she had noted facilitated her growth; it was no accident that Franklin referred to her as his "eyes and ears."

Others confirmed the picture of Eleanor Roosevelt as extraordinariness in the guise of ordinariness. The columnist Bruce Bliven wrote in the *New Republic:* "I have a feeling that the country as a whole likes the sort of person Mrs. Roosevelt has in her column demonstrated herself to be—friendly, unpretentious, possessed of inexhaustible vitality, a broad interest in all sorts of people and a human wish for their welfare." And a Gloucester fisherman once summarized Roosevelt's effect: "She ain't dressed up and she ain't scared to talk."

Roosevelt also embodied the innovative message that a woman could lead a life of independent thought and action, without doing so defiantly and thus alienating the mass of the population. Many individuals questioned one or another of Roosevelt's statements or beliefs during the course of her long career; but the way in which she conducted herself, her respect for others (including members of her large and often-difficult family), and her sensitivity to the times converted many a skeptic into a believer, or at least a tolerant critic.

A final message is especially appropriate for the leader of a nondominant group: One should reach out and try to help those who are less fortunate. Roosevelt truly cared about people, and she particularly cared about the dispossessed, the marginal, and the unentitled—blacks, inhabitants of the third world, young people, Jews, women. Roosevelt did not come by these attitudes naturally— many members of her class were snobs, and her early prejudicial comments revealed her upbringing. Nor could she ever speak as a member of the dispossessed—there was inevitably a touch of noblesse oblige in what she said. But ever attentive to messages from others, Roosevelt was able to transcend the parochialism of her circle and the counterstories of her time to become a genuine advocate for those who could not press their own cause. Her insights came from her experience. As one observer put it: "The personal disasters she had surmounted had taught her that although moments of stress and danger could paralyze and destroy, they could also liberate and strengthen. . . . What distinguished such pleas for benevolence and altruism from sentimental exhortation was the psychological understandings behind them."

The ability to learn from one's experiences is vital for any leader, but particularly so for a person who has few if any role models and lacks a supporting organization. In contrast with institutional leaders, such as George Marshall or Pope John, Roosevelt was literally in the position of having to invent herself and to construct her stories anew. She could only do so by attending carefully to the meanings of her daily experiences and others' reactions to what she said and did, and by publicly describing what she was learning. As noted, she had to reinvent herself a number of times. Most Americans appreciated the extent to which the first lady had gone beyond the prejudices of her past and was addressing new groups, issues, and events on their merits. Her example emboldened many to reach out as well.

Because citizens sensed that Roosevelt was sincere—that she lived a life of charity and that she associated with individuals because of their humanity, rather than because of their social position—she strongly influenced public opinion between 1930 and 1960. She did not merely preach; she acted on her words. For example, she resigned from the Daughters of the American Revolution when that organization refused to let Marian Anderson, the black contralto, sing in Constitution Hall in 1939. In his memorial tribute, Stevenson pointed out that "she walked in the slums and ghettos of the world, not on a tour of inspection . . . but as one who could not feel contentment when others were hungry." One historian noted that "over and over again she answered pleas for help with either a sensitive letter, an admonition to a federal agency to take action, or even a personal check. . . . [She] gave herself emotionally even to distant correspondents who somehow sensed her willingness to listen to their needs."

Although Roosevelt was a bit of a moralist and naturally assumed the role of the teacher, if not the preacher, she was not sanctimonious and she dealt authentically with other human beings. An oft-repeated, though perhaps apocryphal, story illustrates well her feeling for others. On one of her trips during the war, Roosevelt had been sharing a canteen meal with some sailors. An imprudent youth had let an oath slip out. Interrupting the embarrassed silence that ensued, she asserted: "You heard the man—pass the fucking salt."

Roosevelt's key stories were broad and encompassing ones that reached beyond parochialism to a larger humanity. As embodied in the principal stories that she told, one did not need special powers to inspire others; one could fulfill one's socially prescribed roles and maintain one's own ideas and stances; one could (and needed to) learn from one's mistakes and from the parochialism of one's group; and those who were fortunate needed to come to the aid of those who were disadvantaged. Challenging selfishness and insularity, Roosevelt spoke to the more generous impulses in the population, and she often evoked a worthy response. And for every individual in the country who might have been offended by this onslaught on unbridled individualism (and at times people such as President Dwight Eisenhower were threatened or offended by Roosevelt's words and stances), many elsewhere in the world appreciated this acknowledgment of our essential membership in the wider world.

The year after Eleanor Roosevelt died, the writer and activist Betty Friedan published *The Feminine Mystique,* a book that is often regarded as the opening salvo in the modern feminist era. If one were looking for a person who occupies the same role within the women's movement that Martin Luther King, Jr., occupies within the African American community, one would presumably search among figures more recent than Roosevelt. She had come only slowly to feminist concerns, even those that in retrospect seem relatively uncontroversial, such as women's suffrage. Many of her attitudes about women's roles and women's psyches strike us today as dated and were even challenged during her time.

And yet, I feel confident about selecting Roosevelt—along with Margaret Mead and Margaret Thatcher—as a woman who played a seminal role in that rise of women's consciousness (and men's consciousness of women) that has occurred in many nations during the twentieth century. Roosevelt spoke to women, and spoke about women, in a way that made sense to audiences in her time. She thought about dimensions of leadership and said: "Women who are willing to be leaders must stand out and be shot at. More and more they are going to do it and more and more they should do it. . . . Every political woman needs to develop a skin as thick as a rhinoceros hide." And in her attempts to combine the role of wife and mother with an independent mind, a free spirit, and career interests of her own, she provides an example that is difficult to improve on even today.

11

MARTIN LUTHER KING, JR.
Leading in a Rapidly Changing Environment

A great leader must be an educator, bridging the gap between the vision and the familiar. But he must also be willing to walk alone to enable his society to follow the path he has selected.

—Henry Kissinger

Michael King, Jr., the son of an influential Baptist minister, was born in Atlanta in 1929. His father was not without a sense of destiny; in 1934, after a voyage to Europe and the Middle East that had exceeded his high expectations, he changed both his and his son's names to Martin Luther King. Young Martin's early life had its ups and downs; his father had no qualms about beating him, and it appears that the younger Martin twice tried to take his own life. Yet in dramatic, almost paradoxical, contrast to the patrician privileged Eleanor Roosevelt, Martin Luther King, Jr., described a charmed childhood: "The first twenty-five years of my life were very comfortable years, very happy years. I didn't have to worry about anything. . . . I went right through school, [and] I never had to drop out to work or anything."

Young King was a good student. At age fifteen he entered a special program for gifted students at Morehouse College, a historically black* school in Atlanta. After flirting with the idea of a career in law or medicine, he decided to follow the family tradition and enter the ministry. He went on to Crozier Theological Seminary in Pennsylvania, from which he received a bachelor of divinity degree in 1951, and then proceeded to Boston University, from which he received his doctoral degree in 1955. An intellectually oriented student, he immersed himself

---

*In this chapter I use the words *black* and, occasionally, *Negro* because of their common use during King's lifetime.

Martin Luther King, Jr. UPI/Bettmann

in the works of the leading Protestant theologians of the era, including Paul Tillich, Reinhold Niebuhr, and Walter Rauschenbusch. He was also exposed for the first time to the writings of Gandhi and to critiques of the American capitalist system. While King's personal philosophy had not coalesced, he was interested in the connection between the individual's relationship to God and his or her commitment to social activism on earth. He was also attempting to reconcile his personal experiences as a member of the traditional, emotionally suffused black church with the rather abstruse concerns of recent Protestant theologians.

The handsome young King was an eloquent speaker who could move easily in various social circles; his smooth ascent to a pulpit of influence seemed assured. Beginning that ascent in 1954, he accepted an invitation to be the minister of the Dexter Avenue Baptist Church in Montgomery, Alabama.

In all likelihood, King was hardly more prepared than the rest of America for the dramatic event that occurred in Montgomery on December 1, 1955. Rosa Parks, a well-regarded Negro seamstress, refused to leave her bus seat when the bus driver asked her to relinquish it to a white person. Parks was arrested and convicted of violating the city's segregation ordinance. In the wake of the epochal Supreme Court school desegregation decision the previous year in the case of *Brown v. Board of Education of Topeka,* black leaders and their white supporters decided to make a test case of the Parks incident. Within days, they had filed an appeal, organized a boycott of the Montgomery buses, formed a new organization called the Montgomery Improvement Association, and (prompted by King's fellow minister Ralph Abernathy) installed King as the first president.

Just why certain young individuals present themselves as viable candidates for leadership positions is an enigma that we have encountered before. In some cases, such as Robert Maynard Hutchins and J. Robert Oppenheimer, the obvious precocity of the individual stands out. In others, such as George Marshall, it is the willingness to confront authority, irrespective of possible consequences, which helps to authenticate the future leader. In King's case, he apparently was selected to lead the newly formed Montgomery Improvement Association for an ensemble of reasons. As a well-educated and articulate young man, he could be expected to win adherents and minimize opposition to the boycott. His status as a minister of a relatively affluent congregation might elicit support from the traditionally conservative clergy. He had the additional benefit of freshness on the scene; he had not been embroiled in previous political controversies that might have polarized the various audiences he would have to address. And should the boycott fail, he would suffer fewer consequences than would befall more entrenched leaders.

On the night of his selection as president, King had the assignment of delivering a major speech to the thousands of blacks who were involved in the boycott. He had little time to prepare; his remarks presumably reflected thoughts that had formed over a longer period of time, rather than ones assembled afresh for the particular occasion. King began his speech by pointing out that all gathered were American citizens and, as such, were entitled to exercise all the privileges due them. But they were also assembled because of the specific situation involving the bus boycott. He reviewed what had happened and paid tribute to Parks as an individual of integrity and a good Christian. The crowd began to react, greeting his statements with choral responses.

King hit his stride when he declared that patience must yield to protest: "And you know, my friends, there comes a time when people get tired of being trampled over by the iron feet of oppression." The crowd's echo was loud, long, and positive. He built on the same cadences: "There comes a time when people get tired of being pushed out of the glittering sunlight of life's July, and left standing amidst the chill of an Alpine November. We are here because we are tired now." He explained that the boycott would not advocate violence and that the only weapon used would be the weapon of protest. He spoke of the equal importance of Christian love and of justice. As he headed toward the climax of his speech, he said: "We are not wrong in what we are doing. . . . If we are wrong—the Supreme Court of this nation is wrong. . . . If we are wrong, God Almighty is wrong." The crowd exploded with enthusiasm.

As the biographer Taylor Branch chronicled the event:

The boycott was on. King would work on his timing but his oratory had just made him forever a public figure. In the few short minutes of his first political address, a power of communion emerged from him that would speak inexorably to strangers who would both love and revile him, like all prophets.

The well-received appearance in front of thousands of his fellow citizens was clearly a defining moment for King. He had known for some time that he could prepare a speech or sermon and deliver it effectively in front of a congregation. But he had never faced so large a crowd with so little preparation, and he had never been involved in a situation of political drama, where the stakes were high. He later recalled, "I came to see for the first time what the older [preachers] meant when they said, 'Open your mouth and God will speak for you.'"

Playing with the old adage, I suggest that in such cases, "chance favors the prepared tongue." While King had not found himself in such a situation before, he was deeply steeped in the Bible, other religious texts, and important American documents. He had heard hundreds, if not thousands, of sermons before, and he had assimilated their themes and rhythms. Whether he could actually synthesize these experiences into an effective presentation could not have been known beforehand; that is why the speech to the Montgomery boycotters was a high-stakes performance. But without such formative experiences, only a miracle would have enabled King to achieve what he did on that December evening.

King embarked on a course that was to continue for the remainder of his life. He was no longer just another young minister hoping to achieve success with a congregation or in a university teaching position. He had been propelled—willingly or reluctantly—into a position of leadership, where others looked to him for direction and inspiration. He in turn had to monitor his audience, to see which of his words and actions yielded results and which did not. For nearly a year he led fifty thousand blacks who were participating in the Montgomery bus boycott as a means of securing better employment conditions and enhanced civility from their white neighbors.

When city officials decided to break the boycott through arrests on technical violations, King was the first person to go to jail. Released from jail within a few hours, he faced another crisis shortly thereafter when his home was bombed. To his supporters, he declared: "I did not start this boycott. . . . I want it to be known the length and breadth of this land that if I am stopped, this movement will not stop. . . . Kill me, but know that if you do, you have fifty thousand more to kill." The experience of being a target of authority figures strengthened King's resolve; tentative challenges evolved into clear defiance. In 1956 he was arrested and convicted of violating a 1921 statute against boycotts; to his supporters, he boldly announced: "This conviction and all the convictions they can heap on me will not diminish my determination one iota."

King's efforts were rewarded when the Supreme Court decided that Alabama's laws on bus segregation were unconstitutional. The black citizens were euphoric, and King's own role was widely appreciated throughout the country. He made the cover of *Time* magazine in 1957. Significantly and shrewdly, King hailed the decision as a victory for all Americans, and not merely for the black population. Around this time, King reflected on the past year and enunciated a series of lessons for the "new Negro":

1. We can stick together;

2. Our leaders do not have to sell out;

3. Threats and violence do not necessarily intimidate those who are sufficiently aroused and non-violent;

4. Our church is becoming militant;

5. We believe in ourselves—"Montgomery has made me proud to be a Negro";

6. Economics is part of our struggle;

7. We have discovered a new and powerful weapon—non-violent resistance;

8. We now know that the southern Negro has come of age, politically and morally.

After chiding the novelist William Faulkner, who had asked blacks to "stop now for a moment," King concluded by saying: "We do not wish to triumph over the white community. . . . If we can live up to nonviolence in thought and deed, there will emerge an interracial society based on freedom for all."

The simplicity of the list is deceptive. King presumed to speak for—to help define—southern blacks. In creating an interlocking set of identity stories, he was telling his fellow citizens who they were, what they could aspire to, and what means to employ in this quest. Moreover, he was drawing these lessons from concrete realities—for instance, from the roller-coaster events of the bus boycott. The problem of violence formed the centerpiece of his tapestry: he was recognizing that others might be violent and that the church itself would have to become more militant; at the same time, he was embracing the technique of nonviolent resistance and indicating that goals could be pursued through the ploys that had evolved, partly by accident, during the daily struggles of the Montgomery action. Although these themes are now familiar to most Americans, they were decidedly novel—indeed, visionary—when they were first enunciated.

One can discern in King's words the processes by which the first draft of a story of identity coalesces. King identified the various issues on the minds of his audience—race, violence, the church, the economic situation—and wove them together into a coherent account. In each case, there would be questions and counterstories from various players: Could blacks be thought of as a coherent group? Could the church change its characteristic role? What would be the costs of nonviolence and of violence? Rather than ignoring or denying these concerns, King addressed them directly and created an answer that made sense to his direct audience—and to other provisional audiences—of the time.

Having played an instrumental role in launching a new level of militant social protest within Montgomery's black community, King spent the next few years broadening and deepening his experiences. Under the tutelage of the organizer Bayard Rustin, he advanced from familiarity with the ideas of Gandhi to a much more profound and subtle grasp of the principles of peaceful resistance. King, as the head of the newly constituted Southern Christian Leadership Conference (SCLC), went on highly affecting trips to Ghana, where he met Prime Minister Kwame Nkrumah, and to India, where he met Prime Minister Jawaharlal Nehru. In those settings he had the opportunity to observe their political organizations at close range.

Seeing himself (and being seen) as a leader of the national black movement, King also increased the level and variety of his participation in civil rights causes. He directed pointed communications to President Dwight Eisenhower, Vice President Richard Nixon, and Attorney General Herbert Brownell. He continued to be involved in "actions," which now included sit-ins at lunch counters, and he spent his first night in jail. Bomb threats and other attacks continued, and King was also stabbed in New York City by a deranged woman. Having slowly reduced his participation in his Montgomery pastorship, he moved in 1960 to Atlanta, where he became copastor with his father of the large and influential Ebenezer Baptist Church. Upon returning to Atlanta, he announced a broader campaign for equality, one that would include not only voter registration but also an across-the-board attack on discrimination and segregation.

During these formative years as a national leader, King elaborated a fuller vision, one that would thereafter undergird his speeches, writings, and presence. I discern four principal elements in King's emerging message.

First was his fundamental Christianity—the deepest and most pervasive theme in his life. King was knowledgeable about the Bible, the life of Christ, the prophets and the saints, and the more recent theological texts. He identified profoundly with the Christian tradition, with the stories of the Old and New Testaments, and particularly with Christ, whom he called the most influential person who had ever lived. And he also often invoked the figure of Moses, who had confronted the oppressive pharaohs of his era and had declared: "Let my people go."

A second element was King's experiences in the church, and particularly in black churches of the South. For over a hundred years, the church had been the bulwark of the entire black southern society, virtually the only institution with significant power and credibility. King, a scion of ministers on both sides of his family, had been raised in the church and felt its spirit coursing through his body. The church was his natural pulpit, the congregation his natural audience. Even when he addressed other populations in secular settings, the minister was never far from the surface.

A third element included the religious ideas and themes drawn from other traditions. Like Pope John XXIII, King embraced a broad inclusionary vision that was friendly to a variety of intellectual and cultural strands. He was comfortable with ideas and individuals from the Islamic, Catholic, Jewish, and Eastern religious traditions. At this time, Gandhi was the greatest religious influence on him. Gandhi's ideas about *satyagraha,* or nonviolence, seemed to King (as they have to many others in the twentieth century) to be the most legitimate and effective means for dispossessed populations to attain their ends (see chapter 14). Gandhi had shown how Christ's philosophy, worked out primarily at the level of individual human relations, could be transposed to the relations among groups. King was inspired by one of Gandhi's assertions: "It may be through the Negroes that the unadulterated message of nonviolence will be delivered to the world." While King sometimes became despondent about these time-consuming and often painful techniques, he never abandoned his fundamental faith in the Christ-Gandhi examples.

Whatever the shortcomings of his country, King felt deeply committed to the principal ideas on which America had been founded. These constituted the fourth element in his vision. King knew the Declaration of Independence, the Constitution and Bill of Rights, the Emancipation Proclamation, and the pervasive themes and phrases of American history. Like the influential Swedish social scientist Gunnar Myrdal, King saw the plight of American blacks as a unique dilemma that had to be solved in terms of the forces operating in American life. He understood the slave heritage, its relationship to the diverse pockets and ambivalent attitudes of the dominant white population, and the seemingly never-ending series of traumas that had beset the multiracial nation.

These, then, were the ingredients of King's emerging philosophy, one that built on his earlier description of the black identity but placed it in more richly textured settings. Like a masterful artist, such as Margaret Mead with her encyclopedic knowledge of many cultures, King was able to draw on and combine these elements in myriad ways, ways that were appropriate to a given situation, ways that involved and energized those who witnessed what he said, ways that resonated with one another and culminated in a more convincing story. He could introduce a theme through a Christian lens and then refract it through American historical or contemporary events, as appropriate. An increasingly powerful orator, he was able to affect the sentiments of his various audiences; and in turn, he himself was sensitive to, and often affected by, the reactions of those who heard him.

Indeed, as an emerging leader of a nondominant group, King did not have a ready-made audience or institution. Each of these had to be constructed, and often reconstructed, repeatedly within short periods of time. King mastered this highly challenging assignment. He learned how to modulate his words, depending upon whether he was speaking to his home congregation, an unfamiliar congregation, a sympathetic interviewer, a hostile reporter, the viewers of a television talk show, or the readers of an elite magazine. He also had a sense of when to listen, when to compromise, and when to hold his ground.

Initially, by his own testimony, King had not wanted to be a leader. But by 1957, he had come to realize that the decision of what to do with his life was not his alone to make—it had been dictated by forces beyond himself. "I realized that the choice leaves your own hands. The people expect you to give them leadership. You see them growing as they move into action, and then you know you no longer have a choice, you can't decide *whether* to stay in it or out of it, you *must* stay in it." In a manner that evoked parallels with his historical namesake, he spoke of an experience he had had while praying in 1957: "I could hear an inner voice saying to me, Martin Luther, stand for righteousness. Stand up for justice. Stand up for truth. And, lo, I will be with you." In his farewell sermon to his Montgomery congregation, he had wept while telling the congregation: "I can't stop now. History has thrust something upon me which I cannot turn away from."

By 1960, King stood clearly at the forefront of black American leaders. He contrasted sharply with the individuals who had until that point been considered central. The best known and most highly organized groups, the National Association for the Advancement of Colored People (NAACP) and the Urban League, had been relatively conservative bodies. Dependent largely on contributions from the white community, they had sought changes through litigation and other established legal and social service channels. The large Protestant organizations, such as the National Baptist Convention, had proceeded chiefly through exhortation. There were influential individuals in the black community—the audacious New York congressman Adam Clayton Powell, the barrier-breaking baseball player Jackie Robinson, and the elegant performer Harry Belafonte, to name a few—but their impact was idiosyncratic rather than cumulative.

King's SCLC sought to achieve ends through a confrontational approach that did not sit well with some of the rival groups. Leaders such as Roy Wilkins of the

NAACP and J. H. Jackson of the National Baptist Convention saw the SCLC both as an uncomfortable contrast to their previously favored, comfortable modes of operation and as a possible threat to their financial base—either through competition for funds or through a general disaffection with the black cause. The SCLC story of direct confrontation competed with their more traditional stories of gradual change, compromise, and pursuit of legal protests. Of the various leaders, the one who was probably least threatened was A. Philip Randolph, the president of the Brotherhood of Sleeping Car Porters; not only was he acknowledged as the senior member of the black leadership, but he also had been involved in confrontation politics—most notably, in his struggle against job discrimination in the early 1940s.

By virtue of King's personal appeal, the attention that the media devoted to him, and his achievements as leader of protest movements in the South, King and his organization came to occupy the limelight. King's emerging status as the leader of the protest helped increase financial support for the SCLC and advance its various campaigns. Moreover, King was able not only to recruit individuals who might otherwise have clashed with one another but also to get them to work together. His charisma proved crucial in the survival and periodic renewal of his organization. Still, King was not skilled at organizational matters and did not much like the managerial aspects of leadership. Within the SCLC there were many struggles for influence and an unsettling number of difficult situations involving deployment of funds and personnel. King never achieved more than an uneasy truce with the other leaders and organizations involved with black issues.

King found that his personal influence was growing, and he had become engaged in dialogues with many of the most influential individuals and groups in the land. At no point was this more evident than at the time of his jailing in October 1960 in Reidsville State Prison, a maximum security facility in Georgia, on a trumped-up charge of driving with an out-of-state license. Then presidential candidate John F. Kennedy took the calculated risk of telephoning King's wife, Coretta, to express his regret at the jailing and to offer his help. This single phone call, which lasted less than two minutes, along with a phone call from his brother Robert Kennedy to the presiding judge in the case, motivated Martin Luther King, Sr., a lifelong Republican, to throw his influential support in the direction of Kennedy and to issue an election-week pamphlet that reached millions of black voters. Many observers believe that the Kennedys' acts of kindness toward the King family affected enough black votes to make those a deciding factor in Kennedy's narrow victory in 1960.

During the three years that John Kennedy occupied the White House, King campaigned ceaselessly. Like any general presiding over an army, trying to win skirmishes while keeping in mind the overall objectives of the conflict, King and his close associates had to choose their sites carefully. In 1963 alone, King made more than 350 speeches and traveled about 275,000 miles. Opponents were as important as allies and causes; it was extremely useful to be in opposition to heartless officials like Police Commissioner Eugene "Bull" Connor of Birmingham, Alabama, whose acts of wanton cruelty toward protest marchers would either anger or shame those who had even some sympathy toward the black cause. (President Kennedy once remarked, "The civil rights movement owes Bull Connor as much as it owes Abraham Lincoln.") King repeatedly had to decide where to go, whom to confront, how hard to push, when to turn on the heat, and when to allow things to cool off.

But King's campaigns extended well beyond clashes with avowedly racist southern officials. A large part of his task in the early 1960s was to apply pressure on President John Kennedy and Attorney General Robert Kennedy so that they would come to the defense of marchers and throw down the gauntlet to intransigent governors such as George Wallace of Alabama and Ross Barnett of Mississippi. Another part of his task was to work cooperatively with those civil rights leaders whose own efforts were complementary, such as Robert Moses, who was active in voter registration, James Farmer of the Congress of Racial Equality (CORE) and John Lewis and the other key members of the Student Non-Violent Coordinating Committee (SNCC). And, in later years, King also had to contend with black leaders such as Malcolm X and Stokely Carmichael who came to consider him too conservative, too "Uncle Tomish," too much "De Lawd," and who were willing to countenance approaches that were frankly violent.

While it was never possible to modulate these competing forces (and these competing stories) completely, King managed to do so reasonably well during the years of the Kennedy administration. The Kennedy brothers were not fundamentally hostile to the blacks' cause, but they were sufficiently cautious and sufficiently motivated by political opportunism to foster a sustained tension with King. Drawing inspiration from the Reverend Billy Graham and from Gandhi, King and his associates carefully planned marches and protests. They pursued their longer-term goals like desegregation and voter registration, while remaining very flexible in their rhetoric and their tactics. The various protest activities of the early 1960s—in Montgomery, Alabama; Albany, Georgia; and Birmingham, Alabama—were crowned with at least modest success: King's supporters felt it legitimate to introduce their pressure tactics into new arenas.

What lifted King to an unprecedented place in the black community—and in the annals of American political protest more broadly—were the events of 1963: one private and personal, demonstrating indirect leadership; the other, inexorably public, exemplifying direct leadership.

The private event occurred during April when King found himself once again in jail, this time in Birmingham. King happened to read a newspaper article that bore the headline "White Clergymen Urge Local Negroes to Withdraw from Demonstrations." These self-styled liberal clergymen argued that the protests were counterproductive and that blacks should show more patience instead. They favored the traditional story of pursuing gradual, conflict-free change. King was deeply disturbed by this misunderstanding of all that he stood for, and his personal upset led him, in the days ahead, to pen the document now called "Letter from Birmingham City Jail."

In any number of ways, this document stands as the fullest statement of King's position at the height of his powers and influence. King begins by explaining why he is in Birmingham—because there is injustice there. He does not hesitate to compare himself with the Apostle Paul. He endeavors to transport himself into the ministers' minds, to understand where they are coming from, and what has led them to inquire: "Why direct action? Isn't negotiation a better path?" He then tries to educate his audience—which eventually became the entire nation—about why the recommended position of infinite patience is no longer viable. Gathering up all of his accumulated rage, King explains that the experience of the Negro is such that he has suffered far too long:

> We have waited for more than 340 years for our constitutional and God-given rights. The nations of Asia and Africa are moving with jetlike speed toward the goal of political independence and we still creep at horse and buggy pace toward the gaining of a cup of coffee at a lunch counter. I guess it is easy for those who have never felt the stinging darts of segregation to say "wait." But when you have seen vicious mobs lynch your mothers and fathers at will and drown your sisters and brothers at whim; when you have seen hate-filled policemen curse, kick, brutalize and even kill black brothers and sisters with impunity . . . when you suddenly find your tongue twisted and your speech stammering as you seek to explain to your six-year-old daughter why she can't go to the public amusement park that has just been advertised on television, and see tears welling up in her little eyes when she is told that Funtown is closed to colored children . . . then you will understand why we find it difficult to wait.

Having given vent to his frustration, King returns to a calmer rendition of his position. Drawing on traditional views of the law of God, he lays out the difference between a just and an unjust law. He contrasts, on the one hand, angry defiance toward a law that one happens to disagree with and, on the other hand, loving, open disobedience toward an unjust law. He expresses his disappointment that the white church has not more often supported his nonviolent efforts. "We know through painful experience that freedom is never voluntarily given by the oppressor; it must be demanded by the oppressed." He deplores the clergymen's praise of the Birmingham police force and urges that these Christian ministers instead commend the black demonstrators for their "amazing discipline in the midst of the most inhuman provocation." And he calls on the South to recognize its real heroes, those disinherited children of God sitting down at lunch counters who are actually "standing up for the best in the American dream, and the most sacred values in our Judeo-Christian heritage, and thusly, carrying our whole nation back to those great wells of democracy which were dug deep by the Founding Fathers in the formulation of the Constitution and the Declaration of Independence."

The letter took twenty pages; in that space, operating as an indirect leader, King was able to provide background and texture for the picture of heroism and impatience that he was sharing with all other Americans. The reader was able to see with unequaled clarity how the various strands in King's repertoire came together to constitute a coherent story of the blacks' past and a charter for their future action. Even now, citizens of various stripes return to this text as a pivotal statement of the American creed.

The March on Washington of August 28, 1963, constituted the most public opportunity of King's life. This event, devised cooperatively by the leaders of the often-feuding civil rights organizations, was a pivotal one: a large-scale, peaceful effort on the part of civil rights organizations to pressure Congress and the president to pass legislation on voting rights, desegregation of public facilities, and other flashpoint issues. In addition to the two hundred thousand people in attendance, millions of television viewers witnessed the first scheduled national black protest in American history. King had been allotted eight minutes to speak.

The last speaker of the day, King read from a prepared text in which he spoke about a "promissory note" that the Founding Fathers and Lincoln had issued to all Americans, including blacks. In a perhaps shockingly vernacular phrase, he said pithily, "We've come to our nation's capital to cash a check." Harking back to the violence in Birmingham, and with the prospect of civil rights legislation in the national consciousness, he said that the time for action was at hand. He laid out a position for his nonviolent approach, couched between those who would acquiesce in further intolerance and those who were militant or racially separatist. The speech was elevated, positive in spirit, without being unduly optimistic or sentimental.

King's speech was well received from the opening lines, in which he referred to the "greatest demonstration for freedom in the history of our nation." But only toward the end of the formal remarks did he begin to deviate from the script and hit his stride. Finding his voice, which had first broken into public spontaneously in Montgomery eight years before and was now familiar to every American who watched the nightly news, King told the world, "I have a dream." The dream was "deeply rooted in the American dream," and it drew from the Bible and the words of the prophets to touch people in all regions of the country. And the dream culminated—as did the speech—in the refrain of an old Negro spiritual: "Free at last! Free at last! Thank God Almighty, we are free at last!"

King's speech was immediately recognized as a great one. Congratulating him immediately afterward, as he filed into the Cabinet Room at the White House, the president repeated to him the signature phrase "I have a dream." Writing in the *New York Times* the next day, the senior correspondent James Reston commented:

> It will be a long time before [Washington] forgets the melodious and melancholy voice of Rev. Dr. Martin Luther King, Jr., crying out his dreams to the multitude. . . . Dr. King touched all the themes of the day, only better than anybody else. He was full of the symbolism of Lincoln and Gandhi, and the cadences of the Bible. He was militant and sad, and he sent the crowd away feeling that the long journey had been worthwhile.

Winning the hearts of the nation—among whites as well as blacks—as well as the praise of the media was no easy task. King's unique achievements were recognized when he was selected as *Time*'s "Man of the Year" for 1963 and when he was awarded the Nobel Peace Prize in 1964. Whatever tensions had marked King's relationship with other groups and other audiences seemed to recede in importance.

For a brief time, it appeared that King had created—and embodied—a story that went well beyond the boycotters in Montgomery or black southerners as a whole. Perhaps King's "color-blind" story could unite and change a nation—the 19 million blacks and the nearly 200 million others. Perhaps the usually smug citizens of a nation could look beyond their own purview and appreciate the experiences of a group that looked very different from themselves. And perhaps his organization, or a combination of civil rights organizations, could be the permanent trustees of the dream that King had enunciated.

But seeds of trouble, discord, and disarray throughout the country, which had never been far from the surface, began to sprout shortly after the March on Washington. First was the shocking assassination of President Kennedy in November 1963. And there were other brutal killings: of the CORE worker James Chaney and the SNCC workers Andrew Goodman and Michael Schwerner in Mississippi (June 1964), of black children attending a church in Birmingham (September 1964), and of civil rights workers such as the white Detroit homemaker Viola Liuzzo, who was working in Alabama (March 1965). Then there were less conclusive protests, in Selma, Alabama, and in Montgomery, Alabama, where it proved more difficult to determine the political fallout from the bloody confrontations.

Under President Lyndon Johnson's leadership, the Voting Rights Act of 1965 and various other civil rights laws were passed, and the more virulent forms of racism were discredited in the public arena. But the situation in inner cities continued to deteriorate, and summers of urban unrest followed, with much bloodshed and much despair. Convinced that King's pacific approach could not work, a growing number of blacks were electing a militant course; they followed Malcolm X, until his assassination in 1965, and they embraced the escalating rhetoric of Stokely Carmichael, Eldridge Cleaver, and other advocates of separatism and black power. A more radical counterstory exerted pressure on King to revise his Gandhian stance. The Vietnam War was in full swing and many American soldiers, a disproportionate number of whom were black, were dying. Many people felt that the United States, no less than a small, distant land, was being torn asunder by the conflict.

King was shaken by these events. His brave but essentially small-scale actions seemed increasingly paltry in the face of epochal national and international events. One commentator declared that King was "outstripped by his times." We cannot know for sure what brought about changes, but the King of 1967–1968 was a very different man from the King of 1963. Scarred perhaps by growing criticism of his actions in southern states and his focus on southern issues, prompted by a new set of more militant concerns targeted by younger black and white Americans, he attempted to organize in the North. He moved beyond issues of racial discrimination to questions of poverty and economic injustice. Thinking increasingly in terms of a class-structured social movement, he prepared to launch marches of poor people. But his initial efforts in Chicago— where he sought to tackle issues of housing, welfare, education, police brutality, and color discrimination—were not successful. Rebuilding the deteriorating northern ghetto proved to be a task totally different from confronting villainous southern police chiefs.

Passing beyond American domestic issues, King issued increasingly severe and bitter attacks on American foreign policy in Southeast Asia. In April 1967 he publicly denounced the Vietnam War from the pulpit of Manhattan's Riverside Church:

> We have destroyed their two most cherished institutions: the family and the village. We have destroyed their land and their crops. We have cooperated in the crushing of the nation's only non-Communist revolutionary force— the Unified Buddhist Church. We have supported the enemies of the peasants of Saigon. We have corrupted their women and children and killed their men. What liberators! . . . What do they think as we test out our latest weapons on them, just as the Germans tested out new medicine and new tortures in the concentration camps of Europe?

The voice of 1967 was distinct from the voice of 1955, or even 1963.

Each of these shifts was fraught with perils. King had built his reputation and his success through his efforts on ground close to home, where his knowledge was profound and the moral dimensions of his mission least subject to challenge. With each move away from the Deep South, with each issue beyond those associated with race, and, especially, with an attack on foreign policy (a domain that has traditionally been conceived as beyond partisanship), King lost support and risked undermining his entire operation. Moreover, at the very time that these shifts in political focus were taking place, King came under increasingly harsh criticism from the FBI, which had been monitoring his private life for years, and which intermixed allegations that he was under the influence of the Communist Party with a whisper campaign about his supposedly depraved sexual life.

Whether prompted by changes of heart, pressures from other leaders and followers, the events of the external world, or, more likely, some combination of these factors, King was evolving from a reformer into a radical. He said it himself: "For years I labored with the idea of reforming the existing institutions of society, a little change here, a little change there. Now I feel quite differently. I think you've got to have a reconstruction out of the entire society, a revolution of values."

King was getting ready to lead this revolution, though it is far from clear whether he had the requisite followers in his camp. In earlier battles, he had known the terrain, was personally close to the combatants, and had been able to reshape his stories as needed; now he was headed into unknown territory. Ultimately, there was a huge reaction against the Vietnam War, but it came largely from the middle class and was led primarily by disillusioned members of the Democratic Party. And in the increasingly conservative 1970s and the 1980s, the social and economic ills that King had diagnosed throughout the country were never addressed by an enduring political constituency.

This situation serves as a reminder that leaders can become too remote from their audiences. The King of 1960 or 1963 had addressed an audience that was prepared to accept his messages, but the King of 1967 and 1968 faced an unsettling choice. Either he had to listen more carefully to his traditional audience, which was too overwhelmed by its own problems to tackle foreign policy issues, or he had to use his skills of story creation and embodiment to assemble a new audience, essentially from scratch.

The events of King's later years also remind us that leaders almost never behold an unbroken string of successes. Whether it be the attack on Oppenheimer's or Marshall's patriotism, the attempts to ambush Pope John's Vatican Council, or the sudden shift to a foreign policy agenda during the later years of the Roosevelts' era, leaders must confront periods of retrenchment and periods of failure. Indeed, the higher the stakes, and the more daring the vision, the greater the chance of repeated failures. King had sustained many setbacks and frustrations during the early years of his campaigns, and now he was confronting far more serious upheavals. What distinguishes leaders from one another are not the occurrences of reversals of fortune but rather the ways in which they deal with, and recover from, such inevitable constants of their calling.

King had known from his earliest years in the protest movement that his life was tenuous. He spoke often about the possibility of assassination and appeared ready to accept this fate, particularly in the wake of the many murders, bomb threats, bombings, assassination attempts, and assassinations of blacks (and of liberal whites) that had occurred in recent years. When John Kennedy was assassinated, King declared laconically: "This is going to happen to me."

On April 3, 1968, King left Atlanta for Memphis to support a strike among the city's sanitation workers. In his remarks in Memphis that evening, he declared: "Well, I don't know what will happen now. We've got some difficult days ahead. But it doesn't matter with me now. Because I've been to the mountain . . . and I've seen the promised land. I may not get there with you. But I want you to know tonight, that we, as a people, will get to the promised land."

The next day, a right-wing drifter named James Earl Ray assassinated King. Like his hero Gandhi, like the contemporary leader with whom he felt a certain kinship John Kennedy, and like Kennedy's scrappy brother Robert, who (ironically) was in the process of forming bonds to King's traditional constituency, King became a victim of the hatred that he had tried to counter. In death, he was celebrated as an American hero, a moderate who had sought to heal the nation's racial wounds. His more radical closing months were virtually ignored. Perhaps reflecting a wish more than a reality, the journalist Richard Lentz, who covered the Memphis strike, declared:

> It was fitting therefore that King died as he did and where he did, locked in mortal struggle with his foes of old, the white racists of his native South, and not with the larger society, as represented by the national government that was the target of King's most radical and ambitious undertaking.

King wedded a strong, effective visionary message with the embodiment of that message. He was a black man coming from the ministerial heartland of the southern black community, subject to the outrages that had plagued nearly every black person in the society. Yet, rising above the pain and the suffering—perhaps, indeed, strengthened by them—he sought to lay out an approach that blacks, as well as other dispossessed groups, could adopt within America to achieve the place that they merited and had in fact been repeatedly promised. He spoke recurrently and persuasively of a "beloved community" in which blacks and whites could live together harmoniously. He melded together strands and messages from many religions, subcultures, and cultures, in a way that made sense to his contemporaries and that, in the manner of Eleanor Roosevelt, stimulated individuals to be more generous, more humane. Speaking and writing with ever-increasing power and persuasiveness, he was able to establish both indirect and direct links to many audiences.

King was courageous. He told a black reporter in Montgomery: "Once you become dedicated to a cause, personal security is not the goal. What will happen to you personally does not matter. My cause, my race, is worth dying for." His nonviolence reflected his deepest instincts. When attacked at a conference in December 1961, he faced his assailant and dropped his hands "like a newborn baby." This calm in the face of possible injury or even death served as a powerful and powerfully reassuring message to all who knew him or knew of him.

Such courage may have been related to behavior that was less than exemplary. King was humble, but he was also proud and grandiose, and he identified readily with the most illustrious religious leaders of the past. He engaged in personal behavior that was risky and unworthy of a religious leader. Much of his graduate work was plagiarized. The FBI's indefensible effort to ruin King's reputation yielded evidence of his liaisons with many women. King felt guilty about this disloyalty to his family and his creed. It does not excuse King to note that similar exploitation of women has characterized all too many political figures of our day or of days past, nor that it seemed to be a form of camaraderie that he shared with other black ministers. Fortunately, King's personal flaws did not appear to clash with or inhibit his wider political and social agendas; he continued to embody the most central portions of his story.

It is perhaps especially challenging to an individual to occupy a leadership position when that position has no vested authority and depends almost entirely on one's ability to speak and act from conviction and to inspire others to do the same. Like Eleanor Roosevelt, King came to occupy a place in the country for which there had been no predecessor—and, for that matter, no successors. (King's friend Reverend Ralph Abernathy took over leadership of the SCLC, but it slipped into ineffectiveness.) King contributed to greater consciousness of the black role in America and to a more viable definition of what it meant to be a black person in the twentieth century, but his definition could not be sustained after his death. His message inhered primarily in his own person rather than in an enduring organization.

With King, as with Roosevelt, there was a constant interplay among the events of his personal life, events occurring in the groups that he came to represent, and events in the larger society. King's relatively smooth childhood in the Deep South was a necessary contributor to the person he became, the risks he was willing to entertain, and perhaps the limits that he eventually ran up against. Consciousness about blackness had been on the rise during the early part of the century: desegregation of the armed forces and *Brown v. Board of Education of Topeka* had preceded King's ascendancy to a position of influence. But despite various transient heroes and villains, the cause of black Americans had not yet coalesced.

At the core of King's saga is the intersection of the life of a talented individual who was open to growth and the needs of a group that was in search of self-definition. While reflecting on his times, King helped to provide a sense of identity for blacks as well as for the dispossessed, more broadly construed. His message went beyond the familiar categories of the unschooled mind: he (like

Eleanor Roosevelt) asked American citizens to put aside the usual classifications of—and clashes among—groups, to endorse a more inclusionary view of their society, and to attempt to improve the lot of those who were less fortunate. King was not able to establish an organization or a constituency that transcended his death, and so it has been necessary to reinvent his causes and search for new leading individuals and groups. The new forms, however, have built on the indispensable foundations laid by this remarkable leader of a nondominant group.

When one speaks of leaders, one's thoughts most often turn to those individuals who provide leadership to recognized entities as intimate as a college, as broad as the Catholic Church or the U.S. Army. Probably the quintessential leaders of our times are leaders of a nation, such as that ensemble of powerful persons who went to Tehran in 1943 in order to make decisions of fateful consequence. In the next two chapters, I consider such national leaders. In Chapter 12, I turn my attention to Margaret Thatcher—a leader who has had enormous influence in her own time; and then, in Chapter 13, I examine an ensemble of leaders who provided national and international direction during the critical years of the Second World War.

A major goal of this book has been to trace the continuum of leadership, as it is exercised in small, relatively homogeneous groups, to leadership as it operates with larger and relatively heterogeneous groups. As we move now to the stage of national leadership, it is appropriate to take a pause—in the form of a reprise— to review the considerable terrain that has already been traversed and to look ahead to the concluding steps of our journey.

REPRISE

Used without a modifier, the label "leader" generally denotes an individual who serves as the head of a political entity, such as a city, tribe, or nation. Membership in the political entity consists of individuals who represent different domains and statuses but who share a belief that they belong in some sense to the same group. Thus, in the contemporary nation-state, individuals may be drawn from a range of occupations and backgrounds and yet embrace the same credo and institutions.

While the most common national pattern involves individuals who share the same ethnic heritage, an increasing number of nations, including the United States, are composed of individuals from diverse backgrounds. Strife results when conflicting groups living within the same geographical entity wish to have their own political units—as happened in the American Civil War. Equally, conflict ensues when individuals of a given ethnic identity living in dispersed geographical entities wish to join into the same political unit—a chronic situation in the Balkans.

In this and the following chapter, I turn my attention to individuals charged with providing leadership for these large and sometimes quite heterogeneous populations. However elected or appointed to their positions, these individuals must find a way to speak to their population, or at least to those segments of the population from whom they derive their authority and to whom they feel beholden. The larger and more heterogeneous the population, the greater the challenge to craft a story that can speak to the audience; and the more likely it is that the story will need to be a simple, if not a simplistic, one.

To place the task facing the leader of a nation into context, it is helpful to review the ground that has been covered so far in this work. I first considered two individuals whose rise to positions of influence originated in the quality of their work within established academic disciplines. Margaret Mead began as an anthropologist visiting exotic lands; only when her study of human nature came to encompass the women and the men of the United States did her leadership transcend an audience of experts. Similarly, J. Robert Oppenheimer started his career as a physicist; events of the Second World War propelled him to a position where he directed a community of scientists (still experts). Only after the war did he present his ideas—with mixed success—to wider national and international publics.

The next group of individuals headed institutions of varying size and degrees of heterogeneity. Robert Maynard Hutchins led a circumscribed institution—an American university, with its collection of experts representing different disciplines. In the survey of major "estates" Alfred P. Sloan, Jr., directed a business, George C. Marshall provided leadership for the military, and Pope John XXIII stood at the helm of the world's largest church. Estate membership was heterogeneous, particularly in the military and the church, but members were bound by a common allegiance; other, less pertinent realms of experience were "rendered unto Caesar." The vision developed by the leaders could build on earlier "identity stories" within that institution, but it had to be one that the principal interest groups in their membership could appreciate—a vision that helped them understand what it meant to belong to that group at that historical moment.

Eleanor Roosevelt and Martin Luther King, Jr., faced decidedly different challenges. In neither case did there exist a prior audience with its own norms and self-image, nor was there an established route by which they could have traveled to a position of authority in an established institution. There was no "before"; and as it turned out, there was not much "afterward" either. Instead, because of the intersection of their personal histories and the events of their times, both Roosevelt and King found themselves propelled into positions where their words and their practices influenced nondominant groups within their society. Membership in these groups was virtually as diverse as membership in a nation; and yet, the groups were bound together in these instances by their decidedly marginal status and by certain common cultural experiences. The visions put forth by Roosevelt and King helped individuals understand the potential life experiences of women and blacks, respectively, in the twentieth century.

Individuals become leaders of tribes or nations by varied routes, even as they exercise different skills and strategies once they occupy the leadership office. Traditionally, there were two principal routes: an orderly procedure by virtue of lineage—the oldest male (or, less often, female) offspring of the current leader becomes the new head; or a turbulent succession by the exercise of brute power—the strongest individual or the keenest fighter becomes the leader. In recent centuries, leadership of a country has more commonly been achieved through three other avenues: popular election, throughout most of the Western world; consensual discussion and secretive jockeying among an elite, in most nondemocratic societies; or the violent seizure of power by a revolutionary political group, as has happened in less stable countries. Sometimes, the leaders of these groups come from relatively established domains or disciplines: for example, Vaclav Havel, the head of the Czech Republic, is an accomplished playwright, and Ludwig Erhard, the leader of Germany, was an economist. Often the leaders are drawn from the major estates: President Woodrow Wilson was first a historian and then a college president, Prime Minister Silvio Berlusconi of Italy was a successful businessman, President Dwight Eisenhower was a general, and the Ayotallah Khomeini of Iran was a religious leader.

By far the most common route to national leadership has been advancement through political ranks. Most American presidents and Western prime ministers entered into politics fairly early in their adult lives and held a succession of local and national offices. In oligarchic states, most leaders at one time held positions in various governmental jurisdictions. In cases where individuals attained power through revolutionary means, the leaders also had a political background, but one that was more likely to involve secretive, violent, and/or illegal activities. They were more likely to have spent time in jail than terms in recognized political offices. Such disparate leaders as Stalin, Hitler, and Mao Zedong in the earlier part of the twentieth century and

Fidel Castro, Saddam Hussein, and Muramar Qaddafi in the latter part of the century all rose to influence through their control of political entities that they themselves created or whose leadership they seized. To borrow Ronald Heifetz's terms once again, they emerged as leaders long before they attained legitimate authority.

The ways in which such individuals come to attain power need not predict the ways in which they ultimately wield it. An individual may begin as one kind of leader, who relies on one kind of influence, and end up as another kind. The most notorious example is Hitler, who became chancellor of Germany as the result of an election and who immediately ensured that such "free" elections would never again be held. Tyrants are made, not born. There are examples, if less frequent, in the other direction; France's Charles de Gaulle, for example, introduced an elected presidency after he himself had governed by decree; Francisco Franco, himself a dictator, smoothed the way for a constitutional monarchy in Spain after his death. Even individuals who were never involved in an honest election typically had to exhibit a set of personal skills in order to attain their positions: thus, Mao was a superlative organizer and a brilliant debater, while Stalin was a master of propaganda and intrigue. And individuals such as Franklin Roosevelt who continue to be reelected must exercise skills in office that differ from the ones they need to win nominations and elections.

A final consideration involves the extent to which a political leader seeks to transform the sense of identity of the population. Most leaders in most circumstances have been content to assert the same stories and embody the same virtues that their predecessors did; these "ordinary" leaders (the recent American presidents Gerald Ford and George Bush spring to mind) perform a maintenance function. An "innovative leader" takes a set of themes or images that already exist in the society, but that have recently been ignored or minimized, and raises them to high consciousness; such recent leaders as de Gaulle or Ronald Reagan qualify as innovative leaders.

The rarest variety of political leader is an individual who actually creates a new story or image, one that has not been prevalent before, and succeeds in convincing the public of its power and tenability. Such transformative or visionary leadership is difficult to achieve. First, new political ideas are not easy to come by. Moreover, once one addresses a heterogeneous population, one must convince an unschooled, rather than an expert, mind. Thus, while colleagues in physics or in poetry are on the lookout for fresh visions and reward figures who create these novel perspectives, populations within nations are essentially conservative. In the twentieth century, only a few political leaders, such as Lenin and Mao, and only a few ideological innovators, such as Mahatma Gandhi and Jean Monnet, have succeeded in creating stories that merit the epithet "visionary" and in spreading this story beyond their own tight circle of supporters.

12

MARGARET THATCHER
A Clear Sense of Identity

*I never look beyond a battle. It is a culminating event, and
like a brick wall bars all future vision.*

—Winston Churchill

Margaret Thatcher served three times as the prime minister of Great Britain—
the longest continual premiership in twentieth-century British history. Thatcher
accomplished the singular feats of becoming the first female head of a major
British party and then, after her election as the prime minister, changing fundamentally the course of post–Second World War British society. Unlike the leaders described in earlier chapters, Thatcher had the task of addressing an entire
population, with its diverse backgrounds, anxieties, and goals. She did so by presenting a vision of what it meant to be British and inviting her compatriots to
join her; yet, when people chose not to identify themselves with this vision, she
showed little hesitation in cutting them off. Ultimately, in contrast to most of
the leaders considered so far, her vision was exclusionary rather than inclusionary: instead of continuing to seek compromise or rapprochement, Thatcher preferred to dichotomize into "us" and "them." For a surprisingly long period of
time, this tack worked well; but ultimately, Thatcher's penchant for divisiveness
contributed to her own downfall.

Throughout her career, Margaret Thatcher (born Margaret Roberts) represented a fascinating combination of the mundane and the extraordinary. It
would be difficult to envision a less portentous childhood in the 1930s. Her father, Alfred, owned the leading grocery shop in the small town of Grantham in
central England. He was a dedicated member of the Methodist Church and held
various political niches, such as those of alderman and magistrate. He was considered to be a good and dutiful, yet independent-minded, citizen. Alfred doted
on Margaret, the son that he never had. Young Margaret was a good student

Margaret Thatcher. UPI/Bettmann Newsphotos

who, like her father, worked hard and held herself to high standards; but she was certainly not seen as intellectually precocious in the way of, say, Robert Maynard Hutchins or Margaret Mead.

Quite possibly the most extraordinary feature dating back to Thatcher's childhood is the fact that she has virtually denied the existence of her mother, Beatrice. In her public remarks, she has spoken only of her father, and then always in the most glowing terms. When she was selected as the prime minister in 1979, she declared: "Well, of course, I just owe almost everything to my father. He brought me up to believe all the things that I do believe, and they're just the values on which I've fought the election." In her biographical entry in *Who's Who*, she did not list her mother at all. Confronted by this fact in 1988, she acted surprised and commented: "I loved her dearly but after I was 15, we had nothing more to say to each other. It wasn't her fault. She was weighed down by the home, always being in the home." A schoolmate friend once commented that Thatcher "rather despised her mother and adored her father."

Analogous situations in the lives of other achievers spring to mind. Pablo Picasso obliterated his father's name and took his mother's name. As an adult, Charles Darwin stated that he had never lost anyone in his family, repressing the fact that his mother had died when he was eight years old. Michael King changed his and his son's forenames to Martin Luther. One can imagine some kind of deeply embarrassing or wrenching experience, which a growing youth might feel compelled to deny. Perhaps Margaret had a fearful row with her mother, or perhaps Beatrice committed some terrible sin.

It seems far more likely, however, that Thatcher (like Picasso) could not come to terms with the ordinariness of the same-sex parent, whom she repeatedly disparaged as "rather a Martha" (a Freudian might point out the similarity to her own first name). If Thatcher wanted to be extraordinary, the exceptional female who resembled her father in interests and political leanings, the "middle Englishwoman" who led her nation back to greatness, it was necessary for her to expunge the ordinariness in herself—and that ordinariness was epitomized by her downtrodden mother.

Alfred, who had completed no higher education, was determined that his talented daughter attend a university, and she was in due course admitted to Oxford University. At Somerville College, Margaret pursued two different careers. She studied chemistry with the distinguished future Nobel laureate Dorothy Hodgkin. A career in industrial chemistry made sense for an upwardly mobile young woman, and Margaret Thatcher worked briefly in two industrial jobs following her graduation from the university.

But even during her university years, Thatcher's passion was politics. The interest in politics that she had acquired from her father was both sharpened and directed. Margaret read works by leading conservative writers, especially the Austrian-born critic of socialism Friedrich von Hayek, and became a convert to conservative philosophy. Aided by her father, she also gained skills in public speaking and became an excellent debater.

Thatcher's lifelong political stance was strongly colored by her experiences at a critical time in her life. She became truly attuned to the political realm during the years of the Second World War, the time when Britain stood alone for democratic values against the scourge of Nazi Germany. It was a difficult but proud period. Under Churchill's inspiring and implacable leadership, Britain confirmed that it was still a great power and one that represented meritorious values.

I believe that this coming-of-age experience during the Second World War furnished a model for Thatcher of Britain's proper niche in the world; from this defining experience arose her seldom-challenged certainty about her beliefs. Had she achieved her political majority at the time of the Neville Chamberlain defeatism of the 1930s, or during the gradual decline in the 1950s and 1960s of British global influence, Thatcher's political spirit might have been far more tentative or muted.

Turning her back on a profession that was apparently suited for someone of her background, Thatcher took a second degree, in law. She passed her bar examinations in December 1953. As with her other pursuits, Thatcher was a good but not outstanding student; she typically placed at the top of the second rank. Her studies in law figured importantly in her subsequent career, because they introduced her to political and economic issues and governmental procedures. She never forgot her scientific training, however, and often invoked it as a justification for the reasoning that she employed and the stance that she assumed on an issue.

Margaret's choice of a mate appears to have been, in its own way, as calculating as that of Franklin Roosevelt or Bill Clinton. In 1951 she married Denis Thatcher, an older divorcé who had been extremely successful in business. Marrying above her family's social status, Margaret confirmed her Conservative Party ties and also shifted from the Methodist Church to the Church of England. She no longer had to work for a living. But Denis provided more than money and prestige. He has also been a uniquely supportive mate, allowing Margaret the unambiguous limelight, yet providing quiet counsel. The Thatchers had twins in 1953, and Margaret took time off to be with Mark and Carol during their early years.

Still, Thatcher was determined to enter electoral politics. Since her student days, she had been an alert networker, and she began to search for a seat in the House of Commons for which she could run. Not until the late 1950s did she find such an opening—the staunchly conservative London suburb of Finchley. This upwardly mobile community, which valued Thatcher's competent persona and her stance of self-reliance, returned her repeatedly to the House of Commons with high majorities.

By the 1960s Thatcher was a rising star in the ranks of the Conservative Party. Young, attractive, poised, well-briefed, amazingly articulate, and determined yet careful, she impressed both her political allies and the general public. She was mentored by leading Conservative politicians, such as Keith Joseph. As early as 1963 party leader Alec Douglas-Home remarked to his wife, "You know, [Margaret Thatcher's] got the brains of all of us put together and so we'd better look out." Between 1965 and 1970 she held a series of shadow cabinet jobs, and when the Conservatives were returned to power in 1970, she was appointed secretary of state for education by the new prime minister, Edward Heath. She did a creditable job in these posts, mastering the details of her portfolios and seldom making waves; perhaps of greater importance, she learned to take fierce criticism in stride.

While Thatcher's gifts were widely recognized and mostly admired, the question of how far she would rise in the political ranks remained open. The Conservative leadership was overloaded with men from aristocratic backgrounds who had known each other for years and who were basically conservative rather than iconoclastic in temperament. In almost every particular, Thatcher deviated from establishment types such as Douglas-Home, R. A. Butler, Quintin Hogg, and Harold Macmillan. (Actually, in background she resembled only Heath, who had also risen from modest circumstances and was not considered a "true" establishment figure.) She was a woman, she came from the middle of the middle class, she had attended a state-funded grammar school rather than an independent (or public) school, she was the first of her family to attend a university, she had studied a trade rather than a classical discipline, and, above all, she was a true believer in those conservative values that her contemporaries honored more in the breach than in the observance. Indeed, she came eventually to consider Heath a traitor to the true conservative cause.

In such a situation, where the odds do not favor the outsider, a number of circumstances need to fall into place. First, the outsider must be deliberate rather than threatening. Throughout her decade in the shadow cabinet and the cabinet, Thatcher was a good team player and did not openly challenge the other conservative leaders. As a woman, she was already decidedly marginal; she did not have to, and perhaps could not afford to, be any more challenging than she was. Second, the right situation must break. In this case, the opportune moment featured the defeat of Heath in the 1974 election, following a premiership that was seen as weak and ineffective, and a general consensus that more of the same would not do.

Third, the would-be beneficiary must have a skilled sense of timing. Thatcher was realistic about her prospects. She declared in 1974: "It will be years before a woman either leads the party or becomes Prime Minister. I don't see it happening in my lifetime." Yet when a moment presented itself in 1975, Thatcher seized it. Recognizing a situation where possibly stronger—and certainly more predictable—candidates did not dare to break ranks, Thatcher took a risk. She announced that she would be a candidate; and running against the weakened Heath, she became the leader of her party on the second ballot.

In her new position, as head of the opposition to Labor's James Callaghan, Thatcher skillfully walked a fine line. On the one hand, she strove to be inclusive; she tried to keep rival Conservative leaders within the ranks and was deferential to those who might have been inclined to oppose her leadership. Yet at the same time, Thatcher began to impress on the nation (and indeed on the world) that she had her own political philosophy—one much less moderate than that of her contemporaries, whether from the Labor or the Conservative ranks.

The term *Thatcherism* was coined and recognized, within Britain, to denote the conviction that socialism had failed and that Britain had to relinquish governmental interference in favor of privatization and individual initiative. An impatience with labor unions and government civil servants was manifest. Beyond Britain's boundaries, Thatcher was recognized as an unreconstructed cold warrior. After she delivered two belligerent speeches in the mid-1970s, the Russians dubbed her the "Iron Lady." While this title was not meant to be flattering, it probably was of considerable help within Britain. The Russians were not loved, a woman in politics needed to be seen as strong, and the very word *iron* may well have had Churchillian connotations that benefited Thatcher.

At least in retrospect, certain elections are clearly watersheds. In the United States, one thinks of Abraham Lincoln versus Stephen Douglas in 1860, Franklin Roosevelt versus Herbert Hoover in 1932, and Ronald Reagan versus Jimmy Carter in 1980. The 1979 election in Great Britain qualifies as a watershed contest. The government of Callaghan represented the consensual approach that had endured essentially undisturbed since the end of the Second World War: support for, or at least toleration of, socialized institutions; concessions to the unions; efforts to lessen Britain's involvement with its former colonies and to forge stronger links with the emerging European community; and nonrestrictive fiscal policies. While the Conservative prime ministers Macmillan, Douglas-Home, and Heath may have exhibited different emphases from the Labor prime ministers Harold Wilson and Callaghan, the differences among them were even less dramatic than those that distinguished Democratic and Republican American presidents from one another between 1945 and 1980.

In the election campaign of 1979, Margaret Thatcher challenged the conventional wisdom about Great Britain. Her effectively presented poster declared "Labour Is Not Working." She said that Britain was "a great country which seem[ed] to have lost its way." As much by the energy with which she campaigned and the boldness with which she challenged Callaghan ("You no longer have the courage to act. Will you not at least have the courage to resign?") as by the specific proposals that she put forth, Thatcher succeeded in convincing the electorate that it was time for a dramatic change of direction. Callaghan tried to caution the electorate against the risks of a Thatcher revolution: "The question you will have to consider is whether we risk tearing everything up by its roots?" Clearly, a majority of the electorate were willing to answer yes.

Still, when Thatcher and the Tories came to power in 1979, it was not clear whether the changes that her election promised would materialize. Many leaders invoke a powerful rhetoric but cannot convert that rhetoric into action, either because they themselves lack the courage of their convictions or because they cannot convince elected officials, appointed ministers, and entrenched bureaucrats to alter their course. Indeed, the entitled mentality of British civil servants and the collegial atmosphere of the Conservative Party front benches both foretold that Thatcher would not have an easy time forging a new Great Britain.

Perhaps Thatcher's greatest ally in the course that she had set for herself was her own self-confidence. Upon her election, she declared: "The passionately interesting thing to me is that the things I learned in a small town, in a very modest home, are just the things that I believe have won the election." Thatcher was convinced that the virtues of integrity, self-reliance, initiative, and decency that she had absorbed from her father were just the remedies for what ailed Britain. And in a revealing, if immodest, passage in her autobiography, Thatcher says: "Chatham famously remarked: 'I know that I can save this country and that no one else can.' It would have been presumptuous for me to have compared myself to Chatham. But if I am honest, I must admit that my exhilaration came from a similar inner conviction." Like no other political figure since Churchill, Thatcher could embody the self-confidence that she called forth from a demoralized British citizenry. She was prepared to confront others and to meet her own demanding standards.

In general terms, Thatcher fit the pattern of future leaders who see themselves from an early age as figures of destiny and who exhibit an ability to challenge those in positions of authority. It is worth noting, however, that as a woman in a man's world, Thatcher had to walk a fine line between challenge and disruption. Like Eleanor Roosevelt, she only gradually revealed her challenging personality to others—and, perhaps, to herself.

But once she became prime minister, Thatcher made it clear that she would be a very different leader from her immediate predecessors. Conviction dominated over consensus; she stated her goals and mission explicitly; she spoke of "new beginnings," "mandates," and "sea changes." She placed individuals who were loyal to her and to her policies in the most important cabinet positions, particularly in the areas of economics and finance. An instinctive activist, she involved herself deeply—some would say intrusively—in all of the departments and programs. She rose early, worked late, demanded to be fully briefed, and challenged her staff to follow her engaged example. (In this respect, she was closer to activist presidents Carter and Clinton than to the essentially passive Reagan.)

Both in the domestic and in the international arenas, Thatcher established herself as being intransigent—as a person who developed her position, stated it unambiguously, and largely ignored criticism or counsel. At international summit meetings, she nearly always placed herself at the center of controversy. The long-time Laborite Roy Jenkins commented in 1985:

> As a proponent of the British case, she does have the advantage of being almost totally impervious to how much she offends other people. I have seen her when she was a new prime minister surrounded by others who were against her and being unmoved by this in a way that many other people would find difficult to withstand.

A memorable line created in October 1980 by the speechwriter Ronald Millar captured her position perfectly: "The lady's not for turning."

In the first few years of her ministry, Thatcher had decidedly mixed successes. On the one hand, she demonstrated that it was politically acceptable in Britain to adopt a strict monetarist policy and to create high levels of unemployment; the British public appeared prepared to accept the possibility of job loss in order to secure lower inflation and balanced budgets. There was also less loyalty than might have been anticipated to the welfare state; it proved possible to privatize some industries and to curb unions' powers. As in the United States, something of a realignment occurred within the electorate: Laborites-turned-Tories benefited from the opportunity to purchase public housing, even as they felt in tune with the Conservatives' embracing of "old-fashioned" values of family and patriotism.

Yet Thatcher paid a price for these changes of direction. In her cabinet much unhappiness existed, many of the so-called wets (the old consensus Conservatives) threatened to resign, and a number of traumatic shuffles of portfolios occurred. Thatcher did not mind these perturbations. "I am not ruthless," she asserted, "but some things have to be done." Defending her decision to appoint only people who backed her fully, she asserted: "As Prime Minister, I couldn't waste time having any internal arguments." Racial tensions were exacerbated, and Thatcher showed little understanding of, or sympathy for, the poor people and the immigrants who suffered most from her policies.

A major inflammatory agent was Thatcher's own style; she seemed to relish browbeating. She not only wanted to win but seemed to gain satisfaction from winning publicly and dramatically—and humiliating her opposition in the process. As the author David Howell commented:

> While many Tories were aiming to tear down the old consensus in order to build a powerful new one . . . in true Conservative fashion, the Thatcher habit of turning the whole process into one constant upheaval, with constant polarization of every issue, even after events had clearly moved in the right direction anyway, prolonged the turmoil and minimized united support for change.

This confrontational style, perhaps as much as her radical policies, did not endear Thatcher to her electorate. In December 1981, only 23 percent of those polled said that she was doing a good job—the lowest popularity rating to that date ever received by a sitting British prime minister.

Just as there are watershed elections, there are landmark events that change the course of a politician's career and, perhaps, of national political winds as well. Franklin Roosevelt's first one hundred days in office, Churchill's actions during the Battle of Britain, Israel's Six Day War during Golda Meir's tenure, Reagan's firing of the air traffic controllers, and Bush's successful prosecution of the Persian Gulf War are examples from the period covered in this book. No other individual political leader in recent history, however, has had a more dramatic reversal of fortune than did Thatcher at the time of the Falklands War.

On April 1, 1982, the Argentinian military invaded the nearby Falkland Islands, long a British possession. In fact, the Falklands had been an anomalous possession, and British governments had considered from time to time how that territory might be handed over to the Argentinians, who claimed sovereignty over what they called the Malvinas Islands. Nonetheless, nearly all Britons reacted with outrage to this aggressive seizure by a corrupt and fascistic regime; most British political figures demanded that the islands be returned, by force if necessary.

Under Thatcher's determined leadership, the Falklands were indeed reclaimed. Portraying the struggle as a stark one between good and evil, Thatcher declared at once that the invasion had to be ended promptly. She presided over a rapid and powerful marshaling of financial and human resources. She participated actively and enthusiastically in the planning of missions, even getting on her hands and knees alongside the attorney general to measure territorial charts. She authorized the sinking of the *General Belgrano,* an act that resulted in the drowning of 368 Argentinian sailors. When British lives were lost as a consequence of an attack on the destroyer *Sheffield,* she did not deviate from her stated goal—a complete Argentinian surrender. As she declared later: "I do not think that I have ever lived so tensely or intensely as during the whole of the time." And she persisted until the final successful assault on Port Stanley and the capitulation of the Argentinian forces.

As the biographer Hugo Young asserted: "The Falklands war was a seminal event in the life of the Thatcher Administration. Its triumphant end, effacing the many tribulations on the domestic scene, was what guaranteed the Conservatives' political triumph at the next election and on into the measureless future." Speaking in Cheltenham, Thatcher announced in Churchillian tones: "We have ceased to be a nation in retreat. We have instead a newfound confidence—born in the economic battles at home and tested and found true 8,000 miles away. . . . Britain has rekindled that spirit which has fired her for generations past and which today has begun to burn as brightly as before." In her autobiography, Thatcher declares:

> British foreign policy had been one long retreat. . . . Everywhere I went after the war, Britain's name meant something more than it had. . . . Years later I was told by a Russian general that the Soviets had been firmly convinced that we would not fight for the Falklands and that if we fought for the Falklands we would lose. We proved them wrong on both counts and they did not forget the fact.

As at earlier times in her life, Thatcher capitalized on her success. Fully cognizant of its symbolic value, she seized on the Falklands victory as a sign that her policies everywhere were equally justifiable. Momentarily inclusive, she embraced everyone under her own definition of unity: "What matters is that it was everyone together—we all knew what we had to do and went out there and did it." Within her cabinet, she called for and received total allegiance; and benefiting from an outpouring of new support in the electorate, she won a commanding victory in June 1983 by garnering the largest electoral majority of any party since 1945. Thatcher claimed that her election victory was "the single most devastating defeat ever inflicted upon democratic socialism in Britain. . . . The Left could never again credibly claim popular appeal for their programme of massive nationalization, huge increased public spending, greater trade union power, and unilateral nuclear disarmament."

Having secured a comfortable margin in Parliament, Thatcher was able to pursue her policies with fresh confidence and somewhat greater success. On the domestic scene, she risked turmoil by allowing the coal miners to remain on strike for the better part of 1984 and 1985. At the end of that action, she had successfully faced down the incendiary union leader Arthur Scargill and his rather lackluster troops and had significantly weakened the role of labor unions in British life, as her soulmate Reagan had done in America. Despite some setbacks, the privatization of industry continued. And Thatcher rose steadily in the arena of international relations; clearly considering herself a major force, she benefited greatly from her "special relationship" with Reagan and won at least grudging acceptance from other world leaders.

With the Falklands War, her reelection, and the confrontation with the miners behind Thatcher, the major outline of her view of the world—which had one basic premise—was now clear to all. Thatcher's central premise was that human beings could be conceived of as either on the "right side" or the "wrong side." Early in her tenure, Thatcher used to ask of her associates, "Is he one of us?" The referent of "us" might vary somewhat across contexts, but the basic issue was, Did the individual have the same point of view about life as Thatcher and her circle, or was that individual in some fundamental way in opposition? She once declared: "I am in politics because of the conflict between good and evil, and I believe that in the end good will triumph."

This Manichaean view—one that certifiably reflects the unschooled mind at work—was brought to bear in arenas of various scope. Within her cabinet, Thatcher was constantly concerned about whether the individual was a "wet" (one who basically subscribed to the consensual view of Heath) or a "dry" (one who aligned himself or herself with Thatcher's laissez-faire economic and social views). Thatcher was only mildly interested in whether an individual was a Conservative— the question was whether the individual was the "right kind" of Conservative.

Within Britain, Thatcher also took an "us/them" view. Those with whom she had sympathy were small businesspeople, self-made individuals, and those who worked in the engineering and technical spheres. Those whom she considered enemies were government bureaucrats, members of labor unions, and those who worked at universities and/or considered themselves members of the intelligentsia. She believed that people in the former group were hardworking and sympathetic to her philosophy of individualism, while people in the latter group were lazy and enthusiastic about collectivist ideologies. Attractions and repulsions were mutual. Author Julian Barnes commented:

> To the liberal, the snobbish, the metropolitan, the cosmopolitan, she displayed a parochial, small shopkeeper mentality. . . . But to those who supported her, she was a plain speaker, a clear and visionary thinker who embodied no-nonsense, stand-on-your-own-two-feet virtue, a patriot who saw that we had been living on borrowed time and borrowed money for far too long.

Given the facts of Thatcher's life, an inevitable tension existed. Although her background gave her eligibility as a member of the "us," she shared much with the "them"—after all, she was a wealthy university graduate who was comfortable with ideas. A sworn enemy of big government, she had always been on the public payroll. But, like Reagan, she successfully convinced the public that she embodied the virtues of "us" and was fundamentally different in character and worldview from "them." Perhaps the undoubted strength with which she held her convictions, coupled with her authentically humble origins, protected her against the charge of hypocrisy.

In these facets, Thatcher was amazingly similar to the other effective political figure of the 1980s, Reagan. Both put forth a simple nostalgic message in which they personally believed, one that they could articulate persuasively and one that, despite minor inconsistencies, they appeared to embody in their own lives. They were convincing spokespersons for their perspectives. It is important to note how Reagan and Thatcher differed from their successors: neither in the case of Bush nor Clinton nor John Major was it clear what they stood for, and when they took a position, they did not appear to embody it with their entire being.

As part of her clear message, Thatcher saw Britain as having failed under the leadership of "them"—Laborite socialists and Conservative fellow travelers. A true believer in the Hayek tradition, she distrusted any form of collective action. Indeed, in words that raised eyebrows almost everywhere, she claimed that societies do not exist—only individuals do. She looked back nostalgically to the Victorian era of free enterprise and voluntary charity, and to the patriotism of the world wars, while disdaining the collectivist vision of the modern welfare state. An advocate for equality of opportunity but not ultimate equality, she contended that people have the right to keep what they have earned; indeed, she was virtually an unreconstructed social Darwinist. Speaking to aspiring businesspeople, she said: "The only thing I'm going to do for you is to make you freer to do things for yourself. If you can't do it, I'm sorry. I'll have nothing to offer you." She called for a government that allowed "at least some encouragement for work, for skill, for effort, and, above all, for success." And she proudly pointed to Britain's past successes in work, invention, science, and democracy: "With achievements like that, who can doubt that Britain can have a great future and what our friends want to know is whether that future is going to happen."

Against this background, it became easy to identify the enemies of Britain. From within, they were those who disagreed with her philosophy—those who embraced the socialistic counterstory. From without, they were those who threatened to interfere with the British way of life. Thatcher felt that Britain was a special country with a unique relationship to the United States and with increasingly distant relationships to the Commonwealth, to Europe, and to the rest of the globe. Throughout her tenure, she adopted a very cautious stance toward any kind of economic, political, or social connection to Europe. She did not like the centralistic, bureaucratic, and socialistic tendencies of the European Community, and so she opposed those leaders—and especially those from France and Germany—who called for a strong and integrated Europe. (In these respects she was much closer in spirit to de Gaulle than to Jean Monnet.) In her autobiography, she declares tartly: "The idea that other clever people—and Jacques Delors [the president of the European Commission] was one of the cleverest people I met in European politics—can build their Tower of Babel on the uneven foundation of ancient nations, different languages and diverse economies is still more dangerous."

Thatcher's worldview illustrates well the layers that can come to inhere in a dominant story. For those who did not wish to probe deeply, it was sufficient simply to praise Britain and its glorious past and to disdain any attacks on a free-market economy. But Thatcher and her colleagues were prepared to provide further texture for interested parties. Her story could be embraced at different levels of sophistication. As occurred in the Reagan era in the United States, a whole saga came to be written about the proper course that the country had once followed and the various villains who had threatened that course in the last half century. And a sizable group of intellectuals presented themselves as neoconservatives who could provide erudite details of this story and also contribute illustrious future chapters.

Of course, for anyone living in the West during the cold war, the Soviet Union had to serve as the obvious archenemy. And indeed, Thatcher had as little sympathy for communism in Russia as she had for socialism in Britain or in Europe. It is therefore notable that Thatcher was the first Western leader to form a relationship with Mikhail Gorbachev. After meeting him and arguing with him for hours at a stretch, she came to like him and, in a famous phrase, to feel that one could "do business with him." Her recognition that Gorbachev differed from other Soviet leaders and her continuing relationship to him were significant factors in the transformation, if not the collapse, of the Soviet Union. Thus, an individual with unquestionable conservative credentials facilitated a realignment of international political allegiances (as Richard Nixon had done with Communist China in the early 1970s).

Thatcher was fortunate in the succession of opponents who came her way: the weak Conservative leader Edward Heath, the woolly Labor leader Neil Kinnock, the singularly inept Argentinian leader General Leopoldo Galtieri, and the uncouth and extremist miners' union leader Arthur Scargill. Even Gorbachev turned out to be a stroke of luck. But it must be added that, at least for the first years of her prime ministership, Thatcher knew how to choose her enemies, play them expertly, and use them to advance her cause.

Despite her husband's great wealth and her own formidable intellectual powers, Thatcher had no trouble in embodying the story that she told. She was an enthusiastic patriot, a knowledgeable politician, and a tireless worker for the causes in which she believed. In some ways, she never relinquished the simple view of the five-year-old mind. She did see the world in stark black-and-white terms and could not tolerate ambiguity or subtlety. Singularly disinterested in consensus, she went so far as to label consensualists as "quislings" (traitors).

Curiously, Thatcher was able comfortably to maintain her simple worldview along with a quite detailed and sophisticated understanding of political and economic issues. Unlike Reagan, for example, Thatcher was neither lazy nor uninformed. Visitors and opponents were constantly surprised by her detailed knowledge, her superlative memory, her shrewd questions, and her capacity to mobilize information in debates. She liked to argue and respected adversaries who were prepared to state facts and formulate arguments; she had no patience for sentiment or cant. In more than one domain, she qualified as an expert. Yet, with a skill that is seldom encountered in the political realm, Thatcher was able to separate out her expertise from her political instincts, invoking each when needed, but seldom confusing them with each other. Her undoubted intelligence rarely sabotaged her sense of where the public stood. In realms ranging from the Falklands War to fiscal policy, Thatcher illustrated how a political leader can productively synthesize expertise with messages of simplicity and clarity.

Thatcher also possessed personal courage. When Earl Mountbatten was slain, she proceeded directly to Northern Ireland, the scene of the tragedy. When she was almost killed in a terrorist bombing at the Brighton party congress, she continued immediately—even defiantly—with her work, setting an admirable example for her ministers and for the rest of her country. Unlike the many who pay mere lip service to the old adage, Thatcher was clearly prepared to lose on principle and did so on more than one occasion.

Yet, Thatcher's own deficiencies grew all too intimately and integrally out of her strengths. She sought to control everything, rarely delegated authority, slept for only four hours a night, and fixed her eyes on every detail during her waking hours. Her self-confidence slid easily into intolerance, inflexibility, and moralism. She was widely seen, even by supporters, as domineering, mean-spirited, divisive, and unheeding. On television, she appeared as "bossy" to many members of the general public. Intolerant of indecisiveness or reflection, she once dismissed a minister by saying that "his vice was second thoughts." In a related mood, she asserted: "The Old Testament prophets did not go out and ask for consensus." She was famous for insulting individuals gratuitously. Her close associate and minister Kenneth Baker described Thatcher as "personally dominant, supremely self-confident, infuriatingly stubborn . . . a strange mixture of broad views and narrow prejudices." A civil servant said, "She was the only minister I never heard say 'I wonder whether.'"

Finally, there is the issue of Thatcher as a woman. More so than Margaret Mead and Eleanor Roosevelt, Thatcher came to prominence at a time when the role of women was being rethought in Western society; and in all likelihood, she benefited from this reconsideration. It is difficult to imagine Thatcher being elected to high political office in a prefeminist era, even in a country that had long honored women sovereigns. Initially, Thatcher was treated like a woman in politics, being given the predictable socially oriented portfolios and being asked the predictable domestic questions. But Thatcher clearly did not want to be treated like a woman minister and did not in any way accept compartmentalization as a member of the second sex.

Indeed, as a leader, Thatcher is better thought of in the tradition of India's Indira Gandhi (her only declared heroine), Israel's Golda Meir, and Pakistan's Benazir Bhutto—innately adept politicians. On virtually every dimension that one thinks of as "masculine" in politics, Thatcher was capable of defeating her male opponents. She was a better debater, and she was tougher, more analytic, and, when it came to war, more resolute. (According to the political scientist John Stoessinger, women leaders in the twentieth century have never lost a war.) She indeed considered her opponents, nearly all of whom were men, as being more like the women that they derided:

My experience is that a number of the men I have dealt with in politics demonstrate precisely those characteristics which they attribute to women—vanity and an inability to make decisions. . . . If a woman asks no special privileges and expects to be judged solely by what she is and does, this is found gravely and unforgivably disorienting.

Yet, Thatcher was no feminist and had little identification with women's issues (or as she might prefer to express it, she advanced the cause of all women by showing that this woman could make it without apology in a man's world). Still I would be remiss if I failed to point out that Margaret Thatcher is in many ways a very attractive person. Just as leaders of both sexes benefit from charismatic features, women leaders may benefit from their attractiveness in what remains largely a man's world in the political realm.

For the first part of Thatcher's prime ministership, it was unclear whether she would attain her goals. After the Falkland victory and her spectacular reelection, she reached the height of her influence. While neither easier to work with nor more flexible than in earlier years of her ministership, she found—and helped to ensure—that the domestic and international tides were running in her direction. She personally felt, after another electoral victory in 1987, that she might just "go on and on and on." She commented to an interviewer, "I think that I have become a bit of an institution." And she added, "I intend to hang on until I believe there are people who can take the banner forward with the same commitment, belief, vision, strength, and singleness of purpose."

In triumph Thatcher was anything but conciliatory. Rather like Nixon after his unprecedented electoral landslide in 1972, Thatcher wanted her vindication to be complete. She continued to act as if she were the head of a vulnerable guerrilla group rather than the popular choice of the masses. She tolerated no ministers who were not totally loyal. Her opponents were loathe to confront her: "They were intimidated by her. She was bolder, more ruthless, less amenable to reason than they were."

Yet, within three years of her third election victory, on November 22, 1990, Margaret Thatcher resigned because of pressure from members of her own party. How can one account for this swift reversal of fortune? It is tempting to point to specific factors—for example, the increasing discrepancy between the rich and the poor sectors of the British population; Thatcher's virtually single-handed attempt to thwart the creation of an effective European Community; her unrelenting attacks on local government; her perhaps surprising efforts to institute greater central control over education and other traditionally local concerns; and, perhaps especially, her bullying insistence on a regressive poll tax, or "community charge," to be paid by every citizen.

But Thatcher probably would have survived a combination of these miscalculations or misguided policies if she had been a different kind of person. She came to be seen increasingly by members of both parties as an individual who was out of touch with political realities. She had been so convinced of her rightness on every issue that she had begun to act as a reigning monarch rather than as the temporary chosen head of an elected party that would have to win votes of confidence and stand for election again and again. Indeed, once she had convinced herself on an issue, she acted as if she believed that it was no longer necessary to convince others as well. As Geoffrey Howe, her long-time minister, declared in exasperated tones: "The insistence on the undivided sovereignty of her opinion, dressed up as the nation's sovereignty, was her undoing."

Thatcher did not leave office willingly or with equanimity. She resigned only when it became clear that she had lost control of her party. And her memoirs are filled with contempt for those who drove her out of office, and only slightly less disdain for Major, whom she supported as her successor. While others attribute Thatcher's ultimate failure to retain the office to her personal deficiencies, Thatcher herself clearly blames the leaders and followers who did not appreciate her far-sighted policies.

In the years since her departure from office, she has installed herself as a kind of "loyal opposition" to both parties, never hesitating to offer criticism and advice, on both domestic and international issues. In her attempts to mobilize the world to deal with the Bosnian atrocities, one sees her more admirable traits; in her sniping at her former colleagues, one sees Thatcher in her petulant and petty guises.

It is too soon to issue a reliable judgment on the enduring effects of Thatcher's lengthy tenure as the British prime minister. We will not know for decades whether she effected a fundamental reorientation in British political life or only a momentary detour in a process that had begun far earlier in the century and that is likely to continue well into the twenty-first century. Even though Thatcher was the head of a political party that is likely to endure, she is in the position of Martin Luther King, Jr., Eleanor Roosevelt, Pope John XXIII, or indeed any other innovative leader: she cannot be certain that her own legacy will be carried on. She herself recognized this when she declared, after her departure from office:

> Orthodox finance, low levels of regulation and taxation, a minimal bureaucracy, strong defence, a willingness to stand up for British interests wherever and whenever threatened—I did not believe that I had to open windows into men's souls on these matters. The arguments for them seemed to me to have been won. I now know that such arguments are never finally won.

Still, it is possible to speak about Thatcher's interim influence on her country and on her terms—a historical period that has come deservedly to be known as the Thatcher era. On many of her specific goals, Thatcher did not achieve signal success. She did not thwart recession and inflation, significantly reduce public expenditures or the tax burden, secure new sources of revenue, or reduce the high unemployment levels. And during her tenure, regional and racial tensions were exacerbated. Nor was Thatcher entirely consistent in her policies. She defended mortgage tax relief and opposed increases in interest rates because such relatively "wet" policies reflected the interests of her staunchest supporters.

But when it came to affecting how British citizens viewed their country, their options, and their place in the world, Thatcher made considerable strides. She successfully challenged the socialistic trends that had dominated British politics since the Second World War; she conferred power on individual entrepreneurs, small innovative companies, and, more generally, on the market forces; and she undermined consensual views about the once-dominant roles of the unions, nationalized industry, and local government. Like Franklin Roosevelt and Ronald Reagan in the United States, Thatcher changed the terms of the debate in her own country. As the former U.S. secretary of state Henry Kissinger expressed it, in an appreciation of Thatcher: "So great was the transformation that the current official platform of the Labor Party is not very different from what Mrs. Thatcher inherited in 1975 as the Conservative program."

In terms of our discussion, then, Thatcher emerges as an effective direct leader—one who altered the ways in which her contemporaries thought, felt, and acted. Moreover, she deserves to be considered an innovative leader, for she was able to reactivate beliefs and values that had been dormant in her country for many years. She brought about this reorientation, however, in an unschooled way that was often simplistic and divisive—by stressing the difference between Britain and other countries, between Tories and Laborites, and, within her own party, between those who supported her totally and those who were critical of her in any way. Had she sought to build bridges to those who were somewhat critical, she might have been able to weather the political storms of the late 1980s. (Note, in contrast, how well Ronald Reagan's conciliatory gifts stood him during the Iran-Contra crisis of his second term.) However, had she been less dogged, she might never have attained power or, having attained it, redirected the attention, interests, and energies of the British population. Thatcher's failures stemmed from the same factors as did her successes.

In a democratic society definite limits circumscribe what a leader can accomplish. Nearly every issue needs to be debated and voted upon; various constituencies must be considered and satisfied; and, given the prospect of elections, one must always keep an eye on the often-fickle electorate. When an individual leader or group pushes hard in one direction, there is destined to be a reaction, and often that reaction is sufficiently virulent as to undo much of the force of the innovation. One need not subscribe to the historian Arthur Schlesinger, Jr.'s theory of thirty-year cycles in American history or to Thomas Jefferson's (or Mao Zedong's) call for a revolution every ten or twenty years to recognize that trends within a democratic society always have a "term" aspect to them.

Even totalitarian regimes experience some push and pull over the years, and even totalitarian regimes come to an end sooner or later. But while they are running their course, they can proceed much more determinedly in one direction. Stalin's or Mao's or Franco's reigns of several decades find no ready parallel in Western democratic states. Such mobilization is likely to occur in democracies only at times of crisis, as during a major war or a severe depression. Citizens are willing to sacrifice their rights and their personal priorities, at least temporarily, in order to be assured a measure of security and the absence of economic chaos. Thatcher was able to take advantage of such a crisis atmosphere for a time, but it ultimately dissipated and her effectiveness ended. Succeeding generations, however, will more fully judge her contributions as a national and world leader.

13

A GENERATION OF
WORLD LEADERS

When the leader arrives, people are full of panic, uncertain what to do and defeatist about the future. When the authentic leader has spoken, they have been given back their courage.

—William Rees-Mogg

[Franklin Roosevelt] became a scholar and specialist with politics his profession as theoretical physics was Einstein's.

—Thomas Parrish

Looking back and visualizing the whole slow accumulation of inventions that have made us human beings and, finally civilized human beings, we find, salient among them, man's developing ability to include in the conception of his own group ever more people living at greater distance: his clan, his tribe, his nation, his religion, his part of the world.

—Margaret Mead

The leaders present at the Eureka Summit in Tehran at the end of 1943—Franklin Roosevelt (1882–1945) of the United States, Winston Churchill (1874–1965) of Great Britain, and Josef Stalin (1879–1953) of the Union of Soviet Socialist Republics—were a remarkable group. Each presided over a major world power that had been subjected to unprecedented pressures because of their adversaries' military attacks. While the precise details about the end of the Second World War could not be known, it had become clear by the end of November 1943 that victory would be theirs: sooner or later, the rival Axis powers would be defeated and the brutal attacks on Pearl Harbor, London, and

Leningrad would be avenged. Indeed, these powerful men who had never before been gathered as a group had assembled in the Iranian capital in order to reach decisions about the final moves in the war and about the shape of the peace thereafter.

During their meetings, Stalin, Churchill, and Roosevelt came to know and to form personal opinions about one another. As I noted in chapter 1, they discussed the ways in which to defeat Adolf Hitler and the Axis powers efficiently and decisively; they reached final agreement on an Atlantic invasion of Western Europe in the spring of 1944; they made decisions about the battlefronts in the Mediterranean and the Far East; and they weighed territorial and judicial options for the postwar era. While relatively few commitments were made—one thinks of the subsequent controversial meeting at Yalta in 1945 as an occasion at which more fateful agreements were forged—a general compatibility of interests prevailed. The three aging but still-active men returned home to direct their respective countries in war and to prepare for peace.

The summit at Tehran provides a cardinal example of leaders doing what leaders are classically expected to do. Each man had established himself unambiguously as the head of a great nation; each was commanding his troops bravely during war; each was able to commit his nation. Taken together, these men held an unprecedented amount of power—a control over persons and resources that dwarfed the clout associated with such legendary individuals as Alexander, Charlemagne, Genghis Khan, or Napoléon, and even the hated German and Japanese leaders. And they were now engaged in the highest-stakes negotiation, one that had as its twin goals the protection of the prerogatives of their own countries and the forging of a peace that could endure globally.

While these men constituted a unique class, they also represented a generation that consisted of powerful leaders. Joining Roosevelt and Churchill as leaders of a democratic society was Charles de Gaulle (1890–1970), who since 1940 had been the self-proclaimed leader of the Free French forces. The totalitarian leaders of the Axis powers included Adolf Hitler (1889–1945) of Germany, Benito Mussolini (1883–1945) of Italy, and Hideki Tojo (1884–1948) of Japan. Other individuals who could be grouped loosely with the leaders of the war nations included Chiang Kai-shek (1887–1975) and Mao Zedong (1893–1976) of China. Also part of this generation were Stalin and, though no longer surviving, the founding Soviet leader, V. I. Lenin (1870–1924). (Two other relevant figures, Mahatma Gandhi and Jean Monnet are discussed in the next chapter.) Any decision about inclusion or exclusion in this generation of leaders is necessarily arbitrary; for example, Tojo or Lenin could be dropped and Francisco Franco, the Spanish dictator, could be added to my sample. For our purposes, however, these ten men can be considered as representative world leaders of the twentieth century.

In the preceding chapters, I have discussed nine individuals who—by dint of the stories that they told and the lives that they led—may be considered as representative leaders as well. They have ranged from individuals like Margaret Mead, whose leadership derived significantly from the quality of the symbolic products that she issued; to leaders of relatively circumscribed institutions, like Robert Maynard Hutchins; to leaders like Margaret Thatcher, who presided over an entire nation for over a decade. While none of these leaders assumed quite the responsibility or achieved quite the lustre that surrounded the leaders at Tehran, they each have fulfilled the basic criterion of leadership: significantly affecting the thoughts, feelings, and/or actions of a significant number of individuals. Indeed, it might even be argued that some phenomena of leadership may emerge more sharply when one examines individuals who were less extraordinary, less wrapped in legend, than the trio at Tehran.

An examination of these leaders allows me to accomplish two important goals. First, any study of leadership that claims to be comprehensive needs to consider not only a range of representative figures (as I have done) but also paradigmatic cases, such as the ten men just cited. Second, in the course of the study, a number of suggestive themes have emerged. This generation of world leaders provides an opportunity to test out these themes, to see whether, in addition to characterizing the nine representative leaders, they also prove relevant in thinking about ten world-class leaders. Finally, some themes that were muted or absent altogether until now emerge through this survey of ten exceptional people.

Two other points about the scope of this chapter deserve comment. As noted in chapter 1, I conceived the present study of leadership after having completed a similar study of individuals who were considered highly creative in their respective domains. Even as I search for "symptoms" of leadership, I cast a comparative glance at generalizations that emerged from my earlier study, *Creating Minds.* In this respect, Margaret Mead and J. Robert Oppenheimer are especially germane, because they began their professional lives as indirect leaders (in the Einstein/ Picasso tradition) but ultimately became direct leaders (in the Thatcher/Marshall tradition).

I must stress, finally, that this study should not be considered a quantitative one. I lack the tools to measure how much of a rebel each leader was, how many ups and downs marked each career, or how simplistic or complex each person's story was. In the spirit of Howard Gruber's or Erik Erikson's "idiographic" studies of exemplary individuals, I am searching for themes that recur in this population. I look forward to the time when the tentative generalizations that emerge can be placed on firmer "nomothetic" footing.

At the same time, it is important to mention that the themes reported here are not simply scattered impressions. Emma Laskin and I have sought to obtain information on each theme for each individual. To report on a dozen themes in the lives of ten individuals would make for an unwieldy and scientistic document, and so this chapter contains telling examples rather than an exhaustive account. Accordingly, we have prepared appendix II for readers who are interested in a fuller survey of materials relevant to the major themes.

The creators of the modern era came largely from intact bourgeois homes in which dedication to the task—any task—was considered a crucial virtue. Each of these individuals had a comfortable and proper, if not overly loving, relationship with his or her parents. While an ultimate choice of vocation was not always clear, each young creator worked for at least a decade in a domain, thereby attaining an impressive degree of mastery before venturing to more novel applications in the outer regions of that domain.

The direct leaders* examined in this chapter form an instructive contrast to this group. Although they grew up at about the same time and largely in European nations, their backgrounds were far more varied. Very roughly, the leaders fall into two camps: the privileged and the deprived. Roosevelt and Churchill came from essentially aristocratic backgrounds, with a long history of family involvement in political life; de Gaulle's and Lenin's families were upper middle class and scholarly. Interestingly, de Gaulle's family was very patriotic, while Lenin's family opposed the tsarist regime and his brother was actually hanged on account of revolutionary activities.

In contrast, the family backgrounds of the totalitarian leaders were far less privileged. Hitler's father was illegitimate and attained the rank of only a minor customs official; Mussolini's father was a blacksmith who also dabbled in journalism; Stalin's father was an indigent cobbler. The backgrounds of China's leaders anticipated their ultimate opposing stances in the Chinese civil war: the father of left-wing Mao was a peasant (who eventually became well-to-do), while the father of right-wing Chiang was a merchant.

The relationship to their fathers proved crucial and quite problematic for most of the future leaders. Stalin's father beat him savagely; Hitler strongly condemned his tyrannical father for repeatedly beating his beloved mother. Mao's relationship to his father was stormy, and spurning the Chinese filial tradition, Mao left home at an early age. While this group of totalitarian leaders defied their fathers, de Gaulle and Lenin (each with totalitarian impulses) identified with their fathers and sought to carry forward their political leanings. Confirming a pattern reported elsewhere, nearly all of the leaders were quite young when their fathers died. In the absence of a surviving father, ambitious young males (and perhaps young females as well) are challenged to take charge of their own and their families' lives and to create their own moral (or immoral) code.

Experiences in school were equally charged for most of the leaders. While Mead, Oppenheimer, and Hutchins (each reared in educated homes) sailed

---

*In what follows, unless otherwise specified, I use the terms *leaders* and *direct leaders* to refer to the ten leaders portrayed in this chapter.

through school, winning honors and impressing associates with their unusually keen intelligence and their potential to "make a mark as a scholar," most of the world leaders found school to be an uncomfortable, if not disastrous, experience. Hitler was a scholastic failure and could not attain entrance to the art academy he so ardently wanted to attend. At his mother's wish, Stalin went to the Tiflis theological seminary, from which he was expelled for propagating Marxism. Mussolini displayed some academic gifts but was completely unruly in school and twice assaulted fellow students with knives. Mao's experience was similar— academic talent undone by personal tumult. Churchill's personal and academic difficulties in school are well documented. Roosevelt encountered no academic problems in school but basically led the life of the privileged "Gentleman's C" aristocrat rather than that of the young scholar. Of our group of leaders, only de Gaulle and Lenin were exemplary students who might conceivably have ended up pursuing careers as scholars. Indeed, if they had not lived in times of great political upheaval, we might remember them for their indirect leadership (as we remember the German socialist Karl Marx or the French conservative Charles Maurras for their writings).

When it comes to the attainment of expertise, the direct leaders diverge dramatically from the creators. As noted, most creators—and I include Oppenheimer and Mead in these ranks—devote themselves for at least a highly solitary decade to the mastery of the domain or discipline in which they will ultimately make their creative contributions.

The generation of world leaders did not undertake such systematic immersions in a socially organized domain of study. Instead, more adventurous in temperament, they set out to explore and perhaps conquer the wider world of human affairs. The career paths that they selected were typically military (de Gaulle, Chiang, Tojo, Franco, Churchill), journalistic (Mussolini, Churchill, Lenin), or political—either conventional (Churchill, Roosevelt) or revolutionary (Hitler, Mao, Stalin, Lenin). As noted, some followed two or even three of these paths. Nearly all participated actively in one way or another in the First World War; revealingly, none of the creators did.

The decision to travel within one's own country or abroad turns out to be revealing. Churchill traveled the most widely and visited Cuba, India, Sudan, and South Africa as a military reporter in his twenties. Chiang traveled to Japan and the Soviet Union, Tojo completed military training in Berlin, Lenin first traveled voluntarily and then was exiled to Europe, and Roosevelt (like his wife) made the proverbial European tour. What stands out are the individuals who did *not* travel abroad. With the exceptions of the Tehran Summit and his stay in Vienna, Stalin traveled entirely within the Soviet Union, and Mao traveled widely within his own country but did not go abroad. Young Hitler traveled only in Germany and Austria; his first trip to Paris marked the defeat of France in 1940. The biographer Alan Bullock commented, "[Hitler's] grasp of the mood of public opinion in the Western democracies was startling, considering that he had never visited any of them and spoke no foreign language."

Travel abroad in one's youth—of the sort that Mead and Oppenheimer indulged in—opens one up to the perspectives of different cultures and ideologies. (In this regard, Gandhi's twenty-odd years in Europe and South Africa are telling.) It is more difficult to maintain a monolithic perspective—a simplistic, often exclusionary story—when one has been exposed regularly to contrasting viewpoints. Those individuals who have *not* traveled widely are therefore in a more favorable position to see everything from the perspective of their compatriots, most of whom are also parochial, if not xenophobic.

To be sure, the decision to travel is facilitated by the possession of wealth; neither Churchill nor Roosevelt had to scrape up funds to go abroad. But the decision *not* to travel, even when one has the opportunity to do so, may be a marker that one deliberately wishes not to be exposed to experiences that might complicate one's view of the world. It may not be an accident, then, that the three most totalitarian figures of our time—Hitler, Stalin, and Mao—rarely set foot on foreign soil, even after they had ample opportunity to do so, and that their more cosmopolitan colleagues were more open to compromise.

The creators whom I studied did not have the smoothest of early careers. Nearly all of them suffered some setbacks; for instance, Freud was forty years old and had experienced several desultory careers before he finally launched his life's work. Yet, hardly any of the creators of the modern era had lives that could approach those of the leaders in terms of sheer tumult, unexpected opportunities, and sharp reversals.

Many books have been written on the formative years of each of the leaders. It would be impossible—and, given their fame, probably unnecessary—to chronicle the many twists and turns in their lives. But, as a set of illustrations or reminders, consider these extraordinary biographical facts:

Josef Stalin, a native of the Georgian republic, was arrested five times between 1902 and 1913 for revolutionary activities and always escaped. He engaged in many illegal and violent acts as he rose in the Bolshevik ranks. During the years of Lenin's rule in the early 1920s, Stalin, a brilliant organizer, held a number of posts; these allowed him to build up a loyal party apparatus, which he ultimately used after Lenin's death to crush Leon Trotsky and other opponents. He then ruled by increasingly tyrannical means for the next twenty years, during which he annihilated all opposition, formed temporary alliances with Germany and then with the Allied powers, and always strove single-mindedly to make the Soviet Union an invincible industrialized power.

Mao Zedong (Mao Tse-tung) participated in the initial revolutionary activities of the Chinese Communist Party. As early as 1919 he wrote: "The world is ours, the nation is ours, society is ours. If we do not speak, who will speak? If we do not act, who will act?" After joining forces in the early 1920s with the rival Kuomintang faction to fight the oppressive regime in Beijing, he saw nearly all of his colleagues killed in the late 1920s. The few hundred surviving Communists started a new kind of peasant-based revolutionary movement in the countryside, slowly and steadily building up power over twenty years, surviving many clashes and crises, until they seized control over the nation in 1949. As Mao saw it, peasants "would rise like a tornado or tempest—a force so extraordinarily swift and violent that no power, however great, [would] be able to suppress it." For the next twenty-seven years his regime became increasingly tyrannical as he presided over much chaos and contributed to it with his periodic calls for rectification and revolution.

Benito Mussolini was a most difficult child who declared to his mother: "One day I shall make the whole earth tremble." Not without talents, he founded a newspaper, built a trade union, led general strikes, and organized his followers against communism and socialism. Frequently involved in violent activities, he created a new political movement called fascism and marched on Rome in October 1922. After seizing power, he set up a government that, because of its disciplined order, gained admiration throughout much of the rest of the world. Once he became greedy for additional territory and made a "pact of convenience" with Hitler, he embarked on a course that brought ruination to his country and to himself.

Winston Churchill was always an iconoclast who took pleasure in defying convention. Yet his youthful achievements in warfare, journalism, and politics in various corners of the British Empire were so outstanding that he had become a celebrated figure while still in his twenties. Holding high office during the First World War, he laid claim to being the "father of naval aviation." Having been involved in controversial activities and decisions that earned him many enemies, he found himself in 1922 "without an office, without a seat, without a party, and even without an appendix." After flirting with a number of political movements and persistently decrying—to no avail—the rise of Hitler in the 1930s, he was the inevitable choice of his countrymen to provide leadership after France fell to the Nazis in 1940.

In many respects Charles de Gaulle's career resembled Churchill's. De Gaulle was also a gifted military man, political figure, and writer. He, too, was ignored during the 1930s when he anticipated the military tactics of Germany, and he emerged as a leader only after the defeat of France. Although he courageously led Free France during the Second World War, first broadcasting from Britain, then directing forces in North Africa, he did not receive the degree of support that he required after the war and so retired to write his memoirs as "an old man, worn out by all that he [had] gone through, remote from events." French citizens turned to him again in 1958 during the troubled Algerian war, and he undertook a decade of national leadership. Just as Churchill sought to celebrate Britain's grandeur, de Gaulle devoted all of his energies to rebuilding the French sense of worth, even at the cost of alienating the leaders of other countries and the more internationally oriented figures in his own land. After considerable student unrest in the late 1960s, de Gaulle once again voluntarily retired from public office.

Chiang Kai-shek was first influenced by Sun Yat-sen, the Chinese leader who sought to learn from the West. As a young man, Chiang read Marx and Lenin and received military training in the Soviet Union. Convinced that his country was backwards because of its longstanding imperial tradition, he and his Kuomintang Party sought to unify and modernize his country. He became involved for over twenty years in a life-and-death struggle with the Communists—a struggle that was suspended, but not resolved, during the period of the United Front in the Second World War. While China was recognized as a major power by the Allies, Chiang's own government unraveled due to widespread corruption and a loss of support from the general population. In 1949 he and his associates were forced to flee permanently to the small island of Taiwan.

Hideki Tojo, the least well known of the leaders, was the prime minister and military leader of Japan during much of the Second World War. He was trained at the military academy in Tokyo. He served in Berlin after the First World War, where he won a reputation as an effective administrator, a good field commander, and a severe disciplinarian. After assuming a leadership role with the Kwantung Army in Manchuria in the mid-1930s, he returned to Tokyo as the vice minister of war in 1938.

Throughout the latter part of his career, Tojo was among the most militant of Japanese leaders. He advocated an anti-Soviet pact with Germany and Italy, and in 1941 he forced out Prime Minister Konoe Fujimaro, who was more moderate. Proclaiming a "new order" in Asia, he gave final approval for the attack on Pearl Harbor in December 1941.

Styling himself as a fascist leader, Tojo reveled in the early Japanese military victories against the United States. As defeats of Japan began to mount in 1943 and 1944, he became not only the minister of commerce and industry but also the chief of the general staff—a virtual dictator. But he, in turn, was removed from office, along with his entire cabinet, in July 1944. After the Japanese surrender (which he had opposed), Tojo took responsibility for the loss and attempted suicide. He was nursed back to health, only to be tried and hanged as a war criminal in 1948.

As a youth, Adolf Hitler sold postcard sketches, beat carpets, and held a variety of other odd jobs. After first dodging military service, he fought bravely for the

German Army during the First World War. During the early 1920s, frustrated by Germany's defeat in war and its lack of stability during peace, he became one of the first members of the National Socialist (Nazi) Party. Jailed because of a failed putsch, he used the opportunity to write *Mein Kampf,* a remarkable confessional document in which he put forth his personal philosophy of fascist power, mysticism of "the people" (*das Volk*), German purification and grandeur, anti-Semitism, and ultimate world domination. After dissolution of the political system in Germany, he legally gained the chancellorship in 1933. Thereafter, he disassembled what was left of representative government, crushed opposition as decisively as did Stalin, and ruled essentially by decree and force of personality. A massive military buildup in the 1930s was followed by a series of brilliant early military victories in the Second World War, a slow turning of the tide by early 1943, and brutal destruction of Jews, other "non-Aryans," and, ultimately, his followers and much of the German populace.

In the discussion of Eleanor Roosevelt in chapter 10, I noted Franklin Roosevelt's rapid rise to positions of political authority in the United States: a state assemblyman in his twenties, the assistant secretary of the navy in his thirties, an unsuccessful candidate for the vice presidency, the governor of New York in his forties, and then four times elected president of the United States. From one perspective, his career curve was smoother than that of the other contemporary world leaders. But Roosevelt suffered a personal blow as painful as any sustained by his fellow leaders when, just shy of forty, he was struck by polio in 1921. It was not clear for some time whether he would ever walk again or be able to reenter public life. Because of loved ones' help and ample financial resources, Roosevelt was able to re-create himself during this period. His already formidable political skills were more finely honed and directed toward progressive, inclusionary ends. His personal courage not only inspired Americans but also allowed him to project the confidence that was needed to deal, first, with an unprecedented economic depression and, second, with a war that was physically remote from the mainland but that ultimately threatened all of civilization.

V. I. Lenin may have wanted to be a lawyer or a scholar, but events propelled him into the political sphere. After the untimely death of his father in January 1886 from a brain hemorrhage and the hanging of his brother in May 1887 for plotting to kill Tsar Alexandr III, he became a revolutionary follower of Karl Marx. As the leader of the Russian Bolshevik movement, he assumed militant positions with respect to insurgency in Russia and international revolution. A gifted theoretician, polemicist, and political leader, Lenin devised the methods for creating an elite political party and then built up such a powerful organization in the early 1900s. "Give us an organization of revolutionaries and we will overturn Russia," he declared.

Exiled to western Europe, he continued to devote his energies to the revolution in Russia while also promoting the Communist Party as an active political force on the Continent. During the height of the First World War, he was dispatched in a sealed train from Switzerland to Saint Petersburg, where his triumphant return helped to launch the much-anticipated revolution in war-torn imperial Russia. After rival socialistic and imperial armies were defeated, he ruled autocratically in the new USSR. Soon thereafter he became seriously ill, so he never clarified the future course of his regime. He died in 1924, leaving a legacy that his inconstant comrade Stalin extended in unanticipated ways.

Having a background in a domain relevant to political leadership and experiencing a life marked by tumult may turn out to be crucial ingredients in the formation of a national leader. Clearly, however, such a history is not sufficient. Factors of fortune always figure in the equation, and it is quite possible that none of these individuals would have become the leaders of their countries had they been born twenty years earlier or twenty years later. Indeed, a thirty-year-old Hitler in 1919 or a thirty-year-old Stalin in 1909 would have seemed ludicrous candidates for leadership of any kind of a significant political entity. The young de Gaulle and the youthful Churchill were universally recognized as gifted, and yet, had the Second World War not broken out, both might have been writing much briefer memoirs during the early 1940s.

However, one factor, already identified in my earlier portraits, recurs with a vengeance throughout the biographies of these ten titans of leadership: a *conviction* that one is special and a related *readiness* to confront others in positions of power on equal terms. Indeed, one challenges not just leaders in one's own domain of expertise (another physicist, another poet) but leaders with responsibility for entire institutions or political entities. One may recall George C. Marshall speaking up to General Pershing and then to President Roosevelt, or Margaret Thatcher confronting the leaders of her own party. Among the leaders of totalitarian nations, Hitler was haranguing crowds of thousands in the early 1920s and daring to stage a putsch in 1923, and Stalin was amassing power and scheming to eliminate Trotsky while remaining loyal on the surface to Lenin. Mussolini was defying king, army, and church in his march on Rome, and Mao was spending decades in the hinterlands preparing to take over his country. Lenin was confronting the leaders of rival socialist parties with the same intrepidness that he eventually displayed in establishing his Soviet regime in Russia, and Chiang was learning from the Communists in Russia and then using these very techniques to crush Communist factions in his own land. Tojo was leading a coup that unseated Prime Minister Konoe in October 1941.

The same defiance marks individuals who lived in nontotalitarian societies. Willing to face all challengers on nearly every political issue of the century, Churchill often stood alone and was prepared to face repudiation rather than compromise his deeply held opinions. De Gaulle defied the conventional political and military wisdom during the period between the wars, and he twice turned his back on power rather than continue in a position where he felt bereft of sufficient support. Franklin Roosevelt was the most compliant in his early years—perhaps because he did not need to be defiant. But his struggle with polio gave him the strength to risk all in his political life (including a break with his mentor, New York's governor Al Smith)—and to do so repeatedly after his election to the presidency. Like his fellow leaders, Roosevelt was not content to follow precedent. Indeed, for much of the time (from his unprecedented acceptance "in person" of the presidential nomination to his decision to stand for a third term), he was creating precedents. And like his fellow leaders, he was comfortable, even triumphant, in doing so. The insightful British scholar Isaiah Berlin said of Roosevelt, "He was one of the few statesmen of the twentieth century, or any century, who seemed to have no fear of the future."

Now, in noting that the leaders were willing to defy other powerful individuals and previous precedents, both before and during their years in power, it may appear as if I am only stating the obvious. After all, if one finds oneself a leader in unprecedented times, one may be expected to act in novel ways. But consider certain facts: Herbert Hoover was the leader of the United States during the early days of the Great Depression, just as Neville Chamberlain was in office in England and Paul Reynaud was in office in France when the Second World War began. Each of these men is remembered—if at all—precisely for his *failure* to rise to the occasion in the way that his successor did.

Instead, we need to examine a far more important question: Why, well before he had been ensconced as a national leader, did it seem natural—or at least conceivable—that each of the young men under scrutiny could challenge authority and begin to think of himself as an equal of the reigning leader? (Shifting pronouns, one can ask the same question with respect to Margaret Thatcher or Golda Meir, for example.) When it comes to Churchill or Roosevelt, this question is not so difficult to countenance, because both men came from families who had long provided leadership in their own nations. But how could the unemployed Hitler fantasize about a revitalized Germany with himself at the helm? Or the outlaws Lenin and Stalin envision themselves as leaders of the first Communist nation in the world? Or, in various ways, Chiang, Mao, Mussolini, Tojo, or de Gaulle each see himself as a viable leader of his nation?

The definitive clue to this enigma has come from the writings of Erik Erikson, who many years ago began to ponder such questions—most prominently, in his full-length studies of Martin Luther and Gandhi, but also in his more circumscribed musings about many twentieth-century political and ideological leaders. According to Erikson's psychoanalytic perspective, all individuals are involved in working out aspects of their psychosocial identity: who they are, where they come from, what is going to happen to them. It sometimes happens that individuals in the throes of an "identity crisis" arrive at solutions that work not only for them but also seem to hold a key to a wider problem, one that is besetting a significant portion of their society.

Consider, in this light, the conditions of the major countries of the world during the first part of this century. Imperial Russia, war-torn Germany, chaotic Italy, and postimperial China all were in disrepair. Living in these countries were many youths who also shared in the sense of confusion and dispossession—whose anxious feelings arose from the conditions of their families, their generation, and their countries, if not the entire world. At times when the conflicts and uncertainties that beset the individual intersect with those of the polity—and, especially, when the putative solutions also coincide—one has the makings of a potential national leader.

Of course, many young men and women are troubled and devote energies to working out a viable personal solution for their circumstances. What distinguishes the future national leader is that he or she has the ability and the will to think on a wide scale. The ability includes skills or intelligences in talking, writing, analyzing, and influencing other people. The will includes great ambition and a thirst for power, often fueled by a feeling of personal hurt and a sense of destiny. I can envision each of these leaders observing what was happening in his land, feeling deeply unhappy about it, and concluding in his own mind—perhaps grandiosely—that he could actually do a far better job than the current incumbents. He is already thinking as a future leader, challenging the words, the positions, the decisions, and the actions of those paternal figures who are currently in power. In effect, he identifies with current leaders—not in the sense of wanting to resemble the leader but rather in the sense of feeling that he would be comfortable in the leader's shoes. Perhaps because his proposed solution to his nation's problems grows so integrally out of his life's circumstances, that course of action feels intuitively much more powerful and apt than those put forth by leaders reared in an earlier and far different era. And so, when the opportunity arises (or is created) for him actually to confront these individuals—in words, in deeds—he finds in himself the strength, the courage, and perhaps the foolhardiness to do so.

The analysis that I propose in this book complements an Eriksonian approach. Leaders tell stories and embody them; direct leaders who would presume to guide a nation must tell stories that are simple enough to be apprehended by the unschooled mind. Perhaps regrettably, the leaders of the twentieth century provide ample documentation that simple stories can be very successful, and especially so in times of turmoil.

One can think of the twentieth century, politically, as consisting of a number of stories, each vying with rival accounts for a firmer hold on various populations. The story indigenous to the century is fascism. Rooted in certain anti-

Enlightenment attitudes, Mussolini's fascistic story involved a declaration that the state and the nation were the dominant forces in life, to which all individuals had to pledge total allegiance. United under the sign of the fasces, citizens of a fascist state would stand tall; they would be able to meet the threats posed by individualism, democracy, international communism—indeed, any and all rival ideologies that might be superficially appealing but that would undermine the possibility of a strong state. Crucial was the idea of an all-powerful leader—in Mussolini's words, "a man who is ruthless and energetic enough to make a clean sweep." Declared Mussolini when he came to power: "We are Italians and nothing but Italians. Now that steel has met steel, one single cry comes from our hearts: Viva l'Italia!"

If Mussolini created the party line of fascism, Hitler brought it to its complete and awful fruition in Germany. The Nazi story was far more totalistic than the Italian brand of fascism. Germany was not just great; it had to be the mightiest state in the world. Germans were not just mistreated; they were the supreme "race" in the world, and they had to triumph over all others. Shedding pure German blood toward establishing supremacy was a privilege, not a sacrifice. Their all-powerful leader deserved unconditional loyalty and bore responsibility for all that occurred. "The main plan in the Nationalist Socialist programme," Hitler asserted in 1937, "is to abolish the liberalistic concept of the individual and the Marxist concept of humanity and to substitute for them the Volk community, rooted in the soil and bound together by the blood of its common blood." Underscoring the importance of the simple story and the "big lie," Hitler explained: "The art of leadership consists of consolidating the attention of the people against a single adversary and taking care that nothing will split up this attention. The leader of genius must have the ability to make different opponents appear as if they belong to one category."

The unruly aspects of their personal lives and of their compatriots' lives were the background against which the fascistic "solutions" of Hitler and Mussolini made sense. Out of disorder, one must create a grander and all-encompassing order. Hitler called for "a belief which will not abandon [the masses] in these days of chaos, which they will swear and abide by." Mussolini's position was scarcely subtle, yet his own pleasure-seeking tendencies and a certain indolence in execution meant that the fascistic ends were not embodied with total conviction or pursued with equal fanaticism. Even the fascist-leaning Tojo and Chiang tolerated some variation in their systems. No such doubts or ambivalences clouded Hitler's sensibility. He was ready to pursue the fascist story, the fascist ideal, in all its fullness. And far more so than Mussolini, Hitler propounded a synthetic view that could encompass all aspects of his compatriots' lives, from birth to grave, from sports to religion to art to economic life. Hitler's story was truly one that could speak directly—and perhaps with special vividness—to all possible questions residing in the mind of the five-year-old.

In some ways communism presented itself as the polar opposite to fascism. Instead of accepting—or at least tolerating—the given economic order and the prevailing religion, communism directly challenged them; instead of glorifying the individual state, communism saw the contemporary nation-state as anachronistic; instead of reveling in national boundaries, communism called for linkages across geographical borders, as workers from all over the world united against the despised bourgeoisie class. In their writings, Lenin and Mao stressed these points, and even Stalin paid lip service to them. Yet these ideas were unfamiliar to most individuals, and they were particularly alien to the peasants and workers in whose interest they were presumably being articulated. Thus, the details and subtleties of Marxist, Marxist-Leninist, Stalinist, and Maoist thoughts were argued among Communist Party elites but not among broader, less-schooled audiences. Lenin may have written of a "revolutionary democratic dictatorship of the proletariat," but he did not spend much time unpacking this phrase in his popular propagandistic efforts.

Indeed, Communist ideas were often simplified to the point where they were difficult to distinguish from the fascist ideas to which they were putatively opposed. Before wartime, the Communist appeal was a general one to workers and peasants, to overthrow the hostile dominant imperial powers at home and abroad. Stalin essentially dropped the Leninist pretext of Soviet communism as the vanguard of an international movement; revealingly, he stood on the sidelines as the fascists overran Spain in the mid-1930s. And during the time of war, Stalin's appeal to his compatriots was principally to the defense of their Russian homeland, with communist themes virtually unmentioned. The shock of the Nazi-Soviet packet of 1939 can be better understood if one thinks of the two countries not as ideological foes but rather as analogous totalitarian enterprises. And the tormented individual psyche that led Stalin first to embrace revolutionary communism and then to resort to the most brutal moves in its putative defense was far closer to that of Hitler than either man would have liked to acknowledge.

The totalitarian leaders were intent on spreading their messages. Each seized control of the press and set up massive propaganda apparatuses. Of special note, each one came to believe that the survival of his story depended on its adoption—and its embodiment—by members of the younger generation. And so, unprecedented efforts were launched to ensure that the educational system would become the principal purveyor of the current ideology—whether fascism, Nazism, or some brand of communism. In this respect, totalitarian regimes constitute a striking contrast to more democratic ones, where the educational system (perhaps regrettably) is rarely the focus of interest for the leadership.

When one turns from the totalitarian stances of the left and the right to the procedures of the democratic states, one looks expectantly for a more sophisticated set of stories. And indeed, the forms of government involved in constitutional monarchies such as Great Britain's, in parliamentary systems such as France's, or in a congressional-presidential system such as the United States' feature less totalistic solutions. Power is achieved through free election rather than through brazen seizure; issues are debated, and alternative points of view are (at least in principle) tolerated, if not welcomed; the rule of the majority prevails, but the rights of minorities are respected; a balance of power obtains among the various branches of the government; and a nongovernmental press ensures that critique is not stifled.

None of the leaders of the democratic states challenged these precepts of democratic government; in that sense they were political conservatives who sought to defend their systems. Yet, paradoxically, the wartime situation in which they found themselves conferred on them power far greater than would have been available in ordinary times. As the political commentator William Pfaff explained:

> The public turned to Churchill and de Gaulle only after all the combinations of appeasement (and collaboration) had failed. . . . Governments that are passively dependent upon public opinion, as are the democracies, as a general rule are incapable of dealing with long-term threats requiring the sacrifices of life, or even the serious risk of lost lives, even when a reasoned case can be made that this will save lives in the longer term.

Churchill after his selection in 1940, Roosevelt after the attack on Pearl Harbor in 1941, and de Gaulle after the fall of France and, more tellingly, after his ascendancy to the presidency in 1958 were in many respects the beneficiaries of a void that had been created by the democracies' earlier inaction. They were accorded the latitude that more properly is restricted to an autocratic regime. Only their own sense of restraint, plus the knowledge that they would again have to stand for election, served as a brake on their behaviors. In this sense, at least, Roosevelt and Churchill were at a disadvantage in Tehran, since Stalin had to answer to no one.

Rather than aspiring to the new Utopias of fascism or communism, Roosevelt, Churchill, and de Gaulle spoke in terms of the need to protect the freedoms that had been won over the centuries in the West. Roosevelt cited the "arsenal of democracy" and "the four freedoms," Churchill wanted to keep "the world safe for democracy," and de Gaulle called himself the leader of Free France. However, this idealistic appeal was buttressed by more frankly nationalistic and chauvinistic calls. Churchill christened the "battle of Britain"; called on his compatriots to give "blood, toil, tears, and sweat"; and ultimately warned against the "tyranny of the iron curtain." De Gaulle spoke constantly of the "grandeur of France" and the need to resurrect its former greatness. And Roosevelt did not desist from underscoring the special nature of the American dream as he pledged "a new deal for the American people" and promised to "quarantine the aggressor."

In previous chapters, I have illustrated how leaders—including those who at first address only experts within their domain—may fashion a new story, one unfamiliar to the general population, and succeed in impressing it upon that broader group. Alfred P. Sloan, Jr., affected Americans' view of business, Martin Luther King, Jr., facilitated a revolution in thinking about the place of blacks in America, and Margaret Mead helped Americans broaden their conceptions of themselves and of individuals from other lands. Each of these new stories reconfigured individuals' sense of "I" and broadened the sense of "we."

The creation of a new story, and particularly one that is encompassing, poses a formidable challenge to national leaders. After all, their primary task is to maintain legitimacy within their own land, and an adventurous story is likely to stimulate opposition. Roosevelt and Lincoln both became hated men because of their desires to broaden the notion of who should be included within the American family, and de Gaulle weathered numerous assassination attempts as he tried to disengage imperial France from its African colonies.

In times of stress, and particularly in times of war, jingoistic and chauvinistic stories are likely to prevail. As the commentator Michael Korda noted, "Great leaders are almost always great simplifiers who cut through argument, debate, and doubt to offer a solution everyone can understand and remember . . . straightforward but potent messages." Similarly, Mao said, "The only solution lies in promoting ideas simple enough to be grasped by the people." Such unschooled stories stress the special, almost sacred status of the nation and underscore the bond that ties together its citizens.

Time and again one encounters variants of the "Star Wars" story (which I described in chapter 3), in which two groups—good and evil—exist, and those of "us" who resemble one another in racial or ethnic background must stick together so that "we" may prevail. Those individuals or groups that, for one reason or another, cannot be included under the national umbrella are exorcised, often viciously. For example, even in the "melting pot" of the United States, individuals of Japanese background were herded into detention camps during the Second World War, simply because of their ethnic heritage. Even if biologically oriented accounts of the origins of group identity are overstated, it is clear that human beings readily join together with others of similar background to oppose those who appear alien in one or another respect.

At the risk of hyperbole, then, one might say that the leaders of the Second World War were handed their scripts by the embattled circumstances in which they and their populations found themselves. They had little latitude in what to say, if they were going to keep their nations together and rally their constituents effectively for battle. But their success depended as well on two other crucial factors: how effectively they enunciated their scripts and how convincingly they embodied those scripts.

While the majority of the leaders were creditable writers, by and large they were distinguished by their skill at spoken language. They bring to mind President Woodrow Wilson's testimony: "I have a strong instinct of leadership, an unmistakably oratorical temperament. . . . My feeling has been that such literary talents as I have are secondary to my equipment for other things, that my power to write was meant to be a handmaiden to my power to speak and to organize actions." Indeed, if there is a single domain that each can be said to have mastered, it is the domain of public speaking—speaking directly and convincingly to their various audiences. Roosevelt, Churchill, and de Gaulle were all masters of their nations' respective tongues, and all remain much quoted even decades after their death. Mussolini was a dramatic speaker graced by a beautiful voice and impressive theatrical gestures. Mao could electrify a crowd with his vivid images, while Lenin's fiery speeches played a notable role in the launching of the Russian Revolution. Indeed, of the various leaders surveyed here, only Stalin seems not to have been an outstanding speaker on the whole, although his speech to the Soviet people after the surprise Nazi invasion is credited with mobilizing patriotism and helping to ensure Germany's ultimate defeat.

Hitler was the most amazing orator of the era. He had discovered both his ability to argue demagogically in small groups in the years before the First World War and his capacities to arouse a mass audience early in the 1920s. From then on, he worked tirelessly to prove his edict that "to be a leader means to be able to move masses." He was able to work crowds up into a frenzy, with a mixture of appeals to idealism, power, hatred, and action. His live and cinematic use of symbols such as the swastika, the goose step, the "Heil Hitler" salute, and the "Horst Wessel" song have been widely discussed in books on persuasion and propaganda. His one-time Nazi associate Otto Strasser well described Hitler's oratorical genius: "Hitler responds to the vibrations of the human heart with the delicacy of a seismograph . . . enabling him to act as a loudspeaker proclaiming the most serious desires, the least admissible instincts, the sufferings and personal revolts of a whole nation." Scholar Charles Lindholm expressed the same point in a way that helps us understand Hitler's "link of identity" with so many other Germans: "In his speech Hitler re-enacted for his audience his own violent drama of suffering, fragmentation, loss and eventual redemption through the assertion of a grandiose identity and the projection of all evil outside."

When leaders ask their constituents to die for a certain cause, the leaders must appear credible. Leaders must convincingly embody the stories that they tell audiences. I have already suggested that the allegiance to totalitarian ideals and methods grew organically out of the personal experiences of Hitler, Mussolini, Stalin, and Mao. Lenin's initial conversion may have been more intellectual than visceral, but it was no less totalistic for that. Reflecting their military training, Roosevelt, de Gaulle, Churchill, Tojo, and Chiang found it natural to lead the forces of their respective nations during times of battle.

These leaders worked tirelessly at their stations, and their total devotion was known to (and appreciated by) their compatriots. Having the good fortune to live at a time when personal peccadilloes were ignored or forgiven by the press, they loomed as larger than life. Consider, for example, the situation of one woman who had lost her whole family in the Second World War: "Stalin was all that she had left. Like all her generation she knew in her bones, and she was quite right, that without Stalin and his system, they could never have survived the German attack. Stalin personified the Great Patriotic War." It is sobering to realize that Roosevelt was never photographed in a way that made visible his paralysis, that Stalin's tiny stature was also hidden by the photographers, and that such habits as Churchill's drinking and bullying were simply not reported. Much was made of Hitler's personal asceticism. To the extent that a vice such as Mussolini's womanizing was known, it sometimes added to his magnetism; but such self-indulgence may also have undermined his credibility when he called on others to sacrifice.

An element of personal courage is an equally important embodiment. General de Gaulle had been wounded three times in the First World War and had made five unsuccessful attempts to escape from jail. A price lay on his head in the Second World War because he had rejected the peace treaty with Germany. Mussolini had also been wounded in war. Roosevelt's personal courage in overcoming his polio was widely known and admired. Mao, Tojo, and Chiang had been tested in war, and Mao's Long March was a legendary achievement. During the darkest days of the Second World War, when the rest of the government personnel had been evacuated from Moscow, Stalin remained within the Kremlin walls, offering visible support to the beleaguered Soviet people. Interestingly, while Hitler spoke audaciously, he did not rally to his troops in times of defeat, preferring to align himself with them publicly only at moments of military triumph; in the end, he castigated the German people for not being worthy of his leadership.

Churchill came to personify personal courage. From the moment of the outbreak of the Battle of Britain, Churchill was everywhere—working in military headquarters and antiaircraft barracks, visiting scenes of bomb damage, and regularly broadcasting messages of inspiration. He traveled 150,000 miles during the war, often risking death or personal injury, to support the troops and give hope to families. The psychiatrist Anthony Storr declared:

> In that dark time what England needed was not a shrewd, equably balanced leader. She needed a prophet, a heroic visionary, a man who could dream dreams of victory when all seemed lost. Winston Churchill was such a man;

and his inspirational quality owed its dynamic force to the romantic world of fantasy in which he had his true being.

No one doubted that Churchill believed his story to the core.

By virtually any definition, the men chronicled in this chapter must be considered successful leaders. With or without the aid of family background, each managed to attain the most important position in his government and to maintain that position during a period of unparalleled importance and tension. Like the seven creators that I studied earlier, and more so than the other leaders portrayed in this book, they are recognizable simply by their last names—and they will be known a century from now.

Yet, they also embody another theme of this book: Sooner or later, nearly all leaders outreach themselves and end up undermining their causes. Indeed, given their larger-than-life status, these leaders are perhaps especially prone to this hubristic fate. The case is most obvious in the example of the leaders of the defeated nations. Tojo was executed for his leadership of Japan, Hitler killed himself, and Mussolini was shot to death; their extravagant dreams of empire crumbled in the encompassing debris. Chiang lost his deathly struggle with the Communists and ended up on a small island whose very status as a nation remains uncertain. Churchill was turned out of his office almost immediately after the Second World War ended, and his vision of the "thousand-year" British Empire soon disappeared as well. De Gaulle voluntarily withdrew from a leadership role; and while, like Churchill, he was once again called to power, he voluntarily departed from office a second time when he felt that support was ebbing.

Three of the Communist leaders did manage to hold on to their positions until they died of natural causes. Lenin's regime was too brief to reveal his own aspirations or his probable reactions to Stalin's reign of terror. But both Stalin and Mao paid fearsome prices for their longtime survival in office: they ended up with fawning attendants, rather than loving friends or credible advisers, and they are now widely condemned for their murderous regimes and for the many grievous problems they inflicted on their countries. The Soviet Union has disbanded, and Chinese communism is honored in name only. Roosevelt did remain in his office until he died near the end of the war and he continues to be acknowledged as one of America's great presidents. But his decision to run for third and fourth terms has been rejected by American citizens, who pointedly embraced a constitutional amendment that limits the president to two terms. And his much-vaunted New Deal, whose value during the 1930s is now grudgingly conceded, has become a symbol of reflexive governmental intervention that does not necessarily provide tenable solutions to long-term problems. (It is worth noting that recent American leaders Ronald Reagan and Newt Gingrich admired Roosevelt's leadership qualities but devoted their political careers to undoing his legacy.)

To speak of the great leaders' failures is perhaps merely to recognize human imperfection and human finitude. It may be a sign that the notion of a great leader should itself be challenged as excessive. But attention to this phenomenon also reminds us of human promise that is not fully realized. Sometimes the promise lies in the young leader, whose idealistic tendencies sooner or later dissolve in the face of external pressures and the temptations of power for its own sake. Sometimes the promise lies in the audience, which first rises to the calls for sacrifice, but which cannot sustain an altruistic stance over the long haul. There may also be inevitable reactions to any ambitious story, ambitiously told. As the former secretary of state Henry Kissinger put it, "Every political revolution sooner or later reaches its end after the public becomes exhausted from being jolted into one new effort after another." Intriguingly, this kind of reaction seems to occur as predictably in the realm of artistic and scientific creativity as in the realm of political leadership: there has been no generation to succeed Picasso, Stravinsky, and Einstein, just as there has been no cohort to succeed the generation of Stalin, Roosevelt, and Churchill.

PART III

CONCLUSION: LEADERSHIP THAT LOOKS FORWARD

14

JEAN MONNET
AND MAHATMA GANDHI
Leadership beyond National Boundaries

National hatred is strongest and most vehement on the lowest stage of culture. But there is a stage where it totally disappears and where one stands, so to say, above the nations and feels the good fortune or distress of his neighbor people as if it happened to his own.

—Johann Wolfgang von Goethe

Twice in this century, all of Europe has paid a tragic price for the narrow-mindedness and lack of imagination of its democracies.

—Vaclav Havel

Having covered a terrain that stretches from Margaret Mead to Josef Stalin, it may seem as if I have surveyed the full range of leadership. After all, I have considered direct as well as indirect forms, innovative as well as visionary varieties, and a family of identity stories as well as a variety of embodiments. And yet, were I to terminate the study at this point, I would have omitted a type of leadership that may turn out to be crucial for the future.

In this chapter I consider two individuals—Jean Monnet (1888–1979) and Mohandas K. Gandhi* (1869–1948)—who devoted their lives to the creation of forms that did not respect national boundaries. Monnet was interested primarily in international governmental forms; Gandhi, in direct relations among human

---

*As Gandhi became a recognized spiritual leader, he became widely known as "Mahatma" or "great soul."

Jean Monnet. UPI/Bettmann   Mahatma Gandhi. UPI/Bettmann Newsphotos

beings the world over. Although the two differed markedly, both stand out because of their capacities to challenge traditional political entities and methods
and to achieve at least some success in reshaping politics. My discussion of Monnet and Gandhi paves the way for a final chapter in which I summarize the principal findings of the study, discuss the constraints and opportunities that
characterize leadership in the twentieth century, and consider how one might
engender effective leadership in the future.

Jean Monnet, the son of well-to-do parents, was born in the wine region of
Cognac, France, in 1888. The Monnet family was in the brandy business. An indifferent student, Monnet did not pursue a higher education; instead, he traveled widely in Europe, Africa, the United States, and Canada in his late teens
and lived in Britain for a time in his early twenties. Although he came from a
tradition-oriented family and never abandoned his predecessors' accent on comfort and civility, Monnet was deeply influenced by the different attitudes and styles
of life that he encountered during his youthful travels. Reflecting on his life, he
said: "I was daring because I knew no taboos. I was unaware of the importance of
official functions. Like Americans I was trained to think that if something needs
to be changed, every man has the right to point this out."

As the First World War broke out, Monnet (who was medically unfit to serve
in battle) threw himself into the effort to get France and England to work together closely, especially in the joint purchase and distribution of materials. He

developed a new kind of consolidated balance sheet that facilitated the pooling of resources. From this experience Monnet learned that alliances were strengthened when the parties could work together on a concrete economic initiative from which each felt it was getting its fair share. (Monnet's balance sheet had the same kind of liberating effect as the new organizational chart created—for very different purposes—by Alfred P. Sloan, Jr., when he took over the helm at General Motors.)

More generally, Monnet discovered that he had a knack for international diplomacy, for making and maintaining contacts among a wide range of people, and he became respected for his skill and tact. He soon realized that, as a disinterested insider, he could travel easily and effectively through the corridors of power: "My strength was the naïveté of a young man. I had no idea of what a premier really was. . . . He was just a man like any other to me. . . . I arrived on the scene at a time when the men in power were at a loss, when they did not know which way to turn." Showing the self-confidence and boldness characteristic of future innovative leaders, the young Monnet chose not to address leaders by the expected phrase "monsieur le president."

For most of the rest of his life, Monnet focused his energies specifically on building relations among countries. In 1918 he spoke about the need for unity among all the democracies. From 1919 to 1923 he served as the deputy general of the newly formed League of Nations. He then withdrew for a while to the family business, worked as well on Wall Street, and ultimately displayed great skill at rescuing private enterprises all over the world. Alerted by the brutal rise of Hitler and the likelihood of another world war, he directed his talents to amassing arms for France and Britain. He began to think seriously about—and in June 1940 actually proposed—a union between the two nations, including dual citizenship, a single currency, and a pooling of all resources.

Moving first to London, where he was the only French member of the British Supply Council, and then, after the fall of France, to Washington, Monnet sought to work with General Charles de Gaulle, the leader of the Free French. But the two men were destined to be ideological foes: Monnet always worked for international cooperation, the equality of nations, and the attenuation of national boundaries, while de Gaulle devoted himself to the interests of a sovereign, independent, and dominant France. Nonetheless, Monnet aided de Gaulle in 1943 as the general assumed authority in Algeria, and Monnet joined forces with him on several occasions in the next two decades.

The end of the Second World War ushered in the period of Monnet's greatest influence. Monnet knew well the diplomatic and economic mistakes that had been made at the end of the First World War and was determined that they not be repeated. In particular, he knew that vindictiveness against the losers would be catastrophic. At a time when leaders and their nations were exhausted, Monnet—who had been thinking about a revitalized and reconfigured Europe for decades—was brimming with promising ideas for rebuilding Europe and ensuring a lasting peace. In 1947 he proposed a plan for modernizing French industry and agriculture; this scheme fit in well with the blueprint for European recovery that the American secretary of state George Marshall was proposing. Drawing on his unique network of personal relations built up over the decades, Monnet also strove tirelessly to solidify relations among wary France, Britain, and the United States, thereby ensuring the survival of the Atlantic Alliance.

In 1950 Monnet introduced to European leaders another novel set of ideas. The Schuman Plan, as it came to be known, led to the establishment of the first supranational entity—the European Coal and Steel Community (ECSC). This institution represented an important, highly risky, and ultimately successful step in the peaceful reintegration of Germany, economically and politically, into the family of European nations. The new economic entity demonstrated that the countries of Western Europe could constructively and cooperatively share in market, labor, and wealth. Monnet knew that this community was not really about coal and steel, but rather about the beginning of a new Europe. Monnet did not succeed in a parallel effort to create a European Defense Community and had only modest success with Euratom—a third transnational entity centered on the uses of nuclear power.

After completing his term as the president of the ECSC High Authority—the most important official post that he ever held—Monnet organized the Action Committee of the United States of Europe. This group was the forerunner of the European Economic Community, or the Common Market, an institution that did last and that was to change the economic face of Western Europe.

De Gaulle returned to power in 1958, and the friction between de Gaulle and Monnet reemerged. De Gaulle constantly criticized Monnet and ridiculed his idea of a single Europe. "Dante, Goethe, and Chateaubriand belong to Europe only insofar as they are respectively and eminently Italian, German, and French. They would not have served Europe very well had they been without a country, if they had written some kind of Esperanto," declared the general, in one of his frequent evocative comments. "We are no longer in the era when M. Monnet gave orders," he snarled on another occasion. De Gaulle always tilted toward a Europe centered in France and Germany, while Monnet emphasized the importance of including Great Britain in any European scheme. De Gaulle was able to undercut or slow down a number of Monnet's initiatives; for example, he opposed Britain's role in the newly emerging Common Market, insisted on veto power in European councils, and undercut the notion of a multilateral nuclear force. For every chapter of Monnet's new and more inclusionary story, de Gaulle was ready with an equally well articulated counterstory that accentuated the exclusivity of nations.

Nonetheless, Monnet outlasted de Gaulle, not only in the sense of surviving him but also in witnessing the reality of the European Common Market and the beginnings of a single European community, the European Union portrayed in the 1993 Maastricht treaty. In awarding the Freedom Prize to Monnet, President John F. Kennedy declared:

> For centuries, emperors, kings, and dictators have sought to impose unity on Europe by force. For better or worse, they have failed. But under your inspiration, Europe has moved closer to unity in less than twenty years than it had done before in a thousand. You and your associates have built with the mortar of reason and the brick of economic and political interest. You are transforming Europe by the power of a constructive idea.

Kennedy's tribute (which may well have been authored by Monnet's close friend George Ball, then the undersecretary of state) was accurate and apt. Even as a young man, Monnet had become convinced that the future viability of Europe lay in closer ties among its nations. The harrowing events of the first half of the century molded these intuitions into certainty. This was indeed his "one good idea" to which he somewhat self-mockingly referred. What distinguished Monnet from others who might have spoken about the abstract concept of "One Europe" or "One World" was that, without self-aggrandizement, he worked tirelessly and obsessively for decades to help convert that idea into a reality and advanced further than even a bright-eyed optimist might have predicted. As he once put it, "There is always a dream in all enterprise, but the dream if it lasts one day becomes a reality."

Halfway around the world, Mohandas K. Gandhi was born in 1869 at Porbandar, India, on the Arabian Sea. Far less affluent and cosmopolitan than Monnet's forebears, Gandhi's male ancestors had been deeply involved for generations in provincial government. While the ambience in Cognac, France, centered on commercial matters, the preeminent issues on both sides of the Gandhi household were ethical and religious. No more enthusiastic a student than Monnet, young Gandhi was precocious in thinking about issues of morality and was particularly censorious of his own moral transgressions. Ever striving to be a good young Hindu, he berated himself severely for a few youthful sins; he could never forgive himself for leaving the bedside of his dying father in order to have sexual relations with his young bride.

In a move that was much less canonical than Monnet's grand tour, Gandhi countered the advice of the headman in his community and seized the opportunity to study law in England. The exposure to a totally alien culture and to an astonishing range of political, social, and spiritual experiments shocked Gandhi but also deeply influenced his own development. Although mostly a quiet observer in Britain, Gandhi found himself protesting vocally when an attempt was made to punish an individual who was espousing unpopular social doctrines (even though Gandhi himself had little sympathy with iconoclastic views). This assumption of a moral stand on foreign soil was a defining experience for the young law student. The return to India and a predictable life as a provincial lawyer or official was unexpectedly interrupted by an invitation to travel to South Africa to aid in a lawsuit. Leaving his family once again, Gandhi traveled to South Africa in 1893 and remained there for two decades.

During his years in South Africa, Gandhi developed the ideas and practices that ultimately made him into a world figure. Gandhi found himself thrust into the public limelight because of his inability to accept the way in which Indians and other dark-skinned individuals were treated in this Dutch-British outpost. Gandhi felt personally humiliated when he and other Indians were not permitted to sit where they wished, to travel where they desired, or to participate freely in the political and economic life of their chosen country. And so he commenced a life of protest, which included holding meetings, launching organizations and publications, writing petitions, arguing cases, and looking for legal loopholes and maneuvers. For his efforts, Gandhi was beaten, jailed, and constantly attacked by the whites in the power structure, as well as those in the rank-and-file community.

What distinguished Gandhi from other protestors in other parts of the world was his gradual evolution of an innovative philosophy and an original set of methods. Strongly influenced by certain Western writers such as Henry David Thoreau and John Ruskin, by the writings and the personal example of the Russian novelist Leo Tolstoy, and by his own intensive immersion in religious writings from both the East and the West, Gandhi renounced worldly pleasures, as well as the fruits of industrial civilization, and undertook the life of an ascetic. Now reunited with his family, he experimented with matters of diet, schedule, and work, and began to initiate bargains with himself and with those who joined him in Tolstoy Farm, an experimental community that he had set up near Johannesburg in 1910. For Gandhi, a story in itself was never enough; embodiment in one's mode of life was an integral part of the message.

Most important, Gandhi abjured violent confrontation and began to develop a new form of protest. In what ultimately became known as *satyagraha,* those who felt discriminated against would refuse to obey unjust laws but would do so nonviolently and would be prepared to accept any consequence, ranging from arrest to death.

Believing that he had accomplished his mission in South Africa and being sought with increasing frequency by his long-suffering compatriots, Gandhi returned to India at the end of 1914, shortly after the start of the First World War. Like Franklin Roosevelt, Margaret Thatcher, and other leaders I have described, Gandhi had come to feel that he was the only individual who could help "his people." In this case, Gandhi saw that he must aid his native land—a colony that felt increasingly prepared for independence but that had not been able to sever ties from a mighty and tenacious Great Britain. As part of an agreement with a close political ally, Gandhi spent the next year traveling without public comment through India, becoming acquainted with conditions in the land from which he had long been separated. Gandhi supported the British war effort in the First World War; but by war's end, he had already reached the conclusion that India should not—and could not—remain as a possession of Great Britain.

If Monnet's one guiding idea was that the nations of Europe ought to move toward unity, Gandhi's one guiding idea was that India must be able to face Britain as an equal nation, and not as a subordinate colony. In one sense, then, Gandhi's idea can be seen as a nationalist one, in contrast to Monnet's internationalist dream. Yet, almost from the first, much of the rest of the world, if not the British leaders themselves, understood that Gandhi was in fact introducing a different, far more universalistic process.

As demonstrated by his method of peaceful resistance, satyagraha, Gandhi devoted his life to the belief that human beings were united by far more than they were divided. If offered the chance to confront one another directly, they should be able to resolve their differences—in a nonviolent way that confirmed and strengthened the humanity of both sides. Free India was not the cause to which Gandhi devoted his life—rather, it was the prospect of better, more humane relations among human beings everywhere that animated the mission of Gandhi and his followers around the world. Revealingly, he once addressed his adversary Lord Irwin: "I would like to meet not so much the viceroy of India as the man in you."

Monnet operated primarily behind the scenes, and neither his name nor his deeds are particularly well known outside the elite European community in which he operated. Gandhi took precisely the opposite tack, operating in the most public, high-profile manner. Although he was not particularly interested in getting credit for the accomplishments of the movement that he had created, his name, his ideas, and his physical person have been well known for most of the century (and the unexpected success of Richard Attenborough's 1982 biographical movie has helped to ensure that Gandhi's accomplishments will be known by succeeding generations).

As early as 1918, Gandhi tested himself and his ideas on Indian soil by undertaking an organized action in the city of Ahmedabad in west-central India. The ostensible reason for the encounter was a dispute between mill workers and mill owners, both sides in the dispute being personally known to Gandhi. But Gandhi used the occasion to work out methods—including a personal fast—through which both sides could negotiate constructively. His goal in this and subsequent actions was to reach a resolution that would respect the interests of both parties and leave them equally strengthened by their participation in the structured, at times virtually ritualized, conflict.

For a number of reasons, the confrontation in Ahmedabad worked out well and peacefully. This verdict would not apply to all of the subsequent actions in which Gandhi participated over the next thirty years. The protest against the Rowlatt bill (which extended British restraints on Indian life) the following year resulted in violence and culminated in the Amritsar massacre, in which over a thousand people were killed. Gandhi attempted without much success to unite Muslim and Hindu forces in the Khilafat agitation of 1919 and 1920. In 1922, following a variety of acts of resistance to British authority, Gandhi himself was placed on trial for sedition. The proceeding featured a memorable exchange with the judge, in which both men recognized the unprecedented features of their confrontation. Judge Robert Broomfield said: "It will be impossible to ignore the fact that you are in a different category from any person I have ever tried and am likely to have to try. It would be impossible to ignore the fact that in the eyes of millions of your countrymen, you are a great patriot and a great leader." Nonetheless, Gandhi was sentenced to jail for six years. He responded to Broomfield: "So far as the sentence is concerned, I certainly consider that it is as light as any judge would inflict on me, and so far as the whole proceedings are concerned, I must say that I could not have expected greater courtesy."

After his release from jail, Gandhi eagerly reimmersed himself in politics. In 1930 he led his most famous action, the Salt March, in which he and thousands of his followers marched to the sea to carry out an act of great symbolic importance—picking up grains of sand along the shoreline as a means of defying a recently imposed tax on salt. Gandhi expected to be arrested and hoped that thousands of his followers would be similarly incarcerated. What he could not have anticipated was the authorities' violent response.

Armed police struck down hundreds of advancing marchers, who fell to the ground without lifting an arm to fend off the blows. As the United Press reporter Webb Miller chronicled in a famous dispatch:

> There was no fight, no struggle; the marchers simply walked forward till struck down. The police commenced to savagely kick the seated men in the abdomen and testicles and then dragged them by their arms and feet and threw them into the ditches. . . . Hour after hour stretcher-bearers carried back a stream of inert bleeding bodies.

Given the speed of modern journalism, the cruel and bloody quashing of the peaceful protest became known all over the world. While the British had broken the rebellion, their moral hold over India had been permanently shattered.

Gandhi had finally made his case to Great Britain and, perhaps even more, to the rest of the civilized world. What followed was a series of tentative, grudging steps toward the granting of independence to India, greatly sped up by the events of the Second World War. Because of his eminence and moral example, Gandhi was perforce involved in the ultimate dissolution of colonial status, though much of the actual political leadership fell to his protégé Jawaharlal

Nehru. In the mid-1930s Gandhi himself withdrew to some extent from public life, returning, as he had in the middle South African years, to a simple and pointedly exemplary existence in a village.

At the time of the official declaration of independence late in 1947, Gandhi was back in public life, devoting his energies fully to a reduction of the tensions that plagued Muslim-Hindu relations. He spoke, wrote, hectored, bargained, and fasted in the manner of a man decades younger. This struggle was so vicious and so bloody that when someone spoke of a celebration of independence, Gandhi bitterly quipped, "Would it not be more appropriate to send condolences?" In the end, Gandhi himself fell victim to this internecine struggle. In January 1948 one of his own coreligionists, an overzealous Hindu named Nathuram Vinayak Godse, shot Gandhi to death as the leader was walking to a prayerground.

Gandhi's achievements have been respected in India. Despite continuing struggle, much of it bloody, he is recognized there as the preeminent twentieth-century leader. Yet, Gandhi's greatest contributions extended well beyond the Indian subcontinent. Through his inspiring writings and his own embodiment of personal courage, he conveyed to people around the world that it is possible to resist injustice in a way that is honorable, does not involve counterattack, and may even bring about resolutions that empower all concerned.

Among the countless individuals who paid tribute to Gandhi, two twentieth-century leaders—one direct, one indirect—best expressed what millions felt. Martin Luther King, Jr., said that Gandhi provided "the only morally and practically sound methods open to oppressed people in their struggle for freedom." After noting the uncanny temporal coincidence between the development of nuclear weapons and the development of satyagraha, Albert Einstein commented:

> Gandhi had demonstrated that a powerful human following can be assembled not only through the cunning game of the usual political maneuvers and trickeries but through the cogent example of a morally superior conduct of life. In our time of utter moral decadence, he was the only true statesman to stand for a higher human relationship in the political sphere. . . . Generations to come . . . will scarcely believe that such a one as this ever in flesh and blood walked upon this earth.

And King himself insightfully joined together these two titans: "Man has thought twice in our century, once with Einstein, then with Gandhi. Einstein's thought transformed understanding of the physical world, Gandhi's thought transformed understanding of the political world."

The differences between Monnet and Gandhi are pronounced. Monnet was a well-to-do, worldly European with any number of career options open to him.

He decided early on to devote himself to building firmer ties across European nations and, to the extent possible, extending those ties to North America as well. He operated almost entirely behind the scenes. Gandhi was as much an outsider as Monnet was an insider. In South Africa, Gandhi was mistreated as a member of a downtrodden, decidedly nondominant group, considered a troublesome subject population by the mighty British. Rejecting the lot of an obscure Indian official and, later, a career as a successful South African lawyer, Gandhi openly embraced a life of utter simplicity and austerity. Abjuring any work behind the scenes, he instead developed methods of nonviolent resistance that were inherently public and vulnerable; and, a model of courage, he constantly risked death by fasting or suffering injury at the hands of those who were armed.

In grouping these two twentieth-century figures together, I make no effort to minimize such differences. Yet, in terms of the themes of this book, the instructive ways in which Gandhi and Monnet resemble and complement each other are most pertinent. Consider, first, the elemental and single-minded stories they each created. Monnet once asserted, "I had only one good idea but that was enough." As noted earlier, Monnet devoted his life to the proposition that the ties within Europe could and should be strengthened peacefully, and he explained:

> It seemed to me, looking back, that I had always followed the same line of thought, however varied the circumstances, and no matter where I was. My sole preoccupation was to unite men, to solve the problems that divide them, and to persuade them to see their common interest. . . . I have always been drawn towards union, towards collective action. I cannot say why, except that Nature made me that way.

Simple though it was, Monnet's one idea ran counter to the notions—the counterstories—of millions of people over hundreds of years. Europe was seen as a collection of states and nations that vied with one another, sometimes peacefully, sometimes through war. Periodic efforts to unite Europe occurred, but always by virtue of military intervention—the triumphant visions of victory shared by Charlemagne, Napoléon, and Hitler. Monnet challenged this unschooled vision of a Europe under one flag by joining the ideas of peacefulness and union. The very force with which this idea was opposed by individuals like Margaret Thatcher and Charles de Gaulle demonstrates that it was not an easy one to accept; Monnet's accomplishment was to make it so familiar and unthreatening that we now accept as self-evident such practices as a free-trading economic community and ready passage across borders. Biographer François Duchêne summarized Monnet's considerable achievement in terms that echo the argument of this book: "[Monnet was] the one thoroughgoing internationalist so far who has made a marked impact on history. . . . He seized a brief opportunity to achieve one of the rarest feats in history, the deliberate introduction of a new theme."

Gandhi's key idea—his organizing story—was at least as simple and far more ancient. He stressed that human beings belonged to the same species, that their frequent, often-violent struggles were fundamentally illegitimate, and that human beings needed to resolve their conflicts peacefully. It was not right for any human group to subjugate another; members of the species must learn to face one another as equals, unafraid. All these ideas had been spoken before, in so many words, by great religious leaders, chief among them Christ.

Gandhi differed from others of our modern industrial world in the seriousness with which he pursued these ideas. Slavery or subjugation was not just wrong in principle; it was deeply wrong in practice—it had to be opposed. Gandhi called for a resolution of long-time antagonisms through peaceful means, and he developed in detail the methods by which disputes could be handled smoothly and constructively. Indeed, the visionary part of his story inhered in the particular procedures necessary for making satyagraha effective.

Gandhi's ideas met widespread resistance among the subjugated as well as the colonizers; even as Churchill ridiculed the idea of a free India, Gandhi's Indian compatriots scoffed at the notion that independence could be achieved nonviolently. Yet, Gandhi's message was heard in the British Empire and, perhaps even more clearly, in other parts of the world where human rights were being violated. From the American South during the civil rights movement to the People's Republic of China at the time of the Tiananmen Square massacre, Gandhian principles of peaceful resistance have shown their power and their endurance. But Gandhi's vision presupposed a certain humanity among those involved in a confrontation. Gandhi believed—no doubt wrongly—that Hitler's hatred of the Jews could be dissolved if persecuted Jews went peacefully and proudly to their death.

Both Gandhi and Monnet stuck with utmost tenacity to their central idea. At the same time, however, each was flexible about how his idea was pursued or realized, and each actually welcomed periods of instability in which innovation was more likely to be tolerated. They both enjoyed experimenting and were not afraid to try out new tacks, to learn from their mistakes, even to reflect on them publicly. This willingness to change course, while continuing to strive toward the same ends, emboldened others to be resourceful as well.

Until now, I have stressed the importance of the message, the story, more so than the means by which that theme may be achieved. But minimizing the importance of methods in the cases of Monnet and Gandhi would be an enormous mistake. Indeed, we have at least as much to learn from the approaches that the men tried and perfected as from the propositional recounting of their messages. For both Monnet and Gandhi, in the deepest sense, their methods *were* their message.

Monnet's approach, which he developed over the course of half a century, was almost entirely indirect. He spurned the limelight. He was not a good speaker, and he hated political in-fighting. Monnet was the invisible man, the embodiment of impersonality, who spent his time thinking carefully about how to achieve his ends. He built up a small group of trusted associates and made great demands on them as well as on himself; for the most part, Monnet and his team operated in privacy. Capable of technical analysis himself—indeed, a perfectionist in many respects—he largely left technical analysis and writing to others and allowed himself to focus on the big picture, on the broad sweep of events.

Monnet spent his time trying to convince individuals in power that the ideas he and his associates had worked out were worth taking seriously. And he emphasized that if these ideas were enacted, the individuals in power would get the credit. "To get statesmen to listen to you, all you have to do is to give them an idea at the right time, when they are floundering, and ask nothing for yourself," he maintained. Indeed, Monnet made a point of avoiding credit, feeling that such notoriety would ultimately undermine his own ability to get things done. "These men, after all, take the risks; they need the kudos. In my life of work, kudos has to be forgotten." Instead, he sought public recognition for those political figures who dared to pursue the ideas that he had helped them articulate and institute.

Monnet's leadership was indirect, then, but not precisely in the sense used elsewhere in this book. In speaking of the influence exerted by creators like Stravinsky or Einstein or the early Mead, I have pointed out that these individuals operated chiefly through the symbolic products that they created—musical compositions, scientific papers, anthropological essays, and so on. Monnet also worked through a medium—namely, other individuals who were themselves direct leaders. Theoretically, Monnet could have written down his ideas, which might simply have been picked up by one or another leader (and, perhaps, distorted in the process). By working cooperatively with political leaders, however, he not only conveyed the ideas in a conversational way that was comfortable for most of them but also helped shape the ideas and then conferred credit on the leaders.

Labeling Monnet's professional identity is not easy. He himself once declared, "I have never taken a job that I did not myself invent." He spent his time trying to think about political and economic situations that were likely to arise in the future, how these might be dealt with, and how best to mobilize leaders who could create institutions that might deal with these situations. Recognizing the uniqueness of what he was doing, Monnet noted archly, "If there was stiff competition around the centers of power, there was practically none in the area where I wanted to work—preparing the future."

Monnet's own testimony offers the best clues as to how he operated. In his autobiography, he recalls his state of mind in 1945, at the conclusion of the war, when he was fifty-seven:

My life so far had involved a series of actions at the level where contemporary issues are decided. . . . I had constantly been concerned with public affairs; but my work, unlike that of the quintessential politician, had not required an endless succession of fresh choices to be made in the infinitely complex situations that face the Government of a State. What I had undertaken, at every important turning-point in my life, had been the result of one choice and one choice only; and this concentration on a single aim had shielded me from the temptation to disperse my efforts, as from any taste for the many forms of power. . . .

[T]hose who are responsible for all the affairs of state . . . have to look at the whole range of problems. The ability to do so, which is essential to a statesman, itself limits his power to control events. If he were obsessed by only one idea, he would have no time for others. . . . My role for a long time past had been to influence those who held power, and to try to ensure that they used it when the opportunity arose. . . . I have never met a great statesman who was not self-centered, and for very good reason; if he were otherwise, he would not have made his mark. I could not have done it—not that I am modest; simply, that one cannot concentrate on an objective and on oneself at the same time. For me, that objective has always been the same; to persuade men to work together; to show them that beyond their differences of opinion, and despite whatever frontiers divide them, they have a common interest.

Perhaps reflecting his French background, Monnet placed much stock in rationality. In his view, if individuals could be made cognizant of their interests through reason, they would ultimately come to agreement and act for the common good. He placed enormous importance on getting wording exactly right, believing that the precise formulation was crucial to the success or failure of a policy. He believed that one could not change human nature, but that one could help individuals understand the problems that they were confronting, the existing structures that impeded their solutions, and the options (including new structures) that could lead to a solution. He always searched for solutions, rather than for compromises, and tried to turn every setback into an opportunity.

Thus, Monnet worked at the interface of human beings and institutions. Valuing friendships and maintaining them over decades, he pointed out that friendships grew out of joint action. He studied the individuals involved in any negotiation carefully and came to know what was likely to convince them of a proposed course of action. He worked tirelessly, but always straightforwardly, to establish a common bond among them. He did not hesitate to repeat ideas over and over again, and to review the wording of treaties endlessly; yet he understood that the trust people were building among themselves was essential for any agreement to work. At the same time, he knew that any agreement had to transcend individuals. "Nothing is made without men; nothing lasts without institutions," he once shrewdly declared. Indeed, he felt that deeply entrenched habits were most likely to be modified during the opening moments of a new institution. He greatly desired order and imposed it wherever possible in his own life and operations; but he himself came to realize that, in matters of state relations, "there could be no progress without a certain disorder." And perhaps reflecting his background and his time, he valued the unique role played by the great leaders of the major nations.

Gandhi also devoted a great deal of thought to his methods, and particularly so during those times of involuntary isolation in prison. He also depended on the cooperation of a small group of intimate associates, but in Gandhi's case, these individuals directed a much larger and much more public mass of followers. And so Gandhi devoted considerable effort to the buildup and maintenance of organized groups of fellow protestors, or *satyagrahis*.

While Monnet preferred to work behind the scenes with a few carefully chosen leaders, Gandhi's arena was completely public, as noted earlier. Gandhi saw his natural colleagues as the mass of ordinary human beings—"the dumb, semi-starved millions whom I represent," as he once put it. It was part of Gandhi's philosophy that causes had to be articulated, defended, and embodied. And so Gandhi was entirely clear in public about the ends that he and his followers were trying to achieve, and about the aim and purpose of his methods of satyagraha.

Pursuit of satyagraha had been worked out with precision. The satyagrahi had to recognize the opposing views of others and acknowledge his respect for them as persons. Initial efforts to reach agreement in a nonconfrontational manner had to be undertaken. Only if these failed was the satyagrahi entitled to disobey the law, to strike, to fast, or to undertake some other kind of public spectacle that enunciated to all observers the meaning and the stakes of the confrontation. Once an action had been launched, the satyagrahi had to follow strict discipline. Satyagraha was not appropriate for every situation, and it did not always succeed. Compromise was not ruled out, but basic principles had to be honored continually; the satyagrahi had to be prepared to sacrifice much—indeed his life—once the fateful decision to engage had been made.

The arenas in which Monnet and Gandhi operated could not have been more remote from each other. Monnet had little access to ordinary citizens and depended almost entirely on his background interactions with powerful statesmen, many of whom he knew personally. Only rarely did he appear in public to account for his actions. He placed his faith primarily in reason, though he understood as well the role of irrationality and passion in human affairs.

In sharp contrast, Gandhi's identifications were entirely with ordinary human beings, and he felt an instinctive discomfort (and perhaps rivalry with) the high and the mighty. His arena was very public, interrupted only by occasional withdrawals, most of which were involuntary incarcerations. Gandhi's approach had its reasons, but it was based fundamentally on faith and on a spiritual dimension of human relations: for him, the true power was spiritual, and not military. Gandhi and Monnet, between them, eventually had to confront the limits of human reason as well as the limits of human spirituality.

Few people of this era more completely embodied the messages that they promulgated and the methods that they advocated. Monnet's discreteness and trustworthiness were appreciated throughout the world of political and economic figures. "He convinced by shyness rather than by striking attitudes or resounding trumpets," said one observer. He moved as easily between milieus and nations as he hoped that resources, currencies, and citizens might come to circulate in the future. He was infinitely patient in negotiations, never accepted a defeat as permanent, and adhered steadily to the single progressive and inclusionary idea that animated his life.

At least to the same extent, and as befits the leader of a nondominant group, Gandhi focused on messages and methods that grew out of his own life. Only as a result of a lengthy self-examination that involved dozens of personal "experiments" with truth had Gandhi arrived at a position that made sense for his own life, for the Indian subcontinent early in the century, and, with increasing conviction, for dispossessed individuals the world over. Gandhi lived his dreams and his convictions day and night for almost half a century. He passed on these disciplined practices to his associates directly and, by powerful personal example, to millions of devoted followers. When he made errors, he readily conceded them, including the famous "Himalayan blunder" to which he himself confessed after having inappropriately asked his followers to carry out a course of nonviolent action for which they had not yet been adequately prepared. Indeed, in his humor, gentleness, and willingness to admit his own errors and to forgive those of others, as much as in his intrepidness, Gandhi embodied the principal ideas to which he had committed his existence.

Neither Monnet nor Gandhi succeeded in fulfilling his dreams, no more so than did the other redoubtable leaders chronicled in the preceding chapters. After a promising launch in Monnet's later years, the European Economic Community has had its ups and downs. The Maastricht treaty, which promised to move populations and institutions much closer to a single Federation of Europe, had yet to be endorsed by several nations at the time of this writing. The collapse of the Soviet Union has, paradoxically, reactivated long-buried feelings of nationalism in Southern and Eastern Europe and even within some of the Western European democracies.

Examined on its home ground, Gandhi's legacy has had even less clear-cut results. Gandhi's words and examples are honored on the Indian subcontinent far more in the breach than in the observance. Hindu and Muslim tensions continue to run high, and there have been frequent battles within India, as well as occasional military skirmishes with neighboring Pakistan and China. As noted,

Gandhi's personal example has continued to inspire those who espouse the causes of human rights for themselves or for their own people throughout the world. But for every success in the American civil rights movement, for every relatively peaceful transformation such as the one that occurred in South Africa (a full century after Gandhi's arrival in that troubled land), there have been all too many instances in which satyagraha has not been tried, or where it has been tried but has proved ineffective.

The transcendence of national boundaries and the spurning of stereotypical views of other peoples can happen only when an audience is ready to hear and to act on such new messages. Gandhi and Monnet were struggling against attitudes that had endured for centuries, if not millennia. For this reason, each had to express his message in as simple a form as possible and adhere to it steadfastly over decades, in times of crisis and calm. The complex, subtle, and visionary aspects of their messages were vital, but these facets could only begin to be grasped in their fullness once they had gained an initial hearing.

In my personal view, only widespread appreciation of the insights and sensibilities of Monnet and Gandhi may permit our world to endure. Somehow, we need to be able to meld Monnet's faith in reason with Gandhi's reasoned approach to matters of the spirit.

While resembling our other leaders in many particulars, Monnet and Gandhi have also expanded our notion of leadership in many ways. First, they demonstrate that a leader can create a story that is unfamiliar to the unschooled mind and succeed to some extent in promulgating the story to a broad-based constituency. To Europeans who were accustomed to thinking of themselves as citizens of rival nation-states, Monnet said in effect, "We are all Europeans and we must join together for the greater good." To colonizers and colonists, to the powerful and the dispossessed, Gandhi asserted, "We are all, first and foremost, human beings and we must relate to one another on that naked basis." These two approaches to broadening a sense of identity serve as genuine instances of visionary or transformational leadership. While it is true that Monnet spoke mostly to leaders, rather than to ordinary citizens, his plans could not materialize unless they ultimately made sense to the larger population.

Monnet also illustrates that there are various forms of indirect leadership. While most indirect leaders proceed by creating symbolic products, such as books or scientific theories, Monnet instead spoke directly to leading political figures—and, therefore, indirectly to the general public. Ultimately, Monnet's overarching idea did begin to affect the unschooled European mind—but in this instance, the idea had to make its way through one or more intermediaries.

Finally, Monnet and Gandhi illustrate the possibility of achieving success on a broad scale without working through the usual governmental channels, provided that one adheres tenaciously to a single idea. Neither Monnet nor Gandhi craved official accolades and official positions; indeed, they achieved their effects in part by remaining outside the official governmental system—Monnet through his privileged insider status, Gandhi by being the ultimate outsider. In this study, I have already called attention to such extragovernmental influence—for instance, in the cases of Martin Luther King, Jr., and Eleanor Roosevelt, both of whom also eschewed officialdom and determined how to invent their own stories without an institutional base. There are certainly similarities in the cases of these four individuals. But while King and Roosevelt exerted their most pronounced effects on specific nondominant groups, Gandhi and Monnet sought to affect the more general course of history by addressing a broad swathe of humanity. (King and Roosevelt both moved somewhat in this direction in the later years of their lives.) Gandhi and Monnet underscore the importance of putting forth a single idea and of adhering to it compulsively, and with great precision, even in the face of changing conditions. Perhaps this is why their contributions have a strong likelihood of surviving into the next millennium.

15

LESSONS FROM THE PAST, IMPLICATIONS FOR THE FUTURE

We are shaping the world faster than we can change ourselves,
and we are applying to the present the habits of the past.
—Winston Churchill

My survey completed, I can reflect on the overall enterprise. In doing so, I abandon the thematic approach of the preceding chapters and revert to a more systematic method. My stocktaking begins with a sketch of the life of a hypothetical leader—an "ideal-type" description that captures patterns evident from the study.* Next, I review the principal findings with respect to six features imminent in all forms of leadership. For greater perspective, I contrast the eleven leaders on whom I have focused with six "creators" of my earlier study and with the ten leaders of the Second World War. This comparative perspective should illuminate the steps across the Einstein-Eureka continuum that I introduced at the beginning of this book.

In the final pages I focus on a number of issues that remain open. I consider three key questions raised by the study; identify six trends that will affect the shape of leadership in the foreseeable future; and, in conclusion, recommend the courses of action that may facilitate leaders' work in the future.

INTRODUCING AN EXEMPLARY LEADER

As a youth, the exemplary leader (whom I have dubbed E.L.) displays special gifts in two areas: she is a skilled speaker, and she displays a keen interest in, and

---

*An ideal type does not purport to apply in equal measure to every member of a class; rather it seeks to highlight those features that recur prominently in most members of a group and that help others to understand the nature of that group.

an understanding of, other people. Unless she displays a particular strength in schoolwork, she is unlikely to consider a career as a teacher, researcher, or other highly trained professional. Individuals who observe E.L. comment on her general energy and resourcefulness, rather than on her specific talents: there is consensus that she will accomplish something, but it is not yet apparent in which spheres that accomplishment will occur.

The primary exception to this picture comes from the youth with a strong academic bent. That person—one such as Mead, Oppenheimer, or Lenin—is likely initially to pursue some kind of scholarly or professional career. Only gradually does such a person come to realize that he is more likely to achieve his personal goals or to satisfy his community if he addresses a wider audience than if he remains completely within a specific domain.

Among the early markers of the leader's personality, the most telling indication is a willingness to confront individuals in authority. Sometimes this confrontation is abrasive, but it need not be so. Rather, E.L. stands out in that she identifies with and feels herself to be a peer of an individual in a position of authority. To E.L. it therefore feels natural—or at least possible—to address that person directly. Moreover, E.L. has pondered the issues involved in a specific position of leadership and believes that her own insights are at least as well motivated and perhaps more likely to be effective than those of the person currently at the helm. Perhaps this feeling of confidence stems from the fact that E.L.'s proposed solutions to problems grow out of her own life circumstances and thus are more appropriate than solutions conceived in earlier times or in other places. E.L., like many other future leaders, lost her father when she was young. Perhaps this loss empowers her to speak up, whereas another person might allow his or her literal or surrogate father to exercise authority in the public sphere.

This feeling of entitlement, this willingness to challenge, entails risk. Many individuals who, as young adults, have challenged those in power have been slapped down, jailed, or even killed. But future leaders like E.L. are risk takers and do not easily withdraw from the fray. (The principal exceptions to this pattern would be individuals who belong to a highly bureaucratized organization, such as the military, the church, or a large corporation. Here, the future leader must sometimes hold her tongue and wait her turn. Yet, despite their lower profiles, individuals such as George Marshall, Pope John XXIII, and Alfred Sloan, Jr., were all prepared to speak their mind when this proved necessary.) Those individuals who sometimes became ambivalent about asserting themselves, such as J. Robert Oppenheimer, were at risk for attack by those who did not lack such compunctions.

Some other early markers are worth noting. E.L. stands out because of her concern with moral issues. She also tends to be competitive and to enjoy achieving a position of control. Sometimes, power is intoxicating in itself, but most of the leaders on whom I focus in this book sought power in order to attain certain goals.

Whatever her ultimate aspirations are, E.L. begins by working out personal relations with individuals in her own orbit—her family, her neighbors, and other residents of her community. It is the mark of a future leader that the size of these circles increases rapidly, and that the aspiring leader is dealing with hundreds of individuals, rather than a dozen or a score, by the time she has reached her majority. These individuals might be other practitioners in E.L.'s domain, or they might be heterogeneously drawn from a range of domains. Typically, the future leader maintains these heterogeneous contacts. In this respect, she differs from the prototypical creator, who characteristically abandons contacts when they no longer prove relevant to the next project. E.L. readily identifies with individuals who occupy leadership positions; she sometimes imitates them and sometimes challenges them. While interactions with others take varied forms, E.L. exhibits a talent for coming up with explanations or solutions that satisfy the parties in a dispute.

As a young woman, E.L. expands her experiences and viewpoints by traveling outside of her homeland. This choice contrasts with the pattern common among future tyrants, who generally elect not to venture far from their homelands, perhaps because they fear that their well-worked scheme of things may be unduly complexified or uncomfortably challenged by experiences of living in a radically different environment.

In studying creators, I noted that these individuals take at least a decade to master the domain in which each ultimately effects a breakthrough. Many direct leaders do not operate in traditional scholarly or artistic domains and so do not require the daily application that undergirds ultimate mastery. However, no leader is born with the knowledge that she needs to operate effectively in the public sphere. And so, E.L. needs to complete the necessary apprenticeships— whether to gain knowledge of domains, skill in communicating, or mastery of organizational politics. Such training periods may well stretch out for a decade or longer.

Successful leadership requires much more than personal gifts and vaulting ambition. The aspiring leader like E.L.—or an individual, like Martin Luther King, Jr., or Eleanor Roosevelt, who is propelled by circumstances—must be attuned to an audience that is posing basic questions and searching for guidance, particularly regarding issues of identity. E.L. may find that audience either in her professional domain or in a wider or less readily identifiable constituency. At this time, provided that she herself has worked out answers to these basic questions, can express them eloquently, and can embody them in her way of life, E.L. is poised to occupy a position of leadership.

The less well defined the domain, the institution, or the constituency, the more necessary it is for E.L. to invent a life for herself, to reflect on its implications, and then to share the resultant stories with others. The stories that prove effective will differ from circumstance to circumstance, and E.L. must be prepared to revise her story, to combat counterstories, to anticipate future stories (and counterstories), or even to create wholly new ones. She has to develop a position on the extent to which a story is inclusive or exclusive, traditional or innovative, and related chiefly through words or conveyed through some other kind of symbolic system or embodiment. When monitoring the effectiveness of the story, E.L. needs to bear in mind the contours and the limits of the unschooled mind.

Among the stories created by leaders, stories that deal with identity are at a particular premium. Typically, these identity stories have their roots in the personal experiences of the leader in the course of her own development. But it is characteristic of the effective leader that her stories can be transplanted to a larger canvas—that they make sense not only to members of her family and her close circle, but to increasingly large entities, including institutions and, at an extreme, heterogeneously constituted political entities.

Leadership is never guaranteed; it must always be renewed. E.L. witnesses a constant interplay among her favored stories, the audience's reactions, and the often unpredictable events in the society. Leaders succeed, fail, return, and recover, often many times in the course of a career. What operates effectively at one time or in one situation may not be effective in other circumstances, and E.L. must be flexible, though not so flexible that she ceases to stand for anything. At a special premium are the capacities to adjust stories in light of changing circumstances while still adhering to basic principles and remaining—and appearing to remain—an individual of conviction. (President Bill Clinton has had trouble living up to this requirement.)

Leaders cannot create and control their charisma (though image makers certainly strive toward that end). There is little question, however, that from an early age, certain individuals stand out among others for their personal attractiveness, as is true of E.L. Most often, the traits are physical—leaders are often tall, good-looking, and graceful. If they lack these physical characteristics, they may at least have strong defining facial features or piercing eyes. Different traits—such as the power of Oppenheimer's mind, the spirituality surrounding Pope John XXIII, or even the reassuring ordinariness of Eleanor Roosevelt—may captivate different audiences. Invariably, though, leaders find a way to exercise a strong hold over an audience. Leaders must be aware of these charismatic capacities and avoid actions or stories that undermine such power. De Gaulle, for example, conveyed charisma partly through his remoteness from others, and he carefully maintained a studied distance from the fray.

One of the other factors that will affect the course of E.L.'s career is her relationship to institutions and organizations. Such entities serve as the basis for power and support. Indeed, those who find themselves at the helm of well-entrenched organizations have a guaranteed authorized platform from which to issue stories and at least some reason to expect that they will be listened to attentively; the president of any institution commands attention. The maintenance and renewal of organizations is a special kind of skill. If E.L. does not wish to tend this matter herself, if she prefers to focus on her storytelling mission, she must ensure that others maintain and nurture her organizational base. And, of course, if E.L. does not begin with an organizational base, she must either establish one (as did Gandhi and King) or run the risk that her chief messages will quickly disappear in the welter of competing counterstories.

Another feature is the opportunity for reflection. While creators spend most of their time alone and feel the need to mix with other people only occasionally, E.L. confronts the opposite situation. Often the demands for personal attention are so great that she loses the opportunity to reflect, to step back, and to take stock. Yet, in the absence of such time for reflection, the leader risks losing her sense of agency: she may become the tool of other individuals or of forces beyond her control.

The major reason that reflection is so important is that a leader like E.L. must be able to perceive the big picture—its constant features, its changes. No matter how skilled her associates, it is not reasonable to expect that they will have the vantage point of the exemplary leader, who has presumably attained her privileged status because of her special understanding of the situation and her special ties to the audience. The noted political leader and student of leadership John Gardner speaks about the desirability of an "uncluttered mind"—a perspective that is not distracted by the transitory events of the day. The uncluttered mind must constantly remove those obstacles that block vision and scan to identify those issues and trends that are truly important.

Whatever our successes, we must all ultimately face our frailty and our limitations. Perhaps because she aims so high and carries such burdens, E.L. is especially at risk for failure. In many cases, the failure of the leader is not within her control. Opponents may rise, other stories may gain favor, supporters may shield the leader from uncomfortable but vital information, or the particular conditions of popularity or authority may change unpredictably. Indeed, the greater the accomplishment of the leader, the greater the strain on her milieu; strong accomplishments breed strong reactions, and by and large, only those effective leaders who die at a young age are spared the disheartening sight of their accomplishments being severely challenged, if not wholly undone.

It is important to note that E.L., by and large, is not thrown by apparent failures. Tough and robust, she expects that there will be downs as well as ups. Sometimes, indeed, she is energized by setbacks and returns to the fray with new vigor. While some withdraw after defeats or failure, E.L. is likely to follow Jean Monnet's practice of construing every defeat as an opportunity. And indeed, this capacity to place a positive spin on apparently unproductive experiences sends a very important and reassuring message to one's followers.

Yet, despite this capacity to discern the silver lining in a cloud, E.L. often is seen as having failed in her primary mission. And, in a way reminiscent of tragic heroines, E.L. often contributes to her own ultimate downfall. Fiercely ambitious and capable of risk taking, she aims too high, makes overly harsh demands on others, and pays too little attention to those whom she is supposed to nurture. Paradoxically, even those creators with relatively little interest in posterity may continue to exert impact for centuries after their death; conversely, the very leaders with the greatest ambition may end up undermining their own achievements within their lifetime.

Thus, failure may result from a number of different sources: changing conditions, unexpected historical upheavals, a story that proves too inclusionary or too exclusionary, excessive demands by the leader on others, or excessive demands by the leader on herself. Each of the leaders in this study experienced signal successes that make them worthy of study. Yet, in one way or another, all experienced failure: thwarting of their mission, loss of their position, or both. Perhaps only the ordinary leader-manager can reasonably expect to appear successful to her immediate successors, but this success comes at the cost of little significant change. In contrast, the exemplary leader may well appear to have been ineffective immediately after the end of her term; but there remains the chance that she will ultimately prove to have set into operation a series of events that have long-term consequences. Should this prove to be the case, the optimism that characterizes such leaders will have been vindicated.

SIX CONSTANTS OF LEADERSHIP

In the introductory chapters I introduced six key features that have guided my study of effective twentieth-century leadership. I now return to review some of the principal findings that have emerged.

The Story

A leader must have a central story or message. The story is more likely to be effective in a large and heterogeneous group if it can speak directly to the untutored mind—the mind that develops naturally in the early lives of children without the need for formal tutelage. Stories ought to address the sense of individual and group identity, the "we" and the "they," though that sense may actually be expanded or restricted by the story. They should not only provide background, but should help group members to frame future options.

In rare cases, a more novel or transformational story can succeed in persuasiveness even if the group membership extends beyond a single domain. Chances for success are greater if that story becomes the central mission for a leader, if it can be promulgated for a long time, and if it has the opportunity to take hold in a noncrisis situation. Crises (such as a war or an economic depression) demand rapid clarification and typically result in simplification. Leaders benefit from the ability to build on stories that are already known—for example, those drawn from religion or history or those that have already been circulated within an institution—and to synthesize them in new ways, as Martin Luther King, Jr., was able to do.

Most of the leaders in this study put forth stories that were inclusionary, that encouraged individuals to think of themselves as part of a broader community. Among the eleven leaders profiled in-depth, the chief exceptions to this generalization are Robert Maynard Hutchins and Margaret Thatcher, both of whom gained influence—and perhaps pleasure—by encouraging an "in-group/out-group" perspective. Also, the leaders of the Second World War found themselves in a situation where exclusion was as crucial as inclusion.

At first blush, an inclusionary story may seem wholly preferable. More people will feel included, and the leader may feel that she is being a generous, morally praiseworthy individual. The actual situation is more complex, however. To the extent that a story is inclusionary, it denies special status to groups that may have felt so entitled. These groups will eventually come to oppose the leader and her inclusionary story—a story that to them may seem all *too* inclusionary. Thus, Hindus resented Gandhi's efforts to include Muslims in his vision of India. Moreover, when any leader's course is examined at closer range, one can see that there are always inclusionary and exclusionary forces vying with one another. Even Gandhi needed to have opponents; he stood out in his effort to include British imperialists constructively within the stories that he was relating.

The various kinds of stories that leaders tell have many parallels. Yet, each leader is distinguished by the particular stories that, typically on the basis of her own experience, she has created—stories of identity, stories that address other essential questions, stories that obtain within and/or across domains. The stories told by the leaders profiled earlier are summarized in Appendix I.

The Audience

Even the most eloquent story is stillborn in the absence of an audience ready to hear it; even mediocre stories unimpressively related will achieve some effectiveness for an audience that is poised to respond. The relationship between leader and audience is complex and interactive; perhaps especially in the case of leaders of nondominant groups, a dynamic interplay exists between the needs and desires of the audience, on the one hand, and the contours of the leader's story, on the other. Moreover, in the case of leadership of nondominant groups, the leader generally has to create her story afresh and to revise it in accordance with often rapidly changing conditions. Conversely, those authorized to lead an organization with a preexisting hierarchy have a relatively unproblematic time in guiding the audience, so long as they do not require its members to move in new and unexpected directions.

A leader can effect small changes in a large audience fairly easily and some-times effect larger changes in an already dedicated and knowledgeable group, such as other members of her domain, without overwhelming effort. The great-est challenge the leader faces is to bring about significant and lasting changes in a large and heterogeneous group. A leader must not only develop messages in a number of nuanced languages but, in the absence of specialized knowledge, be-gin by addressing an unschooled mind. The examples of Gandhi and Monnet suggest that the best chances for success lie in a steadfast concentration on the same core message, along with flexibility in how it is presented, and openness to the message being apprehended at a number of levels of sophistication.

Note, in contrast, that the traditional creator has an easier task. While he is creating a breakthrough work, he need pay only scant attention to his audience. Once the work has been completed, it may speak for itself, or it can be pro-moted by other individuals. The cross-domain leader has no such luxury. The story cannot be conceived in isolation; and while others can help disseminate the story, the leader will be expected to embody the story personally, at least to some degree.

The Organization

While a leader can sometimes speak directly to a large audience and achieve ini-tial success via the perceived bond between himself and his auditors, enduring leadership ultimately demands some kind of institutional or organizational basis. If the leader already belongs to an organization, such as the church, a corpora-tion, or a political party, it is his job to bring the organization along. While the ascribed leader of an organization can demand initial attention, simply by virtue of his position, there is no guarantee that he will remain a viable vessel of author-ity if he makes significant demands on his membership. And if, as is typically the case with leaders of nondominant groups, no organization is at hand, such an or-ganization must be created and guided. The achievements of twentieth-century totalitarian leaders would have been inconceivable in the absence of the powerful political organizations that they helped to build up and then carefully policed; and nontotalitarian leaders like de Gaulle and Churchill discovered the tenuous-ness of their command after the abatement of the crises that had brought them to the fore.

Leaders of traditional domains such as scholarly disciplines are less dependent on a highly differentiated organization. On the one hand, these domains often organize themselves without the need for much intervention; on the other hand, the actual power of ideas and the existence of seminal work can exert effects in-dependent of the current shape of the domain. Yet, once the leader wishes to guide the fate of her creations, direct forms of leadership become necessary. From the academic examples in chapters 4 and 5, one can see how difficult it is to provide continuing direct leadership to independent scholars. When Robert Maynard Hutchins, as an aspiring direct leader, tried to create new and enduring organizations, he was ineffective; Margaret Mead's decision to avoid organizational commitments may have been personally judicious, but it also assured that there would be no "school of Mead" after her death.

The Embodiment

The creator must in some sense embody his story, although he need not be saintly. Indeed, the credibility of some leaders may actually be enhanced if they have had—and have come to terms with—a rocky or even a counterstory past (as did Saint Augustine). But if the leader seems to contradict the story by the facts of his existence, if he appears hypocritical, the story probably will not remain convincing over the long run.

The story may grow out of the leader's personal experiences and may well have been embodied in his or her daily living before being expressed overtly. Indeed, in selected cases, the actual embodiment by the leader serves as the principal story. George C. Marshall and Pope John XXIII spoke about the kinds of lives they believed in, but their actions "spoke" even more eloquently than their voices.

The issue of embodiment raises the question of authenticity. Just as one can ask whether a story is true, one can ask whether an individual truly embodies what she speaks about. Short of foolproof polygraph examination, it is not possible to determine whether an individual's embodiment is genuine. After all, phonies are never in short supply. Moreover, in the current climate, many individuals are well compensated for helping the leader look credible and convincing. Lacking any magical solution to this enigma, I am content to believe, along with Abraham Lincoln, that one cannot fool all of the people all of the time. The individual who does not embody her messages will eventually be found out, even as the inarticulate individual who leads the exemplary life may eventually come to be appreciated.

Direct and Indirect Leadership

Most creative leaders exert their influence indirectly through the symbolic products that they create; most political leaders relate their stories directly to their audiences. But leaders do have the option of pursuing the alternative course. Some indirect leaders, like Mead and Oppenheimer, attempt to provide direct leadership within their domains; and some direct leaders, like Vaclav Havel of the Czech Republic and Léopold Sédar Senghor of Senegal, have created political or artistic works that influence other people.

Direct leadership is more tumultuous and risky, but in the short run, it can be more efficient and more effective. However, those leaders whose time for considered reflection has vanished—who can no longer "retreat to the mountaintop" to discern "the big picture"—are often in an unfavorable position for making judicious decisions. Indirect leaders have the advantage of more time for reflection and revision; and often their impact proves more enduring, if slower to emerge. It is possible to have a "mixed model"; Jean Monnet, for example, achieved political ends by working through the existing political leadership, rather than by erecting or seizing a direct platform himself.

If there is voluntary movement between these forms, it is almost always from indirect to direct forms of leadership. In general, my study indicates that the transition is most easily effected when the direct and indirect stories and embodiments are relatively similar. Thus, Mead and Sloan were adept at making the transition from leading within their domains to leading a more heterogeneous group, presumably because the content of their stories required relatively little transformation. In contrast, individuals like Oppenheimer and Hutchins, whose initial stories were more specialized, found it more difficult to succeed with a completely nonacademic audience.

Even when the stretch is modest, however, leaders must make a choice. It is almost impossible to meet the quickly changing needs and demands of a specialized domain, on the one hand, and the far less rigorous (though often equally fickle) demands of a heterogeneous unschooled audience on the other. In the end, leaders must cast their primary lot either with a domain or with a wider society. The individual may continue to have some effectiveness in the rejected terrain, but this glory is likely to be reflected, at most.

The Issue of Expertise

In nearly every domain of experience today, there will be important technical knowledge unavailable to most leaders or to most members of an audience. Only those individuals who actually began as domain experts—such as Mead and Oppenheimer—even have the option of continuing to access such knowledge directly. They may call on that knowledge as needed, so long as they can adapt it to the demands of particular situations.

Within a domain, an individual is unlikely to achieve any credibility unless her work is seen as being of high quality. Mead and Oppenheimer could not have become direct leaders within their domains if their colleagues had not esteemed their work. And Hutchins was always considered something of an outsider at faculty meetings because he did not have advanced training in one of the traditional scholarly disciplines.

The more that such individuals become involved in direct leadership, the more difficult it will be for them to retain their technical expertise; and they may well become spurned as popularizers or ex-specialists by the more strict constructionists among their expert colleagues. Most career politicians, of course, lack expertise in any traditional domain, though they may certainly have acquired sophisticated knowledge about political processes and organizations. Thus, a paradox: Direct leaders typically lack direct knowledge, while indirect leaders often can proceed on the basis of direct knowledge. How to attain and maintain expertise is an acute problem for anyone who aspires to direct leadership, and particularly for those who wish to direct a heterogeneous group on the basis of the best current information drawn from the most relevant domains.

QUESTIONS RAISED BY THIS STUDY

In a study of this scope, numerous questions can be posed; and if I did not raise them, readers certainly would—and appropriately so. Of the many issues that have given me pause, I restrict myself here to a discussion of three principal topics.

Conception of Leadership

While my conception of leadership is not unique, I have definitely emphasized certain features and minimized others. From one perspective, the present view might be thought of as traditional. I focus on the single leader—generally recognized as such—and on the considerable agency that that person may gain because of his authoritative position and/or powers of persuasion. I readily acknowledge my belief that individuals matter, and that a few individuals matter a great deal.

Note that I do not question the validity of other views of leadership—views that focus on power, policies, the public, or the personality of the leader (see chapter 1). I have not concerned myself with contemporary revisionist critiques of leadership—leadership as collective; leadership as instigated by the audience, rather than by the nominal leader; leadership on the part of those who have been relatively "without voice" or "without a place at the table"; or a deconstructionist or postmodern critique that would question the entire legitimacy of talk about leadership. I have little sympathy for those who challenge the "great person" theory of leadership but then invoke unspecified "forces of history" in its place. Any serious study of history must take into account human as well as social and economic factors, and the most convincing studies illuminate their continuing interactions.

My study has focused on individuals generally seen as leaders by their contemporaries and, for the most part, on individuals who have had available the customary levers of leadership or who have created effective substitutes. It remains an open question whether leaders defined in a radically different way can still satisfy my criterion of "affecting thoughts, feelings, and behaviors of a significant number of individuals."

While traditional in some respects, however, my conception is iconoclastic in others. In particular, my emphasis on leadership as a cognitive enterprise, as a process occurring and recurring within—and between—the minds of leaders and followers, has few antecedents. The notion of leaders as presenting messages is certainly familiar, but the assertions about various kinds of stories and counterstories, competing with one another in Darwinian fashion, explore new and somewhat controversial ground. The distinction between indirect leadership, through the creation of symbolic products, and direct leadership, through storytelling and embodying, is also novel: I have sought to build bridges between the influence exerted by a creative individual and the influence wielded by a traditional organizational or national leader. Finally, the emphasis throughout on the power of the five-year-old mind, as well as the limits that the unschooled mind imposes on forms of leadership that transcend traditional domain boundaries, also represents a contribution to contemporary considerations of leadership.

The Representativeness of Findings

It is a point of logic that, given any finite number of examples, one can find an infinite number of generalizations that obtain across them. It is also a point of logic that any generalization may be undone by the first counterexample. Given these formidable constraints, what faith can one place in the profile of leadership that is presented here—in my prototype of the exemplary leader and in the various generalizations about the six constants of leadership?

Let me stress once again that the enterprise I have undertaken is not scientific in a strict sense. As I described in *Creating Minds,* I am trying to forge a link between idiographic case studies undertaken by scholars like Howard Gruber and the nomothetic, quantitative studies undertaken by scholars like Dean Keith Simonton. In my earlier study of creativity, I sought generalizations based on seven creators of the modern era; in the present study, my generalizations (and contrasts) are based on studies of eleven leaders. I have provided a modest "test" of these generalizations by noting the ways in which they are modified by a brief examination of the ten "world leaders," and also by occasional contrasts with the profiles of the previously studied creators.

Without doubt, my "sample" is skewed in certain directions. I am aware of some biases—for example, toward voluntary, inclusionary, and innovative leaders—but no doubt unaware of others. Equally, I recognize that each of my leaders operated in a limited set of contexts and that other leaders, operating in other contexts, might well differ in unpredictable ways. And it is worth underscoring that my leaders are all drawn from the modern era, and largely from America and Western Europe. A different kind of inquiry would have to be launched, were one in search of generalizations about leadership in other eras, or from other cultural traditions.

I fully expect that studies of other leaders—direct, indirect, or a Monnet-like amalgam of these two species—will undermine certain generalizations and give rise to others. Thus scholarship advances. Rather than fearing such refutations or modifications, I welcome them. (Indeed, I have been greatly stimulated by exchanges with other scholars who have found my generalizations about extraordinary individuals to be provocative—in both senses of that term!) I hope that the methods developed here and the set of criteria I have applied will prove useful in further comparisons of this sort. Robust characterizations can emerge only if the same set of lenses is applied to additional members of the class of leaders, broadly defined.

The Moral Dimension of Leadership

It has been observed that the word *leader* is often applied in a positive sense, as we praise someone for being a leader, or as we ask, plaintively, "What has become of our leaders?" I should state, then, that my approach to leadership does *not* presuppose a positive view of leadership. Indeed, the stories that leaders tell, the ways in which they embody these stories, and the ways in which they affect others turn out to be as characteristic of reprehensible leaders—the Hitlers and the Stalins—as of leaders whom we might wish to praise.

But while my schematization is meant to be value neutral, I do not deny my own interest in the moral aspects of leadership. It is no accident that, as noted, I have focused in this book on "leaders of choice"—individuals who operate in democratic societies. Nor is it mere coincidence that most of the eleven leaders chose to put forth an inclusionary story, one that enlarged, rather than splintered, the primary human group to which it was addressed. In at least some ways, I admire each of the eleven leaders portrayed in this book.

Leaders who have used their power and their pulpit to turn individuals against one another have wrought incalculable damage. I see this study as one modest effort to examine individuals who have essentially adopted a prosocial perspective—to see what they have accomplished and where they have encountered obstacles. I believe that we are more likely to secure responsible leadership in the future if we can demystify its constituent processes. In that sense, enhanced knowledge about leadership may go hand-in-hand with more morally desirable forms of leadership. However, before uncritically embracing this essentially optimistic point, one should not forget that Machiavelli and Hitler wrote two of the most influential tracts about leadership.

SIX TRENDS AFFECTING
TWENTIETH-CENTURY LEADERSHIP

At least provisionally, one may assume that the six features identified earlier are enduring properties of leadership. But in any consideration of the future, one should take into account a number of additional factors that might influence or even change the ways in which leadership—and leaders—achieve success. I have identified six major trends, each discernible from the beginning of the twentieth century, if not before, and none showing any signs of lessening in recent years. These trends will be familiar to all readers; however, their implications for leadership in the future merit concentrated attention.

The Potential for Global Destruction

Warfare achieved unprecedentedly destructive proportions during the two world wars. And the construction of nuclear weapons now makes it conceivable that, for the first time in recorded history, the entire planet could be effectively destroyed in a matter of days. National leaders must take this possibility into account. They can either use weapons as a threat or implement policies that will help limit or control the spread of these weapons. What they cannot afford to do is ignore the possibility of widespread destruction. The prospect of nuclear annihilation influences not only political leaders but also any other leaders who presume to address the major dimensions of human experience. And while less immediately catastrophic, the possibility of the destruction of the world as we know it—whether through ecological disasters or through uncontrolled population growth—will increasingly affect leaders as well. The possibility of quick or gradual planetary destruction is the often tacit leitmotif of any serious identity story related today.

Instant—Often Simplistic—Communication

With every passing year, it becomes easier for individuals not only to learn almost instantaneously what is happening around the world but also to participate in the "global information super-highway." The broadening and democratizing implications of such flexible transmission of information have often been emphasized. However, an increase in quantity of information and an increase in quality of information are not synonymous. Indeed, more channels often mean more low-grade, spurious, and specious information; and the ubiquitous temptation to transmit easily digested sound bites will come as no surprise to anyone who has explored the powers of the unschooled mind. Such a barrage of undigested and often simplistic information may make it even more difficult to have an uncluttered mind that can discern the big picture.

Absence of Privacy

Hand-in-glove with the ease of information transmission is an ebbing of any sense of privacy. Not only is it easier for governmental (and nongovernmental) agencies to collect detailed information about the lives of all individuals, but traditional respect for the distinction between public and private lives has already been eroded with public figures and is increasingly ignored with private citizens as well.

Ready global communication and the disappearance of privileged information influence the lives of leaders and audiences. Far more individuals have the opportunity to convey their messages quickly and directly—though the din of competing messages may make it more difficult for any specific message to become prevalent. Charges and countercharges, stories and counterstories abound. The speedy revelation of even the most intimate details of the lives of individuals—sometimes with their cooperation, more often against their wishes—means that leaders have increasing difficulty retaining any mystique. It is intriguing—but also alarming—to ponder what would have happened to the leaders of the Second World War if they had had to deal with the kind of public scrutiny of their foibles that has become routine in American (and, increasingly, in all non-totalitarian) political life.

The disappearance of privacy entails another, so far incalculable, cost. Disabused of heroes, audiences come to have less respect for their leaders in general, and many capable individuals no longer consider a career or even a brief stint in public service.

It is worth noting, however, that current or aspiring leaders do not need to accept without protest the increasing invasions of privacy. Individuals retain the right to refuse to reveal information and, in the extreme, to seek legal redress from those who libel them. In my own view, current political leadership in America is far too accepting of impertinent queries—a polite "that is really none of your business" might constitute a promising beginning to an effective new counterstory.

The Rise of Entities That Transcend National Boundaries

At least in many respects, the heyday of the nation-state may have passed. The multinational corporation has been a prominent fact of life for at least a generation. So many issues—aviation, ecology, contagious illnesses, growth and movement of populations, human rights, nuclear inspection and fallout, fuel, disarmament, and trade, just to name a few of the more visible ones—do not neatly respect national boundaries. Consequently, thousands of organizations—some national, some international, many nongovernmental—have arisen in the past few decades, and a number of these have attained a surprising amount of influence. Joining such mainstays as the Red Cross and the World Bank are numerous less well known and less traditionally configured international scientific organizations, computer bulletin boards, commercial entities, and institutions concerned with population control, resource deployment, disease control, preservation of the environment, and human rights.

Newly configured agencies, arising in response to fresh kinds of threats and hitherto-unavailable opportunities, are unlikely to attract leaders of the usual stripe. Some have a much flatter, more heterarchical structure, and others may have no discernible leadership whatsoever. Whether the more established forms of governance will fall into their familiar place over time or whether nonnational entities will evolve new forms of group leadership or audience membership is by no means clear. The political consultant Max Kampelman reflects on the current unsettled situation: "Everything is becoming interconnected and yet in the world of politics, we are still in the Middle Ages."

Nationalistic and Fundamentalist Reactions

Quite possibly in response to the apparent lessening of power of long-standing national organizations, equally powerful pockets of opposition have arisen. The Monnet-inspired movement toward a single Europe has been countered by strong nationalistic currents in nearly all European countries, and by an unexpectedly virulent form of ethnic pride—sometimes leading to calls for "ethnic purity"—in Eastern Europe. Within the United States, nearly all of the aforementioned international tendencies—from nuclear disarmament to human rights to ecological control—are vociferously opposed by individuals who either disdain these themes on principle or feel that they should be handled only by the sovereign state or by an organized religious entity.

Just as a call for nontraditional institutional forms requires a new and flexible viewpoint about identity, the reactions against these innovative organizations exploit the most elemental reservoirs of group identity. In their call for literal embracing of long-standing religious, political, and social verities, fundamentalist leaders speak directly to the least-modulated minds. Given the power of the unschooled mind, it is no easy matter to counter these entrenched beliefs.

Ever More Technical Expertise

In nearly every domain, knowledge continues to accumulate at a spectacular rate, and technical experts are expected to be on top of this accruing knowledge. Nowhere is this trend more evident than in government. Most leaders 150 years ago went about their business with a small staff and could often themselves grasp the details of issues; today the "governmental affairs" wings of even modest-sized entities (ranging from universities to hospitals to municipalities) require a large body of experts, technicians, consultants, and other authorities. Even political figures, expert in politics if in nothing else, depend on teams of consultants who are more expert in the various specializations of politics, from fund-raising to focus groups. Most everyone agrees that one cannot get along without experts; yet recalling George Bernard Shaw's quip that "professions are a conspiracy against the public," experts are often the target of abuse.

Knowing how to take such expert knowledge, judge its importance, and convey it to nonspecialist leaders and then to the more general public is a daunting challenge. The tensions are plain. On the one hand, one wants the best information, and one hopes to base decisions on that information after it has been thoroughly digested and judiciously weighed. On the other hand, neither leaders nor their audiences really have the expertise to master the information. And even if they could achieve such command, there is tremendous pressure to present the information in a simplified way, so that such information can be readily comprehended and readily transmitted to others. The result is often a distortion of the issues. Reflecting on recent political life in America, the sociologist Daniel Bell commented:

> Leadership is a sense of judgment. It is judgment as to what is relevant and how to do things. The result is either people oversimplify, as Reagan did, or you try to lean the other way, become as Dukakis [George Bush's opponent in the 1988 presidential election] did, rather technocratic. So the person who can strike the right balance between the sense of complexity and the sense of judgment is increasingly rare, and that is a problem it seems to me in every society.

Concomitant with the increasing need for technical expertise is an attenuation of the specialists' bonds to the rest of society. Experts must spend so much time focusing on their specialties that they have very little time to devote to issues of the more general good. Many experts have a lessened sense of obligation to the wider society, or even to a wider profession, apart from their own specific area of technical knowledge. The sense of identity of contemporary experts is less frequently rooted in their community or the nation, let alone in the wider world; nor is it, as seems to have been the case a century ago, linked to a morally tinged calling such as the law, medicine, the academy, or the clergy. Particularly because experts are so mobile and the institutions for which they work are so fluid, their bonds are chiefly to the few individuals who know what they know (an exceedingly circumscribed domain) and, equally, to themselves (an exceedingly selfish constituency).

Dating back to Greek times, this tension can be noted. As the historian H. D. F. Kitto has pointed out, "The highly trained expert, the specialist, finds no natural place in the polis, and when he appears, as he did in so many departments of life in the fifth century, the cohesion is weakened or the natural bounds of the polis are overpassed." Confucius, a historical contemporary of the ancient Athenians, noted the problem in another mode: "While the advisers of a great leader should be as cold as ice, the leader himself should have fire, a spark of divine madness." How to harmonize the mind of the specialist with the mind of the five-year-old is a challenge that grows more acute with every passing year. Yet, in my view, unless we can find or form leaders who retain some links to expert knowledge, on the one hand, and some ability to communicate to nonexperts on the other, our world is likely to spin ever further out of control. Far from becoming anachronistic, competent leaders promise to become more crucial than ever before.

GUIDELINES FOR EFFECTIVE LEADERSHIP

In this concluding account, I have identified six enduring themes of leadership and singled out six recent trends that have certainly changed—and in all likelihood have complexified—the tasks of leadership for the twentieth century and, more than likely, for succeeding eras. Were this book a systematic sociological treatise on the training of new leaders, or perhaps a Machiavellian version of the same enterprise, I might examine each of the six constants, in terms of the six trends, coming up with thirty-six points to ponder. It is more in the spirit of this book (and of its author), however, to conclude this study with three lessons that are relevant for the proper training of leaders and for the successful prosecution of their enterprises.

Appreciate Enduring Features of Leadership

Any leader who wishes to be effective must acknowledge, and attempt to deal realistically with, the enduring features of leadership. While leaders will differ from one another in the extent of their ambition, the size of their audiences, and the uniqueness of their message, all of them must confront the six enduring features. A leader is likely to achieve success only if she can construct and convincingly communicate a clear and persuasive story; appreciate the nature of the audience(s), including its changeable features; invest her own (or channel others') energy in the building and maintenance of an organization; embody in her own life the principal contours of the story; either provide direct leadership or find a way to achieve influence through indirect means; and, finally, find a way to understand and make use of, without being overwhelmed by, increasingly technical expertise.

These considerations should constitute part of the training of leaders. They should be monitored by the leader and her associates over the course of a leader's incumbency.

Anticipate and Deal with New Trends

Those who would lead in the world of the future must be aware of, and find ways of coping with, new and often complexifying trends. The trends that affect leadership will of course vary across time, place, and situation. I have suggested that leaders today must directly confront the possibilities of immediate or gradual world destruction; new forms of instant, copious, and often overly simplified forms of communication; the virtual demise of any sense of privacy; the proliferation of entities and concerns that transcend national boundaries; the perhaps predictable reaction to these unsettling trends, in the form of heightened nationalism and fundamentalism; the ever-increasing amount of hermetic knowledge; the unsettling lack of wider commitment that seems to accompany the frenetic and uncertain life of the expert; and, as a result, the leader's greatly complexified task of sifting through what must be communicated to a decidedly nonexpert audience.

While these trends will be reflected in particular domains in distinctive ways, all aspiring leaders need to recognize them. Indeed, in precollegiate education—the domain that I know best—leaders have to consider each of these factors, though they will weigh them in ways different from a business or military leader. For example, a precollegiate educator probably will be particularly affected by the pressure to decide *what* of an increasingly expanded knowledge base merits study and by the temptations of constructing curriculum and pedagogy around instant, but often superficial, forms of communication. In contrast, a businessperson must direct special attention to the proliferation of organizations around the world and the explosion of technical knowledge. And a military leader will probably be preoccupied with the possibilities for world destruction, the dissolution of many national entities, and the correlative rise of vociferous ethnic sects. In any event, any program that educates leaders needs to consider these six facets in light of the domain's dimensions and audiences.

Encourage Recognition of the Problems, Paradoxes, and Possibilities of Leadership

Those concerned with the quality of future leadership must design ways of educating citizens—audiences as well as leaders. Such education must consider not only the constants and the variables of leadership but also the tensions that complicate the leader's role, without in any way rendering that role less essential. An enhanced cadre of future leaders can materialize only if we engender widespread appreciation of the principal issues that surround effective leadership.

Certainly, our society has not ignored the education of leaders. Many institutions, such as professional schools or the military, have as their stated goal cultivating leaders. The seemingly endless stream of books, articles, seminars, workshops, and broadcast programs on political leadership, business leadership, and community leadership testifies to the widespread belief that leadership is important and that we need to prepare potential leaders more effectively.

Yet, despite specific regimens of leadership in specific domains, most of the larger society remains ignorant about leadership—not only about its importance but also about the ways in which it can be effective. To some, leadership is an added ingredient—somewhat like a clever remark that someone can use to spice up an already drafted speech—rather than an essential way of thinking about the thoughts, behaviors, and feelings of human beings. To others, leaders are mysteriously charismatic heroes who operate according to rules of their own devising (or flouting). The very fact that many of the ideas in this book are not (to my knowledge) widely known—and that even when they are known, there exist few avenues for familiarizing individuals with their consequences—testifies to the continuing orphan status of leadership knowledge in our broader society.

The American predilections for egalitarianism and for laissez-faire education exacerbate the situation. Dating back to ancient times, many civilizations have considered it part of their responsibility to provide milieus in which leadership can be identified and fostered. The European and Asian high-prestige professional training schools and long-entrenched civil service have been tried-and-true means of achieving a cadre acquainted with the demands and subtleties of leadership. Margaret Mead used to point out that Americans do not want leaders. By pretending that leadership will happen naturally or that leadership can be inculcated incidentally, we ensure that there will be an unacceptably low number of individuals who can fill the essential desiderata of leadership. And we make it less likely that leaders will emerge from less-dominant groups and less-privileged institutions in the society.

Indeed, if I can be permitted to caricature a bit, it seems that leadership is too often seen as one of two polarities: as unproblematic ("you too can be a leader") or as unreachable ("the born leader" or "the charismatic leader"). Instead, we need to begin to think of leadership as a subject that can be mastered and a role that can be achieved, should one be willing to invest heavily in such enterprises.

But if we desire a leadership that is responsible as well as effective, we must do more than simply train a body of "legitimated" leaders. The "best" leadership training *for* potential leaders, I submit, should be the best training *about* leadership for all—not in a sense of training everyone to be a designated leader of a designated organization, but rather in the sense of familiarizing the population with what is entailed in being a leader, and what can go wrong, as well as what can go right.

I term this knowledge *consciousness about the issues and paradoxes of leadership.* Those close to the phenomena of leadership—and I hope that readers of this book now consider themselves as belonging to those ranks—become intimately aware of a number of issues and paradoxes:

- The tension between the need for technical expertise—which requires sophisticated thinking—and the necessity for broad-based communication skills, so that one can reach the "unschooled mind"

- The need for stories that can speak to many individuals and help them achieve a more satisfying individual and group identity

- The potential of such stories either to broaden or to fragment a sense of community

- The realization that more comprehensive knowledge may well be distributed across members of a group, but that it is much easier to deal with a single authorized leader

- The knowledge that all leaders are limited in what they can accomplish, that all leaders experience failure as well as triumph, and that nearly all leaders eventually encounter obstacles that they cannot overcome

- The alternative possibilities of an audience that is manipulated by a leader, an audience that influences the leader, and an audience that cooperatively molds a message in conjunction with the leader

- The need to aid leaders, or to share their burdens, rather than try to exploit or undermine their authority

- The choice between leadership that is direct (a leader speaking to her audiences) or indirect (a leader achieving effects either through symbolic products or through the education of political leaders), and the possibility of combining both direct and indirect strands in a synergistically effective manner

- The tension between a rational approach and one that is founded on spiritual dimensions, and the desirability of synthesizing these complementary stories

There are other issues and other paradoxes, some contained in this book and others that remain to be identified. No one can be expected to understand and master all of them, but familiarity with some can help individuals appreciate the *possible* and the *probable,* as well as the *problematic* and the *paradoxical* facets of leadership.

Such knowledge can be brought to bear when one considers the leadership that most of us deal with regularly: the leaders of one's workplace, school, and community. But it is equally relevant when one turns one's attention to the broader political scene. As I write in early 1995, we have just witnessed in the United States some of the most vicious political campaigning in recorded history. To characterize the rhetoric as "unschooled" would be to compliment it. While knowledge about leadership cannot be seen as a panacea, I feel confident in asserting that mindless negative campaigning is far more likely to be seen for what it is, if the audience has been educated to understand the aforementioned issues and paradoxes. Within a remarkably short time, American citizens have become more aware of how to enhance their physical health. There is no reason in principle why they cannot become more aware of how to promote (or thwart) their political well-being.

A tension will always exist between those who use their knowledge to manipulate and those who use their knowledge to empower. Political "spin-masters" remind us of this unsettling reality. Yet I believe that the more widely these issues are understood, the less likely it is that irresponsible leadership can rise and prevail in the long run. Moreover, I hope that those who come to appreciate these issues, and who design means of articulating them to a wider audience, will help to usher in a world in which leadership is less coercive, more empowering of the broad citizenry, and better able to achieve constructive ends.

APPENDIX I

The Eleven Leaders Viewed along the
Principal Dimensions of Leadership

	Initial Domain	Stance within Domain	Identity Story within Domain
Margaret Mead, 1901–1978	Anthropology	Inclusionary	We anthropologists have the privilege of chronicling the cultures of the world, demonstrating that none is superior. We bring back the insights and convey them in plain language to our compatriots.
J. Robert Oppenheimer, 1904–1967	Physics (expert and leader of laboratory)	Inclusionary (all should participate in Manhattan Project)	We scientists have the skills to play a major role in prosecution of the all-important war effort. We must bury all differences and be able to work in secrecy.
Robert Maynard Hutchins, 1899–1977	Institutional leader (law dean, college president)	Initially inclusionary, became more exclusionary	We educators must reconstruct the university so that we can produce a liberally educated population rather than gadabouts or narrow specialists. We must avoid frills, progressivism, mindless pluralism, and the worship of science.
Alfred P. Sloan, Jr., 1875–1966	Automotive corporation	Inclusive within corporation; competitive externally	We in business are doing God's work. General Motors knows the best way to conduct business and has produced the most effective corporate family. We in the corporation are willing to help others.
George C. Marshall, 1880–1959	U.S. Army	Inclusionary, but with high standards	We in the military must be disinterested professionals. We must avoid politicization, be ready for any contingency, and inspire others by our exemplary actions.

Pope John XXIII, 1881–1963	Catholic Church	Inclusionary	Catholics and Christians must return to the simple teachings of Christ. We must avoid bureaucratic and political infighting. The spiritual life is all-important.
Eleanor Roosevelt, 1884–1968	Recently enfranchised American women	Inclusionary	We women can and should be full participants in the political life of the nations, and we should stand up for what we believe is right.
Martin Luther King, Jr., 1929–1968	Black Americans, particularly those in the church and those involved in civil rights causes	Inclusionary	We blacks must stand up for our rights and do so nonviolently.
Margaret Thatcher, 1925–	Politics, which is inherently a heterogeneous domain	N.A.	N.A.
Jean Monnet, 1888–1979	Politics, which is inherently a heterogeneous domain	N.A.	N.A.
Mahatma Gandhi, 1869–1948	Politics, which is inherently a heterogeneous domain	N.A.	N.A.

	Counterstories within Domain	Nonidentity Stories within Domain
Margaret Mead, 1901–1978	Certain cultures are superior to others. It is not possible to compare cultures. We should beware of popularization.	1. Racist, evolutionary, and tumultuous portraits of adolescence are wrong. 2. Interdisciplinary work is crucial. 3. We should study families and children. 4. Cultures can be organized according to patterns, such as those found in temperament-and-sex combinations. 5. Samoans have a pleasant adolescence, and Americans can learn from their example.
J. Robert Oppenheimer, 1904–1967	Scientists should stay out of any political or military endeavors. Scientists should serve as a counterweight to the government, and all work should be totally open.	1. Quantum mechanics, relativity, and other features of the new physics are important. 2. We physicists have known sin by unleashing nuclear power.
Robert Maynard Hutchins, 1899–1977	There is no "best way" to educate. We must be open to many electives and a variety of educational philosophies. Beware of a new scholasticism or a new orthodoxy.	1. Be prepared to accept sacrifices such as reductions in salary. 2. American education has lost its way.
Alfred P. Sloan, Jr., 1875–1966	There are many ways to run a business. General Motors is paternalistic and monopolistic, or at least no different from any other large corporation.	1. One can create an organizational chart that combines centralization and decentralization. 2. New ideas about marketing, collaboration, research, and planning are best generated by skilled teams of analysts.
George C. Marshall, 1880–1959	The military is privy to special knowledge and deserves special attention and privileges. Military personnel, however, need not be held to markedly higher standards of behavior than other people are.	1. The military must be strengthened and modernized, and deadwood must be removed.

Pope John XXIII, 1881–1963	Catholics cannot afford to risk interacting with other religious groups. We should trust our hierarchy. Spirituality is an ideal that cannot be achieved by all.	1. Power should reside with the bishops and the people, not the curia. 2. Learn from history, but do not be bound to it. 3. Rethink traditional dogma in terms of contemporary conditions. 4. One can be a good Catholic and a good human being even if one sins.
Eleanor Roosevelt, 1884–1962	Women are better off staying in the background, helping and supporting men.	1. All can participate regardless of rank and background. 2. A president's wife can provide leadership.
Martin Luther King, Jr., 1929–1968	It is hopeless to try to achieve equality in American society. We must be prepared to be violent.	1. It is important to know and to attempt to fuse church traditions, American history, and Gandhian tactics. 2. The Southern Christian Leadership Conference provides a new stance toward racial issues. 3. The time for gradualism is over.
Margaret Thatcher, 1925–	N.A.	N.A.
Jean Monnet, 1888–1979	N.A.	N.A.
Mahatma Gandhi, 1869–1948	N.A.	N.A.

	Other Counterstories within Domain	Direct/Indirect Leadership within Domain
Margaret Mead, 1901–1978	1. The more traditional stories of racial difference, evolution of cultures, and a turbulent adolescence have merit. 2. Interdisciplinary work is perilous. 3. The study of family life and child development should be left to other academic specialties. 4. Beware of generalizations about patterns of culture. 5. Mead's observations in Samoa are suspect.	Both forms
J. Robert Oppenheimer, 1904–1967	1. These new ideas are not yet established truths. 2. We should not dramatize our role in developing nuclear weapons.	Began as indirect leader; with Manhattan Project, became direct leader
Robert Maynard Hutchins, 1899–1977	1. Do not fiddle with faculty members' prerogatives. 2. American education is in decent shape and should not be fundamentally reoriented.	Both forms: effective speaker and writer
Alfred P. Sloan, Jr., 1875–1966	1. Henry Ford's antipathy toward organizational charts, variety of markets, and careful planning and analysis. 2. Durant's laissez-faire attitude. 3. Skilled analysts create more trouble than they are worth.	Began as indirect leader through his organizational plan; became effective direct leader
George C. Marshall, 1880–1959	1. Beware of changes in traditional military practice. 2. Seniority must be honored.	Mostly direct leadership, though could write excellent summaries

Pope John XXIII, 1881–1963	1. It is better to leave power to the Vatican. 2. Tradition should govern all. 3. Catholicism is all-important; punish those who deviate.	Direct
Eleanor Roosevelt, 1884–1962	1. Only certain privileged women can participate fully in American life. 2. A president's wife should stay in the background and support her husband.	Direct, primarily
Martin Luther King, Jr., 1929–1968	1. It is not possible to draw together church, American history, and Gandhian traditions in fashioning a viable approach to effecting change. 2. Blacks should use traditional organizations such as the National Association for the Advancement of Colored People and established strategies such as litigation. 3. Blacks must be prepared to take violent actions.	More direct than indirect
Margaret Thatcher, 1925–	N.A.	N.A.
Jean Monnet, 1888–1979	N.A.	N.A.
Mahatma Gandhi, 1869–1948	N.A.	N.A.

297

	Embodiment within Domain	Ultimate Domain	Stance across Domains
Margaret Mead, 1901–1978	Considerable	American public, especially middle class	Inclusionary
J. Robert Oppenheimer, 1904–1967	Excellent laboratory and institutional leader; not as great a scientist as might have been expected; somewhat intimidating on the personal level	America's educated public, including policy makers	Inclusionary, though with personal remoteness
Robert Maynard Hutchins, 1899–1977	Embodied his educational philosophy at a superficial level, but not clear whether he really favored debate, had strong enduring positions, or was a good listener; may have wanted to stimulate his own interests	American educated public	Some inclusionary, some exclusionary aspects
Alfred P. Sloan, Jr., 1875–1966	Effective model of desired behaviors for his staff and dealers	American public, citizens of other industrialized nations	Inclusionary, but competitive
George C. Marshall, 1880–1959	Exemplary—his life actions constituted a major story	U.S. and world public	Inclusionary, though things became murkier after the Second World War

Pope John XXIII, 1881–1963	Excellent	Citizens of the world	Inclusionary; perhaps appreciated more outside the church
Eleanor Roosevelt, 1884–1962	Increasingly excellent; did not stand on rank or ceremony	The nation and beyond, especially the disadvantaged and those who can help them	Inclusionary
Martin Luther King, Jr., 1929–1968	Excellent	The American nation	Inclusionary
Margaret Thatcher, 1925–	N.A.	British nation and its allies	Exclusionary, for the most part
Jean Monnet, 1888–1979	N.A.	European leaders and others involved in decision making	Inclusionary
Mahatma Gandhi, 1869–1948	N.A.	Indian nation, Great Britain, and rest of the world	Inclusionary

	Identity Story	Counterstories
Margaret Mead, 1901–1978	As human beings, we can make wise decisions about our own lives by studying options that many other cultures pursue.	We Americans are special, and we have little to learn and much to fear from the examples of other cultures.
J. Robert Oppenheimer, 1904–1967	All of us—scientists, policy makers, laypersons—must work together in a new nuclear world. Working as much as possible in tandem with our adversaries, we must voluntarily control weapons of destruction and put nuclear energy to positive use.	Scientists should stay out of politics. The Soviet Union is our moral enemy, and we must oppose the Soviets at all costs. The cold war will continue indefinitely.
Robert Maynard Hutchins, 1899–1977	We educated Americans are the bulwark of a democracy. A certain intellectual heritage, represented by Great Books, is the best way toward such an education.	Great Books are parochial and middle brow.
Alfred P. Sloan, Jr., 1875–1966	Business holds the key to the best life for all of us, and it deserves to be at the center of America's life as a nation.	There is more to life than markets and profits. Life has a spiritual dimension. While business can bring about a more prosperous life, it also leads to market cycles and to a materialistic concern that can be destructive.
George C. Marshall, 1880–1959	We Americans must defend our values, through battle if necessary, but we must also try to share them with the wider world. We must prepare to aid the victims of global war.	Americans must win at all costs. We are special and cannot be compared with other lands. We owe no support to those who have committed aggressive acts against us.

Pope John XXIII, 1881–1963	We are human beings first, religious persons second. We must work together to save the world from disaster and to build a lasting peace.	Religious divisions cannot be mediated. The cold war is inevitable and must be pursued.
Eleanor Roosevelt, 1884–1962	Everybody must work together to help the dispossessed, especially women, blacks, and the citizens of third world countries. We have to be prepared to be confrontational, though not too much so.	This is a social Darwinian world, and there is not much that one can do about it.
Martin Luther King, Jr., 1929–1968	We must be color-blind.	Racial differences will always exist and cannot be ignored or minimized; perhaps some day they can be reduced, but the time is not at hand.
Margaret Thatcher, 1925–	Britain has lost its way in defeatism and socialism. We must reclaim the leadership from "them" (socialists, union troublemakers, and the "wets") and restore earlier grandeur.	Imperial Britain was a mistake and certainly should not be reinstituted. Despite its flaws, the socialist/labor way is still the best way.
Jean Monnet, 1888–1979	Europe must become one society, with close links to America.	The European nations have a long and glorious past and cannot simply jettison this past for a risky and uncertain future.
Mahatma Gandhi, 1869–1948	We in India are equal in status and worth to all other human beings. We should work cooperatively with our antagonists if possible, but be prepared to be confrontational if necessary.	There is inherent inequality between colonizer and colonist. Might is right. If one is going to be confrontational, one must be prepared to be violent.

Other Stories

Margaret Mead,
1901–1978

1. Cultures assume patterns, and one can recognize the pattern of American culture. Human nature is accessible to us, in its unity and its variety.
2. Americans should be prepared to experiment with different lifestyles.

J. Robert Oppenheimer,
1904–1967

1. The world of knowledge and practice is rife with paradoxes (about secrecy, power, knowledge, and science), and we must revel in them.
2. Human knowledge is still frail and limited.

Robert Maynard
Hutchins, 1899–1977

1. Wise men and women should reflect on the great issues and report the results of their reflections.
2. Civil liberties are important.
3. America should be careful about getting involved in international conflicts (before the Second World War).

Alfred P. Sloan, Jr.,
1875–1966

1. Cars are central to life.
2. Anything that opposes business is bad.

George C. Marshall,
1880–1959

1. The cold war should not be allowed to dominate all our actions.
2. It is premature to recognize the State of Israel.

302

Pope John XXIII,
1881–1963

1. It is possible to lead a spiritual life and to ennoble others.
2. We should work to aid the poor.

Eleanor Roosevelt,
1884–1962

1. The ideas of the New Deal must continue within American society and be transported to the rest of the world.
2. An ordinary-appearing and -acting woman can accomplish extraordinary things.

Martin Luther King, Jr.,
1929–1968

1. The sources of disadvantage are economic, and a reallocation of resources is needed.
2. The dispossessed of the world must join forces, and America's belligerent foreign policy stands in the way.
3. Reformers must turn their attention to the northern ghettos.

Margaret Thatcher,
1925–

1. Nationalism is better than internationalism.
2. Privatize as many industries and functions as possible.
3. Maintain the cold war, be firm against all aggressors, but try to do business with the Soviet Union's Mikhail Gorbachev.

Jean Monnet,
1888–1979

1. Reconciliation begins with economics. Place one's faith in reason.
2. One should work with leaders and give them the limelight and the credit.
3. One should pursue a single goal steadfastly.

Mahatma Gandhi,
1869–1948

1. The industrial revolution is inherently destructive; one should go back to a village life. One should follow a certain hygiene.
2. Conflict can strengthen both parties.
3. The dispossessed everywhere should unite.
4. Reform work should be fully public.
5. The spiritual dimension of life is the most important one.

Other Counterstories

Margaret Mead,
1901–1978

1. All cultures can be ranked, or, alternatively, all cultural comparisons are futile.
2. Beware of scientists attempting to tell us about how to lead our lives.
3. Experiments with family and personal lives are dangerous.

J. Robert Oppenheimer,
1904–1967

1. Avoid paradoxes and look for clarity, direction, and solutions.

Robert Maynard
Hutchins, 1899–1977

1. Centers and foundations are inherently elitist and unreliable.
2. We as a society need more conservative thinkers and ideologies, not liberals, who have gotten us into trouble.
3. America needs an activist foreign policy.

Alfred P. Sloan, Jr.,
1875–1966

1. We must be prepared for industries very different from the automobile industry, and for competitors very different from the Big Three auto makers.
2. The union's viewpoint is very different from the management's.
3. Marxism harbors deeper insights than the classical economic analysis.

George C. Marshall,
1880–1959

1. The cold war dwarfs all other issues.
2. Israel merits recognition now.

Pope John XXIII,
1881–1963

1. Religious leaders should stay out of the political arena.
2. Cynicism about genuine spirituality is merited.
3. The poor should accept their lot.

Eleanor Roosevelt,
1884–1962

1. The New Deal is and should be finished.
2. Only a superperson can accomplish extraordinary things.

Martin Luther King, Jr.,
1929–1968

1. The search for economic causes signals that one is a Marxist, and that is dangerous.
2. America is special and has to police the rest of the world.
3. Southerners should stay away from northern urban situations that they cannot understand.

Margaret Thatcher,
1925–

1. Nationalism is anachronistic and dangerous.
2. Many functions are better run by the government.
3. Abandon the cold war, and be wary of Gorbachev.

Jean Monnet,
1888–1979

1. Reconciliation begins with social issues. Spiritual considerations are more important than rational ones.
2. It is bad to work behind the scenes.
3. It is unrealistic to stick to only one goal, especially an international one, given changing conditions and priorities.

Mahatma Gandhi,
1869–1948

1. One cannot turn back the clock. Learn from science.
2. Conflict is a zero-sum undertaking.
3. It is unrealistic for the dispossessed from different societies to feel part of the same population.
4. Do not air your dirty linen publicly; work behind the scenes.
5. Trust reason and analysis, not spirituality.

305

	Direct/Indirect Leadership	Embodiment across Domains	Consonance of Stories within and across Domains
Margaret Mead, 1901–1978	Both forms	Considerable	Considerable
J. Robert Oppenheimer, 1904–1967	Both forms, more problems with direct leadership	Ambivalent, could not defend himself adequately against charges of disloyalty; hauteur was troubling to many	Stretch of domain stories proves problematic, when one deals with a fickle and fearful public
Robert Maynard Hutchins, 1899–1977	Tried both forms, but neither was very effective in later life	Seemed to be all over the map and was not convincing; difficult for ordinary persons to identify with him	Fair degree of consonance at first, but education issues became less important as he addressed the full range of global issues
Alfred P. Sloan, Jr., 1875–1966	Direct leadership	Effective during lifetime, but would rapidly have become anachronistic after 1960	Considerable
George C. Marshall, 1880–1959	Direct leadership	Excellent; more important than story	Considerable

Pope John XXIII, 1881–1963	Direct	Excellent	High consonance
Eleanor Roosevelt, 1884–1962	Direct	Quite convincing, despite her unusual background and position	High
Martin Luther King, Jr., 1929–1968	Direct	Not as effective as within domains	Initially very high; as stories changed, consonance was reduced
Margaret Thatcher, 1925–	Direct	Very convincing	Personally consonant from first days of political life, though she did not reveal her full agenda until she gained high office
Jean Monnet, 1888–1979	Indirect, using leaders as one's vehicle; but primarily direct, in working with leaders	First-rate; cosmopolitan and not parochial; tenacious long-term focus on one issue	N.A.
Mahatma Gandhi, 1869–1948	Both forms	Very convincing	Amazing consistency in long-term goal, flexibility in stories

Areas of Failure

	Areas of Failure
Margaret Mead, 1901–1978	Never set up an enduring organization or a viable program; analysis of Samoa may have been flawed; her progressive ideas lost currency when the society took a more conservative turn in the 1970s and 1980s; her personal life became fragmented
J. Robert Oppenheimer, 1904–1967	Could not convince policy makers to rein in their desire for weapons; judged a security risk during the anti-Communist witch-hunt and forced to withdraw from public life; his experiences suggested the limits of scientists' participation in the hurly-burly world of politics
Robert Maynard Hutchins, 1899–1977	Could not convince his faculty of many of his programs; never succeeded in launching an effective institution or program after leaving the University of Chicago; general public and many faculty members had difficulty in identifying with Hutchins; not clear that he welcomed debate, except on his terms; toward the end, his messages were not distinguishable from those of other pooh-bahs
Alfred P. Sloan, Jr., 1875–1966	Never anticipated the success of Japan or the rise of the information society; erroneously discerned little difference among General Motors, American society, and the rest of the industrialized world
George C. Marshall, 1880–1959	Not selected to lead Operation Overlord; foreign policy after the Second World War was much more vexed than during the war; attacked by Senator Joseph McCarthy and received little support from President Eisenhower; the military that he built up was rapidly demobilized

Pope John XXIII, 1881–1963

Negative reactions within the Catholic Church; successive leaders did not carry forth John's program within the church; most links forged between Khrushchev and Kennedy did not survive their departures from office

Eleanor Roosevelt, 1884–1962

Much of her domestic agenda had to be muted during the Second World War; became seen as increasingly partisan after the war; leadership of the disadvantaged populations shifted to younger and more representative figures; felt herself an unsuccessful mother and had an extremely strained marriage; led a secret life that was never successfully worked through

Martin Luther King, Jr., 1929–1968

Overtaken by militants within the civil rights movement; under personal attack by the FBI; efforts to attack problems in the urban North were frustrated; core constituency was not interested in the problems of faraway nations and peoples; evidence of his plagiarism and sexual promiscuity

Margaret Thatcher, 1925–

Eventually followed her own dictates without even taking into account the views of others; at the end of her tenure in office, political failures were largely self-inflicted; did not achieve many of her goals for Britain, though she did change the nature of the debate

Jean Monnet, 1888–1979

Had difficulty getting support from leaders of many nations; faced great institutional resistance to change; even today, relevant treaties have not yet been ratified, the spirit of "one Europe" seems remote, tribalism has reemerged

Mahatma Gandhi, 1869–1948

India was and remains wracked with conflict; to some extent, more successful outside of India; family life was not harmonious; Gandhiism is more of an ideal than a reality

APPENDIX II

The Leaders of the Second World War

	Family	Education
Chiang Kai-shek, 1887 (Chekiang Province, China)–1975	Wealthy parents; father, a merchant, was cold; mother became intimate only after death of older, favored brother	Private tutor; estranged from academic subjects; attended military academy in Japan, later in USSR
Winston Churchill, 1874 (Oxfordshire, England)–1965	Father was a British lord, mother was an American; politically established but not wealthy family; parents remote; relation to father was tense	Attended several schools, never happy or adjusted; was considered a slow learner; eventually attended military academy; much self-education in later life
Charles de Gaulle, 1890 (Lille, France)–1970	Catholic, Conservative, bourgeois family; warm but demanding	Jesuit education; good student, strong in math and history; attended prestigious military academy at Saint Cyr
Adolf Hitler, 1889 (Branau, Austria)–1945	Father, authoritarian civil servant; mother, indulgent younger woman; father ignored wife and son, died when Hitler was fourteen	Undisciplined in school; rejected from the Academy of Arts; never received high school diploma
Vladimir Ilich Ulyanov (Lenin), 1870 (Volga, Russia)–1924	Supportive and comfortable parents; father died in 1886 when Lenin was sixteen; execution of his beloved older brother in 1887 propelled Lenin into revolutionary politics	Excellent student at *gymnasium*; law degree

Mao Zedong (Mao Tse-tung), 1893 (Shaoshan, Hunan Province, China)–1976	Father was relatively successful rice farmer; beat his son, with whom he clashed repeatedly; mother indulged son and shared belief in Buddhism	Learned Chinese classics at traditional private school; at sixteen, went to modern primary school, but did not succeed; finally received normal school education, where he read works by major Western thinkers
Benito Mussolini, 1883 (Varano di Costa, Italy)–1945	Large family; father was uneducated blacksmith and socialist; mother was teacher; grief-stricken by mother's death in 1905; father died in 1910	Difficult, rebellious student; stabbed other students; eventually performed excellently in history, geography, and Italian studies
Franklin Delano Roosevelt, 1882 (New York, United States)–1945	Wealthy, supportive family; mother incredibly strong-willed; father died in 1900; as only child, was spoiled but also was expected to contribute to community	Tutors and private school; decent but not outstanding student; attended Harvard College and Columbia Law School
Josef Stalin, 1879 (Georgia, Russia)–1953	Illiterate and impoverished parents; father beat wife and son; mother devoted to son, but he showed little gratitude	As student, showed promise and had outstanding memory, but did not become an intellectual; expelled from seminary; scholastic training reflected in dogmatic speeches and writings
Hideki Tojo, 1884 (Tokyo, Japan)–1948	Eldest son of Japanese samurai who had converted to Western-style militarism; mother worked to help with family finances; was doted on by parents	Did not like to study; attended military academy

313

	Personality/Special Feelings	Early Travel
Chiang Kai-shek, 1887 (Chekiang Province, China)–1975	When not ill, was boisterous, liked creating crisis situations; very focused on work; became quite stoic	Japan for study
Winston Churchill, 1874 (Oxfordshire, England)–1965	Energetic, prankish, dissolute; fascinated and energized by war; epic struggles made him feel unique	Europe, United States, commissioned to Cuba, India, and the Sudan
Charles de Gaulle, 1890 (Lille, France)–1970	Stubborn, egotistical; commanded respect at school, in part because of great height; identified with France and announced publicly at military academy that he was destined for great things	Studied in Belgium, served in military in Germany, Poland, Near East
Adolf Hitler, 1889 (Branau, Austria)–1945	Saw self as artist; had difficulty in making friends; felt more rapport with mass audiences; expected one day to overwhelm the world with his deeds	Remained in Germany, Austria
Vladimir Ilich Ulyanov (Lenin), 1870 (Volga, Russia)–1924	Boisterous, bossy, respected by others, but kept his distance; chronically litigious; knew he was gifted as revolutionary leader and felt empowered to dominate	Toured western Europe in 1895; was exiled there during the early 1900s

Mao Zedong (Mao Tse-tung), 1893 (Shaoshan, Hunan Province, China)–1976	Saw self as outsider; proud, resolute, headstrong; had feeling for underdog	Never left China until visit to Moscow in middle age
Benito Mussolini, 1883 (Varano di Costa, Italy)–1945	As youth, a loner and reader; much fighting and bullying; obsessed with making a mark on his era	Switzerland, Germany, as draft evader
Franklin Delano Roosevelt, 1882 (New York, United States)–1945	As youngster, charmed teachers and administrators at school, though had few friends; more buoyant, gregarious as he grew older	Many trips to Europe as a child
Josef Stalin, 1879 (Georgia, Russia)–1953	After early childhood could not tolerate anyone who disagreed with him; no close friends; seen as cruel and vindictive; liked tales of peasant resistance against authority; mother taught him to believe he would do great things	Left Russia for only a month in Vienna in 1913 and then not again until Tehran Summit in 1943
Hideki Tojo, 1884 (Tokyo, Japan)–1948	Spirited, competitive, self-confident; impatient with those who were not quick and decisive; nervous temperament	Served in Siberia, studied in Switzerland and Germany

	Willingness to Challenge Authority/Take Risks	Initial Domain(s)
Chiang Kai-shek, 1887 (Chekiang Province, China)–1975	As boy, hated rules; criticized Manchu court; led protests at school; challenged revolutionary leaders and governmental officials	Military, and writer for military magazine
Winston Churchill, 1874 (Oxfordshire, England)–1965	Defiant at school, and ever after; adventurous in war and peace	Military, journalism, politics
Charles de Gaulle, 1890 (Lille, France)–1970	Insisted on his specialness and personal incarnation of France; would not accept French defeat after German invasion and was sentenced to death in absentia by Vichy government; preferred to leave government rather than to compromise	Served in military and was severely wounded; became history teacher
Adolf Hitler, 1889 (Branau, Austria)–1945	Challenged his priest about methods of Bible analysis; criticized leaders of German government; engaged in arguments and polemics with contemporaries; because of confidence in self (and contempt for others), was willing to entertain enormous risks, such as 1923 putsch	Wandered for ten years, reading, writing, sketching; joined army; identified personally with nationalism and soldiering
Vladimir Ilich Ulyanov (Lenin), 1870 (Volga, Russia)–1924	Known as family daredevil; loved to argue, confront, polarize	Lawyer, defending peasants

Mao Zedong (Mao Tse-tung), 1893 (Shaoshan, Hunan Province, China)–1976	Challenged teachers in schools by refusing to recite maxims; defied father; ultimately showed confrontational tendencies toward peers and opponents	Worked in library at Peking University; set up school to teach illiterate workers how to read
Benito Mussolini, 1883 (Varano di Costa, Italy)–1945	As young revolutionary, fought with police officers; even challenged God to strike him down	Early job as bricklayer; eventually joined Italian Army after being expelled from Switzerland for revolutionary activities
Franklin Delano Roosevelt, 1882 (New York, United States)–1945	Little need or inclination to challenge authority as a youngster; even as youth, believed high office was within his grasp; liked to play devil's advocate and to test others; after contracting polio, became more contemplative and experimented with ideas	Practiced law briefly before becoming state senator in 1910
Josef Stalin, 1879 (Georgia, Russia)–1953	Hated authority and felt compelled to oppose it throughout his life; wanted to crush all opponents, real and imagined; defied both Trotsky's and Lenin's orders in the aftermath of the First World War	After expulsion from seminary, became a Marxist and professional revolutionary agitator
Hideki Tojo, 1884 (Tokyo, Japan)–1948	Known as unusually quarrelsome with young peers	Soldier, attended army war college

	Early Political Career/Relation to Organizations	Language Skills
Chiang Kai-shek, 1887 (Chekiang Province, China)–1975	Joined the Kuomintang Party at an early age; participated in revolutions and assassinations; served directly under leader Sun Yat-sen; after Sun's death, became military leader of Kuomintang; from then on, with few interludes, was involved in lifelong struggle with Communists	As youth, good storyteller; wrote for magazines
Winston Churchill, 1874 (Oxfordshire, England)–1965	Rose to become first lord of admiralty in 1911; held various ministerial posts; ups and downs, including shifting parties and losing his parliamentary seat; seen as talented but unreliable; not much of a party man	Disciplined himself to be outstanding speaker and writer; won Nobel Prize for literature
Charles de Gaulle, 1890 (Lille, France)–1970	After attending École Supérieure de Guerre, was appointed to senior positions in the army; organized Free French forces, and became head of provisional French government after Nazi defeat in 1944	Excellent orator, brilliant lecturer who gave perfectly sculpted and memorized speeches; creative writer in youth; epic stylist in adult years
Adolf Hitler, 1889 (Branau, Austria)–1945	Joined the nascent Nazi Party as member in charge of recruitment and propaganda; rebuilt the party by identifying new constituencies and sources of support; took advantage of economic crisis to insert himself into national leadership; not interested in administration, but was able to work through established organizations; ultimately exercised personal, tyrannical power	Orator of genius, appealing to emotions and irrationality rather than reason; did not enjoy writing and appears to have dictated his books
Vladimir Ilich Ulyanov (Lenin), 1870 (Volga, Russia)–1924	In 1892 and 1893, joined revolutionary Marxist group; talents in speaking, writing, and leading emerged; led the Bolsheviks through their struggles with the more moderate Mensheviks; believed in elite hierarchy and worked closely with a small cadre of like-minded administrators	Aggressive sloganeer and debater, but was more effective as pamphleteer and writer

Mao Zedong (Mao Tse-tung), 1893 (Shaoshan, Hunan Province, China)–1976	Joined revolutionary army under Sun Yat-sen in 1911; founding member of the Chinese Communist Party in the 1920s; headed peasant training institute; showed early leadership capacities and charisma within ranks of peasants and workers; soon engaged in deathly struggle with Kuomintang; eventually led many Communist political and military organizations	Effective conversationalist; prolific writer of political works and poetry
Benito Mussolini, 1883 (Varano di Costa, Italy)–1945	Began revolutionary activities around 1902 or 1903; much early journalism; first ran for office as socialist in 1913; helped define Fascist Party; won and lost elections and finally became national leader in 1921	Authoritative and effective orator, though actual speeches were deficient; wrote many journalistic pieces
Franklin Delano Roosevelt, 1882 (New York, United States)–1945	Rose steadily through the government before and during First World War; always a good Democrat; worked well with party organization	Decent, though not enthusiastic writer; outstanding speaker, especially on radio (fireside chats)
Josef Stalin, 1879 (Georgia, Russia)–1953	Spent much time as revolutionary in jail or on the run; became Lenin's right-hand man in 1911; though frequently removed from positions and censured by Lenin, remained powerful in the party because of his organizational knowledge and acumen; created his own secret department, which helped him to emerge as Lenin's sole successor; knew how to turn administrative skill into political power	Mediocre writer, but able to express arguments in clear, black-and-white terms; effective debater but not good speaker to mass audiences; felt that mystique was enhanced if he seldom spoke publicly; rallied his fellow countrymen effectively during the Nazi siege of 1941–1942
Hideki Tojo, 1884 (Tokyo, Japan)–1948	Officer in Military Affairs Bureau of the army; became involved in public relations and public policy in the early 1930s	Eloquent speaker

319

	Dominant Stories	Counterstories
Chiang Kai-shek, 1887 (Chekiang Province, China)–1975	Make China independent and unified by exorcising foreign elements. China needs a revolutionary army. Personal liberty should be sacrificed to the cause.	Communism and China are part of an international movement. The genius of the peasants will win out. Chiang is an elitist, corrupt dictator who is out of touch with the Chinese people.
Winston Churchill, 1874 (Oxfordshire, England)–1965	Liberty and the rights of individuals are all-important. Britain and the British Empire are grand; there is a special "genius of the English race." Struggle is often necessary.	Internationalism, socialism, and communism are positive. Churchill is a megalomaniac, a warmonger, an imperialist, and a monarchist.
Charles de Gaulle, 1890 (Lille, France)–1970	Mechanized warfare is needed. France should be restored to world stature and to parity with the other Allies. Beware of supranational entities. A strong central government and president are needed.	Monnet's vision of a united Europe is valuable. De Gaulle is an anachronistic chauvinist, bluffer, and dictator.
Adolf Hitler, 1889 (Branau, Austria)–1945	The German "Volk" are a special, superior people who need an omnipotent "Fuehrer." Jews, Communists, and internationalists are villains. Divisiveness used to outflank internal and external opposition is useful. Struggle and war are human imperatives.	Rationality, moderation in internal and foreign affairs, and democratic processes are vital. Internationalism, communism, and non-Aryans should not be rejected. Hitler is a monomaniacal tyrant.
Vladimir Ilich Ulyanov (Lenin), 1870 (Volga, Russia)–1924	Marxism, with a Leninist-Russian flavor, is needed in Russia. Common workers are the vanguards of revolution, but an elite party leadership, with intellectuals playing a key role, is needed. Armed confrontations, with revolutionaries in charge, are inevitable.	Reformist, rather than confrontational, change in government is needed. Lenin is part of a conspiratorial elite; he is an intellectual rather than a genuine man of the people.

Mao Zedong (Mao Tse-tung), 1893 (Shaoshan, Hunan Province, China)–1976

Socialism is the only just cause, the only cause worth dying for. Struggle is endemic in life. Genius lies in the common people. Intellectuals should be treated with suspicion; the proletariat around the world are most important. Knowledge grows out of experience. Power is a key issue in life. Feudalism, moderation, and fascism are valuable, as are traditional Confucian or Buddhist values. The Kuomintang of Chiang Kai-shek should be supported. Mao is a corrupt, warmongering anti-intellectual.

Benito Mussolini, 1883 (Varano di Costa, Italy)–1945

The new masses are the most important element of Italian politics. Fascism, founded on bloody struggle, should reign supreme. Roman virtues should be restored, and an alliance with Germany should be forged. The individual is subordinate to the state. Monarchism, democracy, moderation, free speech, Catholic socialism, and the special role of peasants or workers are each tenable positions. Mussolini is a hypocrite and a bully.

Franklin Delano Roosevelt, 1882 (New York, United States)–1945

The government should be activist, especially in times of crisis. Americans should help one another and their allies oppose fascism. Government intervention is inherently evil. America is better off pursuing an isolationist policy. FDR is greedy and power hungry.

Josef Stalin, 1879 (Georgia, Russia)–1953

A Marxist-Leninist story works best for society. Socialism should be established in one country before world revolution is undertaken. The industrial might of the Soviet Union must be built up. Collectivization of farms must be implemented, irrespective of the hardships involved. All opposition to the party and its leadership must be eradicated. During the Second World War, Marxism needs to be soft-pedaled. There are merits in democratic, evolutionary socialistic, and fascistic governmental forms. International revolutionary efforts must be undertaken. Stalin is a coercive terrorist who is estranged from workers and peasants.

Hideki Tojo, 1884 (Tokyo, Japan)–1948

The Japanese are a superior and invincible race. Germany is an admirable ally. Americans are undisciplined and incapable of sustaining a war. Militarism and war must be supported. A moderate, nonconfrontational policy is best. War with China is more important than war with Europeans and Americans.

Embodiment/Work Habits/Personal Life

Chiang Kai-shek, 1887 (Chekiang Province, China)–1975	Ascetic; importance of decorum and regulated attitude; second marriage to Soong Mei-ling, highly influential Chinese woman who became a full partner in leadership; succeeded in office by his son
Winston Churchill, 1874 (Oxfordshire, England)–1965	Glutton for work; demanding on others; tremendous focus; resilient; his outsized personality and rhetoric, off-putting in earlier decades, proved perfect for embattled Britons during the war; had strong marriage, but tense relations with his children; relaxed by painting and hunting
Charles de Gaulle, 1890 (Lille, France)–1970	Maintained remoteness from public, consistent with French grandeur, contempt for ordinary politics; willingness to resign; physical height signified hauteur; courageous soldier; perfectionist in language; good marriage with Yvonne, who stayed out of politics
Adolf Hitler, 1889 (Branau, Austria)–1945	Regular hours of early political career gave way to idiosyncratic, personally indulgent (though still ascetic) lifestyle; demanded absolute obedience and depended increasingly on personal relations to followers; little personal life; married his mistress just before they committed suicide; in early life, was brave German soldier, but did not exhibit personal bravery or sacrifice during the Second World War
Vladimir Ilich Ulyanov (Lenin), 1870 (Volga, Russia)–1924	Methodical, tireless worker, with leadership of Russia his constant goal; encouraged debate within his circle and was admired by associates; married close political associate Nadya Krupskaya; until late in life, maintained habits of study, chess, walking

Mao Zedong (Mao Tse-tung), 1893 (Shaoshan, Hunan Province, China)–1976	Initially led courageous spartan existence and inspired his colleagues during the Long March; eventually became tyrannical and dissolute, encouraging a cult of personality
Benito Mussolini, 1883 (Varano di Costa, Italy)–1945	Portrayed self as hard worker but actually observed irregular work hours and a dissolute personal life; poseur, though initially gained admiration nationally and internationally for supposed feats; mercurial and liked to surprise his audiences
Franklin Delano Roosevelt, 1882 (New York, United States)–1945	Became a stronger personality after struggle with polio; hard worker; personal courage and fearlessness inspired others; had difficulty in delegating authority and managing smoothly; liked to play advisers off against one another; had political ally in wife, Eleanor, but the two were personally estranged after wife discovered FDR's love affair with Lucy Mercer; little relation with his children
Josef Stalin, 1879 (Georgia, Russia)–1953	Stoic, accepted hardship nonchalantly; difficult to work with because personalized all conflicts; married twice, but had little personal life; second wife killed herself; only daughter left USSR
Hideki Tojo, 1884 (Tokyo, Japan)–1948	Married in 1909; decisiveness faded into impulsiveness; succumbed to cult of personality

Ultimate Successes/Failures

Chiang Kai-shek, 1887 (Chekiang Province, China)–1975

Leadership of China for twenty years; temporary alliance with Communists during Second World War; ultimately forced to withdraw from mainland to island of Taiwan

Winston Churchill, 1874 (Oxfordshire, England)–1965

Many successes and failures in early life and midlife; triumph was leadership of Britain and Allies during Second World War; had limited political success, but great literary success, thereafter

Charles de Gaulle, 1890 (Lille, France)–1970

Represented an unbowed France during dark days of the Second World War; led decolonization of the French Empire; France restored to major European power; ultimately lost the support of his own people

Adolf Hitler, 1889 (Branau, Austria)–1945

Rose against enormous odds, and after many failures, to lead Germany and to conquer almost all of Western Europe; imprudent invasion of Soviet Union spelled the beginning of loss to the Allies; determined that the German people were not worthy of him and was prepared to bring all down along with him

Vladimir Ilich Ulyanov (Lenin), 1870 (Volga, Russia)–1924

Bolshevik revolution succeeded, though with much bloodshed; Lenin became ill shortly thereafter and could not control fight over succession

Mao Zedong (Mao Tse-tung), 1893 (Shaoshan, Hunan Province, China)–1976

Led the largest peasant revolution in history; dominated Chinese scene for thirty years; various policies, such as the Great Leap Forward and the Cultural Revolution, were calamitous, resulting in millions of deaths; legacy of communism in China uncertain at best

Benito Mussolini, 1883 (Varano di Costa, Italy)–1945

Dynamic leader of Fascists who initially was well regarded; wanted Italy to be great, but was not willing to build up military or political strength; alliance with Hitler was ultimately disastrous; was ultimately rejected by his own people

Franklin Delano Roosevelt, 1882 (New York, United States)–1945

Personally triumphed over polio; had unprecedented four electoral victories and presided over the Allied victory in the Second World War; depended too much on personal relations and probably misjudged Stalin fundamentally, thus precipitating conditions for the cold war

Josef Stalin, 1879 (Georgia, Russia)–1953

Changed the face of Russia within a generation, at the cost of millions of lives; ultimately, the Communist state that he created fell into disrepute and collapsed

Hideki Tojo, 1884 (Tokyo, Japan)–1948

Convinced Japan to go to war and presided over early victories; forced to resign when tide went against Japan; took blame, tried unsuccessfully to commit suicide; eventually executed after conviction for war crimes

NOTES

CHAPTER 1.
INTRODUCTION: A COGNITIVE APPROACH TO LEADERSHIP

3 Disraeli, "With words we govern men" is quoted in Blake, 1994, p. 26.

3 Keynes, "Practical men . . . " is from Keynes, 1936.

3 The topics addressed at the Eureka Summit are discussed in Cray, 1990; and Mayle, 1987.

3 For more about Einstein's theories, see Hoffmann, 1975; and Pais, 1982.

4 For more on Einstein's involvement in the Second World War, see Gardner, 1993a.

12 Nixon, "About the time you are writing . . . " is quoted in Kelly, 1993, p. 18.

14 For more on the notion of the human mind as an arena for leadership, see Little, 1985, p. 15.

15 For more on the development of cognitive psychology, see Gardner, 1985.

17 For important contributions to our understanding of the personal traits and personal histories of leaders, see Bell, 1992; Edinger, 1967; Hogan, Curphy, and Hogan, 1994; Korda, 1984; Petrullo and Bass, 1961; Rustow, 1970; Skowronek, 1993; and Zalesnik and Kets de Vries, 1985.

17 For important contributions to our understanding of different forms of leadership, see Barber, 1985; Bennis and Nanus, 1985; Bolman and Deal, 1991; Burns, 1978; Cohen and March, 1984; Gerth and Mills, 1958; Hollander, 1964; Little, 1985, 1988; Neustadt, 1980; Schiffer, 1973; Simonton, 1984; and Sutton and Galunic, 1994.

17 For important contributions to our understanding of the audience's role in leadership, see Armstrong, 1992; Fiedler, 1967; J. Gardner, 1986, 1990; Heifetz, 1994; and Smelser, 1962.

17 For Erikson's contributions, see Erikson, 1958, 1969.

18 For Miroff's use of the term *dissenting,* see Miroff, 1993.

CHAPTER 2. HUMAN DEVELOPMENT AND LEADERSHIP

21 Truman, "A leader is a man who . . . " is quoted in Montgomery, 1958, p. 69.

22 For more on behaviors of male primates, see Dobzhansky, 1962; and Goldberg, 1993.

22 For more on female dominance hierarchies, see Eckholm, 1989.

22 For more on the link between hierarchical shifts and changes in physiological markers, see McDonald, 1994; and Sapolsky and Jay, 1989.

22 For more on primate in-groups and out-groups, see Rushton, 1989.

22 For more on the primate's proclivity to imitate, see Donald, 1991; and Marshack, 1991.

22 For more on features of dominance among young children, see Heifetz, 1994.

23 For more on bonds of attachment between infant and caretaker, see Bowlby, 1969–1980; Harlow and Harlow, 1969; and Kraemer, 1992.

23 For more on the effect of early attachments on individuals' reactions to authority, see Mitscherlich in Edinger, 1967.

23 For more on young children's awareness of their individuality, see Gardner, 1982.

23 For more on identification with role models, see Kagan, 1959.

23 The ability to anticipate what a role model would do is discussed in Gardner, 1982.

24 For Freud's views on the personality of the young child, see Freud, 1952.

25 For Piaget's views on the mind of the child, see Piaget, 1983.

26 For more on experts' ability to relinquish early childhood notions, see Gardner, 1991.

26 For details about children's memories of events, see Bauer, 1993; and Nelson, 1986, 1992.

26 The five-year-old child's openness to new practices is discussed in Cohen and MacKeith, 1991.

28 For details about domains, see Feldman, 1994; and Turiel, 1989.

28 The value of different domains in various cultures is discussed in Gardner, 1993a, 1993b.

29 For more on children gifted in school and in particular domains, see Bloom and Sosniak, 1988; Feldman (with Goldsmith), 1986; and Winner, 1997.

29 For more on the "personal intelligences," see Gardner, 1993b; and Rosnow et al., 1994.

30 For more on the adult's ability to appreciate others' minds and motivations, see Rosnow et al., 1994; and Winner, 1988.

30 The limited ability of people to detect others' motivations is discussed in R. Brown, 1986; Ekman, 1985; and Nisbett and Ross, 1980.

30 Johnson, "The challenge was to learn . . . " is quoted in Heifetz, 1994, p. 229.

30 Loss of a father for leaders-to-be who are young is discussed in Csikszentmihalyi, 1994; and Simonton, 1994.

30 The childhood loss of a parent among 60 percent of British political leaders is discussed in Berrington, 1974.

31 On Sartre's claim that in the absence of a father, one makes one's own choices, see Sartre, 1964, pp. 18–19.

31 The pervasive feeling of loneliness among leaders who have lost a parent is discussed in Berrington, 1974.

31 The fact that Gandhi, Lenin, and Hitler each had a good relationship with one parent and a bad one with the other is discussed in Burns, 1978.

31 On Clinton's tensions with his stepfather, see Kelly, 1994.

31 For more on Clinton's decision to enter politics after realizing he was a good negotiator, see R. Brown, 1993.

31 The attainment of success by some leaders who deviate from socially accepted behavior is discussed in Csikszentmihalyi, 1993b.

31 The leader's propensity for taking risks and striving to get ahead of others is discussed in Burns, 1978; and Simonton, 1994.

31 Implacability in the face of opposition as evidence of one's self-reliance is discussed in Freud, 1921.

31 Churchill, "Famous men are usually . . . " is quoted in Berrington, 1974, p. 385.

32 Leaders' sense of being able to achieve far more than normal individuals is discussed in Gerth and Mills, 1958.

32 For Napoléon's views on his capabilities as a general, see Klein, 1992.

33 Followers' perennial search for an authority figure is discussed in Hoffer, 1951.

33 A leader of the French Revolution, "You know, I must follow the people . . . " has been attributed to various political figures.

33 Followers' differing attitudes toward power are discussed in Fromm, 1941.

33 Morris, "most individuals will placidly accept . . . " is from Morris, 1983, pp. 182–83.

33 For more on the phenomenon of "rescuers," see Oliner and Oliner, 1988.

36 Young children's abilities to master symbol systems are discussed in Gardner, 1991.

37 The description of de Gaulle's political destiny as being dependent on words is from *Encyclopaedia Britannica,* 1974, p. 965.

CHAPTER 3. THE LEADERS' STORIES

39 Cooley, "All leadership takes place . . . " is quoted in Rustow, 1970, p. 24.

39 The Colonel, "I want to be President," and "To do that I have to talk like . . . " are from Allende, 1991, pp. 14–15.

39 "They were dazzled by the clarity . . . " is from Allende, 1991, p. 16.

40 The Colonel, "War's what I know" is from Allende, 1991, p. 16.

40 For Homer's comment about Achilles, see Kitto, 1951, p. 172.

40 For other authors' ideas on the nature of stories, see Aristotle, 1947; Bruner, 1986; Donald, 1991; Mandler, 1984; Propp, 1968; and Schaefer, 1981.

40 For Wittgenstein's analysis of the concept of "games," see Wittgenstein, 1958.

41 For more on children's dualistic form of thinking, see Egan, 1989; and Lévi-Strauss, 1963.

41 For more on children's black-and-white understanding of moral dilemmas, see Fischer, 1984; and Kohlberg, 1969.

41 Thatcher's assessment of Reagan's Star Wars initiative is mentioned in Thatcher, 1993, p. 462.

43 For more on adolescents and relativism, see Damon, 1983, 1988; Kegan, 1982; Kohlberg, 1969; Selman, 1980; Selman and Schultz, 1990; and Turiel, 1989.

45 The unlikelihood of more sophisticated children being dragged down by less sophisticated children is discussed in Kohlberg, 1974.

46 The emotional appeal of stories is discussed in Brown, 1965.

46 The Nixon-Kennedy debate is analyzed in McLuhan, 1964.

47 Allende, "it was not her intention . . . " is from Allende, 1991, p. 12.

48 Malcolm X, "We want to know . . . " is from Malcolm X, 1989, p. 118.

48 Perot, "We owe it to the American people . . . " is quoted in McFarland et al., 1993, p. 310.

48 Trilling, "This is the unresolved question . . . " is quoted in Harris, 1993, p. 99.

48 The Athenian oath, "I inherit from the past . . . " is quoted in Kerr, 1993, p. 5.

49 Diogenes, "I am not an Athenian . . . " is quoted in Smith, 1991, p. 7.

49 For more on children's development of a sense of self, see Damon, 1977, 1983; Gardner, 1982; Kegan, 1982; Kohlberg, 1969, 1974; Selman, 1980; and Selman and Schultz, 1990.

49 For more on competing identities, see Erikson, 1959.

50 For more on the summation of different personality traits in adulthood, see Erikson, 1959.

50 Skowronek, "a coherent and compelling narrative . . . " is from Skowronek, 1993, p. 25.

51 Paine, "the cause of America . . . " is from Paine, 1976, p. 63.

52 For more on the group identity of the rival Serbs and Muslims, see Goleman, 1994; Kinzer, 1993; and Lewis, 1993.

52 Yevtushenko, "Goodbye our Red Flag . . . " is quoted in Schmemann, 1993, p. 4.

54 Two sources for individuals' pictures of the world are discussed in Cassirer, 1953–1957; and Donald, 1991.

54 The endurance of commonsense ideas throughout a person's life is discussed in Gardner, 1991.

56 For a discussion of those who hold moderate worldviews, see Kakutani, 1993.

57 For more on filmmaker Leni Riefenstahl's contribution to the myth of Hitler and the Nazis, see Buruma, 1992.

57 Ailes, "When I die . . . " is quoted in Kolbert, 1992, p. 69.

58 For more on individual differences and the ability to deal with ambiguity, see Adorno et al., 1950.

61 For more on the traditional developmentalist view on stages of development, see Kohlberg, 1969.

CHAPTER 4. MARGARET MEAD: AN OBSERVER OF DIVERSE CULTURES EDUCATES HER OWN

65   Mead, "I have spent . . . " is from Mead, 1972, p. 1.

66   A friend, "She was going to be something . . . " is quoted in Howard, 1984, p. 52.

67   For Hall's theory of adolescence, see Hall, 1904.

68   For more on Mead's rejection of the idea that adolescence has to be turbulent, see Howard, 1984, p. 88.

68   For Mead's assessment of the high price associated with many aspects of American society, see Mead, 1968, p. 178.

68   Mead, "the greatest cause for tears . . . " is from Mead, 1968, p. 146.

69   Mead, "This was the first piece of work . . . " is from Mead, 1968, p. 11.

69   Mead, "In anthropology you only have to show . . . " is quoted in Freeman, 1983, p. 77.

69   Mead, "The life of the day begins . . . " is from Mead, 1968, p. 26.

71   For Mead's description of the role reversals of women and men in the Tchambuli tribe, see Mead, 1972, p. 216.

72   Mead, "We are forced to conclude that human nature . . . " is quoted in Howard, 1984, p. 162.

72   For more on Mead's and Bateson's fourfold scheme, see Bateson, 1984, p. 133.

72   For more on Mead and Bateson having made an epochal discovery, see Mead, 1972, pp. 216–20.

72   Mead's analysis of the Balinese trance state can be found in Mead, 1964a, pp. 38–40.

73   Mead, "Reo had a better ear than I have . . . " is quoted in Howard, 1984, p. 163.

74   Mead, "the biological bases of development . . . " is quoted in Degler, 1991, p. 137.

74   For more on an observer's assessment of Mead as a child at summer camp, see Howard, 1984, p. 175.

75   For a discussion of the ways that Mead broadened the scope and validity of scholarly inquiry within anthropological study, see Bateson, 1984.

75   For the critical scrutiny of Mead's work, see Freeman, 1983; and Geertz, 1988.

76   Mead, "My experience as an anthropologist . . . " is from Mead and Metraux, 1980, pp. 20–21.

77   Mead, " . . . frightened retreat to some single standard . . . " is quoted in Howard, 1984, p. 205.

77   Mead, "What distinguishes human groups . . . " is from Mead and Metraux, 1980, p. 21.

77   For the photographic collection *The Family of Man,* see Steichen, 1955.

78   For more on Mead's public persona, see Bateson, 1994; and Crapanzano, 1993.

78   For more on Mead's overwhelming personality, see Bruner, 1993.

78   Schwartz, " . . . Manhattan project to study the sources of her energy . . . " is quoted in Howard, 1984, p. 308.

79   Mead, "I have become increasingly conscious . . . " is quoted in Bateson, 1984, p. 115.

79   Mead, "It has not been my choice . . . " is quoted in Bateson, 1984, p. 116.

79   For more on Mead's personal religious practices, see Howard, 1984, p. 348.

79   Bateson, "The letter she wrote in 1955 . . . " is from Bateson, 1984, p. 118.

81   Friedan, "symbol of the woman thinker . . . " is from Friedan, 1963, p. 135.

82   For Mead's comment about her relief at being a woman, see Mead, 1972, p. 111.

82   For more on Mead's preference for informal leadership and her feeling that Americans did not crave leaders, see Bateson, 1994.

82   For the 1983 *New York Times* article about Derek Freeman's attack on Mead's work, see McDowell, 1983, p. 1.

83   For more on 1960s feminist assessments of Mead's work, see Friedan, 1963.

CHAPTER 5. J. ROBERT OPPENHEIMER: THE TEACHING OF PHYSICS, THE LESSONS OF POLITICS

85   Brodsky, "Every poet is a bit of a Fuehrer . . . " is from Brodsky, 1986, p. 136.

85   For the cover story photo in *Life* magazine, see Barnett, 1949.

87   Oppenheimer, "unctuous, repulsively good little boy" is quoted in Rhodes, 1986, p. 119.

87   Oppenheimer's suicidal tendency is mentioned in Royal, 1969, p. 35.

87   Oppenheimer, "In the days of my almost infinitely prolonged adolescence . . . " is quoted in Rhodes, 1986, p. 122.

87   Oppenheimer's letter after his mother's death can be found in Goodchild, 1983, p. 17.

88   The psychiatrist's conclusion that Oppenheimer was schizophrenic is mentioned in Smith and Werner, 1980, p. 125.

88   Oppenheimer's early scholarly papers on relativity and quantum mechanics are described in Rabi et al., 1969, pp. 16–17.

88   For more on Oppenheimer's ability to work with his students, see Rabi et al., 1969, p. 17.

89   Rabi, "He was not an original," is quoted in Goodchild, 1983, p. 176.

89   Rabi's view that Oppenheimer romanticized mysteries is mentioned in Rhodes, 1986, p. 149.

89   Oppenheimer, "My friends, both in Pasadena and in Berkeley . . . " is quoted in Goodchild, 1983, p. 30.

90   Oppenheimer, "in late 1936 . . . " is quoted in Rhodes, 1986, p. 445.

90   For more on Oppenheimer's interest in socialist ideas, see Chevalier, 1965, pp. 186–87.

90   Physicists' awareness of the potential of nuclear energy and Einstein's warning to President Roosevelt are described in Rhodes, 1986, pp. 304–12.

90   Oppenheimer's theoretical research on nuclear reactions at Berkeley is mentioned in Smith and Weiner, 1980, p. 224.

91   Groves, "No one with whom I talked . . . " is from Groves, 1962, p. 61.

91 Groves, "much that was not . . . " is from Groves, 1962, p. 63.

91 Bethe, "The success of Los Alamos . . . " is quoted in York, 1989, pp. 165–66.

92 Weisskopf, "continuous and intense presence . . . " is quoted in Smith and Weiner, 1980, p. 104.

92 Horgan, "first class manipulator . . . " is quoted in Smith and Weiner, 1980, p. 221.

92 Rabi, "born leader . . . " is quoted in Rabi et al., 1969, p. 8.

92 Teller, "I don't know how . . . " is quoted in Davis, 1968, p. 129.

92 Chevalier, "From the earliest age . . . " is from Chevalier, 1965, p. 185.

92 For more on Oppenheimer's challenges in organizing the Los Alamos research facility, see Barnett, 1949, p. 132.

93 For more on Oppenheimer's declarations that he could no longer continue to lead Los Alamos, see Smith and Weiner, 1980, p. 261; and Goodchild, 1983, p. 111.

94 Oppenheimer's colleague, "He was so naturally a leader . . . " is quoted in Stern (with Green), 1969, p. 97.

94 For more on Oppenheimer's ability to summarize discussions succinctly, see Smith and Weiner, 1980, pp. 328–29.

94 For more on Oppenheimer quashing the petition for a "trial demonstration" of the bomb, see Halberstam, 1993, p. 28.

95 For Oppenheimer's quoting of the Bhagavad Gita, see Barnett, 1949, p. 133.

95 Oppenheimer, "In some crude sense . . . " is quoted in Barnett, 1949, p. 133.

95 For more on Oppenheimer's support for international control and peaceful use of atomic energy and eventual disarmament, see York, 1989, p. 47.

95 For more on Oppenheimer's minority views about defense issues and politics, see Boyer, 1985.

96 Oppenheimer, "How can human morality . . . " is quoted in Bruner, 1993.

96 Truman, "Don't you bring . . . " is quoted in Goodchild, 1983, p. 172.

97 Oppenheimer, "We are gradually coming . . . " is quoted in Barnett, 1949, pp. 137–38.

98 Oppenheimer, "A subject is much harder . . . " is quoted in Barnett, 1949, p. 123.

98 Oppenheimer, "The peoples of this world . . . " is quoted in Groves, 1962, p. 354.

98 Oppenheimer, "We have devoted effort . . . " is from Oppenheimer, 1984, p. 92.

98 Oppenheimer, "No man should escape . . . " is quoted in Rabi et al., 1969, p. 41.

98 Oppenheimer, "We have made a thing . . . " is quoted in Boyer, 1985, p. 272.

98 Oppenheimer, "The atomic bomb . . . " is from Oppenheimer, 1984, p. 20.

99 For more on the Atomic Energy Commission's withdrawal of Oppenheimer's clearance, see Smith and Weiner, 1980, p. 329.

99 For Oppenheimer's comment about the hearing as a "farce," see Smith and Weiner, 1980, p. 331.

100 Kennan, "Curious mixture . . . " is from Kennan, 1994, p. 8.

100 For more on Rabi's performance at Oppenheimer's hearing, see Goodchild, 1983, p. 246.

100 For more on Oppenheimer making "giants feel like cockroaches," see Stern (with Green), 1969, p. 127.

100 For Oppenheimer's dismissal of Graham, see Halberstam, 1979, p. 159.

101 Latimer, "elements of the mystic" is quoted in Davis, 1968, p. 152.

101 Rabi, "spiritual quality . . . " is from Rabi et al., 1969, p. 8.

101 Brown, "The power of his personality . . . " is quoted in Goodchild, 1983, p. 269.

101 For more on Americans' waning support for restrained use of atomic power, see Boyer, 1985.

102 Oppenheimer, "I think it is just possible . . . " is quoted in Goodchild, 1983, p. 275.

103 For Oppenheimer's comment about his inability to participate in "common discourse," see Oppenheimer, 1960, p. 7.

103 Oppenheimer, "I have been much concerned . . . " is quoted in Rabi et al., 1969, pp. 56–57.

CHAPTER 6. ROBERT MAYNARD HUTCHINS: BRINGING "THE HIGHER LEARNING" TO AMERICA

105 Neustadt, "Presidential power . . . " is quoted in Allison, 1971, p. 148.

105 Cohen and March, "Almost any educated person . . . " is from Cohen and March, 1984, pp. 18–19.

107 For more on Hutchins's abilities as a public speaker during his collegiate days, see Dzuback, 1991, p. 35; and Mayer, 1993, p. 41.

108 Ashmore, "in these public utterances . . . " is from Ashmore, 1989, p. 42.

108 The two projects Hutchins undertook while serving as the acting dean are described in Dzuback, 1991, p. 55; and Mayer, 1993, p. 65.

108 For more on prodigies, see Feldman (with Goldsmith), 1986; Gardner, 1993b; and Winner, 1997.

109 Hutchins, "We do not care much whether . . . " is quoted in Ashmore, 1989, p. 54.

110 The statistics on the University of Chicago can be found in Dzuback, 1991, p. 83.

110 Hutchins's early innovations at Chicago are described by Mayer, 1993, p. 98.

110 Dzuback, "The undergraduate program moved from the fringes . . . " is from Dzuback, 1991, p. 69.

111 For more on Hutchins's and Adler's Great Books seminar, see Adler, 1988, p. xxii; and Rubin, 1992.

111 Hutchins, "The most striking fact . . . " is from Hutchins, 1936, p. 1.

111 Hutchins, "An intellect properly disciplined . . . " is from Hutchins, 1936, p. 63.

111 Hutchins, "the unifying principle of a university . . . " is from Hutchins, 1936, p. 57.

111 Hutchins, "Education implies teaching," is from Hutchins, 1936, p. 66.

112 For more on Hutchins's view that his Great Books course of study would engender a common stock of ideas and common methods for dealing with them, see Hutchins, 1936, p. 85.

112 Hutchins, "Metaphysics then, as the highest science . . . " is from Hutchins, 1936, p. 99.

112 Hutchins, "deal with the same propositions . . . " is from Hutchins, 1936, p. 107.

112 For an assessment of Allan Bloom's stance, see Adler, 1988.

113 Gideonse, "Unity imposed by authority . . . " is from Gideonse, 1937, p. 32.

113 Dewey, "[Such a progressive view] renounces the traditional notion . . . " is from Dewey, 1929, p. 37.

113 Dewey, "I would not intimate that the author . . . " is quoted in Ashmore, 1989, p. 163.

115 Mayer, "The ardent advocate of the scientific approach . . . " is from Mayer, 1993, p. 71.

116 For more on Hutchins's acceptance of many speaking invitations, see Ashmore, 1989, p. 142.

116 Hutchins, "the path to war . . . " is quoted in Ashmore, 1989, p. 214.

116 Hutchins's idea for an article entitled "Where Hitler Is Right" is discussed in Mayer, 1993, p. 234.

116 Hutchins, "Long run activities must be sacrificed . . . " is quoted in Ashmore, 1989, p. 214.

117 For more on Hutchins's pride in the University of Chicago's contribution to wartime military projects, see Ashmore, 1989, p. 225.

117 For more on Hutchins's call for the abolition of tenure and his shock at the reaction to his speech, see Ashmore, 1989, p. 140; and Mayer, 1993, pp. 321–34.

117 For more on the faculty members' reactions to Hutchins's threats to change the groundrules of their employment, see Ashmore, 1989, p. 240.

117 For more on Hutchins's offer to resign and his increased outside activities in the late 1940s, see Dzuback, 1991, p. 69; and Rubin, 1992.

117 Hutchins, "The vital juices . . . " is quoted in Ashmore, 1989, p. 275.

118 Hutchins, "a specialized institution for unspecialized men . . . " is quoted in Mayer, 1993, p. 46.

119 Shils, "prince in exile" is from Shils, 1990, p. 234.

119 Hutchins, "promises fertilizers . . . " "could usher in a new day," and "boredom and suicidal tendencies" are quoted in Boyer, 1985, pp. 112, 142, 261.

120 Hutchins, "Down the hill with Hutchins" is from Cutler, 1994.

120 Dzuback, "In the end, by placing the Center . . . " is from Dzuback, 1991, p. 275.

120 For John Gardner's assessment of Hutchins as too brilliant and too arrogant, see J. Gardner, 1993.

120 Shils, "He always argued like a man . . . " is from Shils, 1990, p. 214.

121 For more on Hutchins's pleasure at going against the grain, see Mayer, 1993, p. 19.

121 Hutchins, "I have come to regard educators . . . " is quoted in Ashmore, 1989, p. xv.

CHAPTER 7. ALFRED P. SLOAN, JR.:
THE BUSINESS OF AMERICA

123 Sloan, "Today it is clear that every man, woman, and child . . . " is from Sloan, 1941, p. 193.

125 Ford, "To my mind there is no bent . . . " is quoted in Byrne, 1993, pp. 170–71.

125 Ford's and General Motors' market shares by the time of the Second World War are quoted in Byrne, 1993, p. 17.

125 For more on GM's status as the richest and largest corporation in the world in the 1950s, see Halberstam, 1993, pp. 118–30.

126 For more on business management before the latter years of the nineteenth century, see Chandler, 1964, 1991; and Jensen, 1993.

127 Chandler, "the major innovation in the American economy . . . " is from Chandler, 1991, p. 73.

127 For more on the corporation becoming the basic industrial unit, see Chandler, 1991, p. 69.

127 Sloan, "I was of two minds about Mr. Durant . . . " is from Sloan, 1972, p. 28.

127 For Sloan's criticisms of Durant and his company policies, see Sloan, 1941, pp. 4, 106.

128 For more on GM writing off $100 million in losses and Durant's $40 million debt, see Chandler, 1964, p. 71.

128 For more on Durant being removed from GM in 1920, see Jacobs, 1992, p. 51.

128 For more on the du Pont family owning 29 percent of GM by 1919, see Sloan, 1972, p. 16.

128 Sloan, "the slow process of getting all the available facts . . . " is from Sloan, 1941, p. 50.

128 Sloan, "Pierre du Pont was the one . . . " is from Sloan, 1972, p. 46.

128 The 101 meetings in 1921 to place GM on an even keel are mentioned in Sloan, 1972, p. 61.

128 For more on Sloan's 1919 memo about the reorganization of GM, see Sloan, 1972, p. 49.

128 Chandler, "an organization for the General Motors Corporation . . . " is from Chandler, 1964, p. 114.

129 Sloan, "a comprehensive plan whereby the organization . . . " is quoted in Chandler, 1964, p. 149.

130 Chandler, "proved to be one of the most costly mistakes . . . " is from Chandler, 1964, p. 68.

130 Sloan, "I never minimized the administrative . . . " is from Sloan, 1972, p. 59.

130 For more on Sloan's treatment of the senior employees, see Sloan, 1941, p. 106.

130 Sloan, "Our management policy decisions . . . " is from Sloan, 1972, p. 510.

131 Ford, "The Ford factories and enterprises . . . " is quoted in Chandler, 1964, p. 15.

131 Sloan, "Much of my life . . . " is from Sloan, 1972, p. 511.

131 For more on Sloan staffing the governing committees with individuals from different divisions, see Sloan, 1972, p. 152.

131 Sloan, "How could we exercise permanent control . . . " is from Sloan, 1972, p. 159.

131 Sloan, "I made it a practice throughout the 1920s . . . " is from Sloan, 1972, p. 283.

132 For more about the donation to cancer research in Sloan's honor, see Sloan, 1972, p. 343.

132 Wilson, "We at General Motors . . . " is quoted in Halberstam, 1993, p. 118.

133 Sloan, "The financial story of General Motors . . . " is from Sloan, 1972, p. 245.

133 Sloan, "development of an industry . . . " is from Sloan, 1941, p. 42.

133 Sloan, "Humanity had never . . . " is from Sloan, 1941, p. 53.

133 Sloan, "The ambition . . . to rank high in the world . . . " is from Sloan, 1941, p. 170.

134 Sloan, "Can anyone see anything . . . " is from Sloan, 1941, p. 153.

134 Sloan, "No greater opportunity for accomplishment . . . " is from Sloan, 1941, pp. 133, 144.

135 For more on Sloan's concern with the styles of each coming year's automobile models, see Halberstam, 1993, p. 127.

136 Gerstner, "The last thing IBM needs now . . . " is quoted in Lohr, 1994, p. C2.

136 Gates, "Being a visionary is trivial . . . " is quoted in Miller and Hays, 1993, p. B1; and Lohr, 1994, p. 1.

136 Gerstner, "[Changing a culture] is not something . . . " is quoted in Lohr, 1994, p. 1.

136 Gerstner, "I'm one of us now" is quoted in Lohr, 1994, p. 1.

CHAPTER 8. GEORGE C. MARSHALL: THE EMBODIMENT OF THE GOOD SOLDIER

137 Montgomery, "My own definition of leadership . . . " is from Montgomery, 1958, pp. 69–70.

137 Marshall, "Yes, General, but we have . . . " is quoted in Mosley, 1982, pp. 57–60.

137 Marshall, "I am sorry, Mr. President . . . " is quoted in Stoler, 1989, pp. 60–70.

137 Morgenthau, "Well, it's been nice knowing you," is quoted in Mosley, 1982, pp. 122–23.

138 Cray, "Two decades earlier he had confronted . . . " is from Cray, 1990, p. 155.

139 Morgenthau, "He [Marshall] stood right up . . . " is quoted in Cray, 1990, p. 155; and Pogue, 1965, pp. 30–31.

139 For more on individuals who exhibit unusual moral responsibility, see Colby and Damon, 1992.

139 For more on creative individuals' expectations for their work, see H. Gardner, 1993a.

140 For more on the influence of Marshall's parents, see Pogue, 1963, pp. 19–23.

140 For more on the Marshall family's financial setback, see Pogue, 1963.

140 Marshall, "I never forget that because . . . " is quoted in Stoler, 1989, p. 5.

141 For more on Marshall always being the senior officer of his class, see "The General," 1944, pp. 15–18.

141 For more on Marshall barging into McKinley's office, see Pogue, 1963, pp. 64–65.

142 Marshall's command of only a small group in the Philippines is discussed in Cray, 1990, p. 42.

142 Marshall, "The absolute stagnation in promotion . . . " is quoted in Mosley, 1982, p. 43.

142 Bullard, "Lt. Col. Marshall's special fitness . . . " is quoted in Cray, 1990, p. 64; and Pogue, 1963, p. 164.

142 For more on Marshall's role in planning the Meuse-Argonne offensive, see "The General," 1944, p. 17; and Pogue, 1963, p. 175.

142 Stoler, "the wizard . . . " and "the most magnificent staff . . . " are from Stoler, 1989, p. 40.

142 For more on Marshall being named Pershing's principal aide, see Pogue, 1963, p. 220.

142 Marshall, "I have never seen a man . . . " is quoted in Cray, 1990, p. 88.

143 For more on Craig appointing Marshall as a brigadier general, see Mosley, 1982, pp. 111–12.

143 For more on Marshall's series of appointments in 1938 and 1939, see Goodwin, 1994b, p. 22.

143 For more on the growth of the U.S. Army to 8.3 million in 1945, see Pogue, 1965, p. 1.

144 Churchill, "the true organizer of victory" is quoted in Pogue, 1973, p. xi.

144 Marshall, "I have but one purpose . . . " is quoted in Stoler, 1989, p. 77.

146 Marshall, "monotonous drilling which, to be honest . . . " is quoted in Cray, 1990, p. 177.

146 Marshall's ability to make successful appointments of high-level officials is discussed in Pogue, 1965, p. 269; and by Bradley in Pogue, 1973, p. ix.

146 Marshall's ability to treat Congressmen as equals and to act like a leader is discussed in Pogue, 1965, p. 149.

147 An observer, "Not one of them could hold a candle to General Marshall . . . " is quoted in Pogue, 1973, pp. 131–32.

147 Sam Rayburn's comment about Marshall is mentioned in Stoler, 1989, p. 77.

147 Marshall, "I have the habit of saying exactly . . . " is quoted in Mosley, 1982, p. 128.

147 For more on Marshall taking careful note of the complaints of officers and front-line soldiers, see Mosley, 1982, p. 242.

147 Marshall, "on the effect of good example, given by officers . . . " is quoted in Cray, 1990, p. 177.

148 Marshall, "To issue an edict . . . " is quoted in Pogue, 1963, p. 249.

148 Marshall, "I cannot afford the luxury of sentiment . . . " is quoted in Pogue, 1965, p. 303.

148 For more on Marshall bawling out his senior staff for failing to disagree with him, see Pogue, 1965, p. ix.

148 Marshall, "Whenever I find these fellows . . . " is quoted in Cray, 1990, p.150.

149 Franklin D. Roosevelt, "I feel I could not sleep . . . " is quoted in Parrish, 1989, p. 416.

150 For more on McCarthy's attempts at the character assassination of Marshall, see Cray, 1990, p. 723.

150 McCarthy, "a conspiracy so immense . . . " is quoted in Stoler, 1989, p. 189.

150 For more on Marshall looking in vain to Eisenhower for a defense, see Halberstam, 1993, pp. 250–51.

150 Marshall, "If I have to explain . . . " is quoted in Cray, 1990, p. 723.

150 Marshall, "It is logical that the United States . . . " is quoted in Freidel, 1990, p. 627; and Cray, 1990, pp. 404–5.

151 Marshall's comment that recovery must follow war is quoted in Cray, 1990, p. 621.

151 Nobel Committee, "the most constructive peaceful work . . . " is quoted in Cray, 1990, p. 730.

152 Truman, "the greatest military man that this country ever produced . . . is quoted in Cray, 1990, p. 555.

152 Truman, "The more I see and talk . . . " is quoted in McCullough, 1992, p. 535.

152 Stimson, "I have seen a great many soldiers . . . " is quoted in Stoler, 1989, p. 130.

152 Recollections from American military leaders and diplomats about the unique effect Marshall had on their lives are discussed in Stoler, 1989, p. 156.

152 For more on how Churchill, Brooke, and Montgomery broke ranks in the processional to shake Marshall's hand, see Cray, 1990, p. 729.

152 Churchill, "the noblest Roman of them all," is quoted in Stoler 1989, p. 130.

152 Churchill, "It has not fallen to your lot . . . " is quoted in Mosley, 1982, p. 341.

CHAPTER 9. POPE JOHN XXIII: REDISCOVERING THE SPIRIT OF THE CHURCH

153 Havel, "All human cultures . . . " is from Havel, 1994.

153 Pope John (Roncalli), "When on 28 October 1958 . . . " is from Pope John XXIII, 1980, p. 324.

154 Pope John, "There was never any bread on our table . . . " is quoted in Hebblethwaite, 1984, p. 8.

154 For more on Pope John's comments about not remembering a time when he did not want to be a priest, see Hebblethwaite, 1984, p. 13.

155 For more analysis on the contents of Pope John's *Journal of a Soul,* see Hebblethwaite, 1984.

155 All of the quotes on ways to behave are from Pope John XXIII, 1980, pp. 427–32.

155 Arendt, "a strangely disappointing and strangely fascinating book . . . " is from Arendt, 1968, p. 57.

155 Arendt, "whatever or whoever . . . " is from Arendt, 1968, p. 67.

156 Arendt, "a bit stupid, not simple . . . " is from Arendt 1968, p. 68.

156 Roncalli (Pope John XXIII), "The life of the spirit . . ." is quoted in Wigginton, 1983, p. 73.

156 For Arendt's comments about Roncalli's success in becoming a spiritual person, see Arendt, 1968, p. 58.

156 Roncalli, "bored stiff with sermons and reading" is quoted in Hebblethwaite, 1984, p. 27.

156 For more on Roncalli being happy to have the "stimulus" of Rome, see Hebblethwaite, 1984, p. 29.

156 For more on Tedeschi founding hostels and soup kitchens, see Hebblethwaite, 1984, p. 32.

157 Roncalli, "I feel a need and a passionate . . . " is quoted in Hebblethwaite, 1984, p. 37.

157 Roncalli, "the forward, upward movement . . . " is quoted in Hebblethwaite, 1984, p. 37.

157 Roncalli, "I shall study new systems of thoughts . . . " is quoted in Hebblethwaite, 1984, p. 44.

157 Roncalli, "In the day of judgment . . . " is quoted in Zizola, 1978, p. 274.

157 Radini Tedeschi, "the hardest moment in the life . . . " is quoted in Hebblethwaite, 1984, p. 47.

157 Roncalli, "It came like a thunderbolt . . . " is quoted in Hebblethwaite, 1984, p. 47.

157 Roncalli, "He did not concentrate . . . " is quoted in Hebblethwaite, 1984, p. 51.

158 Pius X, "In no other diocese . . . " is quoted in Hebblethwaite 1984, p. 71.

158 Cardinal De Lai, "According to information . . . " is quoted in Hebblethwaite, 1984, p. 73.

158 Roncalli, "I have never read more than 15 to 20 pages . . . " is quoted in Hebblethwaite, 1984, p. 74.

159 Roncalli, "It is my nature to talk too much . . . " is from Pope John XXIII, 1980, p. 224.

159 Roncalli, "The truth and the whole truth . . . " is quoted in Hebblethwaite, 1984, p. 68.

159 Roncalli, "I can work in my own style . . . "is quoted in Hebblethwaite, 1984, p. 155.

160 For more on the possibility that Roncalli helped save the lives of thousands of Jews in Turkey, see Zizola, 1978, p. 77; and Hebblethwaite 1984, p. 186.

160 For more on Roncalli's credulousness toward von Papen, see Hebblethwaite, 1984, pp. 186–89.

160 Roncalli, "Could I not, should I not . . . " is quoted in Arendt, 1968, p. 62.

160 Roncalli, "How I dislike politics . . . " is quoted in Zizola, 1978, p. 38.

160 Roncalli, "My own happy nature . . . " is from Pope John XXIII, 1980, p. 274.

160 For more on Roncalli not minding getting old and feeling less prey to temptations, see Pope John XXIII, 1980, pp. 254, 270.

160 Roncalli, "many trials . . . which are not caused by the Bulgarians . . ." is quoted in Arendt, 1968, p. 61.

160 Roncalli, "I feel quite detached from everything . . . " is quoted in Zizola, 1978, p. 51.

161 Roncalli, "My ministry in Greece is once more beset . . . " is from Pope John XXIII, 1980, p. 280.

161 Roncalli, "stress what unites rather than what divides," is quoted in Hebblethwaite, 1984, p. 243.

161 Pope John, "My children, love one another" is quoted in Hebblethwaite, 1984, p. 286; and Wigginton, 1983, p. 62.

161 For more on Pope John's comment on the use of the name John by other popes, see Hebblethwaite, 1984, p. 286; and Tsanoff, 1968, p. 274.

161 For more on Pope John's decision to leave administrative problems to others and to focus on the big picture, see "Man of the Year, Pope John," 1963, p. 50.

161 For more on the number of appointments made and the number of encyclicals Pope John XXIII wrote, see Wigginton, 1983, p. 63.

162 Pope John, "an inspiration which struck us . . . " is quoted in Wigginton, 1983, p. 65.

162 Pope John, "All right, we'll have it in 1962" is quoted in "Man of the Year, Pope John," 1963, p. 51.

162 For more on Pope John XXIII's establishment of the Secretariat for Christian Unity, see Wigginton, 1983, p. 78.

163 Pope John, "There existed a sharp divergence of views . . . " is quoted in Wigginton, 1983, p. 83.

163 Pope John's creation of a special commission for council members with differing views is discussed in Hebblethwaite, 1984, p. 457.

163 Pope John, "to coordinate the work . . . " is quoted in Wigginton, 1983, p. 85.

163 For more on Pope John's calling for the church to go back to its roots and not treat any group as privileged, see Zizola, 1978, p. 208.

163 For more on Pope John's belief that individuals are people first and members of religious groups second, see Zizola, 1978, p. 339.

163 Pope John, "all men of good will," is quoted in Zizola, 1978, p. 105.

164 Yves Congar, "The opening toward the world . . . " is quoted in Zizola, 1978, p. 266.

164 A bishop at the council, "We heard men dare to say things . . . " is quoted in "Man of the Year, Pope John," 1963, p. 52.

165 Pope John, "I always try to show people . . . " is quoted in Zizola, 1978, p. 14.

165 Pope John, "Since you could not come to me . . . " is quoted in *Encyclopaedia Brittanica,* 1974.

165 Pope John, "She should get as close . . . " is quoted in *Encyclopaedia Brittanica,* 1974.

165 Pope John, "I know you are an atheist . . . " is quoted in *Encyclopaedia Brittanica,* 1974.

165 Pope John, "Must you do this? . . . " is quoted in Arendt, 1968, p. 61.

165 Pope John, "Why should people not see me? . . . " is quoted in Arendt, 1968, p. 63.

165 Pope John, "My dear son, stop worrying . . . " is quoted in Arendt, 1968, p. 63.

165 Pope John, "Giovanni, don't take yourself that seriously!" is quoted in Arendt, 1968, p. 65.

166 Pope John, "The Lord is making use . . . " is quoted in Zizola, 1978, p. 111.

166 The ultraconservative Catholic press's description of Pope John as "irresponsible" and "politically unprepared" is quoted in Zizola, 1978, p. 165.

166 Pope John, "The time has come . . . " is quoted in Hebblethwaite, 1984, p. 411.

166 For more on Pope John's quoting of his original texts after being misquoted, see Hebblethwaite, 1984, p. 433.

166 Pope John, "You see, my dear Father . . . " is quoted in Zizola, 1978, p. 179.

167 A cardinal, "the greatest disaster in recent ecclesiastical history . . . " is quoted in Hebblethwaite, 1984, p. 369.

167 Balducci, "the essential modernity of Pope John . . . " is quoted in Zizola, 1978, p. 289.

CHAPTER 10. ELEANOR ROOSEVELT: ORDINARINESS AND EXTRAORDINARINESS

169 Ball, "What are the defining characteristics of a leader? . . . " is from Ball, 1994, p. 20.

169 For more on Heifetz's view that certain leaders attain leadership even though they have no formal authority, see Heifetz, 1994.

171 E. Roosevelt, "My mother was one of the most beautiful women . . . " is from E. Roosevelt, 1992, p. 3.

171 E. Roosevelt, "With my father I was perfectly happy . . . " is from E. Roosevelt, 1992, p. 5.

172 Cook, "The Victorian world of her father . . . " is from Cook, 1992, p. 15.

172 E. Roosevelt, "the ability to think for myself . . . " is from E. Roosevelt, 1992, p. xvi.

172 For more on Eleanor's early command of language and interest in moral issues, see Cook, 1992, p. 96; and Lash, 1973, p. 102.

172 E. Roosevelt, "Whatever I have become . . . " is quoted in Cook, 1992, p. 4.

172 E. Roosevelt, "I had been a solemn girl . . . " is from E. Roosevelt, 1992, p. 36.

173 E. Roosevelt, "I listened to all his plans . . . " is from E. Roosevelt, 1992, p. 63.

173 E. Roosevelt, "I want him to feel that he belongs to someone" is quoted in Lash, 1973, p. 209.

173 Lash, "the state legislature, assistant secretary . . . " is from Lash, 1973, p. 237.

174 For more on Eleanor taking the opportunity to continue her public service in the First World War, see Hoff-Wilson and Lightman, 1984, p. 7; and E. Roosevelt, 1992, p. 87.

174 For more on Eleanor introducing food-saving procedures at home and publicizing these restraints, see Lash, 1973, pp. 287–90.

174 Eleanor's increasingly liberal opinions are discussed in Lash, 1973, p. 289.

174 E. Roosevelt, "The bottom dropped out of my own particular world . . . " is quoted in Lash, 1973, p. 302.

174 For more on Eleanor's decision to stay in the marriage, see Goodwin, 1994b.

175 E. Roosevelt, "made me stand . . . " is quoted in Lash, 1973, p. 373.

175 For more on Eleanor's contributions to issues concerning women's health and the protection of working women, see Goodwin, 1994b.

175 Cook, "Simple networks of shared work and friendship . . . " is from Cook, 1992, p. 299.

176 E. Roosevelt, "To many women, and I am one . . . " is quoted in Hoff-Wilson and Lightman, 1984, p. 9.

176 Goodwin, "a range of abilities she never had any idea of . . . " is from Goodwin, 1994a, p. 44.

176 Perry, "as a result of her experiences . . . " is from Perry, 1984, p. 45.

176 For more on Eleanor being better known in New York political circles than Franklin, see Ware, 1984, p. 49.

177 E. Roosevelt, "I never wanted to be a President's wife . . . " is quoted in Lash, 1973, p. 472.

177 For more on Eleanor's redirecting of her passion, see Goodwin, 1994a.

178 *New York Times,* "the biggest coup for women in years," is quoted in Hoff-Wilson and Lightman, 1984, p. 10.

179 E. Roosevelt, "Why dump all these pigs . . . " is quoted in Lash, 1973, p. 508.

179 Beard, "To an amazing degree . . . " is from Beard, 1933.

179 Tugwell, "No one who ever saw Eleanor Roosevelt . . . " is quoted in Hoff-Wilson and Lightman, 1984, pp. 10–11.

180 E. Roosevelt, "[Franklin] might have been happier . . . " is quoted in Chafe, 1984, p. 22.

180 For more on the American public's approval of Eleanor's performance as the first lady and on her being named as one of the most powerful individuals in Washington, see Lash, 1973, p. 618.

181 E. Roosevelt, "the sorrow of all those to whom . . . " is quoted in Lash, 1973, p. 929.

181 E. Roosevelt, "I am more sorry for . . . " is quoted in Lash, 1973, p. 918.

182 E. Roosevelt, "Is there anything we can do *for you?* . . . " is quoted in Lash, 1973, p. 928.

182 E. Roosevelt, "The story [was] over" is quoted in Lash, 1972, p. 25.

182 Henry Morgenthau, Jr., "now that she was the widow of the President . . . " is quoted in Lash, 1972, p. 27.

182 E. Roosevelt, "If I failed to be a useful member . . . " is quoted in Scharf, 1984, p. 243.

182 Chafe, "In long letters to President Truman . . . " is from Chafe, 1984, p. 22.

183 Stevenson, "What other single human being . . . " is quoted in Lash, 1972, p. 312.

184 Clapper, "the most influential woman of our times" is quoted in Goodwin, 1994a, p. 41.

184 E. Roosevelt, "About the only value the story of my life . . . " is from E. Roosevelt, 1992, p. xix.

184 E. Roosevelt, "I have had only three assets . . . " is from E. Roosevelt, 1992, p. 410.

184 E. Roosevelt, "I do believe that even a few people . . . " is quoted in Lash, 1973, p. 475.

185 For more on Franklin referring to Eleanor as his "eyes and ears," see Goodwin, 1994a, p. 40.

185 Bliven, "I have a feeling that the country as a whole . . . " is quoted in Lash, 1973, p. 563.

185 A Gloucester fisherman, "She ain't dressed up . . . " is quoted in Cook, 1992, p. 498.

185 Lash, "The personal disasters she had surmounted . . . " is from Lash, 1973, p. 507.

186 For more on Eleanor resigning from the Daughters of the American Revolution, see Lash, 1973, p. 684.

186 Stevenson, "She walked in the slums and ghettos of the world . . . " is quoted by Chafe, 1984, p. 27.

186 Chafe, "over and over again she answered pleas . . . " is from Chafe, 1984, p. 27.

187 E. Roosevelt, "Women who are willing to be leaders . . . " is quoted in Cook, 1992, pp. 5–6.

CHAPTER 11. MARTIN LUTHER KING, JR.: LEADING IN A RAPIDLY CHANGING ENVIRONMENT

189 Kissinger, "A great leader must be an educator . . . " is from Kissinger, 1994, p. 382.

189 For more on King, Sr., changing both his and his son's names, see Branch, 1989, p. 44.

189 For more on young King twice trying to take his own life, see "Man of the Year, Martin Luther King, Jr.," 1964, p. 14.

189 King, "The first twenty-five years of my life . . . " is quoted in Garrow, 1989, p. 453.

190 King's attractiveness and eloquence are discussed in Branch, 1989, p. 66.

191 Why King was chosen to lead the boycott is discussed in Lentz, 1990, p. 24.

191 King's speech to those involved in the boycott is described in Branch, 1989, p. 139.

191 King's speech is quoted in Branch, 1989, pp. 139–41.

192 For more on the success of King's first public address, see Branch, 1989, p. 142.

192 King, "I came to see for the first time . . . " is quoted in Miroff, 1993, p. 312.

192 For more on King's having been propelled either willingly or reluctantly into a position of leadership, see A. Young, 1994, pp. C1–2.

192 King, "I did not start this boycott . . . " is quoted in Branch, 1989, p. 166; and Wofford, 1980, p. 105.

193 King, "This conviction and all the convictions . . . " is quoted in Branch, 1989, p. 185.

193 For more on the Supreme Court's decision that segregation on buses was unconstitutional, see Branch, 1989, p. 193.

193 King, "We can stick together . . . " is quoted in Branch, 1989, p. 195; and King, 1992, pp. 76–77.

193 Faulkner, "stop now for a moment," is from King, 1992, p. 81.

193 King, "We do not wish to triumph over the white community . . . " is from King, 1992, p. 81.

194 For more on King's correspondence with Eisenhower, Nixon, and Brownell, see Branch, 1989, p. 213; and Garrow, 1986, p. 86.

194 Bomb threats and the stabbing of King are described in Garrow, 1986, p. 110.

194 King's return to Atlanta and his decision to mount a broader campaign are discussed in Garrow, 1986, p. 123.

194 For more on King's profound identification with the Christian tradition, see Wofford, 1980, p. 234.

195 For more on King invoking the figure of Moses in his speeches, see Callaway-Thomas and Lucaites, 1993, p. 26.

195 Gandhi, "It may be through the Negroes . . . " is quoted in Wofford, 1980, p. 112.

196 For more on King's original feelings about being a leader, see Wofford, 1980, p. 232.

196 King, "I realized that the choice leaves your own hands . . . " is quoted in Garrow, 1986, p. 85.

196 King, "I could hear an inner voice . . . " is quoted in Miroff, 1993, p. 312.

196 King, "I can't stop now . . . " is quoted in Wofford, 1980, p. 232.

197 For more on King's ability to get support for SCLC and to get individuals to work together, see Lentz, 1990, p. 320.

197 For more on King's arrest in October 1960, see Branch, 1989, p. 362.

197 King's number of speeches and miles traveled are described in "Man of the Year, Martin Luther King, Jr.," 1964, p. 27.

198 Kennedy, "The civil rights movement owes Bull Connor . . . " is quoted in "Man of the Year, Martin Luther King, Jr.," 1964, p. 16.

198 For more on King's responsibility for deciding where to go, whom to confront, and so on, see Heifetz, 1994, chapter 9.

198 For more on King having read a newspaper article entitled "White Clergymen . . . " see Branch, 1989, p. 737.

199 For King's comparison of himself with the Apostle Paul, see King, 1992, p. 290.

199 King, "We have waited for more than 340 years . . . " is from King, 1992, pp. 292–93.

199 King, "We know through painful experience . . . " is from King, 1992, p. 292.

199 King, "amazing discipline in the midst . . . " is from King, 1992.

200 King, "standing up for the best in the American dream . . . " is from King, 1992, p. 302.

200 King's "I have a dream" speech is quoted in King, 1992, pp. 217–20.

201 Reston, "It will be a long time before . . . " is from Reston, 1963, pp. 1, 17.

202 For more on King being shaken by the emerging militant faction and the Vietnam War, see Paris, 1991, p. 128.

202 A commentator, "outstripped by his times" is quoted in Wofford, 1980, p. 230.

202 King, "We have destroyed their two most cherished institutions . . . " is quoted in Lentz, 1990, p. 237.

203 King, "For years I labored with the idea . . . " is quoted in *Encyclopaedia Britannica,* 1974.

204 King, "This is going to happen to me" is quoted in Wofford, 1980, p. 175.

204 King, "Well, I don't know what will happen now . . . " is quoted in Miroff, 1993, p. 345.

204 Lentz, "It was fitting therefore that King died as he did . . . " is from Lentz, 1990, p. 341.

204 King's recurrent calling for a "beloved community" is discussed in Callaway-Thomas and Lucaites, 1993, p. 8.

204 King, "Once you become dedicated to a cause . . . " is quoted in Garrow, 1986, p. 84.

205 For more on King being assailed at a conference in December 1961, see Branch, 1989, p. 654.

REPRISE

209 For Heifetz's view that certain leaders emerged long before they attained legitimate authority, see Heifetz, 1994.

CHAPTER 12. MARGARET THATCHER: A CLEAR SENSE OF IDENTITY

211 Churchill, "I never look beyond a battle . . . " is quoted in Blake, 1994, p. 26.

212 Thatcher, "Well, of course, I just owe . . . " is quoted in Little, 1988, p. 100.

212 Thatcher, "I loved her dearly . . . " is quoted in *New York Times,* 1993, p. B2.

213 A schoolmate, "[Margaret Roberts] rather despised her mother . . . " is quoted in Young and Simon, 1986, p. 16.

214 Douglas-Home, "You know, [Margaret Thatcher's] got the brains . . . " is quoted in Young, 1989, p. 27.

215 Thatcher, "It will be years before a woman . . . " is quoted in Little, 1988, p. 108.

216 Thatcher, "a great country which seem[ed] to have lost . . . " is quoted in Little, 1988, p. 48.

216 Thatcher, "You no longer have the courage to act . . . " is quoted in Young, 1989, p. 128.

216 Callaghan, "The question you will have to consider . . . " is quoted in Young, 1989, p. 131.

216 Thatcher, "The passionately interesting thing . . . " is quoted in Little, 1988, p. 91.

217 Thatcher, "Chatham famously remarked . . . " is from Thatcher, 1993, p. 10.

217 Jenkins, "As a proponent of the British case . . . " is quoted in Young, 1989, p. 190.

217 Millar, "The lady's not for turning" is quoted in Young, 1989, p. 209.

218 Thatcher, "I am not ruthless . . . " is quoted in Young, 1989, pp. 104–5.

218 Thatcher, "As Prime Minister I couldn't waste time . . . " is quoted in Little, 1988, p. 72.

218 Howell, "While many Tories were aiming to tear down . . . " is from Howell, 1993.

218 For more on the percentage of people polled in December 1981 who thought Thatcher was doing a good job, see Young, 1989, p. 241.

219 Thatcher, "I do not think that I have ever . . . " is from Thatcher, 1993, p. 173.

219 Young, "The Falklands war was a seminal event . . . " is from Young, 1989, p. 279.

219 Thatcher, "We have ceased to be a nation in retreat . . . " is from Thatcher, 1993, p. 235.

219 Thatcher, "British foreign policy had been . . . " is from Thatcher, 1993, pp. 173–74.

220 Thatcher, "What matters is that it was everyone together . . . " is from a speech by Thatcher, June 15, 1982.

220 For more on Thatcher's 1983 victory, see Thatcher, 1993, p. 345.

220 Thatcher, "the single most devastating defeat . . . " is from Thatcher, 1993, p. 339.

220 Thatcher, "I am in politics because of the conflict . . . " is quoted in Young, 1989, p. 352.

220 For more on Thatcher's contrasting of businesspeople and self-made individuals with government bureaucrats and others, see Cooke, 1989, p. 15.

221 Barnes, "To the liberal, the snobbish . . . " is from Barnes, 1993, p. 82.

221 For more on Thatcher's view that there are only individuals and no real society, see Young, 1989, p. 536.

222 Thatcher, "The only thing I'm going to do for you . . . " is from a speech by Thatcher on May 4, 1979, and is quoted in Cooke, 1989.

222 Thatcher, "at least some encouragement for work . . . " is quoted in Little, 1988, p. 57.

222 Thatcher, "With achievements like that . . . " is quoted in Cooke, 1989, p. 22.

222 Thatcher, "The idea that other clever people . . . " is from Thatcher, 1993, p. 726.

222 Thatcher, "do business with him" is from Thatcher, 1993, p. 463.

223 For more on Thatcher labeling consensualists "quislings," see Young, 1989, p. 224.

224 Thatcher, "his vice was second thoughts" is quoted in Barnes, 1993, p. 85.

224 Thatcher, "The Old Testament prophets did not go out . . ." is quoted in Little, 1988, p. 79.

224 Baker, "personally dominant, supremely self-confident . . ." is quoted in Barnes, 1993, p. 83.

224 A civil servant, "She was the only minister I never heard . . ." is quoted in Little, 1988, p. 43.

224 For Stoessinger's comment on women leaders in the twentieth century, see Stoessinger, 1994.

224 Thatcher, "My experience is that a number of the men . . ." is from Thatcher, 1993, p. 129.

224 For more on Thatcher's femininity, see Young, 1989, p. 304.

225 Thatcher, "go on and on and on . . ." is quoted in Young, 1989, p. 543.

225 Thatcher, "I intend to hang on until I believe . . ." is quoted in Young, 1989, p. 545.

225 Ryan, "They were intimidated by her . . ." is from Ryan, 1993, p. 7.

225 Howe, "The insistence on the undivided sovereignty . . ." is quoted in Riddell, 1993, p. 28.

226 Thatcher, "Orthodox finance, low levels of regulation . . ." is from Thatcher, 1993, p. 755.

227 For more analyses of the Thatcher era, see Barnes, 1993; Riddell, 1993; and Ryan, 1993.

227 Kissinger, "So great was the transformation . . ." is from Kissinger, 1993, p. 1.

CHAPTER 13. A GENERATION OF WORLD LEADERS

229 Rees-Mogg, "When the leader arrives . . ." is from Rees-Mogg, 1993, p. 20.

229 Parrish, "[Franklin Roosevelt] became a scholar and specialist . . ." is from Parrish, 1989, p. 41.

229 Mead, "Looking back and visualizing . . ." is from Mead, 1964b, p. 322.

231 For Gruber's and Erikson's "idiographic" studies, see Gruber, 1981; and Erikson, 1958.

232 The fact that nearly all of the ten Second World War leaders lost their fathers when they were young is discussed by Iremonger, 1970; Eisenstadt et al., 1989; and Simonton, 1984.

232 The fact that young men without fathers take charge of their families and create their own moral code is discussed in Sartre, 1964, pp. 18ff.

233 Bullock, "[Hitler's] grasp of the mood of public opinion . . ." is from Bullock, 1962, p. 337.

234 Mao, "The world is ours . . ." is quoted in *Encyclopaedia Britannica,* 1974.

235 Mao, "would rise like a tornado or tempest . . ." is quoted in *Encyclopaedia Britannica,* 1974.

235 Mussolini, "One day I shall make . . ." is quoted in *Encyclopaedia Britannica,* 1974.

235 Churchill, "without an office, without a seat . . ." is from *Encyclopaedia Britannica,* 1993, vol. 16, p. 372.

235 De Gaulle, "an old man, worn out . . . " is from *Encyclopaedia Britannica,* 1974.

237 Lenin, "Give us an organization of revolutionaries . . . " is quoted in *Encyclopaedia Britannica,* 1993, vol. 22, p. 933.

239 Berlin, "He was one of the few statesmen . . . " is quoted in Goodwin, 1994b, p. 607.

239 For Erikson's writings on Martin Luther and Gandhi, see Erikson, 1958, 1969.

241 Mussolini, "a man who is ruthless and energetic . . . " is quoted in *Encyclopaedia Brittanica,* 1993, vol. 8, p. 452.

241 Mussolini, "We are Italians and nothing but Italians . . . " is quoted in *Encyclopaedia Britannica,* 1974.

241 Hitler, "The main plan in the Nationalist Socialist programme . . . " is quoted in Bullock, 1962, p. 405.

241 Hitler, "The art of leadership consists of consolidating . . . " is quoted in Bullock, 1962, p. 45.

241 Hitler, "a belief which will not abandon . . . " is quoted in Heifetz, 1994, p. 115.

242 For more on the similarities between Hitler's and Stalin's totalitarian regimes, see Bullock, 1991.

243 Pfaff, "The public turned to Churchill and de Gaulle . . . " is from Pfaff, 1993, p. 6.

244 Korda, "Great leaders are almost always great simplifiers . . . " is from Korda, 1984, p. 51.

244 Mao, "The only solution lies in promoting ideas . . . " is quoted in *Encyclopaedia Britannica,* 1974.

245 Wilson, "I have a strong instinct of leadership . . . " is quoted in Barber, 1985, p. 17.

245 For Stalin's impact on the Soviet people after the Nazi invasion, see Stoessinger, 1993.

245 Hitler, "to be a leader means to be able to move masses" is quoted in Bullock, 1962, p. 68.

245 Strasser, "Hitler responds to the vibrations . . . " is quoted in J. Gardner, 1990, p. 90. This quote has also been attributed to Otto's brother Gregor Strasser.

245 Lindholm, "In his speech Hitler re-enacted for his audience . . . " is quoted in Bryman, 1992, p. 38.

246 Bayley, "Stalin was all that she had left" is from Bayley, 1993, p. 4.

246 Storr, "In that dark time what England needed . . . " is from Storr, 1988, pp. 49–50.

248 Kissinger, "Every political revolution sooner or later reaches its end . . . " is from Kissinger, 1993, p. 1.

CHAPTER 14. JEAN MONNET AND MAHATMA GANDHI: LEADERSHIP BEYOND NATIONAL BOUNDARIES

251 Goethe, "National hatred is strongest and most vehement . . . " is quoted in Jaszi, 1966, frontispiece.

251 Havel, "Twice in this century . . . " is from Havel, 1993, p. 3.

252 Monnet, "I was daring because I knew no taboos . . . " is quoted in Bromberger and Bromberger, 1969, p. 13.

252 For more on Monnet learning that alliances are strengthened when parties work together on a concrete economic initiative, see Ball, 1982, pp. 69–91.

253 Monnet, "My strength was the naïveté of a young man . . . " is quoted in Bromberger and Bromberger, 1969, p. 18.

253 For more on Monnet choosing not to address leaders by "monsieur le president," see Duchêne, 1994, p. 348.

254 For Monnet's view that the European Coal and Steel Community was more about the beginning of a new Europe, see Rieben, 1989, p. 28.

254 De Gaulle, "Dante, Goethe, and Chateaubriand belong to Europe . . . " is quoted in Bromberger and Bromberger, 1969, p. 175.

254 De Gaulle, "We are no longer in the era when . . . " is quoted in Duchêne, 1994, p. 315.

255 Kennedy, "For centuries, emperors, kings, and dictators . . . " is quoted in Monnet, 1978, p. 472.

255 Monnet, "one good idea" is quoted in Hackett, 1989, p. 168.

255 Monnet, "There is always a dream in all enterprise . . . " is quoted in Küsters, 1989, p. 45.

255 For more on Gandhi never forgiving himself for having left his father's deathbed, see Mehta, 1977, p. 82; and Payne, 1990, p. 42.

256 For more on Gandhi renouncing worldly pleasures and undertaking an ascetic life, see Gandhi, 1938.

257 Gandhi, "I would like to meet not so much . . . " is quoted in Brown, 1972, p. 248.

257 For more on Gandhi's organized action in Ahmedabad, see Erikson, 1969; and H. Gardner, 1993a.

258 Broomfield, "It will be impossible to ignore the fact . . . " is quoted in Payne, 1990, p. 367.

258 Gandhi, "So far as the sentence is concerned . . . " is quoted in Payne, 1990, p. 367.

258 Miller, "There was no fight, no struggle . . . " is quoted in Mehta, 1977, p. 148; and Shirer, 1979, p. 98.

259 Gandhi, "Would it not be more appropriate . . . " is quoted in Mehta, 1977, p. 171.

259 King, "the only morally and practically sound methods . . . " is quoted in Nanda, 1985, p. 34.

259 Einstein, "Gandhi had demonstrated . . . " is quoted in Fischer, 1950, p. 10.

260 Monnet, "I had only one good idea . . . " is quoted in Hackett, 1989, p. 168.

260 Monnet, "It seemed to me, looking back . . . " is from Monnet, 1978, p. 221.

260 For more on Monnet challenging the unschooled visions of Europe under one flag, see Swedberg, 1994.

260 Duchêne, "[Monnet was] the one thoroughgoing internationalist . . . " is from Duchêne, 1994, pp. 403, 410.

262 For more on Monnet as an indirect leader and as the embodiment of imperson-ality, see Bromberger and Bromberger, 1969, p. 10.

262 Monnet, "To get statesmen to listen to you . . . " is quoted in Bromberger and Bromberger, 1969, p. 101.

262 Monnet, "These men, after all take the risks . . . " is from Monnet, 1978, p. 231.

262 Monnet, "I have never taken a job . . . " is quoted in Duchêne, 1994, p. 346.

262 Monnet, "If there was stiff competition . . . " is quoted in Duchêne 1994, p. 148.

263 Monnet, "My life so far has involved . . . " is from Monnet, 1978, pp. 229–30.

263 For more on Monnet's belief that precise formulation was crucial to a policy's success or failure, see Ball, 1982, p. 73.

264 Monnet, "Nothing is made without men . . . " is quoted in Grosser, 1989, p. 198.

264 For more on Monnet's beliefs about the modification of deeply entrenched habits, see Ball, 1982, p. 81.

264 Monnet, "there could be no progress . . . " is quoted in Hackett, 1989, p. 163.

264 Gandhi, "the dumb, semi-starved millions . . . " is quoted in Shirer, 1979, pp 167–68.

265 Von Simson, "He convinced by shyness . . . " is from von Simson, 1989, p. 33.

265 For more on Gandhi arriving at a position that made sense only after years of self-examination, see Erikson, 1969; and Mamali, 1993.

CHAPTER 15. LESSONS FROM THE PAST, IMPLICATIONS FOR THE FUTURE

269 Churchill, "We are shaping the world . . . " is quoted in Walsh, 1993, p. 21.

273 For more on leaders losing opportunities for reflection, see Sutton and Galunic, 1994.

273 Gardner, "uncluttered mind," is from J. Gardner, 1995.

280 For more information on idiographic and nomothetic studies, see Gruber, 1981; and Simonton, 1984.

283 For more on the types of influential, international organizations that have arisen in the past few decades, see Simmons, 1994.

284 Kampelman, "Everything is becoming interconnected . . . " is quoted in Walsh, 1993, p. 155.

285 Bell, "Leadership is a sense of judgment . . . " is from Bell, 1992, p. 6.

285 Kitto, "The highly trained expert . . . " is from Kitto, 1951, p. 169.

285 Confucius, "While the advisers of a great leader . . . " is quoted by Korda, 1984, p. 63.

BIBLIOGRAPHY

Abse, L. *Margaret, Daughter of Beatrice.* London: Jonathan Cape, 1989.

Adler, M. J. *Reforming Education: The Opening of the American Mind.* Edited by G. Van Doren. New York: Macmillan, 1988.

Adonis, A., and T. Hames, eds. *A Conservative Revolution: The Thatcher–Reagan Decade in Perspective.* Manchester: Manchester University Press, 1993.

Adorno, T. W., E. Frenkel-Brunswick, D. Levinson, and R. N. Sanford. *The Authoritarian Personality.* New York: Harper, 1950.

Allende, I. *The Stories of Eva Luna.* New York: Bantam, 1991.

Allison, G. *Essence of Decision: Explaining the Cuban Missile Crisis.* Boston: Little, Brown, 1971.

Arendt, H. *Men in Dark Times.* New York: Harcourt Brace Jovanovich, 1968.

Aristotle. *Introduction to Aristotle.* Edited by R. McKeon. New York: Random House, 1947.

Armstrong, D. *Managing by Storying Around.* New York: Doubleday, 1992.

Ashmore, H. S. *Unseasonable Truths: The Life of Robert Maynard Hutchins.* Boston: Little, Brown, 1989.

Astin, L., and C. Leland. *Women of Influence, Women of Vision.* San Francisco: Jossey-Bass, 1991.

Astington, J. *The Child's Discovery of Mind.* Cambridge, Mass.: Harvard University Press, 1993.

Ball, G. W. "Kennedy up Close." Review of *President Kennedy: Profile of Power,* by Richard Reeves. *New York Review of Books,* February 3, 1994, pp. 17–20.

———. *The Past Has Another Pattern.* New York: Norton, 1982.

Barber, J. *The Presidential Character.* 3d ed. Englewood Cliffs, N.J.: Prentice-Hall, 1985.

Barnes, J. "The Maggie Years." *New Yorker,* November 15, 1993, pp. 82–89.

Barnett, L. "J. Robert Oppenheimer." *Life,* October 10, 1949, pp. 121–38.

Bateson, M. C. *With a Daughter's Eye: A Memoir of Margaret Mead and Gregory Bateson.* New York: Morrow, 1984.

———. Personal communication with author, August 5, 1994.

Bauer, P. J. "Application of World Knowledge: Examples from Research on Event Memory." Paper presented at the biennial meeting of the Society for Research in Child Development, New Orleans, La., April 1993.

Bayley, J. Review of *Lenin's Tomb* by D. Remnick. *New York Review of Books,* August 12, 1993, p. 4.

Bell, D. "A Conversation with Daniel Bell." *Harvard Gazette,* October 28, 1992, pp. 5–6.

Bennis, W., and B. Nanus. *Leaders: The Strategies for Taking Charge.* New York: Harper and Row, 1985.

Berger, J. *A New Deal for the World: Eleanor Roosevelt and American Foreign Policy.* New York: Social Science Monographs, Columbia University Press, 1981.

Berkov, R. *Strong Man of China: The Story of Chiang Kai-shek.* Boston: Houghton Mifflin, 1938.

Berrington, H. Review of *The Fiery Chariot: A Study of British Prime Ministers and the Search for Love. British Journal of Political Science,* 4 (1974): 345–69.

Bettelheim, B. *The Uses of Enchantment.* New York: Knopf, 1976.

Birke, L., and J. Silvertown, eds. *More than the Parts: Biology and Politics.* London: Pluto Press, 1984.

Blake, R. "A Volatile Greatness." Review of *Churchill,* by N. Rose. *Times Literary Supplement,* April 22, 1994, p. 26.

Blake, R., and W. Louis. *Churchill.* London: Norton, 1993.

Bland, L., J. Bland, and S. R. Stevens, eds. *George C. Marshall: Interviews and Reminiscences for Forrest C. Pogue.* Lexington, Va.: George C. Marshall Research Foundation, 1991.

Bloom, A. *The Closing of the American Mind.* New York: Simon and Schuster, 1987.

Bloom, B., with L. Sosniak. *Developing Talent in Young Children.* New York: Ballantine Books, 1988.

Bok, D. *The Cost of Talent.* New York: Free Press, 1993.

Bolman, L., and T. Deal. *Reframing Organizations: Artistry, Choice, and Leadership.* San Francisco: Jossey-Bass, 1991.

Bouc, A. *Mao Tse-tung: A Guide to His Thought.* Translated by P. Anster and L. Davis. New York: St. Martin's, 1977.

Bowlby, J. *Attachment and Loss.* 3 vols. New York: Basic Books, 1969–1980.

Boyer, P. *By the Bomb's Early Light: American Thought and Culture at the Dawn of the Atomic Age.* New York: Pantheon, 1985.

Branch, T. *Parting the Waters: America in the King Years.* New York: Touchstone Books, 1989.

Brinkley, D., and C. Hackett, eds. *Jean Monnet: The Path to European Unity.* London: Macmillan, 1991.

Brodsky, J. *Less Than One: Selected Essays.* New York: Farrar, Strauss, and Giroux, 1986.

Bromberger, M., and S. Bromberger. *Jean Monnet and the United States of Europe.* Translated by E. P. Halpern. New York: Coward-McCann, 1969.

Brown, J. H. *Gandhi: Prisoner of Hope.* Cambridge, England: Cambridge University Press, 1972.

Brown, Rex. Personal communication with author, August 2, 1993.

Brown, Roger. *Social Psychology.* Glencoe: Free Press, 1965.

———. *Social Psychology.* 2d ed. New York: Free Press, 1986.

Bruner, J. S. *Actual Minds, Possible Worlds.* Cambridge, Mass.: Harvard University Press, 1986.

———. Personal communication, December 3, 1993.

Bryman, A. *Charisma and Leadership in Organizations.* London: Sage, 1992.

Bullock, A. *Hitler: A Study in Tyranny.* London: Penguin Books, 1962.

———. *Hitler and Stalin: Parallel Lives.* New York: Knopf, 1991.

Burns, J. M. *Leadership.* New York: Harper and Row, 1978.

Buruma, I. "A Lethal Thing of Beauty." Review of *The Sieve of Time,* by L. Riefenstahl. *Times Literary Supplement,* October 9, 1992, pp. 3–5.

Butow, R. J. C. *Tojo and the Coming of the War.* Princeton, N.J.: Princeton University Press, 1961.

Byrne, J. A. *The Whiz Kids: The Founding Fathers of American Business—And the Legacy They Left Us.* New York: Currency/Doubleday, 1993.

Byrne, R. W., and A. Whiten. *Machiavellian Intelligence: Social Expertise and the Evolution of Intellect in Monkeys, Apes, and Humans.* Oxford: Clarendon Press, 1988.

Callaway-Thomas, C., and L. Lucaites. *Martin Luther King, Jr., and the Sermonic Power of Public Discourse.* Tuscaloosa, Ala.: University of Alabama Press, 1993.

Cannon, L. *President Reagan: The Role of a Lifetime.* New York: Simon and Schuster, 1991.

Carr, W. *Hitler: A Study in Personality and Politics.* London: Edward Arnold, 1978.

Cassirer, E. *The Philosophy of Symbolic Forms.* 3 vols. New Haven, Conn.: Yale University Press, 1953–1957.

Chafe, W. H. "Biographical Sketch." In J. Hoff-Wilson and M. Lightman, eds., *Without Precedent: The Life and Career of Eleanor Roosevelt.* Bloomington: Indiana University Press, 1984, pp. 3–27.

Chandler, A. D. *The Essential Alfred Chandler: Essays toward a Historical Theory of Big Business.* Edited by T. L. McCraw. Boston: Harvard Business School Press, 1991.

———, ed. *Giant Enterprise: Ford, General Motors, and the Automobile Industry.* New York: Harcourt Brace and World, 1964.

Chandler, A., Jr., and S. Salsbury. *Pierre S. du Pont and the Making of the Modern Corporation.* New York: Harper and Row, 1971.

Chevalier, H. *Oppenheimer: The Story of a Friendship.* New York: George Braziller, 1965.

Chou, E. *Mao Tse-tung: The Man and the Myth.* New York: Stein and Day, 1980.

Clark, R. W. *Lenin: The Man Behind the Mask.* Boston: Faber and Faber, 1988.

Cohen, D., and S. MacKeith. *The Development of Imagination: The Private Worlds of Childhood.* London: Routledge and Kegan Paul, 1991.

Cohen, M., and J. March. "Leadership in an Organized Anarchy." In W. E. Rosenbach and R. L. Taylor, eds., *Contemporary Issues in Leadership.* Boulder, Colo.: Westview Press, 1984, pp. 18–30.

Colby, A., and W. Damon. *Some Do Care.* New York: Free Press, 1992.

Collier, P., and D. Horowitz. *The Rockefellers: An American Dynasty.* New York: Signet, 1976.

Cook, B. W. *Eleanor Roosevelt.* Vol. 1. New York: Penguin Books, 1992.

Cooke, A. B. *Margaret Thatcher: The Revival of Britain.* London: Aurum Press, 1989.

Cousins, N. *The Improbable Triumvirate: John F. Kennedy, Pope John, Nikita Khrushchev.* New York: Norton, 1972.

Craig, G. "Above the Abyss." Review *of Hitler and Stalin,* by Alan Bullock. *New York Review of Books,* April 9, 1992, pp. 3–5.

Crapanzano, V. Personal communication with author, August 24, 1993.

Cray, E. *General of the Army: George C. Marshall, Soldier and Statesman.* New York: Norton, 1990.

Crozier, B. *De Gaulle.* New York: Scribners, 1973.

Csikszentmihalyi, M. *The Evolving Self.* New York: HarperCollins, 1993a.

———. Personal communication with author, August 23, 1993b.

———. Personal communication with author, September 23, 1994.

Cutler, P. Personal communication with author, September 23, 1994.

Damasio, A. *Descartes' Error: Emotion, Reason, and the Human Brain.* New York: Putnam, 1994.

Damon, W. *The Social World of the Child.* San Francisco: Jossey-Bass, 1977.

———. *Social and Personality Development.* New York: Norton, 1983.

———. *The Moral Child.* New York: Free Press, 1988.

Davidson, E. *The Making of Adolf Hitler.* New York: Macmillan, 1977.

Davis, N. P. *Lawrence and Oppenheimer.* New York: Simon and Schuster, 1968.

De Gaulle, C. *The Complete War Memoirs of Charles de Gaulle.* New York: Simon and Schuster, 1964.

———. *Memoirs of Hope: Renewal 1958–62, Endeavor 1962–.* Trans. T. Kilmartin. London: Weidenfeld and Nicolson, 1971.

Degler, C. *In Search of Human Nature.* New York: Oxford University Press, 1991.

Devillers, P. *Mao.* Trans. by T. White. New York: Schocken, 1967.

Dewey, J. *The Quest for Certainty.* New York: Minton, Balch, 1929.

Dobzhansky, T. *Mankind Evolving: The Evolution of the Human Species.* New Haven: Yale University Press, 1962.

Donald, M. *The Origins of the Modern Mind.* Cambridge, Mass.: Harvard University Press, 1991.

Duchêne, F. *Jean Monnet: The First Statesman of Interdependence.* New York: Norton, 1994.

Dzuback, M. A. *Robert M. Hutchins: Portrait of an Educator.* Chicago: University of Chicago Press, 1991.

Eckholm, E. "New Views of Female Primates Assails Stereotypes." *New York Times,* September 18, 1989, p. C1.

Edinger, L., ed. *Political Leadership in Industrialized Societies: Studies in Comparative Analysis.* New York: Wiley, 1967.

Edmonds, R. *The Big Three: Churchill, Roosevelt, and Stalin in Peace and War.* New York: Norton, 1991.

Egan, K. *Teaching as Story Telling: An Alternative Approach to Teaching and Curriculum in the Elementary School.* Chicago: University of Chicago Press, 1989.

Eisenstadt, M., A. Haynal, P. Rentichnick, and P. de Senarchens. *Parental Loss and Achievement.* New York: International Universities Press, 1989.

Ekman, P. *Telling Lies.* New York: Norton, 1985.

Encyclopaedia Britannica. 15th ed. Chicago: Encyclopaedia Brittanica and the University of Chicago, 1974, 1993.

Erickson, P. D. *Reagan Speaks: The Making of an American Myth.* New York: New York University Press, 1985.

Erikson, E. H. *Childhood and Society.* New York: Norton, 1950.

———. *Young Man Luther.* New York: Norton, 1958.

———. "Identity and the Life Cycle." *Psychological Issues,* 1, no. 1 (1959): 1–171.

———. *Gandhi's Truth.* New York: Norton, 1969.

Feldman, D. H. *Beyond Universals in Cognitive Development.* Rev. ed. Norwood, N.J.: Ablex, 1994.

Feldman, D. H., with L. Goldsmith. *Nature's Gambit.* New York: Basic Books, 1986.

Fiedler, F. C. *A Theory of Leadership Effectiveness.* New York: McGraw-Hill, 1967.

Fischer, K., H. H. Hand, M. Watson, M. Van Parys, and J. Tucker. "Putting the Child into Socialization: The Development of Social Categories in Preschool Children." In L. Katz, ed., *Current Topics in Early Childhood Education.* Norwood, N.J.: Ablex, 1984, pp. 27–72.

Fischer, L. *The Life of Mahatma Gandhi.* New York: Harper and Brothers, 1950.

Frank, R. H. *Choosing the Right Pond.* Oxford: Oxford University Press, 1985.

Freedman, D. G. *Human Sociobiology: A Holistic Approach.* New York: Free Press, 1979.

Freeman, D. *Margaret Mead and Samoa: The Making and Unmaking of an Anthropological Myth.* Cambridge, Mass.: Harvard University Press, 1983.

Freidel, F. *Franklin D. Roosevelt: A Rendezvous with Destiny.* Boston: Little, Brown, 1990.

Freud, S. *A General Introduction to Psychoanalysis.* New York: Washington Square Press, 1952.

———. *Group Psychology and the Analysis of the Ego.* In J. Rickman, ed., *A General Selection from the Works of Sigmund Freud.* Garden City, N.Y: Doubleday/Anchor, 1957; originally published in 1921.

Friedan, B. *The Feminine Mystique.* New York: Norton, 1963.

Fromm, E. *Escape from Freedom.* New York: Holt, 1941.

Furuya, K. *Chiang Kai-shek: His Life and Times.* Translated by C. Chang. New York: St. John's University, 1981.

Gandhi, M. *Hind Swaraj, or Indian Home Rule.* Weale, N.H.: Greenleaf Books, 1938.

———. *Autobiography: The Story of My Experiments with Truth.* New York: Dover, 1963.

Gardner, H. *The Shattered Mind: The Person after Brain Damage.* New York: Vintage, 1975.

———. *Developmental Psychology: An Introduction.* Boston: Little, Brown, 1982.

———. *The Mind's New Science: A History of the Cognitive Revolution.* New York: Basic Books, 1985.

———. *The Unschooled Mind: How Children Think and How Schools Should Teach.* New York: Basic Books, 1991.

———. *Creating Minds: An Anatomy of Creativity Seen through the Lives of Freud, Einstein, Picasso, Stravinsky, Eliot, Graham, and Gandhi.* New York: Basic Books, 1993a.

———. *Frames of Mind: The Theory of Multiple Intelligences.* New York: Basic Books, 1993b; originally published in 1983.

Gardner, J. "The Nature of Leadership." Leadership Papers. *The Independent Sector,* 1 (January 1986).

———. *On Leadership.* New York: Free Press, 1990.

———. Personal communication, December 3, 1993.

———. Personal communication, March 15, 1995.

Garrow, D. *Bearing the Cross: Martin Luther King, Jr., and the Southern Christian Leadership Conference.* New York: Morrow, 1986.

———, ed. *Martin Luther King, Jr.: Civil Rights Leader, Theologian, Orator.* Vol. 3. Brooklyn, N.Y: Carlson, 1989.

Geertz, C. *Works and Lives: The Anthropologist as Author.* Stanford, Calif.: Stanford University Press, 1988.

"The General." *Time,* January 3, 1944, pp. 15–18.

Gerth, H., and C. W. Mills. *From Max Weber: Essays in Sociology.* New York: Oxford/Galaxy Books, 1958.

Gideonse, H. D. *The Higher Learning in a Democracy: A Reply to President Hutchins' Critique of the American University.* New York: Farrar and Rinehart, 1937.

Gilbert, M. *Churchill's Political Philosophy.* Oxford: Oxford University Press, 1980.

———. *Churchill: A Life.* London: Heinemann, 1991.

Goldberg, S. *Why Men Rule.* La Salle, Ill.: Open Court, 1993.

Goleman, D. "Studying the Secrets of Child Memory." *New York Times,* April 8, 1993, sec. C, pp. 1, 11.

———. "Amid Ethnic Wars, Psychiatrists Seek Roots of Conflicts." *New York Times,* August 2, 1994, sec. C, p. 1.

Goodchild, P. *Oppenheimer: The Father of the Atom Bomb.* London: British Broadcasting Company/Ariel Books, 1983.

Goodwin, D. K. "The Home Front." *New Yorker,* August 15, 1994a, pp. 38–61.

———. *No Ordinary Time: Franklin and Eleanor Roosevelt—The Home Front in World War II.* New York: Simon and Schuster, 1994b.

Gregory, M. S., A. Silvers, and D. Sutch, eds. *Sociobiology and Human Nature.* San Francisco: Jossey-Bass, 1978.

Gritti, J. *Jean XXIII dans l'opinion publique.* Paris: Editions du Centurion, 1967.

Grosser, A. "La politique extérieure de l'Europe communautaire: tendances et perspectives." In G. Majone, E. Noël, and P. Van den Bossche, eds., *Jean Monnet et l'Europe d'Aujourdhui.* Baden-Baden: Nomos Verlagsgesellschaft, 1989, pp. 191–200.

Groves, L. *Now It Can Be Told: The Story of the Manhattan Project.* New York: Harper, 1962.

Gruber, H. *Darwin on Man.* Chicago: University of Chicago Press, 1981.

Hackett, C. P. "Jean Monnet, Europe, and the United States." In G. Majone, E. Noël, and P. Van den Bossche, eds., *Jean Monnet et l'Europe d'Aujourdhui.* Baden-Baden: Nomos Verlagsgesellschaft, 1989, pp. 163–90.

Hahn, E. *Chiang Kai-shek: An Unauthorized Biography.* New York: Doubleday, 1955.

Halberstam, D. *The Powers That Be.* New York: Knopf, 1979.

———. *The Fifties.* New York: Villard, 1993.

Hall, G. S. *Adolescence.* New York: Appleton, 1904.

Harlow, H., and M. K. Harlow. "Effects of Various Mother-Infant Relationships on Rhesus Monkey Behaviors." In B. M. Foss, ed., *Determinants of Infant Behavior.* Vol. 4. New York: Barnes and Noble, 1969, pp. 15–36.

Harris, L. "Di and Li: Life and Letters of Diana and Lionel Trilling." *New Yorker,* September 13, 1993, pp. 90–91.

Havel, V. "How Europe Could Fail." *New York Review of Books,* November 18, 1993, p. 3.

———. "Transcendent Democracy: The Jackson H. Ralston Lecture." Address delivered at Stanford University Law School, September 29, 1994.

Hebb, D. O. *The Organization of Behavior.* New York: Wiley, 1949.

Hebblethwaite, P. *John XXIII: Pope of the Council.* London: Geoffrey Chapman, 1984.

Heifetz, R. *Leadership without Easy Answers.* Cambridge, Mass.: Harvard University Press, 1994.

Hibbert, C. *Benito Mussolini: A Biography.* London: Longman Green, 1962.

Hitler, A. *Mein Kampf.* Trans. R. Manheim. Boston: Houghton Mifflin, 1962.

Hoffer, E. *The True Believer.* New York: Harper, 1951.

Hoffmann, B. *Einstein.* St. Albans, England: Paladin, 1975.

Hoff-Wilson, J., and M. Lightman, eds. *Without Precedent: The Life and Career of Eleanor Roosevelt.* Bloomington: Indiana University Press, 1984.

Hogan, R., G. Curphy, and J. Hogan. "What We Know about Leadership." *American Psychologist* 49 (1994): 493–503.

Hollander, E. P. *Leadership Dynamics.* New York: Free Press, 1964.

Howard, J. *Margaret Mead: A Life.* New York: Simon and Schuster, 1984.

Howell, D. "Whose Revolution?" Review of *A Conservative Revolution,* edited by A. Adonis and T. Hames. *Times Literary Supplement,* 1993.

Hoyt, E. *Warlord: Tojo against the World.* Lanham, Md.: Scarborough House, 1993.

Hutchins, R. M. *The Higher Learning in America.* New Haven, Conn.: Yale University Press, 1936.

———. "Dark Hours in Our History." Commencement address, University of Chicago, June 10, 1941a. Reprinted in *Vital Speeches of the Day* 7 (July 1, 1941): 69–70.

———. "The Proposition Is Peace: The Path to War Is a False Path to Freedom." Speech delivered in Rockefeller Memorial Chapel, Chicago, Illinois, March 30, 1941b. Reprinted in *Vital Speeches of the Day* 7 (April 15, 1941): 389–92.

Iremonger, L. *The Fiery Chariot: A Study of British Prime Ministers and the Search for Love.* London: Seeker and Warburg, 1970.

Isaacson, W., and E. Thomas. *The Wise Men.* London: Faber and Faber, 1986.

Jacobs, T. *A History of General Motors.* New York: Smithmark, 1992.

Jaeger, W. *Paideia.* 3 vols. Trans. G. Highet. New York: Oxford University Press, 1943–45.

Jaszi, O. *The Dissolution of the Habsburg Monarchy.* Chicago: University of Chicago Press, 1966.

Jean Monnet: Proceedings of Centenary Symposium Organized by the Commission of the European Communities, Brussels, 10 November 1988. Luxembourg: Office for Official Publications of the European Communities, 1989.

Jensen, M. C. "The Modern Industrial Revolution, Exit, and the Failure of Internal Control Systems." *Journal of Finance,* 48, no. 3 (1993): 831–80.

Joes, A. J. *Mussolini.* New York: Franklin Watts, 1982.

Kagan, J. "The Concept of Identification." *Psychological Issues,* 65, no. 5 (September 1958): 296–305.

Kakutani, M. "Books That Make a Case for Shades of Gray." *New York Times,* June 18, 1993, sec. C, pp. 1, 24.

Keating C. F., and K. R. Heltman. "Dominance and Deception in Children and Adults: Are Leaders the Best Misleaders?" *Personality and Social Psychology Bulletin,* 20 (1994): 312–21.

Kegan, R. *The Evolving Self.* Cambridge, Mass.: Harvard University Press, 1982.

Kelly, M. "David Gergen: Master of the Game." *New York Times Magazine,* October 1993, pp. 62–63.

———. "Bill Clinton's Climb." *New York Times Magazine,* July 31, 1994, p. 20.

Kennan, G. F. "In Defense of Oppenheimer." *New York Review of Books,* June 10, 1994, p. 8.

Kerr, D. H. *Beyond Education: In Search of Nurture.* Seattle, Wash.: Institute for Educational Inquiry, 1993.

Keynes, J. M. *The General Theory of Employment, Interest, and Money.* London: Macmillan, 1936.

Kimball, B. *The "True Professional Ideal" in America.* Oxford: Blackwell, 1992.

King, M. L., Jr. *A Testament of Hope: The Essential Writings and Speeches of Martin Luther King, Jr.* Edited by J. M. Washington. San Francisco: HarperCollins, 1986.

———. *I Have a Dream: Writings and Speeches That Changed the World.* San Francisco: HarperSanFrancisco, 1992.

Kinzer, S. "The Nightmare's Roots: The Dream World Called Serbia." *New York Times,* May 16, 1993, p. El.

Kissinger, H. A. "The Right to Be Right." Review of *The Downing Street Years,* by M. Thatcher. *New York Times Book Review,* November 14, 1993, pp. 1, 63–65.

———. *Diplomacy.* New York: Simon and Schuster, 1994.

Kitto, H. D. F. *The Greeks.* London: Penguin, 1951.

Klein, G. Personal communication, August 18, 1992.

Kohlberg, L. "Stage and Sequence: The Cognitive-Developmental Approach to Socialization." In D. A. Goslin, ed., *Handbook of Socialization Theory and Research.* New York: Rand McNally, 1969.

———. *The Psychology of Moral Development.* New York: Harper, 1974.

Kolbert, E. "Test Marketing a President." *New York Times Magazine,* August 30, 1992, pp. 18–20, 68–72.

Korda, M. "How to Be a Leader." In W. E. Rosenbach and R. L. Taylor, eds., *Contemporary Issues in Leadership.* Boulder, Colo.: Westview Press, 1984, p. 61.

Kouzes, J. M., and B. Z. Posner. *Credibility: How Leaders Gain and Lose It, Why People Demand It.* San Francisco: Jossey-Bass, 1993.

Kraemer, G. "A Psychobiological Theory of Attachment." *Behavioral and Brain Sciences,* 15, no. 3 (1992): 493–510.

Kummer, H. *Primate Societies.* Chicago: University of Chicago Press, 1971.

Küsters, H. "Jean Monnet and the European Union: Idea and Reality of the Integration Process." In G. Majone, E. Noël, and P. Van den Bossche, eds., *Jean Monnet et l'Europe d'Aujourdhui.* Baden-Baden: Nomos Verlagsgesellschaft, 1989, pp. 45–60.

Lamb, D. *The Africans.* New York: Vintage Books, 1987.

Lash, J. P. *Eleanor: The Years Alone.* New York: Norton, 1972.

———. *Eleanor and Franklin.* New York: Signet, 1973.

———. *Love, Eleanor: Eleanor Roosevelt and Her Friends.* Garden City, N.Y: Doubleday, 1982.

Lattimore, O. *China Memoirs: Chiang Kai-shek and the War against Japan.* Tokyo: University of Tokyo Press, 1990.

Ledwidge, B. *De Gaulle.* New York: St. Martin's, 1982.

Lenin, V. I. *Essential Works of Lenin: "What Is to Be Done?" and Other Writings.* Ed. H. M. Christman. New York: Dover, 1987.

Lentz, R. *Symbols, the News Magazines, and Martin Luther King.* Baton Rouge: Louisiana State University Press, 1990.

Lévi-Strauss, C. *Structural Anthropology.* New York: Basic Books, 1963.

Lewis, F. "We the Decent People, Saying 'No.'" *International Herald Tribune,* August 28, 1993.

Little, G. *Political Ensembles: A Psychosocial Approach to Politics and Leadership.* Melbourne: Oxford University Press, 1985.

———. *Strong Leadership: Thatcher, Reagan, and an Eminent Person.* Melbourne: Oxford University Press, 1988.

Loh, P. P. Y. *The Early Chiang Kai-shek: A Study of His Personality and Politics, 1887–1924.* New York: Columbia University Press, 1971.

Lohr, S. "IBM Chief Making Drastic Cuts." *New York Times,* July 28, 1993, pp. 1, 6.

———. "On the Road with Chairman Lou." *New York Times,* June 26, 1994, pp. 1, C2.

Lukacs, J. "Benito Mussolini: Back from the Dead." *New York Times Magazine,* July 24, 1994, pp. 14–17.

Luria, A. R. *The Higher Cortical Functions in Man.* New York: Basic Books, 1966.

Lykken, D., M. McGue, A. Tellegen, and T. J. Bouchard. "Emergenesis: Genetic Traits That May Not Run in Families." *American Psychologist,* 47, no. 12 (1992): 1565–77.

Lyttle, R. *Il Duce: The Rise and Fall of Benito Mussolini.* New York: Atheneum, 1987.

Macfarquhar, R., T. Cheek, and E. Wu. *The Secret Speeches of Chairman Mao.* Cambridge, Mass.: Harvard University Press, 1989.

Machiavelli, N. The Prince *and* The Discourses. 1 vol. Trans. L. Ricci and C. E. Detmold. New York: Random House Modern Library, 1950.

Majone, G. E. Noël, and P. Van den Bossche, eds. *Jean Monnet et l'Europe d'Aujourdhui.* Baden-Baden: Nomos Verlagsgesellschaft, 1989.

Malcolm X. *Malcolm X Speaks: Selected Speeches and Statements.* Edited by G. Breitman. New York: Pathfinder, 1989.

Mamali, C. S. "The Gandhian Mode of Becoming: Machiavellianism and Gandhianism as Conflicting Modes of Becoming." Unpublished paper, Iowa City, Iowa, 1993.

Mandler, J. M. *Stories, Scripts, and Scenes: Aspects of Schema Theory.* Hillsdale, N.J.: Erlbaum, 1984.

Maney, P. *The Roosevelt Presence: A Biography of Franklin Delano Roosevelt.* New York: Twayne, 1992.

"Man of the Year, Martin Luther King, Jr." *Time,* January 3, 1964, pp. 13–27.

"Man of the Year, Pope John." *Time,* January 4, 1963, pp. 50–54.

Marshack, A. *The Roots of Civilization.* Mt. Kisco, N.Y: Moyer Bell, 1991.

Marshall, G. C. *The War Reports.* Philadelphia: Lippincott, 1947.

Mayer, M. *Robert Maynard Hutchins: A Memoir.* Edited by J. H. Hicks. Berkeley: University of California Press, 1993.

Mayle, P. D. *Eureka Summit: Agreement in Principle and the Big Three in Tehran, 1943.* Newark: University of Delaware Press, 1987.

McCullough, D. *Truman.* New York: Simon and Schuster/Touchstone, 1992.

McDonald, K., "Biology and Behavior." *Chronicle of Higher Education* (September 14, 1994): A10–11.

McDowell, E. "New Samoa Book Challenges Mead's Conclusions." *New York Times,* January 31, 1983, pp. 1, C21.

McFarland, L. J., L. E. Senn, and J. R. Children, eds. *Twenty-First-Century Leadership: Dialogues with 100 Top Leaders.* New York: Leadership Press, 1993.

McLuhan, M. *Understanding Media.* New York: McGraw-Hill, 1964.

McNeal, R. H. *Stalin: Man and Ruler.* London: Macmillan, 1988.

Mead, M. *Male and Female: A Study of the Sexes in a Changing World.* New York: Dell, 1949.

———. *Sex and Temperament in Three Primitive Societies.* New York: Morrow/Quill, 1963; originally published in 1935.

———. *Anthropology, a Human Science: Selected Papers 1939–1960.* Princeton, N.J.: Van Nostrand, 1964a.

———. *Continuities in Cultural Evolution.* New Haven, Conn.: Yale University Press, 1964b.

———. *Coming of Age in Samoa.* New York: Dell, 1968; originally published in 1928.

———. *Blackberry Winter: My Earlier Years.* New York: Morrow, 1972.

Mead, M., and R. Metraux. *Aspects of the Present.* New York: Morrow, 1980.

Mehta, V. *Mahatma Gandhi and His Apostles.* New York: Viking Press, 1977.

Miller, M., and L. Hays. "Gerstner's Nonvision for IBM Raises a Management Issue." *Wall Street Journal,* July 29, 1993, sec. B, p. 1.

Millis, W., ed. *The War Reports of General of the Army George C. Marshall, General of the Army H. H. Arnold, Fleet Admiral Ernest J. King.* New York: Lippincott, 1947.

Miroff, B. *Icons of Democracy.* New York: Basic Books, 1993.

Monnet, J. *Memoirs.* Translated by R. Mayne. Garden City, N.Y.: Doubleday, 1978.

Montgomery, B. L. *The Memoirs of Field-Marshal Montgomery.* New York: Dell Books, 1958.

Morgan, T. *FDR: A Biography.* New York: Simon and Schuster, 1985.

Morris, R. *Evolution and Human Nature.* New York: Seaview/Putnam, 1983.

Mosley, L. *Marshall: Hero for Our Times.* New York: Hearst Books, 1982.

"Mrs. Roosevelt Takes News Calmly." *New York Times,* February 16, 1933, pp. 1–2.

Mussolini, B. *My Autobiography.* London: Hutchinson, 1939.

Nanda, B. R. *Gandhi and His Critics.* Delhi: Oxford University Press, 1985.

Nelson, K. *Event Knowledge: Structure and Function in Development.* Hillsdale, N.J.: Erlbaum, 1986.

———. "Emergence of Autobiographical Memory at Age 4." *Human Development,* 35, no. 3 (May–June 1992): 172–77.

Neustadt, R. *Presidential Power: The Politics of Leadership from FDR to Carter.* New York: Macmillan, 1980.

New York Times. Chronicle article on Margaret Thatcher. October 19, 1993, p. B2.

Nisbett, R., and L. Ross. *Human Inference.* Englewood Cliffs, N.J.: Prentice-Hall, 1980.

Noble, B. P. "The Debate over *la différence."* *New York Times,* August 15, 1993, Business section, p. 6.

Nye, J. *Bound to Lead: The Changing Nature of American Power.* New York: Basic Books, 1990.

Oliner, S. P., and P. M. Oliner. *The Altruistic Personality: Rescuers of Jews in Nazi Europe.* New York: Free Press, 1988.

Oppenheimer, J. R. *Some Reflections on Science and Culture.* Chapel Hill: University of North Carolina Press, 1960.

———. *Uncommon Sense.* Edited by N. Metropolis, G. Rota, and D. H. Sharp. Boston: Birkhauser, 1984.

Paine, T. *Common Sense.* Edited by I. Kramnick. New York: Penguin, 1976.

Pais, A. *Subtle Is the Lord: The Science and the Life of Albert Einstein.* New York: Oxford University Press, 1982.

Paris, P. *Black Religious Leaders: Conflict in Unity.* Louisville, Ky.: Westminster/John Knox Press, 1991.

Parrish, T. *Roosevelt and Marshall: Partners in Politics and War.* New York: Morrow, 1989.

Paxton, R. "Radicals." Review of *The Birth of Fascist Ideology: From Cultural Rebellion to Political Revolution,* by Z. Sternhell. *New York Review of Books,* June 23, 1994, pp. 51–54.

Payne, R. *The Life and Death of Mahatma Gandhi.* New York: Dutton, 1990.

Pearson, J. *Citadel of the Heart: Winston and the Churchill Dynasty.* London: Macmillan, 1991.

Perlmutter, A. *FDR and Stalin: A Not So Grand Alliance, 1943–1945.* Columbia, Mo.: University of Missouri Press, 1993.

Perry, E. I. "Training for Public Life: ER and Women's Political Networks in the 1920's." In J. Hoff-Wilson and M. Lightman, eds., *Without Precedent: The Life and Career of Eleanor Roosevelt.* Bloomington: Indiana University Press, 1984, pp. 28–45.

Petrullo, L., and B. Bass, eds. *Leadership and Interpersonal Behavior.* New York: Holt, Rinehart, and Winston, 1961.

Pfaff, W. "Passive Government Disarms Democracy." *International Herald Tribune,* June 11, 1993, p. 6.

Piaget, J. "Piaget's Theory." In P. Mussen, ed., *Handbook of Child Psychology.* Vol. 1. New York: Wiley, 1983.

Pogue, F. C. *George C. Marshall: Education of a General, 1880–1939.* New York: Viking Press, 1963.

———. *George C. Marshall: Ordeal and Hope, 1939–1942.* New York: Viking Press, 1965.

———. *George C. Marshall: Organizer of Victory, 1943–1945.* New York: Viking Press, 1973.

Pope John XXIII. *Journal of a Soul.* Trans. by D. White. Garden City, N.Y: Image Books, 1980.

Postbrief, S. "Departure from Incrementalism in U.S. Strategic Planning: The Origins of NSC-68." *Naval College Review* (March–April 1980): 34–57.

Preston, P. *Franco: A Biography.* London: Harper Collins, 1993.

Propp, V. *The Morphology of the Folk Tale.* Austin: University of Texas Press, 1968.

Rabi, I. I., R. Serber, V. Weisskopf, A. Pais, and G. T. Seaborg. *Oppenheimer.* New York: Scribners, 1969.

Rees-Mogg, W. "Our National Malaise." *London Times,* January 28, 1993, p. 20.

Reston, J. "'I have a dream . . .' Preoration by Dr. King Sums Up a Day the Capital Will Remember." *New York Times,* August 29, 1963, pp. 1, 17.

Rhodes, R. *The Making of the Atomic Bomb.* New York: Simon and Schuster, 1986.

Riddell, P. "What We Did and Why We Fell." Review of *The Downing Street Years,* by M. Thatcher. *Times Literary Supplement,* October 29, 1993, p. 28.

Rieben, H. "La naissance de l'idée europeene de Jean Monnet." In G. Majone, E. Noël, and P. Van den Bossche, eds., *Jean Monnet et l'Europe d'Aujourdhui.* Baden-Baden: Nomos Verlagsgesellschaft, 1989, pp. 21–28.

Rieben, H., M. Nathusius, and F. Nicod. *Jean Monnet, Robert Schuman, Correspondence, 1947–1953.* Lausanne: Foundation Jean Monnet Pour L'Europe, Centre de Researches Europeennes, 1986.

Riga, P. *John XXIII and the City of Man.* Westminster, Md.: Newman Press, 1966.

Roland, C., H. Friedlander, and B. Müller-Hill, eds. *Medical Sciences without Compassion: Past and Present.* Arbeitspapiere-Atti-Proceedings, no. 11, fall meeting, Cologne, September 28–30, 1988.

Roosevelt, E. *You Learn by Living.* New York: Harper and Brothers, 1960.

———. *The Autobiography of Eleanor Roosevelt.* New York: Da Capo Press, 1992.

Roosevelt, F. D. *Nothing to Fear: The Selected Addresses of Franklin Delano Roosevelt: 1932–1945.* Edited by B. D. Zevin. Cambridge, Mass.: Riverside Press, 1946.

Rosenbach, W. E., and R. L. Taylor. *Contemporary Issues in Leadership.* Boulder, Colo.: Westview Press, 1984.

Rosenberg, M. "Quixotic Prophet." Review of *Unseasonable Truths,* by H. Ashmore. *Chicago Tribune,* August 27, 1989, sec. 14, p. 33.

Rosener, J. "Ways Women Lead." *Harvard Business Review,* 68 (Nov.–Dec. 1990): 119–25.

Rosnow, R., A. Skleder, M. Jaeger, and B. Rind. "Intelligence and the Epistemics of Interpersonal Acumen: Testing Some Implications of Gardner's Theory." *Intelligence,* 19, no. 1 (1994): 93–116.

Royal, D. *The Story of J. Robert Oppenheimer.* New York: St. Martin's, 1969.

Rubin, J. S. *The Making of Middle-Brow Culture.* Chapel Hill: University of North Carolina Press, 1992.

Rushton, J. P. "Genetic Similarity, Human Altruism, and Group Selection." *Behavioral and Brain Sciences,* 12, no. 3 (September 1989): 503–18.

Rustow, D. A., ed. *Philosophers and Kings: Studies in Leadership.* New York: Braziller, 1970.

Ryan, A. "Yes, Minister." Review of *The Downing Street Years,* by M. Thatcher. *New York Review of Books,* December 2, 1993, pp. 7–12.

Sapolsky, R., and R. Jay. "Styles of Dominance and Their Physiological Correlates among Wild Baboons." *American Journal of Primatology,* 18 (1989): 1–13.

Sartre, J. P. *The Words.* New York: Braziller, 1964.

Schaefer, R. *Narrative Actions in Psychoanalysis.* Worcester, Mass.: Clark University Press, 1981.

Scharf, L. "ER and Feminism." In J. Hoff-Wilson and M. Lightman, eds., *Without Precedent: The Life and Career of Eleanor Roosevelt.* Bloomington: Indiana University Press, 1984, pp. 226–54.

Schiffer, I. *Charisma: A Psychoanalytic Look at Mass Society.* Toronto: University of Toronto Press, 1973.

Schmemann, S. "A Poet Sings Fondly of an Old Enemy." *New York Times,* July 24, 1993, p. 4.

Schram, S. *Chairman Mao Talks to the People.* New York: Pantheon, 1974.

Selman, R. *The Growth of Interpersonal Understanding.* New York: Academic Press, 1980.

Selman, R., and L. H. Schultz. *Making a Friend in Youth: Developmental Theory and Pair Therapy.* Chicago: University of Chicago Press, 1990.

Service, R. *Lenin: A Political Life.* 2 vols. London: Macmillan, 1991.

Shaller, G. *The Mountain Gorilla.* Chicago: Aldine, 1963.

Shils, E. "Robert Maynard Hutchins: Former Controversial President of the University of Chicago and His Educational Philosophy." *American Scholar,* 59, no. 2 (1990): 211–35.

———. "Do We Still Need Academic Freedom?" *American Scholar,* 62, no. 2 (1993): 187–99.

Shirer, W. L. *Gandhi: A Memoir.* New York: Simon and Schuster, 1979.

Simmons, A. "President's Essay: Citizen Groups Are Essential Partners in the New Global Governance." *1993 Report on Activities of the MacArthur Foundation.* Chicago: The MacArthur Foundation, 1994, pp. 2–6.

Simonton, D. K. *Genius, Creativity, and Leadership: Historiometric Inquiries.* Cambridge, Mass.: Harvard University Press, 1984.

———. "Putting the Best Leaders in the White House: Personality, Policy, and Performance." *Political Psychology,* 14, no. 3 (1993): 537–48.

———. *Greatness: Who Makes History and Why.* New York: Guilford Press, 1994.

Skowronek, S. *The Politics Presidents Make: Leadership from John Adams to George Bush.* Cambridge, Mass.: Harvard University Press, 1993.

Sloan, A. P., Jr. *My Years with General Motors.* Garden City, N.Y.: Anchor Books, 1972.

Sloan, A. P., Jr., with Boyden Sparkes. *Adventures of a White-Collar Man.* New York: Doubleday, Doran, 1941.

Smelser, N. *Theory of Collective Behavior.* New York: Free Press, 1962.

Smith, A. K., and C. Weiner. *Robert Oppenheimer: Letters and Recollections.* Cambridge, Mass.: Harvard University Press, 1980.

Smith, D. M. *Mussolini.* New York: Knopf, 1982.

Smith, H. *The World's Religions.* San Francisco: HarperCollins, 1991.

Staw, B., and R. Sutton. "Macro Organizational Society." In J. K. Murnighan, ed., *Social Psychology in Organizations: Advances in Theory and Research.* Englewood Cliffs, N.J.: Prentice Hall, 1992, pp. 350–84.

Steichen, E. *The Family of Man.* New York: Simon and Schuster, 1955.

Stern, P., with H. Green. *The Oppenheimer Case: Security on Trial.* New York: Harper and Row, 1969.

Stoessinger, J. Personal communication, December 6, 1944.

————. *Why Nations Go to War.* 6th ed. New York: St. Martin's, 1993.

Stoler, M. A. *George C. Marshall: Soldier-Statesman of the American Century.* Boston: Twayne, 1989.

Storr, A. *Churchill's Black Dog, Kafka's Mice, and Other Phenomena of the Human Mind.* New York: Grove Press, 1988.

Sutton, R., and D. C. Galunic. "Consequences of Public Scrutiny for Leaders and Their Organizations." Unpublished paper, Stanford University, 1994.

Swedberg, R. "The Idea of 'Europe' and the Origin of the European Union—A Sociological Approach." *Zeitschrift für Soziologie,* 23, no. 5 (1994): 378–87.

Swift, G. *Waterland.* New York: Vintage, 1983.

Tead, O. *The Art of Leadership.* New York: Whittlesly House, 1935.

Terrill, R. *Mao: A Biography.* New York: Harper and Row, 1980.

Thatcher, M. *Margaret Thatcher: The Downing Street Years.* New York: Harper Collins, 1993.

Thompson, K. W. *Winston Churchill's World View: Statesmanship and Power.* Baton Rouge, La.: Louisiana State University Press, 1983.

Toland, J. *Adolf Hitler.* New York: Doubleday, 1976.

Tsanoff, R. *Autobiographies of Ten Religious Leaders: Alternatives in Christian Experience.* San Antonio, Tex.: Trinity University Press, 1968.

Tucker, R. C. *Stalin in Power: The Revolution from Above, 1928–1941.* New York: Norton, 1990.

Turiel, E. "The Social Construction of Social Construction." In W. Damon, ed., *Child Development Today and Tomorrow.* San Francisco: Jossey-Bass, 1989, pp. 86–106.

United States Atomic Energy Commission. *In the Matter of J. Robert Oppenheimer.* Cambridge, Mass.: MIT Press, 1970.

Volkogonov, D. *Stalin: Triumph and Tragedy.* Ed. and trans. H. Shukman. London: Weidenfeld and Nicolson, 1991.

von Simson, W. "Reflections on Jean Monnet's Skillful Handling of Member States and People during the First Years of the Community." In G. Majone, E. Noël, and P. Van den Bossche, eds., *Jean Monnet et l'Europe d'Aujourdhui*. Baden-Baden: Nomos Verlagsgesellschaft, 1989, pp. 29–36.

Walsh, J. "Where Have All the Leaders Gone?" *Time,* July 12, 1993, pp. 17–21.

Walsh, M., and B. Davies, eds. *Proclaiming Justice and Peace: Documents from John XXIII to John Paul II*. London: Collins Liturgical Publications, 1984.

Ware, S. "ER and Democratic Politics: Women in the Postsuffrage Era." In J. Hoff-Wilson and M. Lightman, eds., *Without Precedent: The Life and Career of Eleanor Roosevelt*. Bloomington: Indiana University Press, 1984, pp. 45–60.

White, E., ed. *Sociobiology and Human Politics*. Lexington, Mass.: Lexington Books, 1981.

Wigginton, F. P. *The Popes of Vatican Council II*. Chicago: Franciscan Herald Press, 1983.

Williams, P., and M. Harrison. *De Gaulle's Republic*. Westport, Conn.: Greenwood Press, 1960.

Williams, W. *Mismanaging America: The Rise of the Anti-analytic Presidency*. Lawrence: University Press of Kansas, 1990.

Wills, G. *Certain Trumpets: The Call of Leaders*. New York: Simon and Schuster, 1994a.

———. "What Makes a Good Leader?" *Atlantic Monthly,* April 1994b, pp. 63–80.

Wilson, E. *To the Finland Station*. London: Fontana, 1960.

Wilson, E. O. *Sociobiology*. Cambridge, Mass.: Harvard University Press, 1975.

Winner, E. *The Point of Words: Children's Understanding of Metaphor and Irony*. Cambridge, Mass.: Harvard University Press, 1988.

———. *Gifted Children: Myths and Realities*. New York: Basic Books, 1997.

Wittgenstein, L. *Philosophical Investigations*. Trans. G. E. M. Auscombe. Oxford, England: Blackwell, 1958.

Wofford, H. *Of Kennedy and Kings: Making Sense of the Sixties*. New York: Farrar, Straus, and Giroux, 1980.

York, H. *The Advisors: Oppenheimer, Teller, and the Superbomb*. Stanford, Calif.: Stanford University Press, 1989; originally published in 1976.

Young, A. "Interview with Andrew Young." *New York Times,* May 11, 1994, pp. C1–2.

Young, H. *The Iron Lady: A Biography of Margaret Thatcher*. New York: Farrar, Straus, and Giroux, 1989.

Young, H., and A. Simon. *The Thatcher Phenomenon*. London: BBC Books, 1986.

Zalesnik, A., and M. Kets de Vries. *Power and the Corporate Mind*. Chicago: Bonus Books, 1985.

Zizola, G. *The Utopia of Pope John XXIII*. Maryknoll, N.Y.: Orbis Books, 1978.

NAME INDEX

SUBJECT INDEX

375